Bibliografische Information der Deutschen Nationalbibliothek

Die Deutsche Nationalbibliothek verzeichnet diese Publikation in der Deutschen Nationalbibliografie; detaillierte bibliografische Daten sind im Internet über http://dnb.d-nb.de abrufbar.

ISBN 978-3-8325-2736-5

Logos Verlag Berlin GmbH
Comeniushof, Gubener Str. 47,
10243 Berlin
Tel.: +49 (0)30 42 85 10 90
Fax: +49 (0)30 42 85 10 92
INTERNET: http://www.logos-verlag.de

Self-Calibration of Multi-Camera Systems

Ferid Bajramovic

Dissertation

zur Erlangung des akademischen Grades
doctor rerum naturalium (Dr. rer. nat.)

vorgelegt dem Rat der Fakultät für Mathematik und Informatik
der Friedrich-Schiller-Universität Jena

Special Thanks

I want to express my special thanks to the following people:

- Marcel Brückner for our very fruitful collaboration on several topics.
- Michael Koch for our collaboration on point correspondence extraction.
- Joachim Denzler for his guidance through the jungle of academia.
- Angela Bajramovic and Joachim Kollmer for designing the cover.

Furthermore I want to thank my reviewers:

- Prof. Dr.-Ing. Joachim Denzler, Friedrich-Schiller-Universität Jena
- Prof. Dr.-Ing. Reinhard Koch, Christian-Albrechts-Universität Kiel
- Prof. Kyros Kutulakos, Ph.D., University of Toronto

Abstract

In this dissertation, I develop a novel multi-camera self-calibration method, which neither requires a calibration object nor any user interaction. It estimates intrinsic and extrinsic parameters separately. For the former, it applies rotational self-calibration assuming cameras mounted onto pan-tilt units. I present a novel approach for exploiting (partial) prior knowledge of the camera rotations provided by the pan-tilt units. In order to determine the extrinsic camera parameters, the method first robustly estimates the relative poses of camera pairs using MLESAC, a Monte Carlo maximum likelihood estimator, based on the five-point algorithm. Afterwards the extrinsic calibration is computed from the relative pose estimates. Some of these are more reliable than others—especially if some camera pairs do not have a common field of view. As in general not all relative poses are needed to compute the extrinsic calibration, a method for selecting the best estimates is desirable. I propose three novel uncertainty measures on relative pose estimates. Based on these measures, I formulate the selection of relative poses as a discrete optimization problem and show that it is equivalent to the problem of finding shortest triangle paths in the camera dependency graph. For this problem, I develop a novel, efficient algorithm and prove its correctness. This constitutes the main theoretical contribution of this dissertation. As a complementary supporting technique, I present a novel method for detecting camera pairs that have a common field of view. Pairs without a common field of view can be excluded from the uncertainty-based selection of relative poses in order to further improve the calibration.

In quantitatively evaluated experiments on simulated and real data, I show that my multi-camera self-calibration method gives good results and that each individual contribution of this dissertation improves the calibration. In particular, the evaluation shows that rotational self-calibration clearly benefits from knowing the rotations. The uncertainty-based selection of relative poses greatly outperforms naive or random selection. The common field of view detection method gives better results than an established technique and is suitable for improving the multi-camera calibration results. Furthermore, several existing point correspondence extraction and relative pose estimation methods are compared in the experiments. A proof-of-concept 3D object tracking system demonstrates the practical applicability of my multi-camera self-calibration method.

Zusammenfassung

In der vorliegenden Dissertation wird ein neuartiges Selbstkalibrierverfahren für Multikamerasysteme entwickelt, das weder einen Kalibrierkörper noch Benutzerinteraktion erfordert. Die intrinsischen und extrinsischen Parameter werden separat geschätzt. Erstere werden mittels Rotationsselbstkalibrierung ermittelt unter der Annahme, dass die Kameras auf Schwenk-Neige-Einheiten montiert sind. Hierfür wird ein neuartiger Ansatz vorgestellt, um (partielles) Wissen über die Kamerarotationen zu verwenden, die von den Schwenk-Neige-Einheiten geliefert werden. Um die extrinsischen Kameraparameter zu ermitteln, werden zunächst paarweise relative Posen robust geschätzt. Hierfür wird ein moderner Monte-Carlo-Maximum-Likelihood-Schätzer (MLESAC) auf Basis des Fünf-Punkte-Algorithmus verwendet. Anschließend wird die extrinsische Kalibrierung aus den geschätzten relativen Posen berechnet. Manche dieser Schätzungen sind verlässlicher als andere. Dies gilt insbesondere dann, wenn manche Kamerapaare kein gemeinsames Sichtfeld haben. Da im Allgemeinen nicht alle relativen Posen für die extrinsische Kalibrierung benötigt werden, ist ein Verfahren zur Auswahl der besten Schätzungen wünschenswert. Hierfür werden drei neuartige Unsicherheitsmaße für relative Posen vorgeschlagen. Auf Basis dieser wird die Auswahl relativer Posen als diskretes Optimierungsproblem formuliert. Es wird gezeigt, dass dies äquivalent ist mit der Bestimmung kürzester Dreieckspfade im Kameraabhängigkeitsgraphen. Zur Lösung dieses Problem wird ein neuer, effizienter Algorithmus entwickelt und seine Korrektheit bewiesen. Dies stellt den zentralen theoretischen Beitrag dieser Dissertation dar. Als komplementäre, unterstützende Technik wird ein neuartiges Verfahren zur Detektion von Kamerapaaren mit gemeinsamem Blickfeld präsentiert. Paare ohne gemeinsames Blickfeld können von der unsicherheitsbasierten Auswahl relativer Posen ausgenommen werden, um die Kalibrierung weiter zu verbessern.

Quantitative Experimente auf simulierten und realen Daten zeigen, dass das beschriebene Selbstkalibrierverfahren für Multikamerasysteme gute Ergebnisse liefert, und dass jeder einzelne Beitrag dieser Dissertation die Kalibrierung verbessert. Insbesondere zeigt die Auswertung, dass die Rotationsselbstkalibrierung klar davon profitiert, die Rotationen zu kennen. Die unsicherheitsbasierte Auswahl relativer Posen übertrifft eine naive oder zufällige Auswahl bei weitem. Die Detektion gemeinsamer Ansichten liefert bessere Ergebnisse als ein etabliertes Verfahren und kann die Multikamerakalibrierung verbessern. Außerdem werden verschiedene bestehende Methoden zur Extraktion von Punktkorrespondenzen und zur Schätzung der relativen Pose experimentell verglichen. Die praktische Anwendbarkeit des beschriebenen Selbstkalibrierverfahrens wird im Rahmen eines proof-of-concept 3-D-Objektverfolgungssystems demonstriert.

Contents

Chapter 1

Introduction

Multi-camera systems are becoming increasingly important in computer vision and also in computer graphics. Applications include 3D (video) reconstruction, scene-based rendering, telepresence, surveillance, smart homes, marker less motion capture, etc. (see Section 2.3). In all these cases, there are various methods which differ in the extent of prior knowledge they use (or require) about the setup of the multi-camera system. The most important type of such prior knowledge is the so-called *calibration* of the multi-camera system. It consists of the *intrinsic* model parameters of the individual cameras (e. g. the focal length) and their positions and viewing directions, which are called *extrinsic* parameters.

On the one hand, for most of these applications, there are approaches which do *not require* a calibration of the multi-camera system. On the other hand, if the calibration of the multi-camera system is available, there are often alternative methods or extensions, which are more precise or more robust or produce results with less remaining ambiguity. In the case of multi-camera object tracking e. g., the calibration of the multi-camera system can be used to greatly reduce ambiguities during inter-camera object association (Chang and Gong, 2001; Zimmermann, 2007). In the case of 3D reconstruction, knowing the multi-camera calibration allows us to reconstruct up to a 3D similarity transformation (i. e. effectively up to scale) instead of only up to an unknown 3D projective transformation, which includes anisotropic scaling, further affine deformation and general projective distortion (Hartley and Zisserman, 2003). As indicated by these examples, the improvements gained by knowing and using the calibration of the multi-camera system can have a critical impact on the quality of applications.

The term *(multi-)camera calibration* does not only refer to the set of intrinsic and extrinsic parameters, but also to the task of estimating these parameters. Classical methods use a so-called *calibration object* or *calibration pattern* to solve this problem (see Figure D.1 for an example). This object must (usually) be observed by *all* cameras at the same time. Other methods rely on user interaction instead, such as moving an LED through a dark room. A more detailled overview is given in Chapter 2.

The term *self-calibration* is used by some authors to refer to any method for estimating the intrinsic and/or extrinsic parameters of a single or multiple cameras without using any knowledge about the scene (especially any kind of calibration object/pattern) or any active user support. In this dissertation, I will present a multi-camera self-calibration method in that sense. Note, however, that some other authors use the term self-calibration only for a more specific subset of such methods.

The advantages of self-calibration compared to classical methods based on a calibration object are obvious. On the one hand, it is more comfortable if you do not need a calibration object. On the other hand, in some situations, using a calibration object may not be possible at all, e. g. when calibrating the surveillance system of an entire airport. Calibration methods that require user interaction have similar drawbacks: they are less comfortable than fully automatic methods and in some situations, like multiple mobile robots creating an ad hoc multi-camera system, they may not be applicable at all.

After giving a more precise specification of the multi-camera self-calibration problem in Section 1.1, I will present an overview of my dissertation and its main contributions in Section 1.2.

1.1 Problem Specification

Calibrating a single camera means estimating its intrinsic and possibly also extrinsic parameters with respect to a certain model (Hartley and Zisserman, 2003; Trucco and Verri, 1998; Ma et al., 2004). Ordinary cameras are very often modelled as pinhole cameras. As this approximation is not always precise enough, it is sometimes extended by a model for the radial and possibly also other distortions. The parameters of the pinhole and distortion models are called *intrinsic parameters*, as they describe the internals of the camera. I will focus on the pinhole model, but will also consider radial distortion. Details on these well known camera models are given in Appendix D.1.

The *extrinsic parameters*, on the other hand, represent the viewpoint of the camera by a rigid transformation, which describes its position and orientation. This part of the model is independent of the camera itself. The according parameters are called *extrinsic*, as they describe the relation between the camera and the world.

Calibrating a multi-camera system accordingly means estimating the intrinsic and extrinsic parameters of all cameras. Depending on the application and the input or prior knowledge available, there may be a remaining ambiguity in the resulting calibration. There are two main aspects relevant to this dissertation. First, if we do not know any reference length in the world, which would be available on a calibration object, the scale of the multi-camera system cannot be determined. This effect is well known and widely used in movies: a small model of a ship in a pool may appear as a real ship on the ocean, as there is no absolute information on its size. Second, the extrinsic parameters are expressed with respect to a reference coordinate system, which is also called the world coordinate system. If we do not assume any knowledge about the world, there is accordingly no known world coordinate system. Instead, it is chosen arbitrarily and the resulting multi-camera calibration is known only up to a rigid transformation. In total, there will hence be an unknown 3D similarity transformation.

Difficulty of Wide-Baseline Setups

There is a whole theory relating the images taken by multiple cameras. It is known as *multiple view geometry* (Hartley and Zisserman, 2003; Ma et al., 2004; Faugeras and Luong, 2001). Based on this mathematical description, there are many different approaches for estimating certain entities given knowledge about other entities. In this dissertation, I will focus on point correspondences as input. A *point correspondence* consists of a set of (at least) two image points such that each point is the projection of a common 3D point as observed by (at least) two different cameras. I will present methods for estimating the intrinsic and extrinsic parameters of multiple cameras from such point correspondences.

From a theoretical point of view, assuming a static scene, there is no difference between two cameras taking two images and one camera taking two images from different viewpoints. Accordingly, a moving camera recording a video sequence can be modelled as many cameras. The *structure from motion* problem consists of reconstructing the 3D scene and motion path of the camera (including orientations) from such a video sequence. There are many approaches for solving this problem, some of which give very good results (Hartley and Zisserman, 2003; Kähler, 2009a).

While (extrinsic) multi-camera self-calibration is part of the structure from motion problem, and despite the theoretical multiple view equivalence, there are severe differences between a moving camera and a general multi-camera system. The most important point is that the camera motion between two subsequent frames recorded by a moving camera is very small and that hence two subsequent frames are very similar. The images taken by two different cameras, on the other hand, can be taken from arbitrary viewpoints and under different conditions leading, in general, to very different images.

In multiple view geometry, these differences are usually ignored, as it is based on geometric entities like points and lines. Digital images, on the other hand, consist of a finite set of intensity measurements on a discrete pixel grid (possibly at different wavelengths in the case of a color image). There is hence a gap between having several digital images and being able to apply the theory of multiple view geometry to them. Usually this gap is closed by extracting point correspondences between the images. In the case of a video sequence recorded by a moving camera, due to the usually very limited changes between two subsequent frames, point correspondences can be established by *tracking* points over time (using, e. g., KLT tracking, see Appendix D.6). This problem mainly consists of finding an optimal transformation of a small image patch, which can be found by nonlinear optimization starting from the solution in the previous frame. In the case of two images taken by two different cameras, on the other hand, the difficulty of the point correspondence problem increases drastically depending on several aspects:

- Local optimization or local search usually cannot be applied as corresponding points can be arbitrarily far apart.

- The image patches surrounding two corresponding image points are projectively distorted relative to each other. While under certain assumptions, these changes can be well modelled (by a so-called homography), this poses a global optimization problem with eight degrees of freedom per point correspondence.

- Differences in the illumination conditions, sensor characteristics, etc. are an additional source for variations of the image patches surrounding two corresponding points. These variations are difficult to model.
- The different viewpoints lead to occlusions, which can (a) make a certain 3D point invisible in one of the images and (b) cause additional, possibly very drastic changes of the image patches surrounding corresponding points.

Summarizing these issues, there are two main difficulties: (a) candidates for point correspondences must be searched for globally in the whole images and (b) possibly great differences of the image patches surrounding two corresponding points lead to severe ambiguities. The difficulty of extracting point correspondences between two cameras strongly depends on the difference between their viewpoints. A small vs. great difference is referred to as a *small* vs. a *wide baseline*. Figure 1.1 shows examples of image pairs with increasing baselines.

The difficulties caused by a camera pair with a wide baseline lead to severe degradation of state-of-the-art point correspondence extraction methods. Figure 1.2 shows the point correspondences extracted using methods described in Chapter 3. As far as the resulting point correspondences are concerned, there are two adverse effects caused by a wide baseline. First, due to the interest point detection, we cannot expect the high subpixel precision that tracking methods can provide. In other words, there is more noise on the locations of the point correspondences. Second, false matches lead to point correspondence hypotheses that do not actually correspond. From a statistical point of view, such point pairs are outliers.

In order to get any meaningful results from such input data, we need to employ robust estimation techniques. Additionally, we cannot expect the same precision of the resulting multi-camera self-calibration (or 3D reconstruction) computed from such correspondences that is possible in the case of a moving camera.

1.2 Overview of the Dissertation and its Contributions

I will assume familiarity with the following concepts, most of which are briefly introduced in the appendix: vector spaces, homogeneous coordinates (Appendix A.1), representation of 3D rotations (Appendix A.2), basic graph theoretical concepts (Appendix B), the pinhole camera model (Appendix D.1) and the epipolar geometry (Appendix D.3). The remainder of the Appendices A through D describes methods for solving certain mathematical, graph theoretical or computer vision problems. Knowledge of these topics is *not* required for reading the main part of this dissertation, but can help in understanding and is required for implementing the self-calibration method.

The main part begins with an overview of (self-)calibration methods for a single and multiple cameras and examples of multi-camera applications (Chapter 2). As the most important contribution of my self-calibration method lies in dealing with imperfect point correspondences, state-of-the-art techniques for extracting point correspondences are described in Chapter 3. My multi-camera self-calibration method uses the relative poses of camera pairs and the uncertainties of these estimates. I hence describe state-of-the-art approaches for robustly estimating the epipolar geometry and the relative pose of two cameras in Chapter 4 along with some minor contributions.

The main theoretical and algorithmical contributions of this dissertation can be found in the Chapters 5 and 6. The former is dedicated to estimating the intrinsic camera parameters of a camera which is rotated by a pan-tilt unit. I present a novel approach for using (partial) prior knowledge about the rotations to improve the self-calibration results. Chapter 6 begins by explaining how a multi-camera system can be extrinsically calibrated from known relative poses (Section 6.1). As some relative pose estimates are more trustworthy than others depending on the quality of the point correspondences used to estimate them, I introduce three new uncertainty measures on relative pose estimates along with a method for approximating these measures (Section 6.2). Based on these data, I formulate the selection of good relative poses as a discrete (global) optimization problem (Section 6.3). This leads to the novel problem of finding shortest (i. e. minimum weight) triangle paths in a graph with uncertainties used as edge weights. I present an efficient solution to this problem and prove its correctness (Section 6.4). The exact differences compared to a related method (Vergés-Llahí and Wada, 2008; Vergés-Llahí et al., 2008) are listed in Section 6.5. As a complementary supportive technique, I present a new method for detecting whether two cameras have a common field of view, which is necessary for estimating their relative pose, and show how it can be combined with the uncertainty based selection of relative poses (Section 6.6).

An extensive experimental evaluation of all the methods described in the Chapters 3 through 6 along with a proof-of-concept multi-camera tracking application is presented in Chapter 7. The dissertation concludes with a summary and discussion of its contributions and results as well as ideas for future work (Chapter 8).

Brief Algorithmic Summary of the Multi-Camera Self-Calibration Method

The main algorithmic steps of the multi-camera self-calibration method can be briefly summarized as follows:

1. Assuming cameras mounted onto pan-tilt units, rotate each camera, perform KLT tracking to extract reliable point correspondences and apply the intrinsic self-calibration method described in Chapter 5. Alternatively calibrate the intrinsic parameters of the cameras using some other method before setting up the multi-camera system.

2. Record one image from each camera.

3. For all camera pairs:

   (a) Extract point correspondences using, e. g., the DoG detector, SIFT descriptors and 2NN matching (Chapter 3).

   (b) Optionally detect whether these two cameras have a common field of view (Section 6.6). If they do, estimate their relative pose and its uncertainty (Chapter 4 and Section 6.2).

4. Represent the cameras, the relative poses and their uncertainties as a graph. Compute minimum uncertainty triangle paths to select good relative pose estimates (Sections 6.3 and 6.4).

5. Extract the extrinsic multi-camera calibration from the selected relative pose estimates (Section 6.1).

(a) A single AVT Pike video camera.

(b) Two subsequent frames of an image sequence recorded by a rotating camera. This is a situation with a very small baseline. Note, however, that the images are *not* identical.

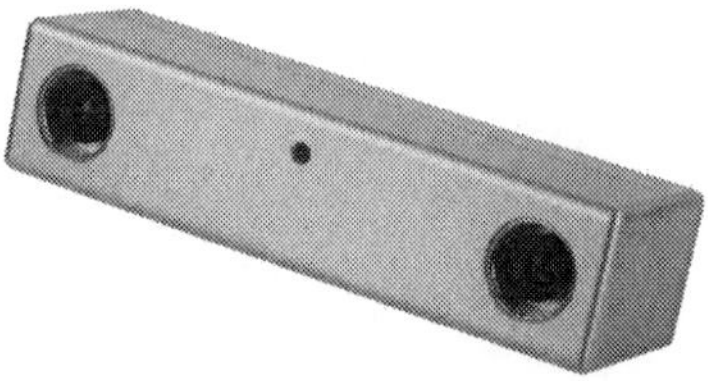

(c) A Point Grey Research Bumblebee stereo camera with a small baseline.

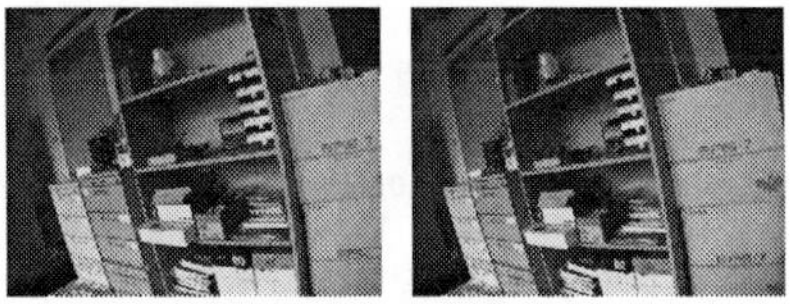

(d) An image pair taken by the Bumblebee camera. Note the severe radial distortion.

(e) Two Sony DFW-VL500 cameras in a wide-baseline setup.

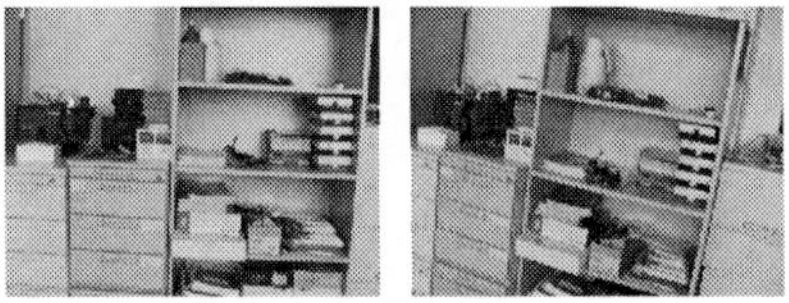

(f) Images taken by the two Sony cameras on the left. Note the different colors caused by different sensor characteristics/settings.

(g) Two Sony DFW-VL500 cameras with a very wide baseline.

(h) Images taken by the two Sony cameras on the left.

Figure 1.1: Examples of small-baseline and wide-baseline setups and image pairs. The baseline increases from top to bottom showing increasing differences in the image pairs.

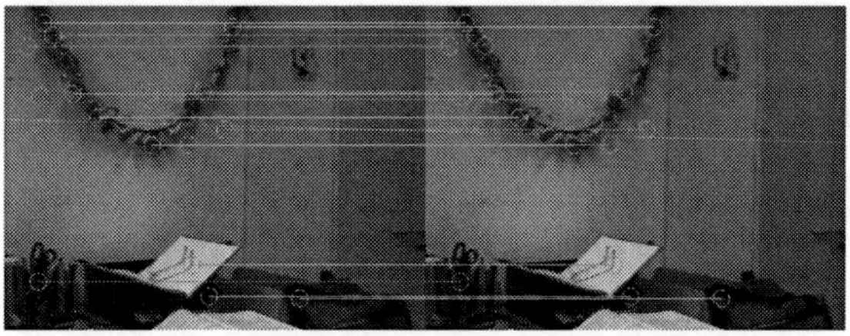

(a) Very small baseline; all correspondences are correct.

(b) Quite small baseline; all correspondences are correct.

(c) Wide baseline; around 30% of the correspondences are false matches.

(d) Very wide baseline; there are no correct correspondences.

Figure 1.2: Point correspondences produced by the DoG detector, the SIFT descriptor and 2NN matching on the image pairs in Figure 1.1. The methods are described in Chapter 3.

Chapter 2

Literature Overview

This chapter gives an overview of the literature concerned with the calibration of multi-camera systems (also known as camera networks). The most important scientific communities involved in the topic are computer vision, photogrammetry, image processing in general and also computer graphics. However, terminology is *not* used consistently throughout these communities. To avoid confusion, I will focus on the computer vision terminology.

Many approaches for multi-camera calibration first calibrate the intrinsic parameters of each camera individually or assume they are known already, before estimating the extrinsic parameters. Thus, the first part of this chapter discusses approaches to calibrate a single camera, focussing on intrinsic calibration.

2.1 Intrinsic Calibration of a Single Camera

The *calibration* of a single camera consists of estimating its intrinsic and usually also extrinsic parameters. An introduction to the pinhole camera model is given in Appendix D.1. This section focuses on intrinsic calibration, as extrinsic calibration of a single camera is of little interest in the context of multi-camera self-calibration, i. e. the estimation of the relative extrinsic parameters of multiple cameras.

Classical Camera Calibration

Classical camera calibration techniques use one or more images of a specifically designed *calibration object* with known geometry. Such a calibration object consists of several easily detectable feature points with known relative 3D positions. Fixating the world coordinate system in the calibration object allows establishing point correspondences between 3D world points and image points. As these have to fulfill the projection equation of the camera model (equation (D.6)), it is possible to compute the model parameters by solving the system of equations resulting from several correspondences.

Since the aim of this dissertation is to fully automatically calibrate a multi-camera system *without* using any dedicated calibration objects, classical calibration is of very limited interest.

There are several text books giving an introduction to the topic, e. g. by Trucco and Verri (1998, Chapter 6), Hartley and Zisserman (2003, Chapter 7), as well as Faugeras (1993, Chapter 3). An example of a classical method using a planar calibration object, which is also called calibration pattern, is presented in Appendix D.5.

As special subproblem of camera calibration is known as *extrinsic calibration* or *camera pose*. It means computing extrinsic parameters of a camera with known intrinsic parameters. Classical solutions of the problem require correspondences between known 3D points and their 2D images, which are typically gained from a calibration object. Such methods are hence of very limited interest to this work. An example of such a method is presented by Ameller et al. (2002, 2000).

Self-Calibration

The term *self-calibration* (also called *auto-calibration*) is used for several related, but nevertheless different concepts. In the broad sense, it refers to any calibration procedure which does not use measurements of known entities of the world, like a calibration object. In the computer vision literature, however, the term self-calibration is sometimes exclusively used for a certain subclass of these methods, which are based on the absolute conic, the absolute quadric, the plane at infinity, the Kruppa equations or a related concept (Hartley and Zisserman, 2003, Chapter 19), (Faugeras and Luong, 2001, Chapter 11). Quan and Triggs (2000) present a unification of such self-calibration methods. The most recent of these approaches first computes a projective 3D reconstruction of the scene from a set of images, which is usually recorded by a moving camera, and then "upgrades" it to a Euclidean reconstruction (so called *stratified methods*). The latter step includes estimating the intrinsic and extrinsic camera parameters. Methods for the preliminary computation of a projective reconstruction typically require point correspondences between the images, often consistently over the whole set of images.

According to Ji and Dai (2004), there are three classes of motion used by different self-calibration approaches: pure translation, pure rotation and general motion. While pure translational approaches do not allow for a rotational motion component and vice versa, general motion approaches require translation *and* rotation. Furthermore, it has been shown by Sturm (1997) that there are classes of degenerate motion paths which only yield an ambiguous calibration. Kahl et al. (2000) analyzed the according problem for a camera with some varying parameters.

As noted by Fusiello (2000) and Triggs (1998), self-calibration methods are typically very sensitive to noise in the localization of the point correspondences. According to the authors, the more recent methods based on a stratified approach are less sensitive, but the general problem is still largely unsolved.

Self-Calibration of a Pan-Tilt Camera

For some special cases, which are degenerate ones for general self-calibration as described above, e. g. pure rotation or planar motion, there are specialized methods, some of which allow self-calibration without a projective reconstruction (Hartley and Zisserman, 2003, Chapter 19). For this dissertation, self-calibration methods for a rotating camera are of special interest, as a pan-tilt camera (i. e. a camera with computer controlable pan and tilt mechanisms) is able to rotate, but cannot perform general motion. The main idea is that an image and a second image acquired after a pure rotation about the optical center (see Appendix D.1) are related by a homography, which can be estimated from the images. Given two or more such homographies, we can compute the intrinsic camera parameters if not all rotations are about the same axis. Details are given in Chapter 5.

In practice, a pan-tilt camera often does *not* perform a pure rotation about the optical center, since the latter often does not coincide with the rotation center (i. e. the intersection of the two rotation axes, assuming they do intersect) of the pan-tilt mechanism. If the distance of the camera to the scene is large compared to the distance between the optical center and rotation center, the errors induced on the intrinsic camera parameters are small, as proven by Hayman and Murray (2003, 2002) under the assumption of known skew, aspect ratio and principal point. A similar error analysis is performed by Wang et al. (2004, 2001). However, as the approximation can also be quite severely violated, as is probably the case for a camera mounted onto a separate pan-tilt unit viewing a close scene, Ji and Dai (2004) proposed a self-calibration method for a rotating camera that allows for a constant translational offset. Their method requires two rotations about the same but unknown angle (and axis). In practice, this means that the pan-tilt control must be able to execute two consecutive rotations by the same angle.

Ignoring radial distortion during self-calibration amounts to systematic errors in correspondence estimations. In other words, the true camera projection function $\boldsymbol{m}$ cannot be described by the pinhole model. It is, hence, not surprising that ignoring radial (and other) distortion will lead to errors in the estimated intrinsic parameters. Assuming zero skew, Tordoff and Murray (2004, 2000) analyse these errors showing that increasing pin-cushion distortion leads to gently worsening underestimation of the focal length, whereas increasing barrel distortion leads to more pronounced overestimation and eventual failure of the calibration. They also propose methods for estimating radial distortion during self-calibration. However, their practical value might be limited, as a high density and quality of image features is required, which natural scenes do not necessarily provide.

Changing Intrinsic Parameters of a Zoom Camera

A camera with computer controlable zoom allows changing the lens configuration of the camera optics. It is not surprising that a change to the zoom setting will alter the focal length parameters in the pinhole camera model. According to Willson (1994a,b), however, a change to the zoom, focus and/or aperture setting of a camera influences the full set of intrinsic and also extrinsic parameters. The change is most pronounced for the focal length and the Z-coordinate of the translation vector. Furthermore, the image center moves systematically by several pixels over the range of zoom settings, and there is a systematic change in the amount of radial distortion. The effects on the other parameters are comparatively small and can probably be ignored in many cases. In accordance with these results, Willson (1994a,b) proposed a parametric model capable of predicting camera model parameters given settings for zoom, focus and possibly also aperture. The calibration of his model is based on classic calibration for many settings of the control parameters and an interpolation of the resulting camera model parameters.

2.2 Multi-Camera Calibration

The multi-camera calibration literature is mainly concerned with estimating extrinsic parameters. Most approaches first compute intrinsic parameters individually for each camera as described in the previous section. Extrinsic parameters are subsequently estimated given the intrinsic parameters. The calibration task is usually formulated such that the world coordinate system may be chosen arbitrarily, which amounts to calibration up to a rigid transformation of the whole system. Furthermore, if no metric measurements are used, the scale of the multi-camera system cannot be determined. This is the case if only correspondences between the cameras are used as input (of the extrinsic calibration).

Virtual Calibration Object with Known Geometry

Calibrating a multi-camera system is theoretically possible by individually calibrating intrinsic and extrinsic parameters of all cameras involved with respect to the same world coordinate system using classical calibration methods. This requires that all cameras observe a common calibration object or that a calibration object is moved to precisely know positions such that every camera can observe it. The first approach imposes very strict limitations on the allowable relative camera poses (i. e. their relative position and orientation) or requires a very large calibration object in the case of a more general camera setup. The second approach requires highly accurate positioning of the calibration object, which is generally complicated and uncomfortable in practice (Chen et al., 2000). As using a calibration object is generally not the aim of this dissertation, such methods will not be reviewed in detail.

An example for such an approach is the work of Kitahara et al. (2001), who use one relatively small calibration plate, which is moved to different locations, and a 3D laser-surveying instrument to measure the positions of the plate. Its multiple positions with known coordinates can be combined to one large *virtual calibration object*, which then allows using classical calibration methods.

Virtual Calibration Object from a Moving Point

One way to avoid the problems mentioned in the previous subsection is to create a virtual calibration object by moving an easily detectable point through the complete working volume, i. e. the space visible to at least one camera. The 3D path of the moving point does not have to be known and it is not required that the point can be observed by all cameras at every point in time. In many approaches, the task of detecting the moving point in the camera images is simplified by darkening the room(s) containing the cameras and moving a modified laser pointer or an LED around. The basic idea is then to establish a point correspondence between all cameras viewing the point at any given point in time.

Baker and Aloimonos (2000) jointly calibrate intrinsic and extrinsic parameters of synchronized cameras. A globally consistent solution up to an unknown, but common projective transformation is achieved by solving a nonlinear eigenvalue minimization problem, which is composed using all point correspondences for all cameras. To allow metric calibration, an additional rod of known length with an LED at each end is moved through the working volume. A nonlinear optimization yields the unknown projective transformation and thus the complete calibration. As a final step, intrinsic and extrinsic parameters can be separated via QR decomposition.

Given the intrinsic calibration of all cameras, Chen et al. (2000) perform structure-from-motion for camera pairs using the observed point correspondences and integrate the results into an extrinsic calibration of the whole network. This rough initial estimate is used as an initialization for an iterative improvement consisting of the following two alternating parts, which are executed until convergence: Firstly, given fully calibrated cameras the 3D path of the point can be reconstructed. Using an extended Kalman filter allows for unsynchronized cameras, which only have to provide a time stamp for each image. Secondly, this point path is used as a huge virtual calibration object, which allows using a classical calibration method for all cameras. Davis and Chen (2003) extend this calibration method to allow for additional cameras with active pan and tilt. During the initial data acquisition, several pan-tilt settings are used to cover the whole range of parameter values. After calibrating the passive cameras, the pan-tilt cameras are calibrated using the virtual calibration object.

Svoboda et al. (2005) (Svoboda, 2003) calibrate intrinsic and extrinsic parameters including radial distortion of a synchronized multi-camera system. After a RANSAC based rejection of incorrectly detected points and filling up of missing points, all point correspondences are used for a projective 3D reconstruction using a factorization method, which is optionally refined by bundle adjustment (see below). This projective reconstruction is upgraded to a Euclidian one by applying self-calibration techniques for varying intrinsic parameters based on the assumption of zero skew. This yields the projection matrices, which can optionally be decomposed into the intrinsic and extrinsic parameters. Based on the 2D reprojection error, another outlier detection on the point correspondences is performed and the previous steps are repeated. Finally, radial distortion parameters are estimated by a standard method using correspondences between image points and reconstructed 3D points as input. As these parameters influence the previous steps, the whole procedure is repeated iteratively. A freely available implementation of the method is described in a separate publication (Svoboda, 2005). There is also an earlier version of the calibration method (Svoboda et al., 2002).

Barreto and Daniilidis (2004) persent a similar approach with several differences in detail. First of all, they assume known projection matrices for at least two cameras. This avoids using a full factorization method, which requires that all correspondences are given for every camera, and thus no filling up of missing points is necessary. Furthermore, direct Euclidian calibration is possible as the initial projection matrices are already Euclidian. The authors claim that this leads to more accurate results. The algorithm incrementally calibrates one camera at a time using a suitable subset of the point correspondences. Hence, a common field of view for all cameras is not required. The incremental calibration scheme as a whole is repeated until convergence to improve the calibration of all cameras, including the initially calibrated ones. Furthermore, the authors present a method for estimating the radial distortion, which is directly integrated into the multiple view equations.

Other Motion Based Methods

A moving point is not the only possibility to create a virtual calibration object with unknown geometry. Baker and Aloimonos (2003) developed an alternative method in order to reach higher stability than their own point based method (Baker and Aloimonos, 2000) described above. For their new method, they use geometric constraints on the images of parallel lines and thus require detectable parallel lines in the scene, which are provided by a planar calibration pattern. Despite parallelism, no metric properties of the calibration pattern must be known. The pattern is arbitrarily moved through the working volume. Detecting the direction of parallel lines in the camera images allows calibrating intrinsic parameters (with the assumption of square pixels and zero skew) including radial distortion as well as rotation matrices, but all of these only up to an affine distortion. A nonlinear optimization is used to improve these estimates. An additional planar, regular grid pattern allows detecting orthogonal lines as well as the center of the pattern, which yields stable point correspondences. This information can be used to remove the affine distortion and also to compute translation vectors. As the calibration object is not stationary, the world coordinate system is identified with one of the camera coordinate systems. Restrictions on the setup of the multi-camera system are not strict, but a detailed analysis is not given.

Sinha et al. (2004) fully calibrate a synchronized multi-camera system using dynamic silhouettes of a moving person. Their incremental algorithm computes a projective calibration from a set of fundamental matrices, which are estimated from the silhouettes. Fundamental matrices are not required for every camera pair as described by Levi and Werman (2003) (see below). The projective calibration is upgraded to a Euclidean one using the self-calibration technique by Pollefeys et al. (2002). A final bundle adjustment (see below) improves the solution and can also compute radial distortion parameters. Sinha and Pollefeys (2004a) also present an extension of their algorithm which can handle unsynchronized cameras by estimating the synchronization.

Lee et al. (2000) track objects moving on a common dominant plane in the scene (e. g. the ground plane). There may be more than one, but not too many objects moving on the plane. Common motion in more than one camera image creates a hypothesis for a correspondence. For every camera pair, these correspondences are used to estimate the homography which relates the dominant plane in both images. Under the assumption that three cameras have an overlapping field of view, these homographies are used to estimate their extrinsic parameters. Experiments on an outdoor traffic scene with a large distance between the cameras and the moving objects are presented.

Multiple Pan-Tilt-Zoom Cameras

As in the case of a single camera, active pan-tilt and also zoom control of the cameras can be exploited for multi-camera calibration. Obviously, it is possible to use a self-calibration method for a rotating camera to calibrate intrinsic parameters and subsequently calibrate the extrinsic parameters of the network. But there are also additional possibilities.

Collins and Tsin (1999) calibrate a system of multiple pan-tilt-zoom cameras in two steps. In the first step, the intrinsic parameters are estimated for each camera using nonlinear optimization to minimize the reprojection error over the intrinsic parameters including radial distortion.

The authors call this "calibration by image warping". Conceptually, this is similar to bundle adjustment (see below) with the main difference that no 3D feature points are used. The first step includes a full zoom calibration, in which a magnification factor and the image center depend on the zoom setting. However, Wilson's work suggests that this is an idealized model not suitable for all cameras (Willson, 1994a). Extrinsic calibration is performed in the second step. An operator has to remotely control pan and tilt settings to point the camera at several landmarks, such that the landmark is in the center of the image. This amounts to manually supplying correspondences between 3D scene points and image points, which can then be used for extrinsic calibration.

Sinha and Pollefeys (2004b) also split the calibration of multiple pan-tilt-zoom cameras into two parts. The first part consists of calibrating the intrinsic parameters including radial distortion, first for the minimum zoom setting and subsequently for the full zoom range. A central part of the approach consists of computing a panorama mosaic for each camera at minimum zoom using the full range of pan and tilt settings. The images required for such a panorama are also used for rotational self-calibration (see Chapter 5). The standard method is slightly modified and combined with two bundle adjustment procedures (see below), which yield a nonlinear improvement of the estimates and also compute radial distortion parameters. Based on this calibration at minimum zoom, a calibration of the full range of zoom parameters is performed. In the second step, the panorama mosaics at minimum zoom are computed and used to estimate the epipolar geometry for "sufficient" camera pairs. The extrinsic parameters are then extracted from the essential matrices of these pairs. Finally, the results have to be integrated into an extrinsic calibration of the whole network (Sinha et al., 2004).

Chippendale and Tobia (2005) calibrate the extrinsic parameters of multiple pan-tilt-zoom cameras with known intrinsic parameters. The setup of the multi-camera system is restricted by the requirement that the cameras have to be able to see each other. The basic idea is that one camera at a time is a "watcher" while the others are "movers". The movers pan around while the watcher actively searches its full pan-tilt range for motion. After detection, the mover is identified by stopping one mover at a time. Then, the mover turns such that the watcher can see and measure the diameter of the image of the mover's lens. Given knowledge of the metric size of the lens diameter, the distance between mover and watcher can be estimated. Relative orientation can be estimated from pan- and tilt-settings and an additional roll estimation. Finally, these pairwise estimates can be combined to form a global extrinsic calibration of the network.

Relative Pose of Two Cameras

The relative extrinsic parameteres of two cameras, also referred to as their *relative pose*, can be estimated up to scale from a set of point correspondences. There are basically two different approaches Hartley and Zisserman (2003); Nistér (2004). The fundamental matrix can be estimated from at least seven point correspondences without knowing the intrinsic parameters. If eight correspondences are known, the simpler, linear eight-point algorithm can be used. Given the fundamental matrix, the essential matrix can be computed and the relative pose can be extracted from that (Section 4.2.6). On the other hand, one of the five-point or six-point algorithms can be used to estimate the essential matrix directly from a least five point correspondences and known intrinsic parameters (Nistér, 2004, 2003; Stewénius et al., 2006; Philip, 1996; Pizarro et al., 2003). Further details are given in Chapter 4.

However, there are degenerate configurations which introduce an ambiguity (Philip, 1998), (Hartley and Zisserman, 2003, Chapter 11). The most important cases are coplanar correspondences and identical camera centers (i. e. pure rotation of a single camera). As mentioned by Nistér (2004), there are specialized homography based methods to compute extrinsic parameters in the coplanar case and approaches which automatically choose the appropriate model depending on the situation.

In practice, it is important to achieve robustness with respect to outliers. Usually, one the algorithms mentioned above is integrated into a sampling algorithm like RANSAC (Fischler and Bolles, 1981) or MLESAC (Torr and Zisserman, 2000). See Section 4.3 for further details.

Extrinsic Calibration of a Multi-Camera System

In a comparatively theoretical work, Brand et al. (2004) perform extrinsic calibration of a multi-camera system given displacement directions between rotationally aligned cameras by solving a graph embedding problem in 3D. The method yields a minimum error solution for overconstrained subgraphs as well as information about underconstrained subgraphs which do not allow for complete calibration due to missing information.

Mantzel et al. (2004) extrinsically calibrate sparse multi-camera systems, which do not require a common field of view for every camera pair. They assume that point correspondences are given as well as intrinsic parameters for each camera and extrinsic parameters for at least two cameras with a common point correspondence. This data is used to triangulate 3D scene points. After the 3D scene points have been computed, cameras which view enough of these can be calibrated. The procedure is iterated until all cameras have been calibrated or no further improvement is possible. Snavely et al. (2008) present a similar approach including an estimation of the extrinsic parameters of the initial camera pair and multiple bundle adjustments. Furthermore, Mantzel et al. (2004) describe an algorithm based on this scheme which only requires local computation at each camera and communication only between neighboring cameras. The advantages are that no central processing unit is required and communication costs can be lower.

As mentioned in the preceeding, extrinsic calibration often computes and uses the epipolar geometry. As a supporting technique, Levi and Werman (2003) describe how missing fundamental matrices can be computed from existing ones, depending on the structure of a certain graph, in which two cameras are connected if their fundamental matrix is known (a variation of the camera dependency graph, see Section 6.1). The authors give an analysis of solvable graph structures for up to six cameras. However, their method is not generally limited to six cameras.

Martinec and Pajdla (2007, 2006) compute extrinsic parameters from pairwise relative poses. They refer to several methods for the two subproblems of rotational and translational alignment/registration and weight the relative poses by a compined support and importance measure. The measure incorporates the number of inliers found by RANSAC a graph theoretical importance based on shortest paths. The approach is roughly similar to the one presented in this dissertation in the sense that pairwise relative poses are combined to the final calibration using a quality measure. The combination algorithm and the measure themselves, however, are very different.

Vergés-Llahí et al. (2008) present a roughly similar approach. They propose an unreliability measure for relative poses and treat them as weights in the camera dependency graph, which contains all cameras and connects them according to known relative poses. In order to compute the calibration of the multi-camera system, the relative poses are concatenated along shortest triangle-connected paths using the unreliabilities as edge weights (lengths). Vergés-Llahí and Wada (2008) present an algorithm for this specific graph-theoretical problem. A detailled analysis of the difference between their approach and mine is given in Section 6.5.

Recalibration

Zomet et al. (2001) and Shashua (1998) present a method for recalibrating a multi-camera system. After calibrating the network and rigidly moving it (e. g. to a different room), they compute a projective reconstruction from point correspondences. Given the relative rotations of the cameras, the projective reconstruction is upgraded to a Euclidean one. That is, intrinsic parameters and relative positions of the cameras can be recalibrated using their approach, but relative orientations have to remain fixed. Furthermore, a certain minimum number of cameras is required, depending on the number of constant intrinsic parameters. Practically, such a method can be applied to a rig carrying multiple fixed zoom cameras.

Bundle Adjustment

Bundle adjustment (Hartley and Zisserman, 2003, Section 18.1), (Triggs et al., 1999) is a nonlinear optimization method which minimizes the (sub)quadratic distances between image points and the reprojections of reconstructed 3D points. The optimization solves for 3D points as well as camera parameters (optionally including intrinsic parameters and distortion), which are needed to project the 3D points. As a local nonlinear optimization algorithm like Levenberg-Marquardt (see Appendix C.2) is used and the problem typically has more than one local minimum, a good initialization is required. This can be provided by a calibration of the multi-camera system and a triangulated set of 2D point correspondences (see Appendix D.4).

Recently, Kahl and Hartley (2007) proposed a new approach for several 3D computer vision problems using the L_∞ distance instead of the Euclidean distance. The advantage is that the global optimum can be found quite efficiently using second-order cone programming. However, in the context of multiple view reconstruction and (extrinsic) calibration, which is (locally) solved by bundle adjustment, the intrinsic parameters and the rotation matrices have to be known in advance. Furthermore, the method is naturally extremely sensitive with respect to outliers.

Generalized Camera Models

Generalized camera models (Sturm and Ramalingam, 2004) can be used to describe a whole multi-camera system as a single camera with multiple projection centers. An example for such an approach is presented by Grossberg and Nayar (2001). They model the projection properties of every pixel individually as the cone in space that this pixel can see. A simplification only considers the central axis of that cone. Pless (2003) applies this model to a multi-camera system. However, there is no calibration method for such a model which does not require a calibration object. Furthermore, it seems impossible to develop a self-calibration method without heavily relying on additional knowledge about the actual camera(s), which severely spoils the advantages of a generalized model as far as the calibration is concerned. Stewénius et al. (2005) present a method for estimating the relative pose of two generalized cameras can be computed given intrinsic parameters and at least six point correspondences.

2.3 Applications

There are several applications of multi-camera systems in various areas. In this section, I will present several examples, whereby this list does not claim to be exhaustive. Depending on the application, a more or less complete calibration of the multi-camera system is required as an initialization. Furthermore, the setup of the multi-camera system may or may not have to fulfill certain restrictions and the cameras may or may not need to be synchronized or allow for an even higher degree of timing control.

Volumetric 3D Reconstruction

Slabaugh et al. (2001, 2004) give a survey of methods for volumetric scene reconstruction based on multiple images. In this context, the term volumetric refers to the representation of the reconstruction, which is typically voxel based as opposed to a surface oriented representation. All methods surveyed in the paper require calibrated cameras. However a few of them do not require a full metric calibration. The methods make up three general classes: volumetric visual hull, voxel coloring and volumetric stereo vision. Volumetric visual hull methods, also known as volume intersection, compute a hull of an object based on a 2D segmentation or silhouette in each of the images of several cameras. Voxel coloring assumes Lambertian surfaces and checks voxels for color consistency: All pixels which can observe a certain voxel are evaluated for color consistency. If the colors are similar, the voxel is marked as an object voxel with according color. Otherwise the voxel is either invisible or transparent. There are several extensions of voxel coloring: space carving, generalized voxel coloring and multi-hypothesis voxel coloring. Projective grid space is a variant of voxel coloring, which only requires epipolar geometry instead of a full camera calibration. The third class, volumetric stereo vision, tries to use a volumetric scene representation to combination with classical stereo vision to handle the problem of robustly finding point matches, which are required for stereo reconstruction.

Multi-Camera Tracking

Khan et al. (2001) perform tracking of humans using multiple uncalibrated cameras. Their system automatically establishes spacial relationships between the fields of view of the individual cameras, which actually amounts to an automatic, partial calibration of the multi-camera system. This information is used during tracking to predict which other cameras can see a person observed by a given camera and also to handle ambiguities. Kim and Davis (2006) present a roughly similar system. The calibration of the system is greatly simplified by assuming that the persons only move on a common ground plane.

Computer Graphics

Wilburn et al. (2005) describe several applications of a certain special multi-camera system called "Stanford multiple camera array", which consists of 128 cameras mounted in a regular planar grid. The details of the setup depend on the application. High dynamic range and high resolution video can be captured if the cameras are set up such that the field of view of neighboring cameras slightly overlaps. From their images a mosaic can be built, which realizes a video camera with high resolution. Furthermore, every camera's exposure time can be set individually, allowing to capture scenes of high dynamic range. The local dynamic range of the virtual camera can be further increased by choosing a greater overlap between the input images. A different arrangement of the camera array with a completely overlapping field of view in a certain depth of interest allows high speed video capture with several thousand frames per second. For this purpose the trigger times of the cameras are linearly staggered. Because of the parallax induced by the placing of the cameras, correcting transformations are required. This approach combined with a spatiotemporal view interpolation algorithm enables time dilation and – arranging the cameras with a reduced overlap in the field of view – virtual camera motion similar to the Bullet Time system used for the movie The Matrix as mentioned in Wilburn's PhD thesis (Wilburn et al., 2005). Using a layout of the camera array similar to the one for high resolution video capture allows for some further interesting applications. One of these, called (nonlinear) synthetic aperture photography, allows to see through a partially occluding object like a bush. Given the different perspectives of the individual cameras, a different part of the virtual focal plane behind the occluding object is unoccluded in each image. This makes it possible to collect only pixels corresponding to 3D points at the desired depth of the virtual focal plane and thus to reconstruct an unoccluded image. A further application is called hybrid aperture photography. It allows creating a virtual camera with short exposure time and high depth of field. The later is realized in a single camera by a small aperture. Combined with the short exposure time, this requires a very bright scene to be able to collect enough light. For less bright scenes, the resulting images are very noisy. The hybrid aperture technique does not have this limitation.

In their above mentioned work on "Virtualized Reality", Kitahara et al. (2001) suggest placing several pan-tilt-zoom cameras around a room, like a soccer stadium for example, in order to create artificial videos from freely chooseable viewpoints. They suggest using a shape from silhouette approach to compute a (partial) 3D reconstruction, which is required for rendering images from new viewpoints.

Telepresence

Gross et al. (2003) present "blue-c: a spatially immersive display and 3D video portal for telepresence". It basically consists of three room-sized 3D display walls and 16 cameras, which are used to capture a 3D video stream of the user inside the "room". That video can be streamed to other similar systems and displayed as part of a common virtual 3D world. As in the work of Kitahara et al. (2001), a shape from silhouette approach is used for (partial) 3D video reconstruction. Possible application of blue-c and similar systems are, amongst others, distributed collaboration and training as well as entertainment.

Prince et al. (2002) describe a somewhat similar augmented reality system. While a head mounted augmented reality display with a frontal camera is used instead of display walls, the system also uses a multi-camera system consisting of, in this case, 15 cameras to capture live 3D video of another person, which is augmented to the live video of the viewer's environment. Acquisition of 3D video data is also based on a shape from silhouette approach. Video-conferencing and entertainment are presented as applications.

Doubek et al. (2003) developed a low-cost multi-camera system called V**i**Room. As an application they present a system for automatic view selection and virtual zoom. That system selects the camera image showing the most of a moving person inside the room and extracts and scales the person from that image. Later, Doubek et al. (2004) present a more sophisticated view selection algorithm, which also applies view interpolation to select views not directly provided by the cameras.

Ambient Intelligence

Brumitt et al. (2000) describe an intelligent environment called "EasyLiving", which is an example of the more general concept of ambient intelligence described by Remagnino and Foresti (2005). An intelligent environment consists of many cooperating electronic devices and sensors. The aim is to realize new ways of human machine interaction and automation. A simple example is automatic light control in a home, which adjusts lighting to the positions of the inhabitants. Of course cameras are a valuable type of sensor for an intelligent environment and typically more than one is needed to cover the whole room or house. Trivedi et al. (2000,?) describe some aspects of using multiple cameras in an intelligent environment.

Similar to an immersive display, Bobick et al. (1999) describe an entertainment environment called "KidsRoom", which also has elements of an intelligent environment. It is used as a multimedial, interactive story telling system. To enable better control of the multimedia equipment, like user aware lighting control, and especially to allow for interaction of the user in the story being told, the system is equipped with four cameras. The main computer vision tasks preformed with these are object tracking, movement detection and action recognition.

Chapter 3

Wide-Baseline Point Correspondence Extraction

The calibration method I present in this thesis (Chapters 4 through 6) requires *point correspondences* between pairs of images as input. The concept of a point correspondence is explained in Appendix D.3. Generally, there are two classes of correspondence extraction techniques. If a video sequence is available, point *tracking* methods, like KLT tracking (Appendix D.6) can be applied. On the other hand, if only two images taken by two cameras with a wide baseline are given, the problem is more difficult and according methods are required.

A pair of cameras is said to have a *wide baseline* if they are placed "far" apart relative to the distance to the scene and/or have a very different orientation. This is meant in opposition to the small baseline in the cases of (a) two subsequent frames in a video and (b) a classical stereo camera setup. Examples of small- and wide-baseline setups and images are given in Figure 1.1. As I focus on a wide-baseline situation in this thesis, I will only present methods suitable for such a situation in this chapter. Only in the experiments regarding the rotational self-calibration of a single camera (Section 7.1), I will apply KLT tracking (Appendix D.6) to a video sequence.

Wide-baseline point correspondence extraction methods typically consist of three steps: (a) detect interest points, (b) compute a descriptor for each interest points and (c) match the descriptors. In the subsequent sections, I will present a few alternative approaches for each step. As correspondence extraction as a whole and interest point detection and point descriptors in particular are mostly treated as black boxes in this dissertation, I will only give brief descriptions focussing on the main ideas. For details, the reader is referred to the literature (see below).

Examples of the output of one of the algorithms are shown in Figure 1.2. Note that the quality of the results highly depends on the imaging conditions.

3.1 Detectors

In this section, I will first describe the task of detecting points of interest in an image and subsequently present a few suitable methods. Note that some of the methods detect regions of interest rather than points. However, as I want to extract point correspondences, there must be a defined reference point within each region, typically the center or center of gravity. Hence, for the sake of simplicity, I will only use the term *interest point*.

There are two reasons for using interest point detectors: (a) to reduce the amount of data considered in the subsequent steps and (b) to only consider image areas which are likely to produce highly discriminative descriptors (Section 3.2), which is important for the matching step (Section 3.3).

For correspondence extraction, the detector is applied to two (or more) images and all subsequent operations are applied to the interest points returned by it. Hence, it is highly desirable that the output of the detector is repeatable even despite a change of the imaging conditions, such as different viewpoints or illumination. In other words, the detector should be *invariant* to such influences. However, due to occlusions (see, e. g. Figure 1.2(d)), full invariance cannot possibly be achieved.

Existing methods, as will be described later on in this section, are invariant to some 2D deformations of the (local) image content, such as translation, scale or full affine deformation and some illumination changes, like additive or multiplicative changes. Let aside occlusions, however, even the best detectors can only handle changes of the imaging conditions to a certain limited extent.

In the remainder of this section, I will briefly present the Harris-Laplace and the Hessian-Laplace detector, their affine region extension, as well as the difference of Gaussian (DoG) detector. This is the same selection I used in (Bajramovic, Koch and Denzler, 2009) and is based on (Mikolajczyk et al., 2005), except for the DoG detector, which is the detector originally suggested in conjunction with the very popular SIFT descriptor (Lowe, 2004).

Harris-Laplace

The Harris-Laplace detector (Mikolajczyk and Schmid, 2002; Mikolajczyk, 2002) is based on the well known Harris-Stephens corner detector (Harris and Stephens, 1988). In addition, it uses a Gaussian and Laplacian of Gaussian scale space (Lindeberg, 1994; Gonzalez and Woods, 2002) to achieve scale invariance. The scale dependent second moment matrix is

$$\boldsymbol{S}(\boldsymbol{x},\sigma_{\mathrm{D}}) \overset{\mathrm{def}}{=} \sigma_{\mathrm{D}}^2 \cdot g(\sigma_{\mathrm{I}}) * \begin{pmatrix} (I_{\mathrm{X}}(\boldsymbol{x},\sigma_{\mathrm{D}}))^2 & I_{\mathrm{X}}(\boldsymbol{x},\sigma_{\mathrm{D}})I_{\mathrm{Y}}(\boldsymbol{x},\sigma_{\mathrm{D}}) \\ I_{\mathrm{X}}(\boldsymbol{x},\sigma_{\mathrm{D}})I_{\mathrm{Y}}(\boldsymbol{x},\sigma_{\mathrm{D}}) & (I_{\mathrm{Y}}(\boldsymbol{x},\sigma_{\mathrm{D}}))^2 \end{pmatrix} , \tag{3.1}$$

where "$*$" denotes convolution, $\boldsymbol{x}$ is the image point, σ_{D} is the scale, σ_{I} specifies the size of the summation window, g is the zero-mean Gaussian function and $I_{\mathrm{X}}(\boldsymbol{x},\sigma_D)$, $I_{\mathrm{Y}}(\boldsymbol{x},\sigma_D)$ denote the image derivatives at resolution σ_{D} of the Gaussian scale space in the X and Y direction, respectively. Based on the second moment matrix, the Harris function is defined as follows:

$$h(\boldsymbol{x},\sigma_{\mathrm{D}}) = \det(\boldsymbol{S}(\boldsymbol{x},\sigma_{\mathrm{D}})) - \alpha \cdot (\mathrm{trace}(\boldsymbol{S}(\boldsymbol{x},\sigma_{\mathrm{D}})))^2 , \tag{3.2}$$

where the constant α is usually set to 0.04. A point $\boldsymbol{x}$ at scale σ_{D} has to fulfill the following conditions in order to be selected as an interest point:

- The point $\boldsymbol{x}$ is a local maximum of the Harris function h with respect to its eight neighbors at scale σ_{D} and the value of the Harris function $h(\boldsymbol{x},\sigma_{\mathrm{D}})$ is above a certain threshold.

- $(\boldsymbol{x}, \sigma_\mathrm{D})$ is a local maximum with respect to its two scale neighbors in the Laplacian of Gaussian scale space and the value of $(\boldsymbol{x}, \sigma_\mathrm{D})$ in that scale space is above a certain threshold.

Additionally, Mikolajczyk (2002) presents an iterative refinement of the location $\boldsymbol{x}$ and scale σ_D.

Hessian-Laplace

For the Hessian-Laplace detector (Mikolajczyk et al., 2005), the second moment matrix $\boldsymbol{S}(\boldsymbol{x}, \sigma_\mathrm{D})$ is replaced by the Hessian

$$\boldsymbol{H}(\boldsymbol{x}, \sigma_\mathrm{D}) \stackrel{\mathrm{def}}{=} \begin{pmatrix} I_\mathrm{XX}(\boldsymbol{x}, \sigma_\mathrm{D}) & I_\mathrm{XY}(\boldsymbol{x}, \sigma_\mathrm{D}) \\ I_\mathrm{XY}(\boldsymbol{x}, \sigma_\mathrm{D}) & I_\mathrm{YY}(\boldsymbol{x}, \sigma_\mathrm{D}) \end{pmatrix} , \tag{3.3}$$

where $I_\mathrm{XX}(\boldsymbol{x}, \sigma_\mathrm{D})$, $I_\mathrm{XY}(\boldsymbol{x}, \sigma_\mathrm{D})$, $I_\mathrm{YY}(\boldsymbol{x}, \sigma_\mathrm{D})$ denote the second image derivatives along the according axes.

Affine Region Extension

The Harris-Laplace and Hessian-Laplace detectors are (approximately) invariant with respect to rotation and scale. The affine region extension (Mikolajczyk and Schmid, 2002; Mikolajczyk, 2002) aims at achieving affine invariance. In contrast to the Harris-Laplace and Hessian-Laplace detectors, the circular region implicitly defined by the convolution with the Gaussian $g(\sigma_\mathrm{I})$ in equation (3.1) may now have general elliptical shape. Accordingly, an affine generalization of the scale space is required. The shape of the region is determined by an iterative algorithm, which optimizes an isotropy measure.

Difference of Gaussian

The difference of Gaussian (DoG) detector described by Lowe (2004) uses a difference of Gaussian scale space (Lindeberg, 1994) to detect scale invariant interest points. A point $\boldsymbol{x}$ at scale σ_D is selected as a preliminary interest point if it is a local extremum in the difference of Gaussian scale space with respect to its 26 neighbors (in the current and the two neighboring scale levels).

Some of the points detected by this approach will lie on edges. As their location is unstable along the edge, a rejection criterion similar to the Hessian detector is used. Instead of the Harris function (using the Hessian instead of the second moment matrix), however, a threshold on the following ratio is used:

$$\frac{(\mathrm{trace}(\boldsymbol{H}(\boldsymbol{x}, \sigma_\mathrm{D})))^2}{\det(\boldsymbol{H}(\boldsymbol{x}, \sigma_\mathrm{D}))} . \tag{3.4}$$

Optionally, the location $\boldsymbol{x}$ is refined to subpixel accuracy by fitting a quadratic model to the 3D neighborhood in the scale space. Also, a threshold on the value of this model at the refined location is used to reject points with a low contrast.

Finally, each interest point is assigned an orientation. First, a gradient orientation histogram weighted by the gradient strength and a Gaussian centered at the interest point is computed at the scale σ_{D} of the interest point (in the Gaussian scale space). The peak of this histogram gives the orientation of the interest point. If there are further dominant local peaks, additional interest points with that orientation (and the same position and scale) are created.

3.2 Descriptors

Once we have detected interest points, we need to extract a description of the image content in a neighborhood of the point in order to be able to match the points in two images. For the matching step, the *interest point descriptors* (also referred to as *local descriptors*) should ideally be identical (or differ only slightly) for corresponding image points and show a pronounced difference otherwise. As the descriptors of two corresponding image points in two *identical* images are obviously identical, we can also formulate the following requirement. The descriptors should be discriminative within the set of interest points of a single image and additionally have the same invariance properties described in Section 3.1 for image point detectors.

In practice, especially in the case of a wide-baseline situation, even the best descriptors show an – arguably – rather poor performance with respect to these ideal requirements. This leads to ambiguities in the matching step (Section 3.3) and, hence, a certain – possibly very high – proportion of false matches. Nevertheless, depending on the situation, the descriptors are often discriminative enough to produce usable or even very good correspondences. However, it is important to keep in mind that this is not always the case and that the quality of resulting correspondences can vary greatly. Note that this problem is also partly caused by the interest point detectors.

In the remainder of this section, I will briefly present the following descriptors: the popular scale invariant feature transform (SIFT), the gradient location and orientation histogram (GLOH), which is an extension of SIFT, steerable filters and moment invariants. This is the same selection I used in (Bajramovic, Koch and Denzler, 2009) and is based on (Mikolajczyk and Schmid, 2005).

Scale Invariant Feature Transform (SIFT)

The scale invariant feature transform (SIFT) descriptor was proposed by Lowe (2004). It basically consists of 16 special gradient orientation histograms with eight bins each giving a vector with 128 entries. The histograms are computed from 4×4 pixel blocks, which are arranged around the interest point in a 4×4 grid. Figure 3.1 visualizes this structure. The histograms are weighted by the gradient strengths and a common Gaussian centered at the interest point. Naturally, the histograms are computed at the scale σ_{D} in the Gaussian scale space (see Section 3.1). Additionally, the gradient orientations are computed relative to the orientation of the interest point. Finally, the descriptor vector is normalized to unit length.

Note that Lowe (2004) proposes some heuristic modifications compared to the simple description given here. They all aim at increasing the robustness with respect to (small) changes of

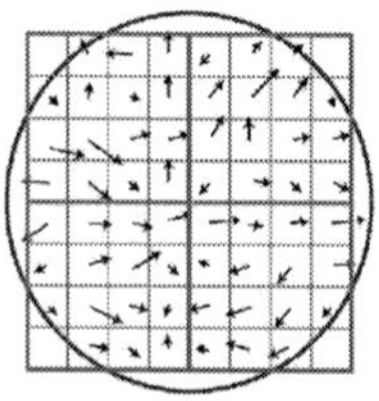

(a) The arrows indicate the image gradients at the scale of the interest point, which is in the center of the grid. The gradients are computed relative to the orientation of the interest point. The figure shows 2×2 (instead of 4×4) blocks of 4×4 pixels each. The circle indicates the common Gaussian weighting function.

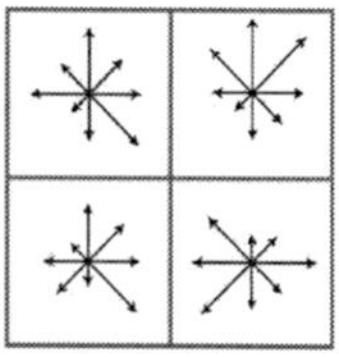

(b) A special gradient orientation histogram is computed for each block.

Figure 3.1: The main structure used to compute the SIFT descriptor. The figures have been taken from (Lowe, 2004).

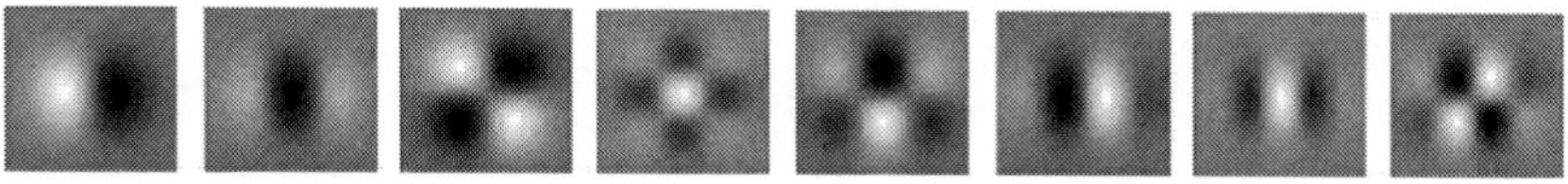

Figure 3.2: Eight of the 14 Gaussian derivative filters. The remaining six filters are 90° rotated versions of these. The figure is based on (Mikolajczyk and Schmid, 2005).

the illumination and the 3D view point.

Gradient Location and Orientation Histogram (GLOH)

The gradient location and orientation histogram (GLOH) descriptor (Mikolajczyk and Schmid, 2005) is an extension of the SIFT descriptor. It computes the SIFT descriptor on a log-polar location grid with various radial and angular directions in a total of 17 parameters for the location. Gradient orientations are quantized to 16 values instead of 8. The dimension of the resulting vector is reduced from 272 to 128 using principal component analysis (Jolliffe, 2002).

Steerable Filters

Steerable filters (Freeman and Adelson, 1991; Mikolajczyk and Schmid, 2005) are based on Gaussian derivative filters up to forth order resulting in a descriptor vector with 14 entries. The filters (or equivalently the image patch around the interest point) are rotated with respect to the gradient to achieve rotation invariance. Figure 3.2 gives an impression of the filters.

Moment Invariants

Moment invariants (van Gool et al., 1996; Mikolajczyk and Schmid, 2005) describe the intensity and shape distribution information surrounding an interest point. They are defined by

$$M_{pq}^{ad} \stackrel{\text{def}}{=} \int_{\Omega} u^p v^q \left(I_d(u,v)\right)^a d(u,v) \ , \tag{3.5}$$

where Ω is an image region around the interest point and I_d with $d \in \{X, Y\}$ denotes the image gradient in X or Y direction, respectively. The moments are discretely approximated as

$$M_{pq}^{ad} \approx \frac{1}{w_\Omega h_\Omega} \sum_{(u,p)\in\Omega\cap\mathbb{Z}^2} u^p v^q \left(I_d(u,v)\right)^a \ , \tag{3.6}$$

where (w_Ω, h_Ω) is the size of the region Ω in pixels. The order of M_{pq}^{ad} is $p+q$, its degree is a.

Mikolajczyk and Schmid (2005) compute the invariant moments up to second order and second degree. Disregarding moments of order zero, the resulting descriptor hence has dimension 20. Note that van Gool et al. (1996) also use color information to compute additional moments.

3.3 Matching

The final step of point correspondence extraction consists of *matching* the interest point descriptors. As input, we have two sets of image points $C_1 = \{\boldsymbol{p}_{1,1}, \ldots, \boldsymbol{p}_{1,m_1}\}$ and $C_2 = \{\boldsymbol{p}_{2,1}, \ldots, \boldsymbol{p}_{2,m_2}\}$ in the two images as produced by the detector and a descriptor $\mathbf{des}(\boldsymbol{p}_k)$ for each point $\boldsymbol{p}_k \in C_k$ $(k = 1, 2)$. The output will consist of a set $\mathcal{D} \subseteq C_1 \times C_2$ of point pairs. Note that the descriptor is of course computed in the first image in the case of $\mathbf{des}(\boldsymbol{p}_1)$ and in the second image in the case of $\mathbf{des}(\boldsymbol{p}_2)$. For the sake of legibility, I do not explicitly denote this aspect.

As the matching is based on the descriptors $\mathbf{des}(\boldsymbol{p}_1)$ and $\mathbf{des}(\boldsymbol{p}_2)$, we need to be able to compare them, e. g. by means of a distance measure $\text{dist}(\cdot,\cdot)$. I will use the Euclidean distance, which is quite common in this context (Mikolajczyk et al., 2005; Mikolajczyk and Schmid, 2005). Note, however, that there are many possible alternatives, like, e. g. the Mahalanobis distance (Mikolajczyk and Schmid, 2005) or the Earth Mover's distance (Rubner et al., 1998). The matching algorithms actually only take these distances into account, which will hence be their (only) input. I denote the pairwise distances by the following abbreviation:

$$d_{ij} \stackrel{\text{def}}{=} \text{dist}(\mathbf{des}(\boldsymbol{p}_{1,i}), \mathbf{des}(\boldsymbol{p}_{2,j})) \ . \tag{3.7}$$

Let $\mathcal{I}_k = \{1, \ldots, m_k\}$ denote the set of indices in C_k $(k = 1, 2)$. For the sake of simplicity, the matching will first be established in terms of indices $\mathcal{J} \subseteq \mathcal{I}_1 \times \mathcal{I}_2$. As a final step, the according point pairs $\mathcal{D}$ have to formed according to $\mathcal{J}$.

Algorithm 3.1 Matching algorithm *exhaustive search.*

Input: descriptor distances $(d_{ij})_{(i,j)\in\mathcal{I}_1\times\mathcal{I}_2}$
Output: pairs $\mathcal{J}$
Parameter: maximum number m of pairs in the output
1: Initialize $\mathcal{J} := \emptyset$
2: **while** $|\mathcal{J}| < m$ and $\mathcal{I}_1 \neq \emptyset$ and $\mathcal{I}_2 \neq \emptyset$ **do**
3: Find the best pair (i, j) according to equation (3.8)
4: Store the pair $\mathcal{J} := \mathcal{J} \cup \{(i, j)\}$
5: Exclude i and j from further consideration $\mathcal{I}_1 := \mathcal{I}_1 \setminus \{i\}$, $\mathcal{I}_2 := \mathcal{I}_2 \setminus \{j\}$

Exhaustive Search

The exhaustive search matching selects the pair (i, j) with the minimal distance d_{ij} as the first correspondence:

$$(i, j) = \operatorname*{argmin}_{(i,j)\in\mathcal{I}_1\times\mathcal{I}_2} d_{ij} \tag{3.8}$$

The indices i and j are then disregarded from further consideration and the pair with the smallest distance within the remaining sets is chosen. This procedure is repeated until there are enough pairs or one of the remaining sets is empty. Details are given in Algorithm 3.1

Nearest Neighbor

Nearest neighbor (NN) matching is quite similar to exhaustive search. In the first step, a set of candidate pairs $\mathcal{J}'$ is constructed as follows. To each $j \in \mathcal{I}_2$, we assign the nearest neighbor in $\mathcal{I}_1$ with respect to the descriptor distances:

$$\mathrm{NN}_1(j) \overset{\text{def}}{=} \operatorname*{argmin}_{i\in\mathcal{I}_1} d_{ij} \ . \tag{3.9}$$

From the candidate set

$$\mathcal{J}' = \{\, (i, j) \in \mathcal{I}_1 \times \mathcal{I}_2 \mid i = \mathrm{NN}_1(j) \,\} \ , \tag{3.10}$$

we repeatedly choose the best (remaining) pair (i, j) and remove all pairs involving i (or j) from $\mathcal{J}'$. Details are given in Algorithm 3.2.

Next, I will explain the difference between the nearest neighbor matching algorithm and the exhaustive search algorithm. I will begin with an example.

Example 3.1 *Assume we only have two interest points in each image:* $m_1 = m_2 = 2$. *Let the descriptor distance be given by the matrix* $\boldsymbol{D} = (d_{ij})_{(i,j)\in\mathcal{I}_1\times\mathcal{I}_2}$*:*

$$\boldsymbol{D} = \begin{pmatrix} 3 & 5 \\ 5 & 9 \end{pmatrix} \ . \tag{3.11}$$

Algorithm 3.2 The matching algorithms *nearest neighbor* (NN) and *two nearest neighbors* (2NN).

Input: descriptor distances $(d_{ij})_{(i,j)\in\mathcal{I}_1\times\mathcal{I}_2}$
Output: pairs $\mathcal{J}$
Parameter: maximum number m of pairs in the output
Parameter: 2NN acceptance threshold $0 \leq \theta_{2NN} \leq 1$ (e. g. $\theta_{2NN} = 0.8$) ▹ only for 2NN

```
Initialize 𝒥 := ∅ and 𝒥' := ∅
for all j ∈ ℐ₂ do
    Find the nearest neighbor i := NN₁(j) according to equation (3.9)
    Find the second nearest neighbor i' := argmin_{i'∈ℐ₁\{i}} d_{i'j}      ▹ only for 2NN
    if d_{ij}/d_{i'j} ≤ θ_2NN then                                      ▹ condition only for 2NN
        Store the candidate pair 𝒥' := 𝒥' ∪ {(i, j)}
while |𝒥| < m and 𝒥' ≠ ∅ do
    Find the best pair (i, j) := argmin_{(i,j)∈𝒥'} d_{ij}
    for all (i', j') ∈ 𝒥' with i' = i do
        Remove (i', j') from the candidate pairs: 𝒥' := 𝒥' \ {(i', j')}
    Store the matched pair 𝒥 := 𝒥 ∪ {(i, j)}
```

The exhaustive search will find the global minimum, which is 3, and produce the first pair $(1, 1)$. *The first row and column of* $\boldsymbol{D}$ *are removed and the only remaining pair* $(2, 2)$ *is chosen. The result is* $\mathcal{J} = \{(1, 1), (2, 2)\}$.

The nearest neighbor algorithm first finds the minimum within each column (the nearest neighbors):

$$\boldsymbol{D} = \begin{pmatrix} \boxed{3} & \boxed{5} \\ 5 & 9 \end{pmatrix}, \tag{3.12}$$

where nearest neighbors (i. e. the members of $\mathcal{J}'$*) are marked by a box. Subsequently, only the boxes are considered. From the set of boxes,* $(1, 1)$ *is selected, which is also the global minimum. All boxes in the first row and column are removed, leaving no further choices. Hence, in this example, the nearest neighbor matching only produces a single correspondence* $\mathcal{J} = \{(1, 1)\}$.

As may or may not be obvious from the example, the difference mainly consists of the way ambiguities are resolved. In both cases, the first correspondence (i, j) has globally minimal distance d_{ij} (see equation (3.8)). The next correspondence produced by the exhaustive search algorithm is again the one with minimal distance d_{ij} within the reduced set $(\mathcal{I}_1 \setminus \{i\}) \times (\mathcal{I}_2 \setminus \{j\})$. The nearest neighbor algorithm, on the other hand, only considers the set of pairs consisting of points in $\mathcal{I}_2 \setminus \{j\}$ and their nearest neighbors in the full set $\mathcal{I}_1$—provided that nearest neighbor is not yet part of a pair in the result $\mathcal{J}$. I. e. it considers the set $\mathcal{J}' \cap ((\mathcal{I}_1 \setminus \{i\}) \times (\mathcal{I}_2 \setminus \{j\}))$.

In other words, the exhaustive search iteratively considers new partners for the remaining indices in $\mathcal{I}_2$ within the set of remaining points in $\mathcal{I}_1$. The nearest neighbor algorithm, on the other hand, initially establishes a potential partner $\text{NN}_1(j) \in \mathcal{I}_1$ for each index $j \in \mathcal{I}_2$. If, during the iterative selection of pairs, that partner $\text{NN}_1(j)$ has already been finally assigned to another partner, the index j is disregarded and will not be part of any pair in the result. Hence, the nearest neighbor matching performs a stricter rejection of ambiguities than the exhaustive search.

Two Nearest Neighbors

Two nearest neighbor (2NN) matching is an extension of nearest neighbor matching described by Lowe (2004). It introduces an additional rejection of ambiguous pairs. When matching $j \in \mathcal{I}_2$ to its nearest neighbor $i = \mathrm{NN}_1(j) \in \mathcal{I}_1$, we also find the second nearest neighbor $i' \in \mathcal{I}_1$. A candidate pair in $\mathcal{J}'$ is only established if the ratio of the two distances is below a certain threshold $\theta_{2\mathrm{NN}}$. Details are given in Algorithm 3.2.

Chapter 4

Relative Pose Estimation

In this chapter, I will describe techniques for estimating the relative pose of two cameras from known point correspondences (Chapter 3) and known intrinsic parameters (Chapter 5) of the pinhole camera model. After defining the precise problem to be solved (Section 4.1), I will describe basic relative pose estimation algorithms, which require correspondences free of outliers (Section 4.2). As minor novel contributions of this dissertation, I will propose two improvements to these algorithms (Sections 4.2.7 and 4.2.8). After that, I will present two robust approaches, which can handle data containing outliers (Section 4.3). The second one (Section 4.3.2) will contain another minor novel contribution of this dissertation.

4.1 Background and Notation

In this section, I will very briefly introduce the pinhole camera model, the relative pose of two cameras, the essential matrix, and related notation. Further details can be found in Appendix D and in the literature, e. g. in the textbooks by Hartley and Zisserman (2003), Ma et al. (2004), or Trucco and Verri (1998).

Pinhole Camera Model

The *pinhole camera model* is a function, which maps a 3D point to the 2D location of its image in the picture according to perspective projection:

$$\boldsymbol{p} \cong \boldsymbol{K}\boldsymbol{q}_{\mathrm{C}} \ , \tag{4.1}$$

where $\cong$ denotes equality up to scale as defined in equation (A.6), $\boldsymbol{q}_{\mathrm{C}} \in \mathbb{R}^3$ is a 3D point in the camera coordinate system, $\boldsymbol{p} \in \mathbb{P}^2$ is the imaged point in homogeneous 2D pixel coordinates (cf. Section A.1), and $\boldsymbol{K}$ is the camera calibration matrix

$$\boldsymbol{K} \stackrel{\text{def}}{=} \begin{pmatrix} f_{\mathrm{x}} & s & o_{\mathrm{x}} \\ 0 & f_{\mathrm{y}} & o_{\mathrm{y}} \\ 0 & 0 & 1 \end{pmatrix} , \tag{4.2}$$

where f_x and f_y are the effective focal lengths, s is the skew parameter, and $(o_x, o_y)^T$ is the principal point. The entries of $\boldsymbol{K}$ are known as the *intrinsic camera parameters*.

The rigid transformation of a 3D point from world coordinates $\boldsymbol{q} \in \mathbb{R}^3$ to camera coordinates $\boldsymbol{q}_C \in \mathbb{R}^3$ is expressed as follows:

$$\boldsymbol{q}_C = \boldsymbol{R}\boldsymbol{q} + \boldsymbol{t} \ , \tag{4.3}$$

where $\boldsymbol{R}$ is a 3D rotation matrix defining the orientation of the camera and $\boldsymbol{t} \in \mathbb{R}^3$ is a translation vector. Together, $(\boldsymbol{R}, \boldsymbol{t})$ is called the *pose* of the camera and is also known as its *extrinsic parameters*. By the equations (4.1) and (4.3), we get the following formula for the 2D image $\boldsymbol{p}$ of a 3D point $\boldsymbol{q}$ in world coordinates:

$$\boldsymbol{p} \cong \boldsymbol{K}(\boldsymbol{R}\boldsymbol{q} + \boldsymbol{t}) \ . \tag{4.4}$$

A pinhole camera can hence be described by the tuple $(\boldsymbol{K}, \boldsymbol{R}, \boldsymbol{t})$. Further details are given in Appendix D.1.

Relative Pose and Essential Matrix

Let $(\boldsymbol{R}_{\text{rel}}, \boldsymbol{t}_{\text{rel}})$ denote the relative pose between two cameras. The *essential matrix* $\boldsymbol{E}$ encodes the *epipolar geometry* and is very closely related to the relative pose:

$$\boldsymbol{E} \cong [\boldsymbol{t}_{\text{rel}}]_\times \boldsymbol{R}_{\text{rel}} \ , \tag{4.5}$$

where $[\boldsymbol{t}_{\text{rel}}]_\times$ denotes the *skew symmetric matrix* of $\boldsymbol{t}_{\text{rel}}$ (see equation (A.16)). The essential matrix has several important properties. The best-known one is the *epipolar constraint*

$$\hat{\boldsymbol{p}}_1^T \boldsymbol{E} \hat{\boldsymbol{p}}_2 = 0 \tag{4.6}$$

for two corresponding image points $\hat{\boldsymbol{p}}_1, \hat{\boldsymbol{p}}_2$ expressed in *camera normalized coordinates*, i. e.

$$\hat{\boldsymbol{p}}_i \overset{\text{def}}{\cong} \boldsymbol{K}_i^{-1} \boldsymbol{p}_i, \quad i = 1, 2 \ . \tag{4.7}$$

Furthermore, the essential matrix fulfills the following two equations (Nistér, 2004):

$$\det(\boldsymbol{E}) = 0 \tag{4.8}$$

$$\boldsymbol{E}\boldsymbol{E}^T\boldsymbol{E} - \frac{1}{2}\text{trace}\left(\boldsymbol{E}\boldsymbol{E}^T\right)\boldsymbol{E} = 0 \ . \tag{4.9}$$

For further details, please see Appendix D.3.

4.2 Basic Relative Pose Estimation Algorithms

In this section, I will describe algorithms that estimate the essential matrix of two cameras from a set of m point correspondences $\mathcal{D} = \{(\boldsymbol{p}_{1,j}, \boldsymbol{p}_{2,j}) \in \mathbb{P}^2 \times \mathbb{P}^2 \mid 1 \leq j \leq m\}$ and known intrinsic camera parameters: the well known eight-point and seven-point algorithms, a simple six-point algorithm, and the quite recent five-point algorithm. After a note on improving the stability in the presence of noise, I will explain how the relative pose can be extracted from the essential matrix. Finally, I will propose two improvements of the basic relative pose estimation algorithms, which I have published in (Brückner, Bajramovic and Denzler, 2008).

4.2.1 Eight-Point Algorithm

The well known eight-point algorithm (Hartley and Zisserman, 2003, Section 11.1) estimates the *fundamental matrix* $\boldsymbol{F}$ (defined in Appendix D.3) from $m \geq 8$ point correspondences based on the epipolar constraint (equation (D.20)). By expressing the corresponding points in camera normalized coordinates $(\hat{\boldsymbol{p}}_{1,j}, \hat{\boldsymbol{p}}_{2,j})$ for $1 \leq j \leq m$, the epipolar constraint is also valid for the essential matrix $\boldsymbol{E}$ (equation (4.6)). Hence, the eight-point algorithm can also be used to directly estimate the essential matrix.

The epipolar constraint can be written as a scalar product

$$\boldsymbol{a}_j^{\mathrm{T}} \boldsymbol{e} = 0 \ , \tag{4.10}$$

with

$$\boldsymbol{a}_j \stackrel{\text{def}}{=} \left(\hat{u}_{2,j}\hat{u}_{1,j}, \hat{v}_{2,j}\hat{u}_{1,j}, \hat{w}_{2,j}\hat{u}_{1,j}, \hat{u}_{2,j}\hat{v}_{1,j}, \hat{v}_{2,j}\hat{v}_{1,j}, \hat{w}_{2,j}\hat{v}_{1,j}, \hat{u}_{2,j}\hat{w}_{1,j}, \hat{v}_{2,j}\hat{w}_{1,j}, \hat{w}_{2,j}\hat{w}_{1,j}\right)^{\mathrm{T}} \ , \tag{4.11}$$

$$\boldsymbol{e} \stackrel{\text{def}}{=} (e_{11}, e_{12}, e_{13}, e_{21}, e_{22}, e_{23}, e_{31}, e_{32}, e_{33})^{\mathrm{T}} \ , \tag{4.12}$$

where $\hat{\boldsymbol{p}}_{i,j} = (\hat{u}_{i,j}, \hat{v}_{i,j}, \hat{w}_{i,j})^{\mathrm{T}}$ and $\boldsymbol{E} = (e_{ij})_{i,j}$. The row vectors $\boldsymbol{a}_j^{\mathrm{T}}$ for $1 \leq j \leq n$ can be stacked to form an $m \times 9$ data matrix $\boldsymbol{A}$ with

$$\boldsymbol{A}\boldsymbol{e} = \boldsymbol{0} \ . \tag{4.13}$$

For $m = 8$, $\boldsymbol{A}$ has rank defect 1 and $\boldsymbol{e}$ is in its right nullspace. Let $\boldsymbol{A} = \boldsymbol{U}\operatorname{diag}(\boldsymbol{s})\boldsymbol{V}^{\mathrm{T}}$ be the singular value decomposition (SVD, Appendix A.3) of $\boldsymbol{A}$. Then $\boldsymbol{e}$ is the last column of $\boldsymbol{V}$ (assuming a decreasing order of the singular values in $\boldsymbol{s}$). Finally, the essential matrix $\boldsymbol{E}$ can be formed from $\boldsymbol{e}$ according to equation (4.12).

Note that due to the definition of $\boldsymbol{V}$, the resulting vector $\boldsymbol{e}$ will have norm $\|\boldsymbol{e}\| = 1$. This is no problem, as the essential matrix $\boldsymbol{E}$ is defined only up to scale. For $m > 8$, the same procedure gives the least squares approximation with respect to $\|\boldsymbol{e}\| = 1$.

4.2.2 Seven-Point Algorithm

The seven-point algorithm (Hartley and Zisserman, 2003, Section 11.1) is very similar to the eight point algorithm, but additionally uses and enforces equation (4.8). It hence needs only seven point correspondences. As in the eight point algorithm, the SVD of the data matrix $\boldsymbol{A}$ is computed. For $m = 7$, $\boldsymbol{A}$ has rank defect 2, and $\boldsymbol{e}$ is in its two dimensional right nullspace, which is spanned by the last two columns of $\boldsymbol{V}$. These two vectors are transformed back into the matrices $\boldsymbol{Z}$ and $\boldsymbol{W}$ according to equation (4.12). Then we have

$$\boldsymbol{E} \cong z\boldsymbol{Z} + w\boldsymbol{W} \ , \tag{4.14}$$

where z and w are unknown real values. Given the arbitrary scale of $\boldsymbol{E}$, we can set $w = 1$. To compute z, substitute equation (4.14) into equation (4.8). This results in a third degree polynomial in z. Each of the up to three real roots gives a solution for $\boldsymbol{E}$. The roots can be computed using the companion matrix method (see Appendix A.6). In case of $m > 7$, the algorithm is identical and the computation of the nullspace becomes a least squares approximation.

4.2.3 Six-Point Algorithm

There are various six-point algorithms (Philip, 1996; Pizarro et al., 2003). Here, I will only present a simple one. For $m = 6$, the data matrix has rank defect 3 and $\boldsymbol{e}$ is in its three dimensional right nullspace, which is spanned by the last three columns of $\boldsymbol{V}$. These three vectors are transformed back into the matrices $\boldsymbol{Y}$, $\boldsymbol{Z}$, and $\boldsymbol{W}$ according to equation (4.12). Then we have:

$$\boldsymbol{E} \cong y\boldsymbol{Y} + z\boldsymbol{Z} + w\boldsymbol{W} \ , \tag{4.15}$$

where y, z, and w are unknown real values. Given the arbitrary scale of $\boldsymbol{E}$, we can set $w = 1$. To compute y and z, substitute equation (4.15) into equation (4.9). This results in nine third degree polynomial equations in y and z:

$$\boldsymbol{B}\boldsymbol{v} = \boldsymbol{0}, \quad \text{with} \quad \boldsymbol{v} \stackrel{\text{def}}{=} \left(y^3, y^2z, yz^2, z^3, y^2, yz, z^2, y, z, 1\right)^{\mathrm{T}} \ , \tag{4.16}$$

where the 9×10 matrix $\boldsymbol{B}$ contains the coefficients of the polynomials. The common root (y, z) of the nine multivariate polynomials can be computed by various methods. As the solution is unique, we can use a very simple one: compute the right nullvector $\boldsymbol{b}$ of $\boldsymbol{B}$ via SVD and extract the root $y = b_8/b_{10}$, $z = b_9/b_{10}$. Note, however, that this method ignores the structure of the vector $\boldsymbol{v}$. According to equation (4.15), this finally gives $\boldsymbol{E}$. For $m > 6$, the same algorithm can be applied.

4.2.4 Five-Point Algorithm

The first part of the five-point algorithm is very similar to the six-point algorithm. For $m = 5$, $\boldsymbol{A}$ has rank defect 4 and we get the following linear combination for $\boldsymbol{E}$:

$$\boldsymbol{E} \cong x\boldsymbol{X} + y\boldsymbol{Y} + z\boldsymbol{Z} + w\boldsymbol{W} \ , \tag{4.17}$$

where x, y, z, w are unknown scalars and $\boldsymbol{X}, \boldsymbol{Y}, \boldsymbol{Z}, \boldsymbol{W}$ are formed from the last four columns of $\boldsymbol{V}$ according to equation (4.12). Again, we set $w = 1$. Substituting equation (4.17) into the equations (4.8) and (4.9) gives ten third degree polynomial equations

$$\boldsymbol{M}\boldsymbol{m} = \boldsymbol{0} \tag{4.18}$$

in three unknowns, where the 10×20 matrix $\boldsymbol{M}$ contains the coefficients and the vector $\boldsymbol{m}$ contains the monomials:

$$\boldsymbol{m} = \left(x^3, x^2y, x^2z, xy^2, xyz, xz^2, y^3, y^2z, yz^2, z^3, x^2, xy, xz, y^2, yz, z^2, x, y, z, 1\right)^{\mathrm{T}} . \tag{4.19}$$

The multivariate problem can be transformed into a univariate problem, which can then be solved using the companion matrix or Sturm sequences (Nistér, 2004). A more efficient variant of the five-point algorithm (Stewénius, 2005; Stewénius et al., 2006) directly solves the multivariate problem by using Gröbner bases (Appendix A.7). Despite the non-trivial theory of Gröbner basis, the main aspect is simply that the polynomials in equation (4.18) will be transformed into a new system which has the same set of common roots and is easier to handle.

First, the well known Gauss Jordan elimination with partial pivoting is applied to $\boldsymbol{M}$ (Press et al., 1994, Section 2.1). This results in a matrix $\boldsymbol{M}' = (\boldsymbol{I}|\boldsymbol{B})$, where $\boldsymbol{I}$ is the 10×10 identity matrix and $\boldsymbol{B}$ is a 10×10 matrix. The ten polynomials defined by $\boldsymbol{M}'$ are a Gröbner basis and have the same common roots as the original system in equation (4.18). Now, form the 10×10 action matrix

$$\boldsymbol{C} = (c_{ij})_{1 \le i,j \le 10}, \quad c_{ij} = \begin{cases} b_{ji} & \text{if } j \le 6 \\ 1 & \text{if } (i,j) \in \{(1,7),(2,8),(3,9),(7,10)\} \\ 0 & \text{otherwise} . \end{cases} \tag{4.20}$$

The eigenvectors $\boldsymbol{u} = (u_1, u_2, \ldots, u_{10})^{\mathrm{T}}$ corresponding to real eigenvalues of $\boldsymbol{C}^{\mathrm{T}}$ give the up to ten common real roots

$$\begin{pmatrix} x_i \\ y_i \\ z_i \end{pmatrix} = \frac{1}{u_{i,10}} \begin{pmatrix} u_7 \\ u_8 \\ u_9 \end{pmatrix} . \tag{4.21}$$

An explanation of eigenvalues and eigenvectors can be found in Appendix A.5. By substituting into equation (4.17), each root $(x, y, z)^{\mathrm{T}}$ gives a solution for $\boldsymbol{E}$. For $m > 5$, the same algorithm can be applied.

4.2.5 Numerical Aspects

In this section, I will describe two well known possibilities of improving the numeric stability of the essential matrix estimation algorithms in the presence of noise. As the input point correspondences will always contain at least a minor amount of noise, these improvements are generally advisable.

Constraint Enforcement

Let $\boldsymbol{E} = \boldsymbol{U}\mathrm{diag}(\boldsymbol{s})\boldsymbol{V}^{\mathrm{T}}$ be the singular value decomposition of $\boldsymbol{E}$ (Appendix A.3). Assuming the relative translation $\boldsymbol{t}_{\mathrm{rel}}$ is non-zero, the singular values have to fulfill the condition $\boldsymbol{s} \cong (1, 1, 0)^{\mathrm{T}}$

(Hartley and Zisserman, 2003, Section 9.6.1). This constraint may be violated by an essential matrix estimate $\boldsymbol{E}$. Hence, it should be enforced after the estimation by setting

$$\boldsymbol{E}' = \boldsymbol{U}\text{diag}(1, 1, 0)\boldsymbol{V}^{\mathrm{T}} \ . \tag{4.22}$$

Note that this operation also normalizes the scale of $\boldsymbol{E}'$ such that $\|\boldsymbol{E}'\|_2 = \sqrt{2}$, where $\|\cdot\|_2$ denotes the Frobenius norm. I apply this constraint enforcement to the results of the basic estimation algorithms in Section 4.2.

Normalization

According to Hartley and Zisserman (2003, Section 11.2), the point correspondences $\mathcal{D}$ should be normalized before applying the eight-point or the seven-point algorithm to improve stability. The normalization is applied to the points of each image individually such that (a) their third homogeneous coordinates equal one, (b) their centroid is in the origin, and (c) their average norm in Euclidean coordinates is $\sqrt{2}$. When using camera normalized coordinates to estimate the essential matrix instead of the fundamental matrix, the same normalization can be used. Note that the terms "normalized" and "camera normalized" have a very different meaning and should not be mixed up.

Let

$$\hat{\mathcal{D}} = \left\{ (\boldsymbol{K}_1^{-1}\boldsymbol{p}_1, \boldsymbol{K}_2^{-1}\boldsymbol{p}_2) \,\middle|\, (\boldsymbol{p}_1, \boldsymbol{p}_2) \in \mathcal{D} \right\} \tag{4.23}$$

denote the camera normalized correspondences. Make sure that the third coordinate of all homogeneous points in $\hat{\mathcal{D}}$ is 1:

$$\hat{\mathcal{D}}' = \left\{ \left(\frac{1}{w_1}\boldsymbol{p}_1, \frac{1}{w_2}\boldsymbol{p}_2 \right) \,\middle|\, (\boldsymbol{p}_1, \boldsymbol{p}_2) \in \hat{\mathcal{D}} \right\} \quad \text{with} \quad \boldsymbol{p}_i = \begin{pmatrix} x_i \\ y_i \\ w_i \end{pmatrix} \text{ for } i = 1, 2 \ . \tag{4.24}$$

This operation assumes that all w_1 and w_2 are nonzero. Note that only the homogeneous *representations* of the points are affected. Next, we compute the means

$$\boldsymbol{c}_i = \frac{1}{m} \sum_{(\boldsymbol{p}_1, \boldsymbol{p}_2) \in \mathcal{D}} \boldsymbol{p}_i \quad \text{for } i = 1, 2 \ , \tag{4.25}$$

where $m = |\mathcal{D}|$. Additionally, we need the average norms of the centered points:

$$\alpha_i = \frac{1}{m} \sum_{(\boldsymbol{p}_1, \boldsymbol{p}_2) \in \mathcal{D}} \left\| \begin{pmatrix} x \\ y \end{pmatrix} - \begin{pmatrix} c_{\mathrm{x}} \\ c_{\mathrm{y}} \end{pmatrix} \right\| \quad \text{for } i = 1, 2 \text{ with } \boldsymbol{c}_i = \begin{pmatrix} c_{\mathrm{x}} \\ c_{\mathrm{y}} \\ 1 \end{pmatrix} \text{ and } \boldsymbol{p}_i = \begin{pmatrix} x \\ y \\ 1 \end{pmatrix} \ . \tag{4.26}$$

The transformation performs a translation by $-\boldsymbol{c}_i$ followed by a scaling by

$$\beta_i = \sqrt{2}/\alpha_i \ . \tag{4.27}$$

Interpreting the homogeneous points as vectors in $\mathbb{R}^3$, this is a linear transformation and can be expressed by the following matrix:

$$T_i \overset{\text{def}}{=} \begin{pmatrix} \beta_i & 0 & -\beta_i c_x \\ 0 & \beta_i & -\beta_i c_y \\ 0 & 0 & 1 \end{pmatrix} \quad \text{for } i = 1, 2 \text{ with } \boldsymbol{c}_i = \begin{pmatrix} c_x \\ c_y \\ 1 \end{pmatrix} . \tag{4.28}$$

The normalized correspondences are hence:

$$\hat{\mathcal{D}}'' = \left\{ (\boldsymbol{T}_1 \boldsymbol{p}_1, \boldsymbol{T}_2 \boldsymbol{p}_2) \,\middle|\, (\boldsymbol{p}_1, \boldsymbol{p}_2) \in \hat{\mathcal{D}}' \right\} . \tag{4.29}$$

After estimating the essential matrix $\boldsymbol{E}'$ from normalized point correspondences $\hat{\mathcal{D}}''$, we have to compensate for the normalization as follows to get the essential matrix for unnormalized correspondences $\mathcal{D}$:

$$\boldsymbol{E} = \boldsymbol{T}_1^{\mathrm{T}} \boldsymbol{E}' \boldsymbol{T}_2 . \tag{4.30}$$

Note that for the six-point and five-point algorithms, the normalization presented above cannot be used, as it does not preserve equation (4.9).

4.2.6 Extracting the Relative Pose from the Essential Matrix

In order to compute the relative pose $(\boldsymbol{R}_{\text{rel}}, \boldsymbol{t}_{\text{rel}})$ of two cameras, we can first estimate the essential matrix $\boldsymbol{E}$ and subsequently extracted $(\boldsymbol{R}_{\text{rel}}, \boldsymbol{t}_{\text{rel}})$ from $\boldsymbol{E}$ as described by Hartley and Zisserman (2003, Section 9.6.2). Let $\boldsymbol{E} = \boldsymbol{U}\text{diag}(\boldsymbol{s})\boldsymbol{V}^{\mathrm{T}}$ be the singular value decomposition of $\boldsymbol{E}$. Then we have

$$\boldsymbol{t}_{\text{rel}} \cong \boldsymbol{u}_3 \quad \text{and} \quad \boldsymbol{R}_{\text{rel}} \in \left\{ \boldsymbol{U}\boldsymbol{W}\boldsymbol{V}^{\mathrm{T}}, \boldsymbol{U}\boldsymbol{W}^{\mathrm{T}}\boldsymbol{V}^{\mathrm{T}} \right\} , \tag{4.31}$$

where $\boldsymbol{u}_3$ denotes the last column of $\boldsymbol{U}$ and

$$\boldsymbol{W} = \begin{pmatrix} 0 & -1 & 0 \\ 1 & 0 & 0 \\ 0 & 0 & 1 \end{pmatrix} . \tag{4.32}$$

As the scale of $\boldsymbol{t}_{\text{rel}}$ cannot be determined without additional information, I normalize it such that $\|\boldsymbol{t}_{\text{rel}}\| = 1$. (Note that $\|\boldsymbol{u}_3\| = 1$ is already ensured by the singular value decomposition.) There are four remaining possibilities:

$$(\boldsymbol{R}_{\text{rel}}, \boldsymbol{t}^*_{\text{rel}}) \in \left\{ (\boldsymbol{U}\boldsymbol{W}\boldsymbol{V}^{\mathrm{T}}, \boldsymbol{u}_3), (\boldsymbol{U}\boldsymbol{W}\boldsymbol{V}^{\mathrm{T}}, -\boldsymbol{u}_3), (\boldsymbol{U}\boldsymbol{W}^{\mathrm{T}}\boldsymbol{V}^{\mathrm{T}}, \boldsymbol{u}_3), (\boldsymbol{U}\boldsymbol{W}^{\mathrm{T}}\boldsymbol{V}^{\mathrm{T}}, -\boldsymbol{u}_3) \right\} \tag{4.33}$$

Note that $\boldsymbol{t}_{\text{rel}}$ can be determined up to a *positive* scale factor. I emphasize the unknown positive scale factor by a star: $\boldsymbol{t}^*_{\text{rel}}$. Equation (4.33) is typically summarized as "up to (positive) scale and a fourfold ambiguity".

The ambiguity can be resolved up to positive scale by the *cheirality constraint*, which exploits that reconstructed 3D points need to be *in front of both cameras* (as they would not be visible

Algorithm 4.1 Extract the relative pose from the essential matrix up a fourfold ambiguity and positive scale.

Input: essential matrix $\boldsymbol{E} \neq \boldsymbol{0}$
Input: point correspondences $\mathcal{D}$
Input: intrinsic camera parameters $\boldsymbol{K}_1$, $\boldsymbol{K}_2$
Output: four possible solutions $\left(\boldsymbol{R}_{\text{rel}}^{(1)}, \boldsymbol{t}_{\text{rel}}^{*(1)}\right)$, $\left(\boldsymbol{R}_{\text{rel}}^{(1)}, \boldsymbol{t}_{\text{rel}}^{*(2)}\right)$, $\left(\boldsymbol{R}_{\text{rel}}^{(2)}, \boldsymbol{t}_{\text{rel}}^{*(1)}\right)$, $\left(\boldsymbol{R}_{\text{rel}}^{(2)}, \boldsymbol{t}_{\text{rel}}^{*(2)}\right)$ with $\|\boldsymbol{t}_{\text{rel}}^*\| = 1$
Ensure: the correct translation is $\lambda \boldsymbol{t}_{\text{rel}}^{*(1)}$ or $\lambda \boldsymbol{t}_{\text{rel}}^{*(2)}$ with $\lambda > 0$

Compute the singular value decomposition $\boldsymbol{E} = \boldsymbol{U}\text{diag}(\boldsymbol{s})\boldsymbol{V}^{\text{T}}$ ▹ Appendix A.3
Set $\boldsymbol{t}_{\text{rel}}^{*(1)} := \boldsymbol{u}_3$ and $\boldsymbol{t}_{\text{rel}}^{*(2)} := -\boldsymbol{u}_3$ ▹ $\boldsymbol{u}_3$ is the last column of $\boldsymbol{U}$
Set $\boldsymbol{R}_{\text{rel}}^{(1)} := \boldsymbol{U}\boldsymbol{W}\boldsymbol{V}^{\text{T}}$ and $\boldsymbol{R}_{\text{rel}}^{(2)} := \boldsymbol{U}\boldsymbol{W}^{\text{T}}\boldsymbol{V}^{\text{T}}$ ▹ $\boldsymbol{W}$ is defined in equation (4.32)

Algorithm 4.2 Check whether the cheirality constraint holds.

Input: point correspondence $(\boldsymbol{p}_1, \boldsymbol{p}_2)$
Input: relative pose $(\boldsymbol{R}_{\text{rel}}, \boldsymbol{t}_{\text{rel}}^*)$
Input: intrinsic camera parameters $\boldsymbol{K}_1$, $\boldsymbol{K}_2$
Output: true if cheirality constraint holds

Set $(\boldsymbol{R}_1, \boldsymbol{t}_1) := (\boldsymbol{I}, \boldsymbol{0})$ and $(\boldsymbol{R}_2, \boldsymbol{t}_2) := (\boldsymbol{R}_{\text{rel}}, \boldsymbol{t}_{\text{rel}}^*)$
Triangulate $\boldsymbol{q}$ from $(\boldsymbol{p}_1, \boldsymbol{p}_2)$ ▹ Appendix D.4
if $[\boldsymbol{q}]_3 > 0$ and $[\boldsymbol{R}_2\boldsymbol{q} + \boldsymbol{t}_2]_3 > 0$ **then** ▹ $[\cdot]_3$ denotes the third entry of a vector
    return true
else
    return false

otherwise). In order to use this constraint, choose one of the possibilities and triangulate the 3D point $\boldsymbol{q}$ given a point correspondence $(\boldsymbol{p}_1, \boldsymbol{p}_2) \in \mathcal{D}$ (see Appendix D.4). If the choice was correct, the z coordinates of $\boldsymbol{q}$ expressed in the two camera coordinate systems will be positive. Otherwise, try another possibility according to equation (4.33). As the point correspondences $\mathcal{D}$ might contain outliers, I let the correspondences vote for the four possible relative poses according to the cheirality constraint and choose according to the majority of votes. Details are given in Algorithm 4.3.

4.2.7 Selecting a Single Solution for the Essential Matrix

The seven- and five-point algorithms can produce more than one solution, which I will call solution *candidates*. In this section, I will propose a method for automatically selecting the single correct solution from these candidates. For each solution candidate, the deviation of each correspondence from the epipolar constraint is measured and summed up over all correspondences $\mathcal{D}$:

$$g(\boldsymbol{E}) \stackrel{\text{def}}{=} \sum_{(\boldsymbol{p}_1, \boldsymbol{p}_2) \in \mathcal{D}} d_{\boldsymbol{E}}(\boldsymbol{p}_1, \boldsymbol{p}_2) \ . \tag{4.34}$$

Algorithm 4.3 Extract the relative pose from the essential matrix up to positive scale.

Input: essential matrix $E \neq 0$
Input: point correspondences $\mathcal{D}$
Input: intrinsic camera parameters K_1, K_2
Output: relative pose $(R_{\text{rel}}, t^*_{\text{rel}})$ with $\|t^*_{\text{rel}}\| = 1$
Ensure: the correct translation is λt^*_{rel} with $\lambda > 0$

Extract the possible rotations $R^{(1)}_{\text{rel}}, R^{(2)}_{\text{rel}}$ and translations $t^{*(1)}_{\text{rel}}, t^{*(2)}_{\text{rel}}$ from E ▹ Algorithm 4.1
Initialize $c_{\text{best}} := 0$
for all $(R'_{\text{rel}}, t^{*\prime}_{\text{rel}}) \in \left\{\left(R^{(1)}_{\text{rel}}, t^{*(1)}_{\text{rel}}\right), \left(R^{(1)}_{\text{rel}}, t^{*(2)}_{\text{rel}}\right), \left(R^{(2)}_{\text{rel}}, t^{*(1)}_{\text{rel}}\right), \left(R^{(2)}_{\text{rel}}, t^{*(2)}_{\text{rel}}\right)\right\}$ **do**
    Initialize $c := 0$
    for all $(p_1, p_2) \in \mathcal{D}$ **do**
        if (p_1, p_2), $(R'_{\text{rel}}, t^{*\prime}_{\text{rel}})$ and K_1, K_2 fulfill the cheirality constraint **then** ▹ Algorithm 4.2
            Increase $c := c + 1$
    if $c > c_{\text{best}}$ **then**
        Set $(R_{\text{rel}}, t^*_{\text{rel}}) := (R'_{\text{rel}}, t^{*\prime}_{\text{rel}})$
        Set $c_{\text{best}} := c$

The solution candidate E with the smallest error $g(E)$ is selected. There are various possibilities to measure the deviation d_E from the epipolar constraint, which are also referred to as *epipolar distance* measures (Hartley and Zisserman, 2003, pp. 284–288):

1. The algebraic error is

$$d^{(A)}_E(p_1, p_2) \stackrel{\text{def}}{=} \left|p_1^{\mathrm{T}} F p_2\right| \ , \tag{4.35}$$

   where $F = K_1^{-\mathrm{T}} E K_2^{-1}$ denotes the fundamental matrix (see Section D.3).

2. The symmetric squared distance from the epipolar line (see Section D.3) is

$$d^{(L)}_E(p_1, p_2) \stackrel{\text{def}}{=} \frac{\left(p_1^{\mathrm{T}} F p_2\right)^2}{[F p_2]_1^2 + [F p_2]_2^2} + \frac{\left(p_1^{\mathrm{T}} F p_2\right)^2}{\left[F^{\mathrm{T}} p_1\right]_1^2 + \left[F^{\mathrm{T}} p_1\right]_2^2} \ , \tag{4.36}$$

   where $[\cdot]_i^2$ denotes the squared ith entry of a vector.

3. The squared reprojection error is

$$d^{(R)}_E(p_1, p_2) \stackrel{\text{def}}{=} d_2(p_1, \check{p}_1)^2 + d_2(p_2, \check{p}_2)^2 \ , \tag{4.37}$$

   where d_2 denotes the Euclidean distance, and $\check{p}_1$ and $\check{p}_2$ are the reprojections of the reconstructed 3D point $\check{q}$:

$$\check{p}_i = K_i(R_i \check{q} + t_i) \ , \tag{4.38}$$

   where $R_1 = I$, $t_1 = 0$, $R_2 = R_{\text{rel}}$, and $t_2 = t_{\text{rel}}$. A suitable triangulation algorithm for computing $\check{q}$ is presented in Section D.4.

4. The Sampson error is the first order Taylor approximation of the squared reprojection error (equation (4.37)):

$$d_E^{(S)}(p_1, p_2) \stackrel{\text{def}}{=} \frac{\left(p_1^T F p_2\right)^2}{[F p_2]_1^2 + [F p_2]_2^2 + \left[F^T p_1\right]_1^2 + \left[F^T p_1\right]_2^2} . \tag{4.39}$$

4.2.8 Combining Algorithms

There is no single best algorithm for all situations. This makes it difficult to choose one, especially if there is no prior knowledge about the camera motion (see Section 7.2.1). Hence, I propose the novel approach of combining two or more algorithms, which exploits their combined strengths. Several algorithms are applied on the same data to produce a set of candidate solutions. The automatic selection procedure (Section 4.2.7) is used to select the best solution. I will call this approach *combining algorithms for relative pose estimation.*

4.3 Robust Relative Pose Estimation

The basic essential matrix or relative pose estimation algorithms presented above are sensitive to outliers in the data. As point correspondences automatically extracted from images will almost always contain false matches, robustness with respect to outliers is very important. In this section, I will describe two sampling-based methods.

4.3.1 Adaptive RANSAC

To achieve robustness with respect to false correspondences, the well known (adaptive) RANdom SAmple Concensus (RANSAC) approach (Fischler and Bolles, 1981; Hartley and Zisserman, 2003) can be applied. RANSAC is a very generic, voting-based method for handling outliers. Here, I will describe a robust essential matrix estimation algorithm based on RANSAC and any one of the basic estimation algorithms in Section 4.2.

The main idea of the algorithm consists of repeatedly sampling a small subset $\mathcal{D}_S \subseteq \mathcal{D}$ containing M point correspondences, and generating a hypothesis for the solution using only the sample $\mathcal{D}_S$. When using the five-point algorithm to generate hypotheses, M has to be at least five. Each of the multiple solution candidates generated by the five-point (or seven-point) algorithm can be treated as a single hypothesis.

Each hypothesis is evaluated by counting how many point correspondences are consistent with it. A correspondence $(p_1, p_2) \in \mathcal{D}$ is considered *consistent* with a hypothesis E if a suitable distance or error measure $d_E(p_1, p_2)$, as presented in Section 4.2.7, is below a certain threshold θ. The set of all consistent correspondences

$$\mathcal{S} = \{ (p_1, p_2) \in \mathcal{D} \mid d_E(p_1, p_2) < \theta \} \tag{4.40}$$

is called the *support set* of E. The hypothesis with the largest support set $\mathcal{S}_L$ found during the iterations could be returned as the result of RANSAC. However, as the influence of noise is typically lower when estimating from a large set of data (as opposed to the very small samples $\mathcal{D}_S$). Hence, in the final step, the result is usually estimated from $\mathcal{S}_L$. Note, however, that this approach is based on the assumption that $\mathcal{S}_L$ is outlier-free, which in general cannot be guaranteed.

The number of iterations of the RANSAC algorithm can optionally be adapted on-line based on the following observation. Assume the data $\mathcal{D}$ contain a proportion ε of outliers. The probability of drawing at least one outlier-free sample $\mathcal{D}_S$ is

$$p_{\text{free}} = 1 - (1 - (1 - \varepsilon)^M)^N \ , \tag{4.41}$$

where N denotes the number of RANSAC iterations. In order to get at least one outlier-free sample with a probability of (at least) p_{free}, we hence need to perform at least

$$N \geq \log_{1-(1-\varepsilon)^M}(1 - p_{\text{free}}) \tag{4.42}$$

iterations. Typically, the proportion of outliers ε is unknown. However, the largest support set $\mathcal{S}_L$ found during previous iterations can be used to derive an upper bound for ε:

$$\varepsilon \leq \frac{|\mathcal{S}_L|}{|\mathcal{D}|} \tag{4.43}$$

Hence, the required number of iterations is:

$$N_{\mathcal{S}_L} \stackrel{\text{def}}{=} \left\lceil \frac{\log(1 - p_{\text{free}})}{\log\left(1 - \left(1 - \frac{|\mathcal{S}_L|}{|\mathcal{D}|}\right)^M\right)} \right\rceil \ . \tag{4.44}$$

If there are very many outliers, however, $N_{\mathcal{S}_L}$ might always stay very large leading to a very long running time. In order to enforce a certain limit on the running time, we can specify a maximum number of iterations in the beginning and make sure that N will not be increased by using the following adaptation rule:

$$N := \min(N, N_{\mathcal{S}_L}) \ . \tag{4.45}$$

Selecting a Single Solution and Combining Algorithms

The selection of a single solution described in Section 4.2.7 is inappropriate during RANSAC iterations due to outliers. Instead, I suggest computing the support set for *each* solution candidate. Note that this can be interpreted as a robust selection of a single solution. For the final estimation from the best support set, which is assumed to be free of outliers, the non-robust selection (Section 4.2.7) may of course be used.

In the context of RANSAC, the combination of basic relative pose algorithms (Section 4.2.8) can be used in a straight forward fashion. However, we also have the possibility to use a single algorithm during RANSAC iterations and a combination of algorithms for the final estimation

Algorithm 4.4 RANSAC algorithm for estimating the essential matrix of two cameras.

Input: point correspondences $\mathcal{D}$
Input: known intrinsic camera parameters $\boldsymbol{K}_1, \boldsymbol{K}_2$
Output: essential matrix estimate $\boldsymbol{E}$
Parameter: maximum number of iterations N (e. g. $N = \infty$)
Parameter: probability p_{free} (e. g. $p_{\text{free}} = 0.999$)
Parameter: an epipolar distance measure d_E from Section 4.2.7 (e. g. the Sampson error $d_E^{(\mathrm{S})}$)
Parameter: threshold θ (e. g. $\theta = 2$)
Parameter: essential matrix estimation algorithm(s) (e. g. the five-point algorithm)
Parameter: final essential matrix estimation algorithm(s) (e. g. five-point and eight-point)
Parameter: sample size M (e. g. $M = 5$)

Initialize the largest support set $\mathcal{S}_\mathrm{L} := \emptyset$
for N times **do** ▷ note that N changes during the iterations
  Randomly select M point correspondences $\mathcal{D}_\mathrm{S}$ from $\mathcal{D}$
  Estimate the essential matrix from $\mathcal{D}_\mathrm{S}$ ▷ multiple solution candidates allowed
  for all resulting solution candidates $\boldsymbol{E}$ **do**
    Compute the support set $\mathcal{S}$ according to equation (4.40)
    if $|\mathcal{S}| > |\mathcal{S}_\mathrm{L}|$ **then**
      Set $\mathcal{S}_\mathrm{L} := \mathcal{S}$
      Update N according to equation (4.45) ▷ optional adaptation of N
Estimate the final solution $\boldsymbol{E}$ from $\mathcal{S}_\mathrm{L}$ ▷ with automatic selection (Section 4.2.7)

from the best support set $\mathcal{S}_\mathrm{L}$. I will call this approach *final combination*. It has the advantage that the five-point algorithm can be used during iterations with a small sample size $m = 5$ and the five-point and eight-point algorithms can be combined for the final estimation.

The adaptive RANSAC algorithm described above (including these two modifications) is summarized in Algorithm 4.4. In order to estimate the relative pose, I first estimate the essential matrix (Algorithm 4.4) and subsequently extract the relative pose using the cheirality constraint (Algorithm 4.3).

4.3.2 MLESAC

The threshold θ of the RANSAC algorithm is somewhat undesirable, as it strictly distinguishes between inliers and outliers, i. e. correspondences that are (not) consistent with the epipolar geometry. So called M-estimators (Huber, 2004; Zhang, 1998) avoid this decision. While the term *M-estimator* refers to a very broad class of statistical methods, I will only present one specific M-estimator for robustly estimating the essential matrix. The main idea is to model the problem as a probability density function (pdf) such that its maximum describes the solution and also such that outliers only have a minor (or ideally no) influence on the location of the maximum.

The Maximum Likelihood Estimation SAmple Concensus (MLESAC) algorithm (Torr and Zisserman, 2000) uses a Monte Carlo sampling procedure similar to RANSAC to find the maximum of the pdf. As I also want to extract information about the global uncertainty of the resulting relative pose (Section 6.2), I use a variant of MLESAC, which is very similar to the one described by Engels and Nistér (2005). The full algorithm will be presented in Section 6.2.1. In the current section, I will focus on robustly estimating the essential matrix and the relation of the algorithm to RANSAC.

Engels and Nistér (2005) model the pdf of the fundamental matrix $\boldsymbol{F}$ given the point correspondences $\mathcal{D}$ using the *Cauchy distribution*. Instead, I will model the pdf of the essential matrix $\boldsymbol{E}$ given the point correspondences (and assuming known intrinsic parameters $\boldsymbol{K}_1, \boldsymbol{K}_2$). Also, I will make a minor simplification, which is irrelevant for estimating the essential matrix. I will add this missing bit in equation (6.8). The probabilistic model is

$$p(\boldsymbol{E} \mid \mathcal{D}) \propto p(\mathcal{D} \mid \boldsymbol{E})p(\boldsymbol{E}) \tag{4.46}$$

$$\text{with} \quad p(\mathcal{D} \mid \boldsymbol{E}) \propto \prod_{(\boldsymbol{p}_1, \boldsymbol{p}_2) \in \mathcal{D}} p(\boldsymbol{p}_1, \boldsymbol{p}_2 \mid \boldsymbol{E}) \tag{4.47}$$

$$\text{and} \quad p(\boldsymbol{p}_1, \boldsymbol{p}_2 \mid \boldsymbol{E}) \propto \frac{\alpha}{\alpha^2 + d_E(\boldsymbol{p}_1, \boldsymbol{p}_2)} \ , \tag{4.48}$$

where α is the scale parameter of the Cauchy distribution and $d_E(\boldsymbol{p}_1, \boldsymbol{p}_2)$ denotes an epipolar distance measure (Section 4.2.7). Note that the Cauchy distribution, as opposed to, e. g. the Gaussian distribution, has so called *heavy tails*. This means that the pdf converges more "slowly" towards zero and hence models outliers.

In order to further increase the robustness in the presence of very many outliers, I alternatively use the Blake-Zisserman distribution[1] instead of the Cauchy distribution. This is a slight variation of the model proposed by Torr and Zisserman (2000). In the experiments in Section 7.2.2, I will show that this pdf actually leads to better results than the Cauchy distribution. The change consists of replacing equation (4.48) by

$$p(\boldsymbol{p}_1, \boldsymbol{p}_2 \mid \boldsymbol{E}) \propto \exp\left(-\frac{d_E(\boldsymbol{p}_1, \boldsymbol{p}_2)}{\sigma^2}\right) + \epsilon \ , \tag{4.49}$$

where $\sigma^2/2$ is the variance of the Gaussian component and ϵ defines the weight of the uniform component.

The maximum a posteriori estimate, which can be interpreted as an M-estimate due to the heavy tails of the pdf, is given by:

$$\hat{\boldsymbol{E}} = \operatorname*{argmax}_{\boldsymbol{E}} p(\boldsymbol{E} \mid \mathcal{D}) \ . \tag{4.50}$$

As mentioned before, a sampling procedure similar to RANSAC is used to approximate that maximum in Algorithm 4.5. As in the case of RANSAC (Algorithm 4.4), in order to estimate the relative pose, I first estimate the essential matrix (Algorithm 4.5) and subsequently extract the relative pose using the cheirality constraint (Algorithm 4.3).

[1] If we make the reasonable assumption that outlier points only occur within the image area, the uniform part of the distribution can be limited to finite support and we actually get a valid probability density function.

Algorithm 4.5 Variant of the MLESAC algorithm for estimating the essential matrix.

Input: point correspondences $\mathcal{D}$
Input: known intrinsic camera parameters $\boldsymbol{K}_1, \boldsymbol{K}_2$
Output: approximate solution $\hat{\boldsymbol{E}}$ to equation (4.50)
Output: $\beta = p(\hat{\boldsymbol{E}} \mid \mathcal{D})$
Parameter: number of iterations N (e. g. $N = 3000$)
Parameter: an epipolar distance measure d_E from Section 4.2.7 (e. g. the Sampson error $d_E^{(S)}$)
Parameter: essential matrix estimation algorithm(s) (e. g. the five-point algorithm)
Parameter: sample size M (e. g. $M = 5$)

```
1: Initialize β := 0                               ▹ used to store the maximum value of p(E | D)
2: for N times do
3:     Randomly select M point correspondences D_S from D
4:     Estimate the essential matrix from D_S        ▹ multiple solution candidates allowed
5:     for all resulting solution candidates E do
6:         if β < p(E | D) then
7:             Set β := p(E | D)
8:             Set Ê := E
```

A Note on the Selection of the Most Suitable Solution Candidate

Note that the lines 5–8 of Algorithm 4.5 implement a selection of the most suitable solution candidate, which is very similar to the procedure in Section 4.2.7. To verify that, take a look at the negative logarithm of equation (4.46):

$$-\log p(\boldsymbol{E} \mid \mathcal{D}) = -\log p(\mathcal{D} \mid \boldsymbol{E}) - \log p(\boldsymbol{E}) - \log \lambda \ , \tag{4.51}$$

where λ denotes the missing normalization factor in equation (4.46). By the equations (4.47) and (4.49), we get

$$\begin{aligned} -\log p(\boldsymbol{E} \mid \mathcal{D}) &= -\log \prod_{(\boldsymbol{p}_1,\boldsymbol{p}_2)\in\mathcal{D}} \left(\exp\left(-\frac{d_E(\boldsymbol{p}_1,\boldsymbol{p}_2)}{\sigma^2}\right) + \epsilon\right) - \log p(\boldsymbol{E}) - \log\lambda \\ &= \sum_{(\boldsymbol{p}_1,\boldsymbol{p}_2)\in\mathcal{D}} \left(-\log\left(\exp\left(-\frac{d_E(\boldsymbol{p}_1,\boldsymbol{p}_2)}{\sigma^2}\right) + \epsilon\right)\right) - \log p(\boldsymbol{E}) - \log\lambda \\ &\underset{\epsilon=0}{=} \sum_{(\boldsymbol{p}_1,\boldsymbol{p}_2)\in\mathcal{D}} \frac{d_E(\boldsymbol{p}_1,\boldsymbol{p}_2)}{\sigma^2} - \log p(\boldsymbol{E}) - \log\lambda \\ &= \frac{1}{\sigma^2} \sum_{(\boldsymbol{p}_1,\boldsymbol{p}_2)\in\mathcal{D}} d_E(\boldsymbol{p}_1,\boldsymbol{p}_2) - \log p(\boldsymbol{E}) - \log\lambda \ . \end{aligned} \tag{4.52}$$

Hence, in the case of a flat prior $p(\boldsymbol{E})$ and the Blake-Zisserman distribution with $\epsilon = 0$, which is actually a Gaussian distribution, the selection criterion is identical to the one in equation (4.34). (The constants σ, $p(\boldsymbol{E})$, and λ do not influence the selection.)

Incorporating the Cheirality Constraint

As described above, in order to estimate the relative pose, I first estimate the essential matrix and subsequently extract the relative pose using the cheirality constraint. Alternatively, I suggest using a model $p(\boldsymbol{R}_{\text{rel}}, \boldsymbol{t}^*_{\text{rel}} \mid \mathcal{D})$ instead of $p(\boldsymbol{E} \mid \mathcal{D})$. Then the MAP estimate for the relative pose is (cf. equation (4.50)):

$$(\hat{\boldsymbol{R}}_{\text{rel}}, \hat{\boldsymbol{t}}^*_{\text{rel}}) = \operatorname*{argmax}_{(\boldsymbol{R}_{\text{rel}}, \boldsymbol{t}^*_{\text{rel}})} p(\boldsymbol{R}_{\text{rel}}, \boldsymbol{t}^*_{\text{rel}} \mid \mathcal{D}) \ . \tag{4.53}$$

The model for the relative pose can simply be defined as

$$p(\boldsymbol{R}_{\text{rel}}, \boldsymbol{t}^*_{\text{rel}} \mid \mathcal{D}) \stackrel{\text{def}}{=} p(\boldsymbol{E} \mid \mathcal{D}) \quad \text{with} \quad \boldsymbol{E} = [\boldsymbol{t}^*_{\text{rel}}]_\times \boldsymbol{R}_{\text{rel}} \ . \tag{4.54}$$

However, this approach only uses the epipolar constraint and ignores the cheirality constraint (Section 4.2.6). For a given relative pose $(\boldsymbol{R}_{\text{rel}}, \boldsymbol{t}^*_{\text{rel}})$ with $\|\boldsymbol{t}^*_{\text{rel}}\| = 1$, there are three other relative poses $(\boldsymbol{R}'_{\text{rel}}, \boldsymbol{t}^{*\prime}_{\text{rel}})$ with $\|\boldsymbol{t}^{*\prime}_{\text{rel}}\| = 1$ which give the same essential matrix $\boldsymbol{E} = [\boldsymbol{t}^*_{\text{rel}}]_\times \boldsymbol{R}_{\text{rel}} = [\boldsymbol{t}^{*\prime}_{\text{rel}}]_\times \boldsymbol{R}'_{\text{rel}}$ (cf. equation (4.33)). These four relative poses all have the same value $p(\boldsymbol{E} \mid \mathcal{D})$. The model $p(\boldsymbol{R}_{\text{rel}}, \boldsymbol{t}^*_{\text{rel}} \mid \mathcal{D})$ hence has (at least) four global minima and the MAP estimate is ambiguous.

I suggest using the cheirality constraint to resolve this ambiguity. Note that there are several approaches combining the cheirality constraint with the RANSAC algorithm (Xu and Mulligan, 2008). To the best of my knowledge, however, the cheirality constraint has not yet been integrated into the MLESAC algorithm. I propose adding the cheirality constraint to the posterior density as follows:

$$p(\boldsymbol{R}_{\text{rel}}, \boldsymbol{t}^*_{\text{rel}} \mid \mathcal{D}) \propto p(\mathcal{D} \mid \boldsymbol{R}_{\text{rel}}, \boldsymbol{t}^*_{\text{rel}}) p(\boldsymbol{R}_{\text{rel}}, \boldsymbol{t}^*_{\text{rel}}) \tag{4.55}$$

$$\text{with} \quad p(\mathcal{D} \mid \boldsymbol{R}_{\text{rel}}, \boldsymbol{t}^*_{\text{rel}}) \propto \prod_{(\boldsymbol{p}_1, \boldsymbol{p}_2) \in \mathcal{D}} p(\boldsymbol{p}_1, \boldsymbol{p}_2 \mid \boldsymbol{R}_{\text{rel}}, \boldsymbol{t}^*_{\text{rel}}) \tag{4.56}$$

$$\text{and} \quad p(\boldsymbol{p}_1, \boldsymbol{p}_2 \mid \boldsymbol{R}_{\text{rel}}, \boldsymbol{t}^*_{\text{rel}}) \propto \begin{cases} p(\boldsymbol{p}_1, \boldsymbol{p}_2 \mid [\boldsymbol{t}^*_{\text{rel}}]_\times \boldsymbol{R}_{\text{rel}}) & \text{cheirality constraint holds} \\ \epsilon & \text{otherwise} \ , \end{cases} \tag{4.57}$$

where $p(\boldsymbol{p}_1, \boldsymbol{p}_2 \mid \boldsymbol{E})$ (with $\boldsymbol{E} = [\boldsymbol{t}^*_{\text{rel}}]_\times \boldsymbol{R}_{\text{rel}}$) is defined in equation (4.49) and ϵ is the same parameter as in the Blake-Zisserman distribution in that equation. The cheirality constraint is checked by using Algorithm 4.2. Note that the model based on the Cauchy distribution in equation (4.48) could of course also be used for $p(\boldsymbol{p}_1, \boldsymbol{p}_2 \mid \boldsymbol{E})$.

Algorithm 4.6 Variant of the MLESAC algorithm for estimating the relative pose.

Input: point correspondences $\mathcal{D}$
Input: known intrinsic camera parameters K_1, K_2
Output: approximate solution $(\hat{R}_{\text{rel}}, \hat{t}^*_{\text{rel}})$ to equation (4.53)
Output: $\beta = p(\hat{R}_{\text{rel}}, \hat{t}^*_{\text{rel}} \mid \mathcal{D})$
Parameter: number of iterations N (e. g. $N = 3000$)
Parameter: an epipolar distance measure d_E from Section 4.2.7 (e. g. the Sampson error $d_E^{(S)}$)
Parameter: essential matrix estimation algorithm(s) (e. g. the five-point algorithm)
Parameter: sample size M (e. g. $M = 5$)
1: Initialize $\beta := 0$ ▷ used to store the maximum value of $p(R_{\text{rel}}, t^*_{\text{rel}} \mid \mathcal{D})$
2: **for** N times **do**
3:    Randomly select M point correspondences $\mathcal{D}_S$ from $\mathcal{D}$
4:    Estimate the essential matrix from $\mathcal{D}_S$ ▷ multiple solution candidates allowed
5:    **for all** resulting solution candidates E **do**
6:       Extract the possible rotations $R^{(1)}_{\text{rel}}, R^{(2)}_{\text{rel}}$ and translations $t^{*(1)}_{\text{rel}}, t^{*(2)}_{\text{rel}}$ ▷ Algorithm 4.1
7:       **for all** $(R_{\text{rel}}, t^*_{\text{rel}}) \in \left\{\left(R^{(1)}_{\text{rel}}, t^{*(1)}_{\text{rel}}\right), \left(R^{(1)}_{\text{rel}}, t^{*(2)}_{\text{rel}}\right), \left(R^{(2)}_{\text{rel}}, t^{*(1)}_{\text{rel}}\right), \left(R^{(2)}_{\text{rel}}, t^{*(2)}_{\text{rel}}\right)\right\}$ **do**
8:          **if** $\beta < p(R_{\text{rel}}, t^*_{\text{rel}} \mid \mathcal{D})$ **then**
9:             Set $\beta := p(R_{\text{rel}}, t^*_{\text{rel}} \mid \mathcal{D})$
10:            Set $(\hat{R}_{\text{rel}}, \hat{t}^*_{\text{rel}}) := (R_{\text{rel}}, t^*_{\text{rel}})$

Chapter 5

Intrinsic Rotational Self-Calibration with Partially Known Rotations

For relative pose estimation (Chapter 4) and hence also multi-camera calibration (Chapter 6), the intrinsic parameters of the pinhole camera model (Appendix D.1) are assumed to be known. In this chapter, I will describe how they can be estimated in the case of a rotating camera—without needing a calibration pattern or any other knowledge about the scene. This is known as *rotational self-calibration*. With a camera mounted onto a stationary pan-tilt unit in mind, I will present a novel method for using partial rotation knowledge to improve the rotational self-calibration. I have published this improvement in (Bajramovic and Denzler, 2007).

First, I will present a known linear approach for rotational self-calibration (Section 5.1) and a nonlinear refinement procedure (Section 5.2). Afterwards, I will show how the nonlinear method can be extended to make use of partial rotation knowledge. As this knowledge has to be expressed in the camera coordinate system, I will show how the information gained from a pan-tilt unit can be used in this context, (a) by making certain assumptions or (b) by integrating a model of the pan-tilt unit into the optimization problem (Section 5.4).

5.1 Linear Rotational Self-Calibration

Let a camera take an image, rotate about its optical center, and take another image. This situation can be modelled as two cameras with a relative pose $(\boldsymbol{R}_{\text{rel}}, \boldsymbol{0})$. In the case of a pinhole camera, corresponding points $(\boldsymbol{p}_1, \boldsymbol{p}_2) \in \mathbb{P}^2 \times \mathbb{P}^2$ in the two images are mapped onto each other by a so called *homography*, i. e. a two-dimensional projective mapping. In homogeneous coordinates, it can be expressed as a matrix multiplication

$$\boldsymbol{p}_2 \cong \boldsymbol{H}\boldsymbol{p}_1 \ , \tag{5.1}$$

where $\cong$ denotes equality up to scale as defined in equation (A.6) and $\boldsymbol{H}$ is a 3×3 matrix, which is also called homography. In the self-calibration literature, the special homography relating two images of a rotating camera is known as the *infinite homography* $\boldsymbol{H}_\infty$ (Hartley and Zisserman, 2003, Chapter 19). An introduction to 3D computer vision basics, including the pinhole camera model, its optical center, the relative pose of two cameras, and the concept of a point correspondence, is given in Appendix D.

For rotational self-calibration, we need (in general) $n \geq 2$ rotations of the camera about at least two axes (Hartley and Zisserman, 2003, Section 19.6). The first step is to estimate the infinite homographies $\boldsymbol{H}_{\infty,i}$ for all consecutive image pairs $1 \leq i \leq n$, i. e. for all rotations. I use a linear homography estimation method as described in Section 5.1.1. Once we have the infinite homographies, we can estimate the intrinsic pinhole parameters using, e. g. the image of the absolute conic (Section 5.1.2).

5.1.1 Homography Estimation

A homography $\boldsymbol{H}$ can be estimated from $m \geq 4$ point correspondences $(\boldsymbol{p}_{1,j}, \boldsymbol{p}_{2,j})$ with $1 \leq j \leq m$. In this section, I will present the linear algorithm described by Hartley and Zisserman (2003, Section 4.1). The cross product can be used to circumvent the unknown scale factor in equation (5.1):

$$\boldsymbol{p}_{2,j} \times \boldsymbol{H}\boldsymbol{p}_{1,j} = 0 \ . \tag{5.2}$$

This can be written as three scalar equations, two of which are linearly independent:

$$\begin{aligned} v_{2,j}h_{31}u_{1,j} + v_{2,j}h_{32}v_{1,j} + v_{2,j}h_{33}w_{1,j} - w_{2,j}h_{21}u_{1,j} - w_{2,j}h_{22}v_{1,j} - w_{2,j}h_{23}w_{1,j} &= 0 \ , \\ w_{2,j}h_{11}u_{1,j} + w_{2,j}h_{12}v_{1,j} + w_{2,j}h_{13}w_{1,j} - u_{2,j}h_{31}u_{1,j} - u_{2,j}h_{32}v_{1,j} - u_{2,j}h_{33}w_{1,j} &= 0 \ , \\ u_{2,j}h_{21}u_{1,j} + u_{2,j}h_{22}v_{1,j} + u_{2,j}h_{23}w_{1,j} - v_{2,j}h_{11}u_{1,j} - v_{2,j}h_{12}v_{1,j} - v_{2,j}h_{13}w_{1,j} &= 0 \ , \end{aligned} \tag{5.3}$$

where $\boldsymbol{p}_{i,j} = (u_{i,j}, v_{i,j}, w_{i,j})^{\mathrm{T}}$ for $i = 1, 2$ and $\boldsymbol{H} = (h_{jk})_{1 \leq j,k \leq 3}$. The first two equations can be written as a matrix multiplication as follows:

$$\boldsymbol{A}_j \boldsymbol{h} = \boldsymbol{0} \ , \tag{5.4}$$

with

$$\boldsymbol{A}_j = \begin{pmatrix} 0 & 0 & 0 & -w_{2,j}u_{1,j} & -w_{2,j}v_{1,j} & -w_{2,j}w_{1,j} & v_{2,j}u_{1,j} & v_{2,j}v_{1,j} & v_{2,j}w_{1,j} \\ w_{2,j}u_{1,j} & w_{2,j}v_{1,j} & w_{2,j}w_{1,j} & 0 & 0 & 0 & -u_{2,j}u_{1,j} & -u_{2,j}v_{1,j} & -u_{2,j}w_{1,j} \end{pmatrix} \ , \tag{5.5}$$

$$\boldsymbol{h} = (h_{11}, h_{12}, h_{13}, h_{21}, h_{22}, h_{23}, h_{31}, h_{32}, h_{33})^{\mathrm{T}} \ . \tag{5.6}$$

The matrices $\boldsymbol{A}_j$ with $1 \leq j \leq m$ can be stacked to form a $2m \times 9$ matrix $\boldsymbol{A}$ with

$$\boldsymbol{A}\boldsymbol{h} = \boldsymbol{0} \ . \tag{5.7}$$

For $m = 4$, $\boldsymbol{A}$ has rank defect 1 and $\boldsymbol{h}$ is in its right nullspace. Let $\boldsymbol{A} = \boldsymbol{U}\mathrm{diag}(\boldsymbol{s})\boldsymbol{V}^{\mathrm{T}}$ be the singular value decomposition of $\boldsymbol{A}$ (Appendix A.3). Then $\boldsymbol{h}$ is the last column of $\boldsymbol{V}$ (assuming a decreasing order of the singular values in $\boldsymbol{s}$). For $m > 4$, the same procedure gives the least squares approximation with respect to $\|\boldsymbol{h}\| = 1$. The homography $\boldsymbol{H}$ can be formed from $\boldsymbol{h}$ according to equation (5.6).

Coordinate Normalization

In order to improve stability, the coordinates of the point correspondences should be normalized as described in Section 4.2.5 before applying the linear homography estimation algorithm (Hartley and Zisserman, 2003, Section 4.4.4). In order to denormalize the resulting homography, however, we need to use the following formula instead of equation (4.30):

$$H = T_2^{-1} H' T_1 \ . \tag{5.8}$$

In the context of rotational self-calibration, I will suggest a slight variation of the normalization in Section 5.1.3.

Enforcing Constraints on the Infinite Homography

The infinite homography can be expressed in the following form (Hartley and Zisserman, 2003, Section 19.6):

$$H_\infty \cong K R_{\text{rel}} K^{-1} \ , \tag{5.9}$$

where $\cong$ denotes equality up to scale (cf. equation (A.6)). Note that $\cong$ is used for vectors as well as matrices. Despite being defined only up to scale, the infinite homography is similar (adjunct) to R_{rel}. As the absolute values (complex moduli) of all eigenvalues of a rotation matrix equal 1, the absolute values of the eigenvalues of H_∞ must all be equal (not necessarily 1).

As this property is not guaranteed by the homography estimation algorithm, I enforce it afterwards as follows. Let $\lambda_1, \lambda_2, \lambda_3 \in \mathbb{C}$ denote the eigenvalues of H_∞. The constraint requires that

$$|\lambda_1| = |\lambda_2| = |\lambda_3| \overset{\text{e.g.}}{=} 1 \ . \tag{5.10}$$

I use eigendecomposition to enforce the following eigenvalues (Appendix A.5):

$$\frac{\lambda_1}{|\lambda_1|}, \frac{\lambda_2}{|\lambda_2|}, \frac{\lambda_3}{|\lambda_3|} \ . \tag{5.11}$$

Note that the eigendecomposition of H_∞ is always defined. This is easy to see. The eigenvalues $\lambda'_1, \lambda'_2, \lambda'_3$ of R_{rel} must all have absolute value 1. Hence, we either have $\lambda'_1 = \lambda'_2 = \lambda'_3 = 1$, i. e. $R_{\text{rel}} = I$, or $\{\lambda'_1, \lambda'_2, \lambda'_3\} = \{1, a + ib, a - ib\}$ with $a, b \in \mathbb{R}$ and $b \neq 0$. In the first case, H_∞ is symmetric and the eigendecomposition is hence defined. Otherwise, we have three distinct eigenvalues, which guarantees that the eigendecomposition is defined.

5.1.2 The Image of the Absolute Conic

The infinite homographies are closely related to the so called *image of the absolute conic (IAC)* (Hartley and Zisserman, 2003, Sections 8.5.1 and 19.5.2)

$$\omega \overset{\text{def}}{=} K^{-T} K^{-1} \tag{5.12}$$

as follows:

$$\omega \cong \boldsymbol{H}_{\infty,i}^{-\mathrm{T}} \omega \boldsymbol{H}_{\infty,i}^{-1} \ . \tag{5.13}$$

The equality (5.13) is given only up to scale. Nevertheless, in this case, the unknown scale factor can be resolved. If the scale of $\boldsymbol{H}_{\infty,i}$ is normalized such that

$$\det(\boldsymbol{H}_{\infty,i}) = 1 \ , \tag{5.14}$$

then we have

$$\omega = \boldsymbol{H}_{\infty,i}^{-\mathrm{T}} \omega \boldsymbol{H}_{\infty,i}^{-1} \ . \tag{5.15}$$

The normalization of $\boldsymbol{H}_{\infty,i}$ is performed as follows:

$$\boldsymbol{H}_{\infty,i} := (\det(\boldsymbol{H}_{\infty,i}))^{-\frac{1}{3}} \boldsymbol{H}_{\infty,i} \ , \tag{5.16}$$

where ":=" denotes replacement (or assignment), i. e. this is *not* meant to express equality or recursion.

Equation (5.15) can be written as a homogeneous linear equation

$$\boldsymbol{B}_i \boldsymbol{b} = 0 \ , \tag{5.17}$$

where

$$\boldsymbol{b} = (\omega_{11}, \omega_{12}, \omega_{13}, \omega_{22}, \omega_{23}, \omega_{33})^{\mathrm{T}} \tag{5.18}$$

contains the entries of the IAC

$$\omega = \begin{pmatrix} \omega_{11} & \omega_{12} & \omega_{13} \\ \star & \omega_{22} & \omega_{23} \\ \star & \star & \omega_{33} \end{pmatrix} \ , \tag{5.19}$$

where $\star$ denotes symmetric entries, and the 6×6 matrix $\boldsymbol{B}_i$ is computed from $\boldsymbol{H}_{\infty,i}$ as follows:

$$\boldsymbol{B}_i = \begin{pmatrix} h_{11}^2 - 1 & 2h_{11}h_{21} & 2h_{11}h_{31} & h_{21}^2 & 2h_{21}h_{31} & h_{31}^2 \\ h_{12}h_{11} & h_{12}h_{21} + h_{22}h_{11} - 1 & h_{12}h_{31} + h_{32}h_{11} & h_{22}h_{21} & h_{22}h_{31} + h_{32}h_{21} & h_{32}h_{31} \\ h_{13}h_{11} & h_{13}h_{21} + h_{23}h_{11} & h_{13}h_{31} + h_{33}h_{11} - 1 & h_{23}h_{21} & h_{23}h_{31} + h_{33}h_{21} & h_{33}h_{31} \\ h_{12}^2 & 2h_{12}h_{22} & 2h_{12}h_{32} & h_{22}^2 - 1 & 2h_{22}h_{32} & h_{32}^2 \\ h_{13}h_{12} & h_{13}h_{22} + h_{23}h_{12} & h_{13}h_{32} + h_{33}h_{12} & h_{23}h_{22} & h_{23}h_{32} + h_{33}h_{22} - 1 & h_{33}h_{32} \\ h_{13}^2 & 2h_{13}h_{23} & 2h_{13}h_{33} & h_{23}^2 & 2h_{23}h_{33} & h_{33}^2 - 1 \end{pmatrix} \ , \tag{5.20}$$

where $\boldsymbol{H}_{\infty,i}^{-1} = (h_{kl})_{1 \le k,l \le 3}$. The matrices $\boldsymbol{B}_i$ with $1 \le i \le n$ can be stacked to form a $6n \times 6$ matrix $\boldsymbol{B}$ such that

$$\boldsymbol{B}\boldsymbol{b} = \boldsymbol{0} \ . \tag{5.21}$$

If not all rotations are about the same axis, in theory, $\boldsymbol{B}$ will have rank defect 1 and $\boldsymbol{b}$ is in its right nullspace. Let $\boldsymbol{B} = \boldsymbol{U}\mathrm{diag}(\boldsymbol{s})\boldsymbol{V}^{\mathrm{T}}$ be the singular value decomposition of $\boldsymbol{B}$ (Section A.3). Then $\boldsymbol{b}$

is the last column of $\boldsymbol{V}$. In practice, $\boldsymbol{B}$ will often have full rank and the same procedure is used to compute a least squares approximation with respect to $\|\boldsymbol{b}\| = 1$. The IAC $\boldsymbol{\omega}$ is constructed from $\boldsymbol{b}$ according to the equations (5.18) and (5.19).

As this determines $\boldsymbol{\omega}$ only up to scale, we have to normalize it such that $\omega_{11} > 0$ to ensure that $\boldsymbol{\omega}$ is positive definite instead of negative definite. Finally, we can compute the Cholesky decomposition (Appendix A.4) of $\boldsymbol{\omega}$ to get $\boldsymbol{K}^{-1}$ and thus $\boldsymbol{K}$. Note, however, that in practice, the estimate for $\boldsymbol{\omega}$ is not necessarily definite due to noise. In that case, the Cholesky decomposition cannot be performed and the self-calibration fails.

5.1.3 Numerical Stability

As mentioned by Quan and Triggs (2000), self-calibration methods in general are numerically delicate. However, the various methods differ in the extent of numerical sensitivity. For self-calibration of a rotating camera, the same has been noted by Hartley and Zisserman (2003, Section 19.5.2). For this special case, only relatively few methods have been presented in the literature, as the problem is comparatively simple and does not seem to offer fundamental reformulations.

Nevertheless there are some possibilities to improve the stability of rotational self-calibration: (a) normalize coordinates (see below), (b) assume some intrinsic parameters to be known (see below), (c) apply nonlinear refinement (Section 5.2), or (d) assume additional knowledge about the rotations (Section 5.3).

Coordinate Normalization

I have already mentioned coordinate normalization in the context of homography estimation (Section 5.1.1). Instead of denormalizing the homographies (equation (5.8)), however, we can directly use the homographies estimated from normalized correspondences and denormalize the resulting intrinsic parameters $\boldsymbol{K}'$. However, this requires that the same normalizing transformation $\boldsymbol{T}$ is used for all images. In this case, the denormalization is performed as follows:

$$\boldsymbol{K} = \boldsymbol{T}^{-1}\boldsymbol{K}' \quad . \tag{5.22}$$

I use the following transformation $\boldsymbol{T}$ for all images:

$$\boldsymbol{T} = \frac{1}{s_{\mathrm{m}}}\begin{pmatrix} 2 & 0 & -s_{\mathrm{x}} \\ 0 & 2 & -s_{\mathrm{y}} \\ 0 & 0 & s_{\mathrm{m}} \end{pmatrix} \quad \text{with} \quad s_{\mathrm{m}} = \max(s_{\mathrm{x}}, s_{\mathrm{y}}) \ , \tag{5.23}$$

where $(s_{\mathrm{x}}, s_{\mathrm{y}})$ denotes the size of the images (width, height). This transformation normalizes the points such that their X and Y coordinates are each within $[-1, 1]$.

In order to analyze the difference between this normalization and the one presented in Section 4.2.5, let us assume that the points (in Euclidean coordinates) are uniformly distributed within the image area and that the image is square (i. e. $s_{\mathrm{x}} = s_{\mathrm{y}}$). Hence, after the normalization according to equation (5.23), the points are uniformly distributed in $[-1, 1] \times [-1, 1]$. Their centroid is

$$E\begin{pmatrix} x \\ y \end{pmatrix} = \int_{-1}^{1} \frac{1}{2} \int_{-1}^{1} \frac{1}{2} \begin{pmatrix} x \\ y \end{pmatrix} dx\,dy = \begin{pmatrix} 0 \\ 0 \end{pmatrix} \tag{5.24}$$

as in Section 4.2.5. Their average norm

$$E\left(\left\| \begin{matrix} x \\ y \end{matrix} \right\|\right) = \int_{-1}^{1} \frac{1}{2} \int_{-1}^{1} \frac{1}{2} \sqrt{x^2 + y^2} dx\,dy \tag{5.25}$$

is difficult to compute. I hence use Maple™ for a numerical approximation:

$$E\left(\left\| \begin{matrix} x \\ y \end{matrix} \right\|\right) \approx 0.7651957165 \ . \tag{5.26}$$

In order to achieve an average norm of $\sqrt{2}$ (as in Section 4.2.5), we can use the following transformation:

$$\boldsymbol{T} = \frac{1}{s'_{\mathrm{m}}} \begin{pmatrix} 2 & 0 & -s_{\mathrm{x}} \\ 0 & 2 & -s_{\mathrm{y}} \\ 0 & 0 & s'_{\mathrm{m}} \end{pmatrix} \quad \text{with} \quad s'_{\mathrm{m}} = \frac{\sqrt{2}}{0.7651957165} s_{\mathrm{m}} \approx 1.848172346 \cdot s_{\mathrm{m}} \ . \tag{5.27}$$

As the factor 1.848172346 is quite close to 1, it will probably only have a minor impact on the results.

Known Intrinsic Parameters

Examples of known intrinsic parameters are: (a) zero skew, i. e. $s = 0$, (b) square pixels, i. e. $s = 0$ and $f_{\mathrm{x}} = f_{\mathrm{y}}$, or that the principal point is in the center of the image. For modern cameras, especially the zero skew assumption is usually valid. In the case of the nonlinear algorithms, known intrinsic parameters can easily be kept constant during the optimization. In the case of the linear algorithm presented above, such knowledge leads to constraints on the IAC ω or the closely related DIAC ω^{-1} (Hartley and Zisserman, 2003, Section 19.5.2). I will only describe the zero skew situation in more detail.

As noted by Harley and Zisserman (Hartley and Zisserman, 2003, Section 19.5.2), when assuming zero skew (i. e. $s = 0$), the IAC becomes:

$$\omega = \begin{pmatrix} \omega_{11} & \omega_{12} & \omega_{13} \\ \star & \omega_{22} & \omega_{23} \\ \star & \star & \omega_{33} \end{pmatrix} = \boldsymbol{K}^{-T}\boldsymbol{K}^{-1} = \begin{pmatrix} \frac{1}{f_x^2} & 0 & -\frac{o_x}{f_x^2} \\ \star & \frac{1}{f_y^2} & -\frac{o_y}{f_y^2} \\ \star & \star & 1 + \frac{o_x^2}{f_x^2} + \frac{o_y^2}{f_y^2} \end{pmatrix} , \tag{5.28}$$

where $\star$ denotes symmetric entries. As in this case, $\omega_{12} = 0$, the matrix $\boldsymbol{B}_i$ can be simplified to refect this, i. e. the second column in equation (5.20) can be left out.

Inversion of Homographies

Note that the inversion of the infinite homographies $\boldsymbol{H}_{\infty,i}$ is not actually necessary. On the one hand, instead of inverting the homographies numerically, we can simply exchange the input images by using swapped correspondences $(\boldsymbol{p}_2, \boldsymbol{p}_1)$ instead of $(\boldsymbol{p}_1, \boldsymbol{p}_2)$. On the other hand, the inverse homographies correspond to inverse rotations:

$$\boldsymbol{H}_{\infty,i}^{-1} = \left(\boldsymbol{K}\boldsymbol{R}_{\text{rel,i}}\boldsymbol{K}^{-1}\right)^{-1} = \boldsymbol{K}\boldsymbol{R}_{\text{rel,i}}^{\text{T}}\boldsymbol{K}^{-1} \ . \tag{5.29}$$

As this change of the rotations is irrelevant for the linear rotational self-calibration method presented above, it actually does not matter, whether the homographies are inverted at all. Hence, from a numerical point of view, we should use $\boldsymbol{H}_{\infty,i}$ instead of $\boldsymbol{H}_{\infty,i}^{-1}$ to build the equation system (5.21).

5.2 Nonlinear Self-Calibration

The equations (5.9) and (5.1) can be combined to get

$$\boldsymbol{p}_2 \cong \boldsymbol{K}\boldsymbol{R}_{\text{rel}}\boldsymbol{K}^{-1}\boldsymbol{p}_1 \ . \tag{5.30}$$

This equation can be used to express the self-calibration problem for a rotating camera as the following optimization problem (Hartley and Zisserman, 2003, Section 19.6):

$$\boldsymbol{K} = \underset{\boldsymbol{K}}{\operatorname{argmin}} \quad \min_{\substack{(\boldsymbol{R}_{\text{rel,i}})_{1\le i\le n} \\ \text{with } \boldsymbol{R}_{\text{rel,i}} \in \mathcal{SO}(3)}} \quad \sum_{i=1}^{n}\sum_{j=1}^{m_i} d\left(\boldsymbol{K}\boldsymbol{R}_{\text{rel,i}}\boldsymbol{K}^{-1}\boldsymbol{p}_{1,i,j}, \boldsymbol{p}_{2,i,j}\right)^2 \ , \tag{5.31}$$

where m_i denotes the number of point correspondences $(\boldsymbol{p}_{1,i,j}, \boldsymbol{p}_{2,i,j})$ for the ith rotation,

$$\mathcal{SO}(3) \stackrel{\text{def}}{=} \left\{ \boldsymbol{R} \in \mathbb{R}^{3\times3} \;\middle|\; \boldsymbol{R}\boldsymbol{R}^{\text{T}} = \boldsymbol{R}^{\text{T}}\boldsymbol{R} = \boldsymbol{I} \wedge \det(\boldsymbol{R}) = 1 \right\} \tag{5.32}$$

is the 3D rotation group, and

$$d\left(\begin{pmatrix} x_1 \\ y_1 \\ w_1 \end{pmatrix}, \begin{pmatrix} x_2 \\ y_2 \\ w_2 \end{pmatrix}\right) \stackrel{\text{def}}{=} \sqrt{\left(\frac{x_1}{w_1} - \frac{x_2}{w_2}\right)^2 + \left(\frac{y_1}{w_1} - \frac{y_2}{w_2}\right)^2} \tag{5.33}$$

denotes the Euclidean distance of 2D points in homogeneous coordinates (assuming $w_1 \neq 0$ and $w_2 \neq 0$). There are two advantages of the nonlinear formulation of the problem. First, the distance $d(\cdot,\cdot)$ is a geometrically meaningful measure on the point correspondences. Second, the constraint that $\boldsymbol{K}$ is identical for all rotations is enforced directly, which is impossible for the homography estimation part of the linear algorithm.

The nonlinear optimization problem in equation (5.31) can be solved by finding a good initial approximation to the solution and refining that using a local nonlinear optimization algorithm, like, e. g. the trust-region algorithm described in Appendix C.1. The initial solution for $\boldsymbol{K}$ is provided by the linear self-calibration method described in Section 5.1. The rotation matrices $\boldsymbol{R}_{\text{rel,i}}$ can be initialized as follows: compute $\boldsymbol{R}_{\text{rel,i}} = \boldsymbol{K}^{-1}\boldsymbol{H}_{\infty,i}\boldsymbol{K}$ and enforce the constraint $\boldsymbol{R}_{\text{rel,i}} \in \mathcal{SO}(3)$ by setting all singular values of $\boldsymbol{R}_{\text{rel,i}}$ to one (see Appendix A.3).

For the optimization, we need to determine the gradient and the Hessian of the objective function in equation (5.31) (or accordingly of the variants that will follow in the Sections 5.3 and 5.4.4). After the following simple reformulation, I use the computer algebra system Maple™ to automatically compute symbolic expressions (and generate C code) for the remaining derivation operator inside of the sum:

$$\frac{\partial}{\partial x}\sum_{i=1}^{n}\sum_{j=1}^{m_i} d\left(\boldsymbol{K}\boldsymbol{R}_{\text{rel,i}}\boldsymbol{K}^{-1}\boldsymbol{p}_{1,i,j}, \boldsymbol{p}_{2,i,j}\right)^2 = \sum_{i=1}^{n}\sum_{j=1}^{m_i} \underbrace{\frac{\partial}{\partial x} d\left(\boldsymbol{K}\boldsymbol{R}_{\text{rel,i}}\boldsymbol{K}^{-1}\boldsymbol{p}_{1,i,j}, \boldsymbol{p}_{1,i,j}\right)^2}_{\text{via Maple}^{\text{TM}}} , \tag{5.34}$$

where x denotes any parameter of $\boldsymbol{R}_{\text{rel,i}}$ or $\boldsymbol{K}$. This also works for second order derivatives.

Parameterization

A suitable parameterization should be used to represent the rotations $\boldsymbol{R}_{\text{rel,i}}$ in equation (5.31). I use *rotation vectors*, which are also known as exponential parameters, as suggested by Ma et al. (2004, Section 2.3):

$$\text{Rod}(\boldsymbol{w}) \stackrel{\text{def}}{=} \boldsymbol{I} + \frac{[\boldsymbol{w}]_\times}{\|\boldsymbol{w}\|}\sin(\|\boldsymbol{w}\|) + \frac{([\boldsymbol{w}]_\times)^2}{\|\boldsymbol{w}\|^2}(1 - \cos(\|\boldsymbol{w}\|)) , \tag{5.35}$$

where $\boldsymbol{w} \in \mathbb{R}^3$ is the rotation vector and $[\boldsymbol{w}]_\times$ denotes the skew symmetric matrix of $\boldsymbol{w}$ (see equation (A.16)). Equation (5.35) is known as *Rodrigues' formula*. Further details can be found in Appendix A.2.1.

One benefit of rotation vectors is that they implicitly enforce the constraint $\boldsymbol{R}_{\text{rel,i}} \in \mathcal{SO}(3)$. Furthermore, rotation vectors provide an elegant way of integrating partial rotation knowledge into the nonlinear optimization problem (Section 5.3). In some cases, the closely related *axis-angle* parameterization is preferable. It separates the rotation axis $\boldsymbol{v}$ and angle α explicitly at the cost of one additional parameter and the constraint $\|\boldsymbol{v}\| = 1$:

$$\text{Rod}(\boldsymbol{v}, \alpha) \stackrel{\text{def}}{=} \text{Rod}(\alpha\boldsymbol{v}) = \boldsymbol{I} + [\boldsymbol{v}]_\times \sin(\alpha) + ([\boldsymbol{v}]_\times)^2(1 - \cos(\alpha)) \quad \text{for} \quad \|\boldsymbol{v}\| = 1 . \tag{5.36}$$

I prefer the axis-angle parameterization over rotation vectors only if there is appropriate priori knowledge (e. g. if $\boldsymbol{v}$ is known).

For the following reasons, I do not use unit quaternions, even though they are very popular:

- They do not provide a minimal parameterization, as they have four parameters and require the unit quaternion constraint (similar to axis-angle).
- The close relationship between rotation vectors and the axis-angle representation helps pinpoint the precise differences between the various cases of partial rotation knowledge (cf. Section 5.3).

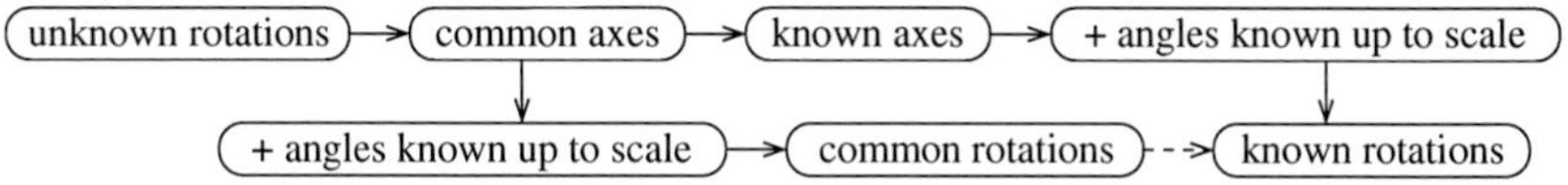

Figure 5.1: Cases of partially known rotations. The arrows indicate additional rotation knowledge and "+ known angles up to scale" means that, additionally, rotation angles are known up to a common scale factor. Further explanations can be found in the text.

- There is no clear agreement as to which parameterization of 3D rotations is best (Schmidt and Niemann, 2001).

The experiments in Section 7.1 will show that rotation vectors work well for rotational self-calibration.

Using rotation vectors, I formulate the optimization problem in equation (5.31) as follows:

$$\boldsymbol{K} = \underset{\boldsymbol{K}}{\operatorname{argmin}} \min_{(\boldsymbol{w}_i)_{1\leq i\leq n}} \sum_{i=1}^{n} \sum_{j=1}^{m_i} d\left(\boldsymbol{K}\mathrm{Rod}(\boldsymbol{w}_i)\boldsymbol{K}^{-1}\boldsymbol{p}_{1,i,j}, \boldsymbol{p}_{2,i,j}\right)^2 , \tag{5.37}$$

For the initialization of this optimization problem, we need to compute the rotation vectors $\boldsymbol{w}_i$ from the rotation matrices $\boldsymbol{R}_{\mathrm{rel,i}}$ (see Appendix A.2.1).

5.3 Using Partial Rotation Knowledge

Due to the numerical problems of rotational self-calibration, I suggest using (partial) rotation knowledge to improve the calibration results. Such knowledge is typically available in the case of a camera mounted onto a pan-tilt unit. The extent of knowledge about the rotations depends on the situation, i. e. mostly on the pan-tilt unit.

The various cases of partially known rotations are summarized in Figure 5.1. I will subsequently explain these cases, and show how each type of prior knowledge can be incorporated into the nonlinear self-calibration procedure by presenting appropriate variants of equation (5.37) with modified parameterizations of the rotations. Even though the new formulations may look more complicated, decreasing the dimension of the parameter space is likely to reduce the over-adaptation to noise. Despite that, in the cases with known values of some parameters, the algorithms simply cannot introduce errors by misestimating them.

5.3.1 Suitable Optimization Problems

Common Rotation Axes

The minimum case of partial rotation knowledge consists of knowing that certain rotations have a common rotation axis (Figure 5.1: "common axes"). e. g. a pan-tilt unit can be actively controlled such that only one of the two physical rotation axes is used *at the same time* (see also

Section 5.4). In this case, rotations only have one parameter each (the rotation angle) and there are two additional degrees of freedom for each rotation axis. If there are $r \leq n$ distinct rotation axes, we have $n + 2r + 5$ parameters in total instead of $3n + 5$ for the general case.

To obtain a suitable version of the optimization problem in equation (5.37), I replace the rotation vectors by the axis-angle parameterization and use only r instead of n rotation axes. I add constant indices k_i as prior knowledge, which assign the correct rotation axis $\boldsymbol{v}_{k_i}$ to the rotation with index i. The resulting optimization problem is

$$\boldsymbol{K} = \underset{\boldsymbol{K}}{\operatorname{argmin}} \min_{\substack{(\alpha_i)_{1\leq i\leq n},(\boldsymbol{v}_k)_{1\leq k\leq r}\\ \|\boldsymbol{v}_k\|=1 \text{ for all } k}} \sum_{i=1}^{n}\sum_{j=1}^{m_i} d\left(\boldsymbol{K}\mathrm{Rod}(\alpha_i,\boldsymbol{v}_{k_i})\boldsymbol{K}^{-1}\boldsymbol{p}_{1,i,j},\boldsymbol{p}_{2,i,j}\right)^2 . \tag{5.38}$$

Note that this formulation uses one parameter too much for each axis $\boldsymbol{v}_k$. In this one case, I trade minimality for simplicity and ignore the constraints $\|\boldsymbol{v}_k\| = 1$ during the optimization.

To initialize the common rotation axes, I take the average over all (independent) initial estimates that belong to the same axis. An according strategy is applied in the subsequent cases of partial rotation knowledge whenever two or more rotations have common parameters.

Known Rotation Axes

If the rotation axes are known (Figure 5.1: “known axes”), the parameters $\boldsymbol{v}_k$ in equation (5.38) are constant and do not have to be optimized. We get the following optimization problem with a minimal parameterization of $n + 5$ parameters:

$$\boldsymbol{K} = \underset{\boldsymbol{K}}{\operatorname{argmin}} \min_{(\alpha_i)_{1\leq i\leq n}} \sum_{i=1}^{n}\sum_{j=1}^{m_i} d\left(\boldsymbol{K}\mathrm{Rod}(\alpha_i,\boldsymbol{v}_{k_i})\boldsymbol{K}^{-1}\boldsymbol{p}_{1,i,j},\boldsymbol{p}_{2,i,j}\right)^2 . \tag{5.39}$$

Rotation Angles Known up to Scale

Using a pan-tilt unit, relative rotation angles are often known in some device specific unit. If the pan-tilt unit is calibrated and provides a mapping from its internal unit to radians, we get the actual angles. Otherwise, I assume a linear mapping from angles γ_i in machine units to angles α_i in radians:

$$\alpha_i = \eta_{k_i}\gamma_i , \tag{5.40}$$

where η_{k_i} is the unknown scale factor, which may be specific to each of the r rotation axes.

This results in a total of $3r + 5$ parameters for r unknown, but fixed rotation axes (Figure 5.1: “common axes + known angles up to scale”). To formulate an appropriate optimization problem, I start with equation (5.37). I encode each axis *and* scale factor by *one* vector $\boldsymbol{u}_k$. For each actual rotation, the appropriate vector $\boldsymbol{u}_{k_i}$ is multiplied by the known angle in machine units γ_i to produce the rotation vector $\boldsymbol{w}_i$. Accordingly, I now minimize over the vectors $\boldsymbol{u}_k$:

$$\boldsymbol{K} = \underset{\boldsymbol{K}}{\operatorname{argmin}} \min_{(\boldsymbol{u}_k)_{1\leq k\leq r}} \sum_{i=1}^{n}\sum_{j=1}^{m_i} d\left(\boldsymbol{K}\mathrm{Rod}(\gamma_i\boldsymbol{u}_{k_i})\boldsymbol{K}^{-1}\boldsymbol{p}_{1,i,j},\boldsymbol{p}_{2,i,j}\right)^2 . \tag{5.41}$$

If the rotation axes are also known (Figure 5.1: "known axes + known angles up to scale"), I start with the formulation in equation (5.38). The angles α_i are replaced by $\eta_{k_i}\gamma_i$, and the values η_k are the new optimization parameters ($r + 5$ parameters in total):

$$\boldsymbol{K} = \underset{\boldsymbol{K}}{\operatorname{argmin}} \min_{(\eta_k)_{1\leq k\leq r}} \sum_{i=1}^{n}\sum_{j=1}^{m_i} d\left(\boldsymbol{K}\operatorname{Rod}(\eta_{k_i}\gamma_i, \boldsymbol{v}_{k_i})\boldsymbol{K}^{-1}\boldsymbol{p}_{1,i,j}, \boldsymbol{p}_{2,i,j}\right)^2 . \tag{5.42}$$

As a further variant of the previous two cases, it is possible that some or all factors η_{k_i} are equal. Exploiting this knowledge seems most interesting if there are many rotation axes (leading to many parameters η_{k_i}). This can easily be integrated in equation (5.42) by having fewer parameters η_{k_i}. In equation (5.41), things are a bit more complicated, as combining η_{k_i} and $\boldsymbol{v}_{k_i}$ in the vector $\boldsymbol{u}_{k_i}$ is no longer possible. I will, however, not treat these cases any further.

Common Rotations

A further situation consists of knowing that certain rotations are identical (Figure 5.1: "common rotations"). Mathematically, this situation is a special case of equation (5.41) if we set $\gamma_i = 1$ for all i. Thus, there is again a total of $3r + 5$ parameters. This case is also a direct special case of equation (5.37) with fewer rotation parameters:

$$\boldsymbol{K} = \underset{\boldsymbol{K}}{\operatorname{argmin}} \min_{(\boldsymbol{w}_k)_{1\leq k\leq r}} \sum_{i=1}^{n}\sum_{j=1}^{m_i} d\left(\boldsymbol{K}\operatorname{Rod}(\boldsymbol{w}_{k_i})\boldsymbol{K}^{-1}\boldsymbol{p}_{1,i,j}, \boldsymbol{p}_{2,i,j}\right)^2 . \tag{5.43}$$

Known Rotations

Finally, rotations can be known completely (Figure 5.1: "known rotations"). In practice, such data can be provided by a dedicated rotation sensor or a calibrated pan-tilt unit. To get an appropriate optimization problem, observe that this is a special case of *each* case presented above. For the sake of simplicity, I choose equation (5.37). The rotation parameters $\boldsymbol{w}_i$ are now constant and do not have to be optimized:

$$\boldsymbol{K} = \underset{\boldsymbol{K}}{\operatorname{argmin}} \sum_{i=1}^{n}\sum_{j=1}^{m_i} d\left(\boldsymbol{K}\operatorname{Rod}(\boldsymbol{w}_i)\boldsymbol{K}^{-1}\boldsymbol{p}_{1,i,j}, \boldsymbol{p}_{2,i,j}\right)^2 , \tag{5.44}$$

This situation with only five parameters is briefly mentioned by Hartley (1997), who uses a similar nonlinear formulation. Frahm and Koch investigate this case in more detail and present a linear algorithm (Frahm and Koch, 2003; Frahm, 2005). Note, however, that their approaches cannot benefit from only *partially* known rotations.

5.4 Partial Rotation Knowledge from a Pan-Tilt Unit

In order to make (partial) rotation knowledge acquired from a pan-tilt unit usable in the sense of Section 5.3, it has to be expressed as a relative rotation in the first camera coordinate system of each respective image pair. There are two aspects to this problem. First, a tilt motion typically rotates the pan axis (or vice versa) relative to the camera coordinate system. Second, for the cases "known axes", "known axes + known angles up to scale", and "known rotations", we need to know how the camera is mounted onto the pan-tilt unit.

In order to handle these problems, the pan-tilt unit can be modelled as an open kinematic chain. I will present such a model in Section 5.4.2. I will use it to express relative rotations in the camera coordinate system (Section 5.4.3). Based on that, I will develop new variants of the optimization problem in equation (5.37), which explicitly model the pan-tilt unit (Section 5.4.3). Note, however, that this model is comparatively complex and adds additional parameters to the optimization problems presented above. I will hence first present a simpler practical approach, which allows to directly gain partial rotation knowledge expressed in the camera coordinate system from a pan-tilt unit if certain assumptions are made. In the experiments (Section 7.1), I will only use this simple approach.

5.4.1 A Simple Practical Approach

For the simple approach, the idea is to avoid changing the rotation axes of the pan-tilt unit relative to the camera coordinate system. Assume that the pan-tilt unit is constructed such that the camera is rigidly connected to the tilt axis. In this case, a tilt motion will change the pan axis relative to the camera coordinate system. In order to avoid that, we can control the pan-tilt unit such that we first perform multiple pure pan rotations and subsequently pure tilt rotations (or vice versa). This leads to two distinct rotation axes in total. Depending on our knowledge about the rotation angles, this strategy allows us to use the cases "common axes", "common axes + known angles up to scale", or "common rotations", respectively.

For the other cases, we need to know the rotation axes expressed in the camera coordinate system. There are two requirements for this. First, we need to know how the camera is mounted onto the pan-tilt unit expressed as a rigid transformation $(\boldsymbol{R}_{\mathrm{H}}, \boldsymbol{t}_{\mathrm{H}})$. This is known as the *hand-eye transformation*. Second, we need to know the state of the tilt axis.

The assumption that the rotation center coincides with the optical center of the camera implies $\boldsymbol{t}_{\mathrm{H}} = \boldsymbol{0}$. In the more complex models in Section 5.4.4, the rotation $\boldsymbol{R}_{\mathrm{H}}$ will be part of the new optimization problems in the equations (5.58)–(5.61). Here, in contrast to that, I will assume that the camera is mounted onto the pan-tilt unit such that the rotation $\boldsymbol{R}_{\mathrm{H}}$ is very simple to determine manually. Let us assume that the tilt axis coincides with the X axis of the camera coordinate system, and that the pan axis coincides with the Y axis in the case of a suitable tilt angle β_{ref}. Hence, the rotation of the hand-eye transformation is given by the identity matrix:

$$\boldsymbol{R}_{\mathrm{H}} = \boldsymbol{I} \ . \tag{5.45}$$

In this situation, a tilt motion is always about the X axis and a pan motion with the tilt angle set to β_{ref} is about the Y axis. If we do not perform any other rotations, we thus know all rotation axes. Depending on our knowledge about the rotation angles, we can use the cases "known axes", "known axes + known angles up to scale", or "known rotations", respectively.

For further details on this simple approach, please note that at the end of Section 5.4.4, the simple approach will be presented as a special case of the general model, which is described more formally.

5.4.2 General Kinematic Chain Model

In this section, I will develop an open kinematic chain model for a pan-tilt unit under the assumption that the pan and the tilt axis intersect. Their intersection point is called *rotation center*. An *open kinematic chain* is basically a series of coordinate systems together with appropriate rigid transformations. In robotics, there is one fixed initial coordinate system and each joint (pan/tilt axis) introduces one or two new coordinate systems. Except for the initial one, each coordinate system i is defined by the relative rigid transformation $(\boldsymbol{R}_{i,i-1}, \boldsymbol{t}_{i,i-1})$, which transfers a point $\boldsymbol{q}_{i-1}$ from the previous coordinate system $i-1$ to the current one:

$$\boldsymbol{q}_i = \boldsymbol{R}_{i,i-1}\boldsymbol{q}_{i-1} + \boldsymbol{t}_{i,i-1} \ . \tag{5.46}$$

I choose the initial coordinate system with its origin in the rotation center and arbitrary but fixed orientation. In computer vision terminology, this can be interpreted as the world coordinate system. The first transformation $(\boldsymbol{R}_\text{P}(\alpha), \boldsymbol{0})$ expresses the current state of the pan joint and thus depends on the pan angle α. The second transformation $(\boldsymbol{R}_\text{T}(\beta), \boldsymbol{0})$ handles the tilt axis and depends on the tilt angle β. The final coordinate system is the camera coordinate system. The according transformation $(\boldsymbol{R}_\text{H}, \boldsymbol{t}_\text{H})$ is known as the *hand-eye transformation.* It is constant, as the camera is assumed to be rigidly mounted onto the pan-tilt unit. Assuming that the optical center coincides with the rotation center is equivalent to $\boldsymbol{t}_\text{H} = \boldsymbol{0}$. The complete kinematic chain is:

$$\boldsymbol{q}_\text{C} = \boldsymbol{R}_\text{H}\boldsymbol{R}_\text{T}(\beta)\boldsymbol{R}_\text{P}(\alpha)\boldsymbol{q} + \boldsymbol{t}_\text{H} \ , \tag{5.47}$$

where $\boldsymbol{q}$ and $\boldsymbol{q}_\text{C}$ donate a scene point in world and camera coordinates, respectively. The current state of the pan-tilt unit and thus the pose of the camera can be described by the pair of angles (α, β). Note that the order of the transformations is *not* arbitrary, but determined by the hardware. The above formulation assumes that panning also rotates the tilt axis, but not vice versa. In the opposite case, $\boldsymbol{R}_\text{P}$ and $\boldsymbol{R}_\text{T}$ have to be interchanged. If the two axes are independent (should this mechanically be possible at all), this formulation might be inappropriate. Also note that Davis and Chen (2003) present a similar model of a pan-tilt unit. However, they do not assume that the rotation axes intersect. Furthermore, they do not model $\boldsymbol{R}_\text{H}$.

For typical pan-tilt units, the model in equation (5.47) can be simplified further. Pan and tilt axes can often be assumed to be orthogonal. In this case, the orientation of the initial coordinate system can be chosen as follows: the Y axis equals the pan axis, the X axis equals the tilt axis in its initial position, and the Z axis is chosen appropriately. In this situation, panning rotates about the Y axis and tilting about the X axis.

Furthermore, the camera can often be assumed to be mounted onto the pan-tilt unit such that the X axis of the camera coordinate system is parallel to the tilt axis and the Y axis is parallel to the pan axis in the configuration $\boldsymbol{R}_\text{T}(\beta) = \boldsymbol{I}$, where $\boldsymbol{I}$ is the identity matrix. In this case, the Z axis of the initial coordinate system can be chosen equal to the optical axis of the camera in the configuration $\boldsymbol{R}_\mathrm{P}(\alpha) = \boldsymbol{R}_\mathrm{T}(\beta) = \boldsymbol{I}$. This finally leads to $\boldsymbol{R}_\mathrm{H} = \boldsymbol{I}$ and the following kinematic chain:

$$\boldsymbol{q}_\mathrm{C} = \boldsymbol{R}_\mathrm{X}(\beta)\boldsymbol{R}_\mathrm{Y}(\alpha)\boldsymbol{q} + \boldsymbol{t}_\mathrm{H} \ , \tag{5.48}$$

where $\boldsymbol{R}_\mathrm{X}(\cdot)$ and $\boldsymbol{R}_\mathrm{Y}(\cdot)$ denote rotations about the X and Y axis, respectively.

5.4.3 Relative Transformation for Pan-Tilt Motion

Now, the relative transformation from a pan-tilt configuration (α,β) to a new configuration $(\alpha',\beta') = (\alpha + \bar{\alpha}, \beta + \bar{\beta})$ can be derived. To achieve this, transfer the point $\boldsymbol{q}_{\mathrm{C}_1}$ from the camera coordinate system C_1 back to the world coordinate system and then forward to the new camera coordinate system C_2 to get $\boldsymbol{q}_{\mathrm{C}_2}$:

$$\begin{aligned} \boldsymbol{q} &= \boldsymbol{R}_\mathrm{P}(-\alpha)\boldsymbol{R}_\mathrm{T}(-\beta)\boldsymbol{R}_\mathrm{H}^\mathrm{T}(\boldsymbol{q}_{\mathrm{C}_1} - \boldsymbol{t}_\mathrm{H}) \\ \boldsymbol{q}_{\mathrm{C}_2} &= \boldsymbol{R}_\mathrm{H}\boldsymbol{R}_\mathrm{T}(\beta')\boldsymbol{R}_\mathrm{P}(\alpha')\boldsymbol{q} + \boldsymbol{t}_\mathrm{H} \\ \Rightarrow \boldsymbol{q}_{\mathrm{C}_2} &= \boldsymbol{R}_\mathrm{H}\boldsymbol{R}_\mathrm{T}(\beta')\boldsymbol{R}_\mathrm{P}(\alpha')\boldsymbol{R}_\mathrm{P}(-\alpha)\boldsymbol{R}_\mathrm{T}(-\beta)\boldsymbol{R}_\mathrm{H}^\mathrm{T}(\boldsymbol{q}_{\mathrm{C}_1} - \boldsymbol{t}_\mathrm{H}) + \boldsymbol{t}_\mathrm{H} \\ &= \boldsymbol{R}_\mathrm{H}\boldsymbol{R}_\mathrm{T}(\beta + \bar{\beta})\boldsymbol{R}_\mathrm{P}(\bar{\alpha})\boldsymbol{R}_\mathrm{T}(-\beta)\boldsymbol{R}_\mathrm{H}^\mathrm{T}(\boldsymbol{q}_{\mathrm{C}_1} - \boldsymbol{t}_\mathrm{H}) + \boldsymbol{t}_\mathrm{H} \ . \end{aligned} \tag{5.49}$$

The last reformulation uses $\boldsymbol{R}_\mathrm{P}(\alpha')\boldsymbol{R}_\mathrm{P}(-\alpha) = \boldsymbol{R}_\mathrm{P}(\alpha' - \alpha)$, which is valid because both rotations are about the same axis. Note that, as expected, in case the pan-tilt unit rotates about the optical center (i. e. $\boldsymbol{t}_\mathrm{H} = \boldsymbol{0}$), the above equation is a pure relative rotation.

For the simplified situation of equation (5.48), the relative transformation is:

$$\boldsymbol{q}_{\mathrm{C}_2} = \boldsymbol{R}_\mathrm{X}(\beta + \bar{\beta})\boldsymbol{R}_\mathrm{Y}(\bar{\alpha})\boldsymbol{R}_\mathrm{X}(-\beta)(\boldsymbol{q}_{\mathrm{C}_1} - \boldsymbol{t}_\mathrm{H}) + \boldsymbol{t}_\mathrm{H} \ . \tag{5.50}$$

To get a better understanding of the rotational part of this relative transformation, assume $\boldsymbol{t}_\mathrm{H} = 0$:

$$\boldsymbol{q}_{\mathrm{C}_2} = \boldsymbol{R}_\mathrm{X}(\beta + \bar{\beta})\boldsymbol{R}_\mathrm{Y}(\bar{\alpha})\boldsymbol{R}_\mathrm{X}(-\beta)\boldsymbol{q}_{\mathrm{C}_1} \ . \tag{5.51}$$

I will subsequently call this situation "XY rotation". Now, knowing both relative rotation angles $\bar{\alpha}$ and $\bar{\beta}$, there is still the unknown angle β. In the case of a pure pan or pure tilt motion (i. e. $\bar{\beta} = 0$ or $\bar{\alpha} = 0$, respectively), the transformations are

$$\boldsymbol{q}_{\mathrm{C}_2} = \boldsymbol{R}_\mathrm{X}(\beta)\boldsymbol{R}_\mathrm{Y}(\bar{\alpha})\boldsymbol{R}_\mathrm{X}(-\beta)\boldsymbol{q}_{\mathrm{C}_1} \tag{5.52}$$

and

$$\boldsymbol{q}_{\mathrm{C}_2} = \boldsymbol{R}_\mathrm{X}(\bar{\beta})\boldsymbol{q}_{\mathrm{C}_1} \ , \tag{5.53}$$

respectively. In the tilt case, the relative tilt angle $\bar{\beta}$ defines the complete transformation. In the pan case, however, it does not only depend on the relative pan angle $\bar{\alpha}$, but also on the tilt angle β.

Simplified Relative Transformation without Explicit Kinematic Chain

The relative transformation between two pan-tilt configurations can be expressed by a somewhat simpler equation. The idea is to express a pan motion as a rotation about a certain axis which depends on the tilt state. This can be viewed as an alternative approach to the open kinematic chain. Nevertheless, in the following, the alternative formulation will be derived from the kinematic chain.

In order to express equation (5.49) in a simpler form, first use rotation vectors to explicitly denote the pan and tilt rotation axes:

$$\boldsymbol{q}_{\mathrm{C}_2} = \boldsymbol{R}_{\mathrm{H}}\mathrm{Rod}(\boldsymbol{v}_{\mathrm{T}},\beta+\bar{\beta})\mathrm{Rod}(\boldsymbol{v}_{\mathrm{P}},\bar{\alpha})\mathrm{Rod}(\boldsymbol{v}_{\mathrm{T}},-\beta)\boldsymbol{R}_{\mathrm{H}}^{\mathrm{T}}(\boldsymbol{q}_{\mathrm{C}_1}-\boldsymbol{t}_{\mathrm{H}})+\boldsymbol{t}_{\mathrm{H}} \ , \tag{5.54}$$

where $\boldsymbol{v}_{\mathrm{T}}$ is the tilt axis and $\boldsymbol{v}_{\mathrm{P}}$ is the pan axis such that $\mathrm{Rod}(\boldsymbol{v}_{\mathrm{T}},\beta) = \boldsymbol{R}_{\mathrm{T}}(\beta)$ and $\mathrm{Rod}(\boldsymbol{v}_{\mathrm{P}},\alpha) = \boldsymbol{R}_{\mathrm{P}}(\alpha)$. Now, Corollary A.3 can be used to simplify the expression:

$$\begin{aligned}
\boldsymbol{q}_{\mathrm{C}_2} &= \boldsymbol{R}_{\mathrm{H}}\mathrm{Rod}(\boldsymbol{v}_{\mathrm{T}},\bar{\beta})\mathrm{Rod}(\boldsymbol{v}_{\mathrm{T}},\beta)\mathrm{Rod}(\boldsymbol{v}_{\mathrm{P}},\bar{\alpha})(\mathrm{Rod}(\boldsymbol{v}_{\mathrm{T}},\beta))^{\mathrm{T}}\boldsymbol{R}_{\mathrm{H}}^{\mathrm{T}}(\boldsymbol{q}_{\mathrm{C}_1}-\boldsymbol{t}_{\mathrm{H}})+\boldsymbol{t}_{\mathrm{H}} & \\
&= \boldsymbol{R}_{\mathrm{H}}\mathrm{Rod}(\boldsymbol{v}_{\mathrm{T}},\bar{\beta})\mathrm{Rod}(\mathrm{Rod}(\boldsymbol{v}_{\mathrm{T}},\beta)\boldsymbol{v}_{\mathrm{P}},\bar{\alpha})\boldsymbol{R}_{\mathrm{H}}^{\mathrm{T}}(\boldsymbol{q}_{\mathrm{C}}-\boldsymbol{t}_{\mathrm{H}})+\boldsymbol{t}_{\mathrm{H}} & \text{(Corollary A.3)}\\
&= \boldsymbol{R}_{\mathrm{H}}\mathrm{Rod}(\boldsymbol{v}_{\mathrm{T}},\bar{\beta})(\boldsymbol{R}_{\mathrm{H}}^{\mathrm{T}}\boldsymbol{R}_{\mathrm{H}})\mathrm{Rod}(\mathrm{Rod}(\boldsymbol{v}_{\mathrm{T}},\beta)\boldsymbol{v}_{\mathrm{P}},\bar{\alpha})\boldsymbol{R}_{\mathrm{H}}^{\mathrm{T}}(\boldsymbol{q}_{\mathrm{C}}-\boldsymbol{t}_{\mathrm{H}})+\boldsymbol{t}_{\mathrm{H}} & (\boldsymbol{R}_{\mathrm{H}}^{\mathrm{T}}\boldsymbol{R}_{\mathrm{H}}=\boldsymbol{I})\\
&= \mathrm{Rod}(\boldsymbol{R}_{\mathrm{H}}\boldsymbol{v}_{\mathrm{T}},\bar{\beta})\mathrm{Rod}(\boldsymbol{R}_{\mathrm{H}}\mathrm{Rod}(\boldsymbol{v}_{\mathrm{T}},\beta)\boldsymbol{v}_{\mathrm{P}},\bar{\alpha})(\boldsymbol{q}_{\mathrm{C}}-\boldsymbol{t}_{\mathrm{H}})+\boldsymbol{t}_{\mathrm{H}} & \text{(Corollary A.3)} \ .
\end{aligned} \tag{5.55}$$

If there is only a pan or only a tilt motion, the situation simplifies further:

$$\boldsymbol{q}_{\mathrm{C}_2} = \begin{cases}\mathrm{Rod}(\boldsymbol{R}_{\mathrm{H}}\boldsymbol{v}_{\mathrm{T}},\bar{\beta})(\boldsymbol{q}_{\mathrm{C}_1}-\boldsymbol{t}_{\mathrm{H}})+\boldsymbol{t}_{\mathrm{H}} & \bar{\alpha}=0\\ \mathrm{Rod}(\boldsymbol{R}_{\mathrm{H}}\mathrm{Rod}(\boldsymbol{v}_{\mathrm{T}},\beta)\boldsymbol{v}_{\mathrm{P}},\bar{\alpha})(\boldsymbol{q}_{\mathrm{C}_1}-\boldsymbol{t}_{\mathrm{H}})+\boldsymbol{t}_{\mathrm{H}} & \bar{\beta}=0 \ .\end{cases} \tag{5.56}$$

5.4.4 Optimization Problems Modeling a Pan-Tilt Unit

In order to use partial rotation knowledge by reducing the number of unknown parameters, the above formulation does not help much in case of a single rotation. However, the number of parameters per rotation can be reduced if a *series* of pan-tilt rotations is performed. The idea is to have only one common parameter β for all rotations.

First, define the notation for a series of rotations. Let (α_i,β_i) denote the ith pan-tilt configuration, starting with 0 for the initial configuration. Set $\bar{\alpha}_i \stackrel{\mathrm{def}}{=} \alpha_i - \alpha_{i-1}$ and $\bar{\beta}_i \stackrel{\mathrm{def}}{=} \beta_i - \beta_{i-1}$. For the ith rotation, the relationship with the notation used above is as follows: $(\alpha,\beta) = (\alpha_{i-1},\beta_{i-1})$, $(\bar{\alpha},\bar{\beta}) = (\bar{\alpha}_i,\bar{\beta}_i)$, and $(\alpha',\beta') = (\alpha_i,\beta_i)$. The critical value is $\beta = \beta_{i-1}$. Given a sequence of rotations, the following equation holds:

$$\beta_{i-1} = \beta_0 + \sum_{j=1}^{i-1}\bar{\beta}_j \ . \tag{5.57}$$

The non-linear rotational self-calibration problem can now be expressed in the following form (assuming $t_{\mathrm{H}} = \mathbf{0}$):

$$\boldsymbol{K} = \underset{\boldsymbol{K}}{\operatorname{argmin}} \min_{\boldsymbol{w}_{\mathrm{H}},\boldsymbol{v}_{\mathrm{T}},\boldsymbol{v}_{\mathrm{P}},\beta_0,(\bar{\alpha}_i,\bar{\beta}_i)_{1\le i\le n}} \sum_{i=1}^{n}\sum_{j=1}^{m_i}$$

$$d\left(\boldsymbol{K}\mathrm{Rod}\left(\mathrm{Rod}(\boldsymbol{w}_{\mathrm{H}})\boldsymbol{v}_{\mathrm{T}},\bar{\beta}_i\right)\mathrm{Rod}\left(\mathrm{Rod}(\boldsymbol{w}_{\mathrm{H}})\mathrm{Rod}\left(\boldsymbol{v}_{\mathrm{T}},\beta_0+\sum_{k=1}^{i-1}\bar{\beta}_k\right)\boldsymbol{v}_{\mathrm{P}},\bar{\alpha}_i\right)\boldsymbol{K}^{-1}\boldsymbol{p}_{1,i,j},\boldsymbol{p}_{2,i,j}\right)^2 , \tag{5.58}$$

where $\boldsymbol{R}_{\mathrm{H}} = \mathrm{Rod}(\boldsymbol{w}_{\mathrm{H}})$. Hence, for a sequence of n pan-tilt rotations, there are $2n + 15$ parameters ($\boldsymbol{v}_{\mathrm{T}}$ and $\boldsymbol{v}_{\mathrm{P}}$ are expressed by three parameters, even though they only have two degrees of freedom). There is an important special case in which each rotation is only about one of the two axes (pan and tilt). I will be called this the *two axes case*. There are $n + 15$ remaining parameters:

$$\boldsymbol{K} = \underset{\boldsymbol{K}}{\operatorname{argmin}} \min_{\boldsymbol{w}_{\mathrm{H}},\boldsymbol{v}_{\mathrm{T}},\boldsymbol{v}_{\mathrm{P}},\beta_0,(\bar{\alpha}_i)_{i\in\mathcal{I}_{\mathrm{P}}},(\bar{\beta}_i)_{i\in\mathcal{I}_{\mathrm{T}}}}$$

$$\sum_{i\in\mathcal{I}_{\mathrm{P}}}\sum_{j=1}^{m_i} d\left(\boldsymbol{K}\mathrm{Rod}\left(\mathrm{Rod}(\boldsymbol{w}_{\mathrm{H}})\mathrm{Rod}\left(\boldsymbol{v}_{\mathrm{T}},\beta_0+\sum_{k=1}^{i-1}\bar{\beta}_k\right)\boldsymbol{v}_{\mathrm{P}},\bar{\alpha}_i\right)\boldsymbol{K}^{-1}\boldsymbol{p}_{1,i,j},\boldsymbol{p}_{2,i,j}\right)^2$$

$$+\sum_{i\in\mathcal{I}_{\mathrm{T}}}\sum_{j=1}^{m_i} d\left(\boldsymbol{K}\mathrm{Rod}\left(\mathrm{Rod}(\boldsymbol{w}_{\mathrm{H}})\boldsymbol{v}_{\mathrm{T}},\bar{\beta}_i\right)\boldsymbol{K}^{-1}\boldsymbol{p}_{1,i,j},\boldsymbol{p}_{2,i,j}\right)^2 , \tag{5.59}$$

where $\mathcal{I}_{\mathrm{T}} \stackrel{\mathrm{def}}{=} \{\, i \in \{1,\ldots,n\} \mid \text{rotation } i \text{ is tilt} \,\}$ and $\mathcal{I}_{\mathrm{P}} \stackrel{\mathrm{def}}{=} \{\, i \in \{1,\ldots,n\} \mid \text{rotation } i \text{ is pan} \,\}$ denote the sets of tilt and pan rotation indices, respectively. The assumption that each rotation is only about one of the two axes translates to $\mathcal{I}_{\mathrm{T}} \cap \mathcal{I}_{\mathrm{P}} = \emptyset$.

If the relative rotation angles $(\bar{\alpha}_i,\bar{\beta}_i)_{1\le i\le n}$ are known, there are 15 remaining parameters. As noted in Section 5.3, in practice, the rotation angles may be known in some unknown machine specific unit only. Assuming a linear transformation between machine units and radians while allowing a separate transformation per axis, there are two additional parameters for the scale of the angles. Replace $\bar{\alpha}_i$ by $\eta_{\mathrm{P}}\bar{\gamma}_i$, $\bar{\beta}_i$ by $\eta_{\mathrm{T}}\bar{\delta}_i$, and (optionally) β_0 by $\eta_{\mathrm{T}}\delta_0$, where η_{P} and η_{T} denote the unknown scale parameters and $(\bar{\gamma}_i,\bar{\delta}_i)_{1\le i\le n}$ denote the angular values known up to scale. This leads to 17 parameters. The optimization problem in equation (5.58) becomes:

$$\boldsymbol{K} = \underset{\boldsymbol{K}}{\operatorname{argmin}} \min_{\boldsymbol{w}_{\mathrm{H}},\boldsymbol{v}_{\mathrm{T}},\boldsymbol{v}_{\mathrm{P}},\delta_0,\eta_{\mathrm{P}},\eta_{\mathrm{T}}} \sum_{i=1}^{n}\sum_{j=1}^{m_i}$$

$$d\left(\boldsymbol{K}\mathrm{Rod}\left(\mathrm{Rod}(\boldsymbol{w}_{\mathrm{H}})\boldsymbol{v}_{\mathrm{T}},\eta_{\mathrm{T}}\bar{\delta}_i\right)\mathrm{Rod}\left(\mathrm{Rod}(\boldsymbol{w}_{\mathrm{H}})\mathrm{Rod}\left(\boldsymbol{v}_{\mathrm{T}},\eta_{\mathrm{T}}\left(\delta_0+\sum_{k=1}^{i-1}\bar{\delta}_k\right)\right)\boldsymbol{v}_{\mathrm{P}},\eta_{\mathrm{P}}\bar{\gamma}_i\right)\boldsymbol{K}^{-1}\boldsymbol{p}_{1,i,j},\boldsymbol{p}_{2,i,j}\right)^2 . \tag{5.60}$$

In the two axes case, there are still the same 17 parameters, but the optimization problem can be written in the following, slightly more suitable form:

$$\boldsymbol{K} = \underset{\boldsymbol{K}}{\operatorname{argmin}} \min_{\boldsymbol{w}_{\mathrm{H}},\boldsymbol{v}_{\mathrm{T}},\boldsymbol{v}_{\mathrm{P}},\delta_0,\eta_{\mathrm{P}},\eta_{\mathrm{T}}}$$

$$\sum_{i\in\mathcal{I}_{\mathrm{P}}}\sum_{j=1}^{m_i} d\left(\boldsymbol{K}\mathrm{Rod}\left(\mathrm{Rod}(\boldsymbol{w}_{\mathrm{H}})\mathrm{Rod}\left(\boldsymbol{v}_{\mathrm{T}},\eta_{\mathrm{T}}\left(\delta_0+\sum_{k=1}^{i-1}\bar{\delta}_k\right)\right)\boldsymbol{v}_{\mathrm{P}},\eta_{\mathrm{P}}\bar{\gamma}_i\right)\boldsymbol{K}^{-1}\boldsymbol{p}_{1,i,j},\boldsymbol{p}_{2,i,j}\right)^2$$

$$+\sum_{i\in\mathcal{I}_{\mathrm{T}}}\sum_{j=1}^{m_i} d\left(\boldsymbol{K}\mathrm{Rod}\left(\mathrm{Rod}(\boldsymbol{w}_{\mathrm{H}})\boldsymbol{v}_{\mathrm{T}},\eta_{\mathrm{T}}\bar{\delta}_i\right)\boldsymbol{K}^{-1}\boldsymbol{p}_{1,i,j},\boldsymbol{p}_{2,i,j}\right)^2 . \tag{5.61}$$

In the XY rotation case, some values are known: $\boldsymbol{w}_{\mathrm{H}} = \boldsymbol{0}$, $\boldsymbol{v}_{\mathrm{T}} = (1,0,0)^{\mathrm{T}}$ and $\boldsymbol{v}_{\mathrm{P}} = (0,1,0)^{\mathrm{T}}$. There are hence 9 parameters less in all of the above cases.

Relation to the Simple Practical Approach

The simple practical approach (Section 5.4.1) is a special case of the two axes case (equations (5.59) and (5.61)). By first performing only pan motion and subsequently only tilt motion, for all $k \in \mathcal{I}_{\mathrm{P}}$, $\bar{\beta}_k = 0$ and $\bar{\delta}_k = 0$. Hence, there are only two rotation axes (expressed in the respective camera coordinate systems):

$$\boldsymbol{v}'_{\mathrm{P}} = \mathrm{Rod}(\boldsymbol{w}_{\mathrm{H}})\mathrm{Rod}\left(\boldsymbol{v}_{\mathrm{T}},\beta_0+\underbrace{\sum_{k=1}^{i-1}\bar{\beta}_k}_{=0}\right)\boldsymbol{v}_{\mathrm{P}} \tag{5.62}$$

$$\boldsymbol{v}'_{\mathrm{T}} = \mathrm{Rod}(\boldsymbol{w}_{\mathrm{H}})\boldsymbol{v}_{\mathrm{T}} . \tag{5.63}$$

After substituting these two simplifications into equation (5.59) and replacing the optimization parameters $\boldsymbol{w}_{\mathrm{H}}, \boldsymbol{v}_{\mathrm{T}}, \boldsymbol{v}_{\mathrm{P}}, \beta_0$ by $\boldsymbol{v}'_{\mathrm{P}}, \boldsymbol{v}'_{\mathrm{T}}$, it is obvious that equation (5.38) is a special case.

The simple practical approach with known rotation axes is the XY rotation case with the additional assumption $\beta_0 = 0$. Hence, we have $\boldsymbol{v}'_{\mathrm{T}} = (1,0,0)^{\mathrm{T}}$ and $\boldsymbol{v}'_{\mathrm{P}} = (0,1,0)^{\mathrm{T}}$. This shows that equation (5.39) is a special case of equation (5.59).

By the same argumentation, the cases with known angles (up to scale), i. e. all remaining cases in Section 5.3, are special cases of equation (5.61).

Chapter 6

Uncertainty-Based Extrinsic Multi-Camera Self-Calibration

In this chapter, I will present an extrinsic multi-camera self-calibration procedure that only requires a single image from each camera along with its intrinsic parameters as input. I have published the method itself and additional aspects in (Bajramovic and Denzler, 2008b,a, 2009; Brückner, Bajramovic and Denzler, 2009; Bajramovic, Brückner and Denzler, 2009, 2011). I will first give an overview of the method. Afterwards, I will describe the individual steps in detail.

After extracting point correspondences between camera pairs (Chapter 3), I estimate their relative poses (Chapter 4) and the uncertainty of each relative pose (Section 6.2). This information is represented by the *camera dependency graph* (Section 6.1). An example is given in Figure 6.1(a). The remaining task consists of composing the relative poses to the extrinsic calibration of the whole system (Section 6.1), by treating one triangle in the camera dependency graph at a time.

In order to improve the results of this process, I propose a novel, discrete two-stage optimization criterion for selecting relative poses (Section 6.3):

1. For a given reference camera pair, the total uncertainty with respect to all other cameras is minimized.

2. The reference pair is chosen such that the total uncertainty of all selected relative poses is minimal.

I will show that the first stage is equivalent to a shortest triangle paths problem, for which I will present a novel, efficient algorithm and prove its correctness (Section 6.4). The second stage consists of selecting the shortest triangle paths subgraph with minimum total uncertainty. Note that the two stages can be interpreted as solving a single discrete optimization problem with respect to certain structural constraints.

If a camera pair does not have a common field of view, it is not possible to correctly estimate the relative pose from point correspondences and their uncertainties will usually be high. Hence, as long as there are only few such camera pairs, my uncertainty-based selection of relative poses

Algorithm 6.1 A brief overview version of my extrinsic multi-camera calibration Algorithm 6.2.

Input: an image and intrinsic parameters per camera

Output: the absolute pose of each camera (up to a common similarity transformation)

1: Use Algorithm 6.3 to optionally detect camera pairs with a common fields of view, extract point correspondences, estimate relative poses and uncertainties, and construct the camera dependency graph

2: Assume that the camera dependency graph is triangle-connected ▹ Algorithm 6.5

3: Select relative poses with minimum total uncertainty by computing shortest (i. e. minimum weight) triangle paths in the camera dependency graph ▹ Sections 6.3 and 6.4

4: Estimate missing scale factors and absolute poses along shortest triangle paths ▹ Section 6.1

can often avoid the according edges in the camera dependency graph. On the other hand, common field of view detection can be used to detect such camera pairs in a preprocessing step. I present a novel method for detecting camera pairs with a common field of view in Section 6.6. If there are only few camera pairs without a common field of view, this preprocessing step supports the uncertainty-based selection of relative poses (Section 6.6.4) and can improve the calibration results (see experiments in Section 7.5.1). However, if there are too many such camera pairs, e. g. because the cameras are in two separate rooms, the preprocessing is actually required for calibration (Section 6.6.5).

A brief overview summary of the whole calibration procedure including common field of view detection is given in Algorithm 6.1, details are presented in Algorithm 6.2. A motivation for and an explanation of the individual steps will be given in the remainder of this chapter.

6.1 Multi-Camera Calibration from Relative Poses

In this section, I assume that the relative poses between some cameras pairs are known up to scale. After describing the relationship between relative and absolute poses, I will specify the task of extrinsically calibrating a multi-camera system from known relative poses. Afterwards, I will present the elementary operations for solving the problem, followed by a basic calibration algorithm (Section 6.1.1).

Relative and Absolute Poses

The relative pose between two cameras i and j is denoted by $(\boldsymbol{R}_{ij}, \boldsymbol{t}_{ij})$ (cf. Appendix D.3). It is defined such that it maps a 3D point $\boldsymbol{q}_{\mathrm{C},i}$ from the ith camera coordinate system to the jth one as follows:

$$\boldsymbol{q}_{\mathrm{C},j} = \boldsymbol{R}_{ij}\boldsymbol{q}_{\mathrm{C},i} + \boldsymbol{t}_{ij} \ . \tag{6.1}$$

The absolute poses of the $k$the camera is denoted by $(\boldsymbol{R}_k, \boldsymbol{t}_k)$ (cf. Appendix D.1). It transforms a 3D point $\boldsymbol{q}$ in world coordinates to kth camera coordinates as follows:

$$\boldsymbol{q}_{\mathrm{C},k} = \boldsymbol{R}_k\boldsymbol{q} + \boldsymbol{t}_k \ . \tag{6.2}$$

Algorithm 6.2 My extrinsic multi-camera calibration procedure.

Input: an image and intrinsic parameters per camera

Output: the absolute pose $(\boldsymbol{R}_k, \boldsymbol{t}_k)$ of each camera k (up to a common similarity transformation)

Use Algorithm 6.3 to optionally detect camera pairs with a common fields of view, extract point correspondences, estimate relative poses and uncertainties, and construct the camera dependency graph $\mathcal{G}_\mathrm{R}$
Assume that $\mathcal{G}_\mathrm{R}$ is triangle-connected (or treat each component separately) ▹ Algorithm 6.5
Construct the edge-triangle-vertex graph $\mathcal{G}_\mathrm{E}$ with w_2 edge weights ▹ Algorithm 6.9
for all edges e in $\mathcal{G}_\mathrm{R}$ **do**
    Find shortest paths from the entry vertex $v_{e\rightarrow}$ to all exit vertices in $\mathcal{G}_\mathrm{E}$ ▹ Appendix B.2
    Compute the total uncertainty $\omega(\mathcal{S}_e)$ of all involved relative poses ▹ Section 6.3
Choose the edge $e = (i, j)$ with minimum total uncertainty $\omega(\mathcal{S}_e)$ ▹ equation (6.18)
Set $\|\boldsymbol{t}_{ij}\| := 1$, $\boldsymbol{R}_i := \boldsymbol{I}$, and $\boldsymbol{t}_i := 0$
for all cameras k **do** ▹ all loop cycles must be independent of each other
    ▹ use local variables within the following loop (or restore $\mathcal{G}_\mathrm{E}$ afterwards)
    for all triangle vertices along the shortest triangle path from $v_{e\rightarrow}$ to $v_{\rightarrow k}$ **do**
        Estimate missing scale factors and concatenate relative poses ▹ Section 6.1
    Store the absolute pose $(\boldsymbol{R}_k, \boldsymbol{t}_k) = (\boldsymbol{R}_{ik}, \boldsymbol{t}_{ik})$

Note that relative poses have a double subscript, whereas absolute poses have a single one. When estimating relative poses from images only, i. e. without additional information like a reference length, the translation $\boldsymbol{t}_{ij}$ can only be determined up to a positive scale factor (Section 4.2.6). I emphasize the unknown positive scale by a star: $\boldsymbol{t}^*_{ij}$.

I represent a multi-camera system together with the set of known relative poses as the *camera dependency graph* $\mathcal{G}_\mathrm{R}$ (Vergés-Llahí et al., 2008), which is also known as the *image connectivity graph* (Snavely et al., 2008): each camera is a vertex and camera i is connected to camera j iff their relative pose $(\boldsymbol{R}_{ij}, \boldsymbol{t}^*_{ij})$ is known. Note that edges are directed, to distinguish $(\boldsymbol{R}_{ij}, \boldsymbol{t}^*_{ij})$ from $(\boldsymbol{R}_{ji}, \boldsymbol{t}^*_{ji})$. As relative poses can be easily inverted, however, all edges will be treated as bidirectional. An algorithm for constructing the camera dependency graph $\mathcal{G}_\mathrm{R}$ from images and known intrinsic parameters is given in Algorithm 6.3. An example graph is given in Fig. 6.1(a).

Extrinsic Calibration Task from Relative Poses

From a set of relative poses $(\boldsymbol{R}_{ij}, \boldsymbol{t}^*_{ij})$ known up to positive scale, I seek to compute absolute poses $(\boldsymbol{R}_k, \boldsymbol{t}_k)$ expressed in an arbitrary (but common) world coordinate system up to only one common unknown scale factor. In other words, I want to extrinsically calibrate the multi-camera system up to a 3D similarity transformation.

Actually, this is not always possible. In order to formulate a more precise statement, I need to define a few graph-theoretical concepts. Let $\mathcal{G}$ be an undirected graph without self-loops. I denote its vertices by $\mathcal{V}(\mathcal{G})$ and its edges by $\mathcal{E}(\mathcal{G})$.

Definition 6.1 (triangle path) *Let $i, j \in \mathcal{V}(\mathcal{G})$ be vertices in the graph $\mathcal{G}$. A sequence $\mathcal{P}$ =*

Algorithm 6.3 An algorithm for constructing the camera dependency graph from images and known intrinsic parameters.

Input: an image and intrinsic parameters per camera
Output: the camera dependency graph $\mathcal{G}_\mathrm{R}$

```
Initialize the camera dependency graph G_R = (∅, ∅)
for all cameras i do
    Add a vertex i to G_R
for all camera pairs (i, j) do
    if i and j have a common field of view then          ▷ condition is optional, Section 6.6
        Extract point correspondences D_ij                                      ▷ Chapter 3
        Estimate the relative pose R_ij, t*_ij and its uncertainty ω(R_ij, t*_ij)  ▷ Section 6.2
        Insert the edge (i, j) into G_R with weight ω(R_ij, t*_ij) and additional data (R_ij, t*_ij)
```

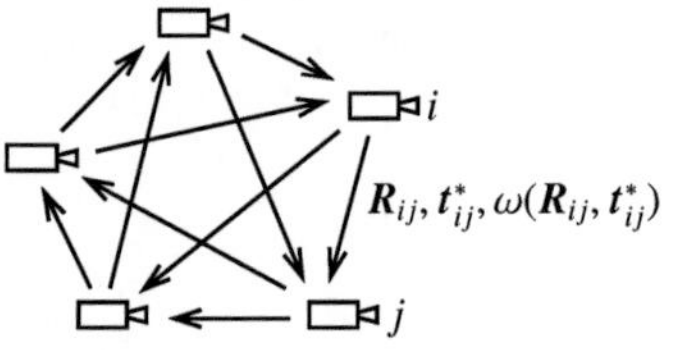

(a) An example of a camera dependency graph containing cameras i, j, relative poses $(\boldsymbol{R}_{ij}, \boldsymbol{t}^*_{ij})$, and uncertainties $\omega(\boldsymbol{R}_{ij}, \boldsymbol{t}^*_{ij})$.

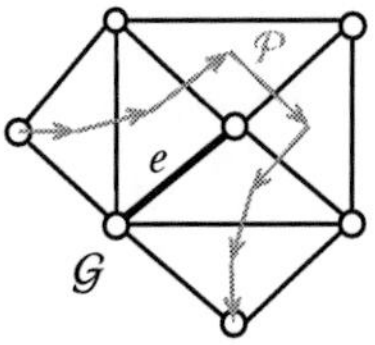

(b) A graph $\mathcal{G}$ and a triangle path $\mathcal{P}$ (blue / gray).

Figure 6.1: Examples of a camera dependency graph and a triangle path.

$(i, \mathcal{T}_1, \ldots, \mathcal{T}_n, j)$ *is called a* triangle path from i to j *iff* $\mathcal{T}_k \subseteq \mathcal{G}$ *is a triangle (i. e. a clique of size three) for all* $1 \le k \le n$, $|\mathcal{E}(\mathcal{T}_k) \cap \mathcal{E}(\mathcal{T}_{k+1})| = 1$ *for all* $1 \le k < n$, $i \in \mathcal{V}(\mathcal{T}_1)$ *and* $j \in \mathcal{V}(\mathcal{T}_n)$.

In other words, a triangle path consists of a sequence of triangles such that consecutive triangles have exactly one common edge. An example is given is Figure 6.1(b).

Definition 6.2 (triangle-connected) *A subgraph* $\mathcal{G}'$ *of a graph* $\mathcal{G}$ *is called* triangle-connected *iff for all vertices* $i, j \in \mathcal{V}(\mathcal{G}')$, *there is a triangle path from* i *to* j *in* $\mathcal{G}'$. *A* triangle-connected component *is a maximal triangle connected subgraph.*

These definitions allow to precisely state to which extent the extrinsic parameters of a multi-camera system can be computed from given relative poses, which are known up to positive scale. There will be one unknown 3D similarity transformation per triangle-connected component in the camera dependency graph $\mathcal{G}_\mathrm{R}$ (Mantzel et al., 2004). Subsequently, I will assume that the camera dependency graph is triangle-connected. Otherwise the calibration can be applied to each component separately. A method for detecting the triangle-connected components is given in Algorithm 6.5.

6.1.1 A Simple Extrinsic Calibration Algorithm

A *triangle* $\mathcal{T}$ in $\mathcal{G}_R$ consists of three cameras and three known relative poses. Let $\{i, j, k\} = \mathcal{V}(\mathcal{T})$. If one of the scales $\|\boldsymbol{t}_{ij}\|$ is known (or fixed), the remaining two scales can be computed by triangulation (Appendix D.4) as follows. The cameras i and j are treated as a stereo camera pair. The relative positions of the third camera, $\boldsymbol{c}^*_{ik} = -\boldsymbol{R}_{ik}\boldsymbol{t}^*_{ik}$ and $\boldsymbol{c}^*_{jk} = -\boldsymbol{R}_{jk}\boldsymbol{t}^*_{jk}$, form a point correspondence in camera normalized coordinates (Appendix D.3). By triangulating the position of the third camera, we get the scales of $\boldsymbol{c}_{ik}$ and $\boldsymbol{c}_{jk}$ (and hence $\boldsymbol{t}_{ik}$ and $\boldsymbol{t}_{jk}$) relative to $\boldsymbol{t}_{ij}$. Note that, as the correspondence to be triangulated is given in camera normalized coordinates, the intrinsic pinhole camera parameters to be used for the triangulation are $\boldsymbol{K}'_i = \boldsymbol{K}'_j = \boldsymbol{I}$ (identity matrix). An alternative method for estimating the scale factors is described in (Vergés-Llahí and Wada, 2008).

By treating one triangle after the other such that each triangle has a common edge with a previously treated triangle, all scales can be computed up to one common unknown scale parameter. Once the scales have been estimated, the absolute poses can be extracted from the relative poses based on the following two equations:

$$\begin{aligned} \boldsymbol{R}_j &= \boldsymbol{R}_{ij}\boldsymbol{R}_i \\ \boldsymbol{t}_j &= \boldsymbol{R}_{ij}\boldsymbol{t}_i + \boldsymbol{t}_{ij} \ . \end{aligned} \tag{6.3}$$

In order to formulate an explicit algorithm for this procedure, I define the following auxiliary graph.

Definition 6.3 (triangle graph) *The* triangle graph $\mathcal{G}_T$ *of a graph* $\mathcal{G}$ *is defined as follows. There is a vertex* $v_{\mathcal{T}}$ *for each triangle* $\mathcal{T}$ *in* $\mathcal{G}$. *For each two triangles* $\mathcal{T}, \mathcal{T}' \subseteq \mathcal{G}$ *with* $|\mathcal{E}(\mathcal{T}) \cap \mathcal{E}(\mathcal{T}')| = 1$, *there are two edges* $(v_{\mathcal{T}}, v_{\mathcal{T}'})$ *and* $(v_{\mathcal{T}'}, v_{\mathcal{T}})$ *in* $\mathcal{G}_T$.

An example and an efficient algorithm for constructing the triangle graph $\mathcal{G}_T$ are given in Figure 6.2 and Algorithm 6.4, respectively. In order to calibrate the multi-camera system, Algorithm 6.6 applies the steps described above while traversing $\mathcal{G}_T$, e. g. via breadth first search.

Note that Algorithm 6.6 assumes that $\mathcal{G}_R$ is triangle-connected. Otherwise the algorithm can be independently applied to each triangle-connected component. Algorithm 6.5 can be used to find the triangle-connected components of $\mathcal{G}_R$. It does so by detecting the connected components of the triangle graph $\mathcal{G}_T$, which directly correspond to the triangle-connected components of $\mathcal{G}_R$.

Obviously, there are many possible traversals of $\mathcal{G}_T$. Also, except for very sparse camera dependency graphs, only a subset of the triangles actually has to be visited in order to compute all scale factors and absolute poses. Hence, the traversal order implies a selection of triangles and thus relative poses. As the quality of the relative pose estimates varies between camera pairs, a more sophisticated selection is desirable. After introducing the uncertainty measures (Section 6.2), I will present such a selection criterion (Section 6.3).

6.2 Uncertainty Measures

I use *uncertainty measures* to assess the quality of a relative pose estimate. Such a measure should not only capture the local precision, but also the global uncertainty caused by ambigui-

Algorithm 6.4 An efficient algorithm for constructing the triangle graph $\mathcal{G}_\mathrm{T}$.

Input: a graph $\mathcal{G}$
Output: the triangle graph $\mathcal{G}_\mathrm{T}$ of $\mathcal{G}$

```
Initialize G_T := (∅, ∅)
for all e ∈ E(G) do
    Initialize Δ(e) := ∅                          ▹ sequence of triangles containing edge e
for all e ∈ E(G) do
    for all i ∈ V(G) do
        if e and i form a triangle T in G then
            Add the vertex v_T to G_T
            for all e' ∈ E(T) do
                for all v_T' ∈ Δ(e') do
                    Add two edges connecting v_T to v_T' and vice versa to G_T
            for all e' ∈ E(T) do
                Insert v_T into Δ(e')
```

ties. Furthermore, it should be well suited for a theoretically sound formulation of relative pose selection as an optimization problem.

The uncertainty measures are based on the probability density function $p(\boldsymbol{R}_\mathrm{rel}, \boldsymbol{t}^*_\mathrm{rel} \mid \mathcal{D})$. In Section 4.3.2, I have proposed two alternative definitions for $p(\boldsymbol{R}_\mathrm{rel}, \boldsymbol{t}^*_\mathrm{rel} \mid \mathcal{D})$ in the equations (4.54) and (4.55). The former is based on the epipolar constraint, whereas the latter additionally uses the cheirality constraint. As equation (4.55) does not give better results in the experiments (Section 7.2.2), but requires roughly 70 times more computation time, I will only consider equation (4.54) in the current section.

Note that equation (4.54) suffers from a fourfold ambiguity as explained in Section 4.3.2. In Section 6.2.1, I will give an argument, why this ambiguity, which could be avoided by using equation (4.55) instead, is acceptable in the context of the approximations I will present there.

I use one of the following three measures, which I have published in (Bajramovic and Denzler, 2008b), to model the uncertainty $\omega(\hat{\boldsymbol{R}}_\mathrm{rel}, \hat{\boldsymbol{t}}^*_\mathrm{rel})$ of the relative pose estimate $(\hat{\boldsymbol{R}}_\mathrm{rel}, \hat{\boldsymbol{t}}^*_\mathrm{rel})$.

1. The *information* is defined as

$$\omega_\mathrm{I}(\hat{\boldsymbol{R}}_\mathrm{rel}, \hat{\boldsymbol{t}}^*_\mathrm{rel}) \stackrel{\mathrm{def}}{=} -\log p(\hat{\boldsymbol{R}}_\mathrm{rel}, \hat{\boldsymbol{t}}^*_\mathrm{rel} \mid \mathcal{D}) \ . \tag{6.4}$$

2. The *entropy* is defined as

$$\omega_\mathrm{E}(\hat{\boldsymbol{R}}_\mathrm{rel}, \hat{\boldsymbol{t}}^*_\mathrm{rel}) \stackrel{\mathrm{def}}{=} -\int\int p(\boldsymbol{R}_\mathrm{rel}, \boldsymbol{t}^*_\mathrm{rel} \mid \mathcal{D}) \log p(\boldsymbol{R}_\mathrm{rel}, \boldsymbol{t}^*_\mathrm{rel} \mid \mathcal{D}) \mathrm{d}\boldsymbol{R}_\mathrm{rel} \mathrm{d}\boldsymbol{t}^*_\mathrm{rel} \ . \tag{6.5}$$

3. The *smoothed information* is defined as the information

$$\omega_\mathrm{S}(\hat{\boldsymbol{R}}_\mathrm{rel}, \hat{\boldsymbol{t}}^*_\mathrm{rel}) \stackrel{\mathrm{def}}{=} -\log p'(\hat{\boldsymbol{R}}_\mathrm{rel}, \hat{\boldsymbol{t}}^*_\mathrm{rel} \mid \mathcal{D}) \tag{6.6}$$

Algorithm 6.5 An algorithm for detecting the triangle-connected components of a graph.

Input: a graph $\mathcal{G}$
Output: a set $\mathcal{S}_\mathrm{T}$ containing the triangle-connected components of $\mathcal{G}$
Output: is $\mathcal{G}$ triangle-connected?

Initialize $\mathcal{S}_\mathrm{T} := \emptyset$
Construct the triangle graph $\mathcal{G}_\mathrm{T}$ ▹ Algorithm 6.4
Detect the connected components of $\mathcal{G}_\mathrm{T}$ ▹ Algorithm B.1
for all connected components C_C of $\mathcal{G}_\mathrm{T}$ **do**
  Initialize a new triangle-connected component $C_\mathrm{T} := (\emptyset, \emptyset)$
  for all vertices $v_\mathcal{T} \in \mathcal{V}(C_\mathrm{C})$ **do**
    Set $\mathcal{V}(C_\mathrm{T}) := \mathcal{V}(C_\mathrm{T}) \cup \mathcal{V}(\mathcal{T})$ and $\mathcal{E}(C_\mathrm{T}) := \mathcal{E}(C_\mathrm{T}) \cup \mathcal{E}(\mathcal{T})$
  Add C_T to the result $\mathcal{S}_\mathrm{T} := \mathcal{S}_\mathrm{T} \cup \{C_\mathrm{T}\}$
$\mathcal{G}$ is triangle-connected iff $|\mathcal{S}_\mathrm{T}| \leq 1$

Algorithm 6.6 A simple extrinsic multi-camera calibration algorithm based on breadth first search.

Estimate relative poses and construct the camera dependency graph $\mathcal{G}_\mathrm{R}$ ▹ Algorithm 6.3
Assume that $\mathcal{G}_\mathrm{R}$ is triangle-connected (or treat each component separately) ▹ Algorithm 6.5
Construct the triangle graph $\mathcal{G}_\mathrm{T}$ ▹ Algorithm 6.4
Choose a starting vertex $v_\mathcal{T} \in \mathcal{V}(\mathcal{G}_\mathrm{T})$
Let $\{i, j, k\} = \mathcal{V}(\mathcal{T})$
Set $\|\boldsymbol{t}_{ij}\| := 1$, $\boldsymbol{R}_i := \boldsymbol{I}$, and $\boldsymbol{t}_i := 0$
while traversing $\mathcal{G}_\mathrm{T}$ **do** ▹ e. g. via breadth first search (BFS), Appendix B.1
  if visiting a triangle vertex **then**
    Estimate missing scale factors and extract missing absolute poses ▹ Section 6.1

of the smoothed density function

$$p'(\hat{\boldsymbol{R}}_\mathrm{rel}, \hat{\boldsymbol{t}}^*_\mathrm{rel} \mid \mathcal{D}) = \mathcal{N}(\boldsymbol{R}_\mathrm{rel}, \boldsymbol{t}^*_\mathrm{rel}; \hat{\boldsymbol{R}}_\mathrm{rel}, \hat{\boldsymbol{t}}^*_\mathrm{rel}, \boldsymbol{\Sigma}) * p(\boldsymbol{R}_\mathrm{rel}, \boldsymbol{t}^*_\mathrm{rel} \mid \mathcal{D}) \ , \tag{6.7}$$

where $*$ denotes the convolution operation and $\mathcal{N}(\boldsymbol{R}_\mathrm{rel}, \boldsymbol{t}^*_\mathrm{rel}; \hat{\boldsymbol{R}}_\mathrm{rel}, \hat{\boldsymbol{t}}^*_\mathrm{rel}, \boldsymbol{\Sigma})$ is the normal distribution with mean $(\hat{\boldsymbol{R}}_\mathrm{rel}, \hat{\boldsymbol{t}}^*_\mathrm{rel})$ and covariance $\boldsymbol{\Sigma}$.

I will use an extension of the MLESAC algorithm (Section 4.3.2) proposed by Engels and Nistér (2005) to approximate these measures (see Section 6.2.1).

An Extension of the Probabilistic Model

I extend the likelihood function $p(\mathcal{D} \mid \boldsymbol{E})$ defined in equation (4.47) as proposed by Engels and Nistér (2005):

$$p(\mathcal{D} \mid \boldsymbol{E}) \propto \left(\prod_{(\boldsymbol{p}_1, \boldsymbol{p}_2) \in \mathcal{D}} p(\boldsymbol{p}_1, \boldsymbol{p}_2 \mid \boldsymbol{E}) \right)^{|\mathcal{D}|^{-\phi}} \ , \tag{6.8}$$

where $p(\boldsymbol{p}_1, \boldsymbol{p}_2 \mid \boldsymbol{E})$ is defined according to either equation (4.48) or (4.49). The new exponent $|\mathcal{D}|^{-\phi}$ can be used to change the shape of the distribution without shifting the positions of its maxima. It can be interpreted as a "non-linear scaling" and $\phi = 0$ corresponds to assuming independence as in equation (4.47). Engels and Nistér (2005) suggest using $\phi = 0.5$, which also gives good results in my experiments (Section 7.3). Note that $p(\boldsymbol{R}_{\mathrm{rel}}, \boldsymbol{t}^*_{\mathrm{rel}} \mid \mathcal{D})$ is directly affected by this extension (cf. equations (4.54) and (4.46)).

For some additional insight into the role of ϕ, substitute the Blake-Zisserman distribution according to equation (4.49):

$$\begin{aligned} p(\mathcal{D} \mid \boldsymbol{E}) &\propto \left(\prod_{(\boldsymbol{p}_1,\boldsymbol{p}_2)\in\mathcal{D}} \exp\left(-\frac{d_E(\boldsymbol{p}_1, \boldsymbol{p}_2)}{\sigma^2}\right) + \epsilon \right)^{|\mathcal{D}|^{-\phi}} \\ &= \prod_{(\boldsymbol{p}_1,\boldsymbol{p}_2)\in\mathcal{D}} \left(\exp\left(-\frac{d_E(\boldsymbol{p}_1, \boldsymbol{p}_2)}{\sigma^2}\right) + \epsilon \right)^{|\mathcal{D}|^{-\phi}} \\ &\underset{\epsilon=0}{=} \prod_{(\boldsymbol{p}_1,\boldsymbol{p}_2)\in\mathcal{D}} \exp\left(-\frac{d_E(\boldsymbol{p}_1, \boldsymbol{p}_2)}{|\mathcal{D}|^{\phi}\sigma^2}\right) . \end{aligned} \tag{6.9}$$

This shows that in the special case $\epsilon = 0$, choosing $\phi \neq 0$ simply changes the variance of the Gaussian depending on $|\mathcal{D}|$. If $\epsilon > 0$ or if the the Cauchy distribution is used instead of the Blake-Zisserman distribution, the influence of ϕ is more complicated.

6.2.1 Approximating the Uncertainty Measures

I use an extension of MLESAC (Section 4.3.2) to approximate the uncertainty measures in the equations (6.4)–(6.6). To facilitate the latter, I reduce the problem from five to two dimensions by using the marginal density

$$p(\boldsymbol{t}^*_{\mathrm{rel}} \mid \mathcal{D}) = \int p(\boldsymbol{R}_{\mathrm{rel}}, \boldsymbol{t}^*_{\mathrm{rel}} \mid \mathcal{D}) \mathrm{d}\boldsymbol{R}_{\mathrm{rel}} \tag{6.10}$$

instead of $p(\boldsymbol{R}_{\mathrm{rel}}, \boldsymbol{t}^*_{\mathrm{rel}} \mid \mathcal{D})$. This simplification can be expected to still give useful uncertainties as the errors in the translation $\boldsymbol{R}_{\mathrm{rel}}, \boldsymbol{t}^*_{\mathrm{rel}}$ and the orientation $\boldsymbol{R}_{\mathrm{rel}}$ of a relative pose estimate is usually highly correlated (Engels and Nistér, 2005).

Engels and Nistér (2005) approximate the integral in equation (6.10) using Laplace's method. I use the simpler approximation

$$p(\boldsymbol{t}^*_{\mathrm{rel}} \mid \mathcal{D}) \propto \max_{\boldsymbol{R}_{\mathrm{rel}}} p(\boldsymbol{R}_{\mathrm{rel}}, \boldsymbol{t}^*_{\mathrm{rel}} \mid \mathcal{D}) , \tag{6.11}$$

which equals the Laplace approximation if $\det(\nabla^2_{\boldsymbol{R}_{\mathrm{rel}}} \log p(\boldsymbol{R}_{\mathrm{rel}}, \boldsymbol{t}^*_{\mathrm{rel}} \mid \mathcal{D}))$ is independent of $\boldsymbol{t}^*_{\mathrm{rel}}$ (MacKay, 2003, Chapter 27).

Like Engels and Nistér (2005), I further simplify the problem by using a discrete approximation of the density $p(\boldsymbol{t}^*_{\mathrm{rel}} \mid \mathcal{D})$. Note that $\boldsymbol{t}^*_{\mathrm{rel}}$ has only two degrees of freedom. Furthermore, $\boldsymbol{t}^*_{\mathrm{rel}}$ and $-\boldsymbol{t}^*_{\mathrm{rel}}$ cannot be distinguished based on the epipolar constraint (cf. equation (4.54)). Hence,

t^*_{rel} can be restricted to lie on the upper unit hemisphere and the first two coordinates of t^*_{rel} suffice as a representation. In other words, I orthographically project the unit hemisphere onto the unit circle. I discretize $[-1, 1]^2$ into a regular grid $\{-d, -d+1, \dots, d-1\}^2$ and use the function $\psi : \{-d, -d+1, \dots, d-1\}^2 \to \mathbb{R}$ as a discrete approximation of $p(t^*_{rel} \mid \mathcal{D})$:

$$\psi(a, b) \propto \max_{R_{rel} \in \mathcal{SO}(3), t^*_{rel} \in \mathcal{Z}(a,b)} p(R_{rel}, t^*_{rel} \mid \mathcal{D}) \ , \tag{6.12}$$

where $\mathcal{SO}(3)$ denotes the set of 3D rotations as defined in equation (5.32) and

$$\mathcal{Z}(a, b) = \left\{ (x, y, z)^T \in \mathbb{R}^3 \;\middle|\; x \in \left[\frac{a}{d}, \frac{a+1}{d}\right[, y \in \left[\frac{b}{d}, \frac{b+1}{d}\right[, z > 0, \left\|(x, y, z)^T\right\| = 1 \right\} \ . \tag{6.13}$$

Note that $\mathcal{Z}(a, b)$ is empty for some (a, b) outside the unit circle. In such cases, the maximum in equation (6.12) is set to 0 (the smallest possible probability). I use data driven sampling to approximate equation (6.12) and at the same time also equation (4.53). The resulting Algorithm 6.7 can be interpreted as an extension of Algorithm 4.5.

The uncertainty measures can now be approximated as follows:

1. $\omega_I(\hat{R}_{rel}, \hat{t}^*_{rel}) \approx -\log \psi(\hat{a}, \hat{b})$, where $(\hat{a}, \hat{b})$ corresponds to $\hat{t}^*_{rel}$ as described above in the lines 7–11 of Algorithm 6.7.

2. $\omega_E(\hat{R}_{rel}, \hat{t}^*_{rel}) \approx -\sum_{a,b} \psi(a, b) \log \psi(a, b)$.

3. $\omega_S(\hat{R}_{rel}, \hat{t}^*_{rel}) \approx -\log \sum_{a,b} \mathcal{N}(\alpha(a, b, \hat{t}^*_{rel}); 0, \gamma^2) \psi(a, b)$, where $\alpha(a, b, \hat{t}^*_{rel})$ denotes the angle between $\hat{t}^*_{rel}$ and $\left(a, b, \sqrt{1 - a^2 - b^2}\right)^T$ and γ^2 is the variance of the normal distribution $\mathcal{N}$.

Note that due to the discretization step, these approximations are guaranteed to be non-negative. This – arguably – appears to be more intuitive than the definitions in the equations (6.4)–(6.6), which could lead to negative uncertainties. Furthermore it is advantageous for finding shortest triangle paths (Section 6.4). On the other hand, the non-negativity of course shows that the approximations cannot be arbitrarily good in all situations.

6.3 Selection of Relative Poses as a Discrete Optimization Problem

I propose a two-stage optimization criterion for selecting relative poses. I begin by motivating the first stage. The calibration of the pose of a camera j relative to a reference camera i involves a triangle path from i to j in the camera dependency graph $\mathcal{G}_R$. As noted above, there are often several alternative triangle paths $\mathcal{P}$ consisting of different sets of relative poses. I want to choose a triangle path that minimizes the total uncertainty of all involved relative poses. Hence, I need a measure for the total uncertainty of a triangle path $\mathcal{P}$—or more generally of a set $\mathcal{S}$ of relative poses.

Algorithm 6.7 An extension of MLESAC (Algorithm 4.5) for estimating the relative pose and its uncertainty.

```
Input: point correspondences 𝒟
Input: known intrinsic camera parameters K_1, K_2
Output: essential matrix estimate Ê as approximate solution to equation (4.50)
Output: according relative pose estimate (R̂_rel, t̂*_rel)
Output: β = p(Ê | 𝒟)
Parameter: number of iterations N (e. g. N = 3000)
Parameter: essential matrix estimation algorithm(s) (e. g. the five-point algorithm)
Parameter: a model for the density p(E | 𝒟) and its parameters
Parameter: sample size M (e. g. M = 5)
Parameter: resolution d of the function ψ
Initialize ψ(a, b) := 0 for all (a, b)
Initialize β := 0                ▷ used to store the current maximum value of p(E | 𝒟)
for c times do:
    Draw a sample of (at least) five point correspondences from 𝒟
    Apply the five point algorithm to estimate the essential matrix E      ▷ Section 4.2.4
    Extract the translation t*_rel := t*(1)_rel from E up to (arbitrary!) scale   ▷ Algorithm 4.1
    Normalize t*_rel to length 1
    Let t*_rel = (x, y, z)^T
    if z < 0 then        ▷ sign of z unknown, restrict t*_rel to upper unit hemisphere
        Set x := −x and y := −y
    Compute discrete grid positions a = ⌊dx⌋ and b = ⌊dy⌋
    Set ψ(a, b) := max(ψ(a, b), p(E | 𝒟))
    if β < p(E | 𝒟) then
        Set β := p(E | 𝒟) and Ê := E
Normalize ψ such that Σ_{a,b} ψ(a, b) = 1
Extract the relative pose (R̂_rel, t̂*_rel) from Ê                       ▷ Algorithm 4.3
```

Assuming independence, we have

$$p(\mathcal{S} \mid \mathcal{D}) = \prod_{(\boldsymbol{R}_{\text{rel}}, \boldsymbol{t}^*_{\text{rel}}) \in \mathcal{S}} p(\boldsymbol{R}_{\text{rel}}, \boldsymbol{t}^*_{\text{rel}} \mid \mathcal{D}) \ . \tag{6.14}$$

This leads to the following expression for the information measure in equation (6.4) and the entropy measure in equation (6.5):

$$\omega(\mathcal{S}) = \sum_{(\boldsymbol{R}_{\text{rel}}, \boldsymbol{t}^*_{\text{rel}}) \in \mathcal{S}} \omega(\boldsymbol{R}_{\text{rel}}, \boldsymbol{t}^*_{\text{rel}}) \ . \tag{6.15}$$

In the case of the information measure, the derivation is simple:

$$\omega_{\text{I}}(\mathcal{S}) = -\log p(\mathcal{S} \mid \mathcal{D}) = -\log \prod_{(\boldsymbol{R}_{\text{rel}}, \boldsymbol{t}^*_{\text{rel}}) \in \mathcal{S}} p(\boldsymbol{R}_{\text{rel}}, \boldsymbol{t}^*_{\text{rel}} \mid \mathcal{D})$$

$$= \sum_{(\boldsymbol{R}_{\text{rel}},\boldsymbol{t}^*_{\text{rel}})\in\mathcal{S}} -\log p(\boldsymbol{R}_{\text{rel}}, \boldsymbol{t}^*_{\text{rel}} \mid \mathcal{D}) = \sum_{(\boldsymbol{R}_{\text{rel}},\boldsymbol{t}^*_{\text{rel}})\in\mathcal{S}} \omega_{\text{I}}(\boldsymbol{R}_{\text{rel}}, \boldsymbol{t}^*_{\text{rel}}) \ . \tag{6.16}$$

In the case of the entropy measure, I refer to the fact that the joint entropy of independent random variables equals the sum of the individual entropies (MacKay, 2003, Section 8.1). Assuming

$$p(\mathcal{S} \mid \mathcal{D}) = \prod_{(\boldsymbol{R}_{\text{rel}},\boldsymbol{t}^*_{\text{rel}})\in\mathcal{S}} p'(\boldsymbol{R}_{\text{rel}}, \boldsymbol{t}^*_{\text{rel}} \mid \mathcal{D}) \ , \tag{6.17}$$

we also get equation (6.15) for the smoothed information measure in equation (6.6).

As a measure for the total uncertainty of a triangle path $\mathcal{P}$, I use the total uncertainty $\omega(\mathcal{E}_1(\mathcal{P}))$ of all its relative poses $\mathcal{E}_1(\mathcal{P})$ (cf. equation (6.20)). By the sum in equation (6.15), the problem of finding a triangle path with minimum total uncertainty is equivalent to the w_1 *shortest triangle path problem*, which will be treated in detail in Section 6.4, using the uncertainties as edge weights: $w(i, j) = \omega(\boldsymbol{R}_{ij}, \boldsymbol{t}^*_{ij})$. This provides a theoretical justification for using shortest triangle paths.

Using this approach to calibrate a whole multi-camera system involves shortest triangle paths from i to all other cameras. While the common reference camera ensures that the set of all involved relative poses $\mathcal{S}_i$ is connected, by using a common reference edge $e \in \mathcal{E}(\mathcal{G}_{\text{R}})$ instead, it is actually guaranteed that $\mathcal{S}_e$ is *triangle*-connected. As this is required for the calibration (cf. Section 6.1), I use w_1 shortest triangle paths from a common relative pose (edge) to all cameras (cf. Section 6.4.2).

The second stage of the optimization consists of selecting the reference relative pose $e \in \mathcal{E}(\mathcal{G}_{\text{R}})$ and hence also the set $\mathcal{S}_e$ of relative poses used for the extrinsic multi-camera calibration. I choose $e \in \mathcal{E}(\mathcal{G}_{\text{R}})$ such that the *total* uncertainty $\omega(\mathcal{S}_e)$ is minimized:

$$\operatorname*{argmin}_{e\in\mathcal{E}(\mathcal{G}_{\text{R}})} \omega(\mathcal{S}_e) \tag{6.18}$$

In other words, the two stages of the optimization select the *shortest* triangle-connected subgraph consisting of w_1 *shortest* triangle paths. Even though the optimization consists of two stages, it can be interpreted as solving a single discrete optimization problem with respect to certain structural constraints.

Interpretation and Alternatives

One effect of the selection of relative poses is the avoidence of outliers (within the set of relative pose estimates). However, there is no explicit outlier classification. Instead, a small (not necessarily minimal) number of relative poses is selected such that the total uncertainty is minimized (with respect to the shortest triangle paths condition) while ensuring that all cameras can still be calibrated up to one common unknown 3D similarity transformation (assuming a triangle-connected camera dependency graph). Alternatively, each relative pose could independently be classified as inlier or outlier. I will present such an approach based on common field of view detection in Section 6.6 as a supportive technique for the uncertainty-based selection of relative poses.

6.4 Shortest Triangle Paths

In this section, I will present the shortest triangle paths problem from a graph theoretical point of view and propose an efficient algorithm. Let $\mathcal{G}$ be a non-negatively edge-weighted, undirected graph without self-loops. I denote its vertices by $\mathcal{V}(\mathcal{G})$, its edges by $\mathcal{E}(\mathcal{G})$ and its edge weights by $w : \mathcal{E}(\mathcal{G}) \to [0, \infty[$.

I consider three alternative definitions for the length of a *triangle path* (Definition 6.1). In order to easily express their differences, I will use multisets, i. e. sets that allow for duplicate elements. I will use standard set notation with an M subscript and "$\sqcup$" for multiset union. For example, $\{b, b\}_\mathrm{M} \sqcup \{a, b, b\}_\mathrm{M} = \{a, b, b, b, b\}_\mathrm{M}$, $\sum_{x \in_\mathrm{M} \{b,b,b\}} x = 3b$. I use the notation $\mathcal{U}(\mathcal{A})$ to denote the *set* containing all elements in a multiset $\mathcal{A}$, i. e. the elements without duplicates. For example, $\mathcal{U}(\{a, b, b, b\}_\mathrm{M}) = \{a, b\}$.

Definition 6.4 (length of a triangle path) *For $k \in \{1, 2, 3\}$, the "w_k* length*" of a triangle path $\mathcal{P}$ is defined as*

$$w_k(\mathcal{P}) \stackrel{\text{def}}{=} \sum_{e \in_\mathrm{M} \mathcal{E}_k(\mathcal{P})} w(e) \tag{6.19}$$

$$\textit{with } \mathcal{E}_1(\mathcal{P}) \stackrel{\text{def}}{=} \bigcup_{a=1}^{n} \mathcal{E}(\mathcal{T}_a) \tag{6.20}$$

$$\mathcal{E}_2(\mathcal{P}) \stackrel{\text{def}}{=} \mathcal{E}(\mathcal{T}_1) \sqcup \bigsqcup_{a=2}^{n} \mathcal{E}(\mathcal{T}_a) \setminus \mathcal{E}(\mathcal{T}_{a-1}) \tag{6.21}$$

$$\mathcal{E}_3(\mathcal{P}) \stackrel{\text{def}}{=} \bigsqcup_{a=1}^{n} \mathcal{E}(\mathcal{T}_a) \; . \tag{6.22}$$

Example 6.5 *Figure 6.1(b) shows a graph $\mathcal{G}$ and a triangle path $\mathcal{P}$. Let all edges $e' \in \mathcal{E}(\mathcal{G})$ have weight $w(e') = 1$. Then the lengths of the triangle path are $w_1(\mathcal{P}) = 12$, $w_2(\mathcal{P}) = 13$, $w_3(\mathcal{P}) = 18$. The difference between $w_1(\mathcal{P})$ and $w_2(\mathcal{P})$ is due to the edge e.*

Definition 6.6 (shortest triangle path) *A triangle path $\mathcal{P}$ from i to j is called a w_k* shortest triangle path from *i* to *j iff all triangle paths $\mathcal{P}'$ from i to j are at least as long as $\mathcal{P}$, i. e. $w_k(\mathcal{P}) \leq w_k(\mathcal{P}')$.*

6.4.1 Shortest Triangle Paths Algorithm

Our efficient shortest triangle paths algorithm is based on an auxiliary directed graph, which I call the *vertex-triangle-vertex graph $\mathcal{G}_\mathrm{V}$*. It is an extension of the triangle graph $\mathcal{G}_\mathrm{T}$. The structure of $\mathcal{G}_\mathrm{V}$ is identical for all three triangle path lengths, but we will need specific edge weights.

Definition 6.7 (vertex-triangle-vertex graph) *The* vertex-triangle-vertex graph *$\mathcal{G}_\mathrm{V}$ of a graph $\mathcal{G}$ is defined as follows: for every vertex x in $\mathcal{G}$, there is a corresponding* entry vertex *$v_{x\to}$ and also a corresponding* exit vertex *$v_{\to x}$ in $\mathcal{G}_\mathrm{V}$. Furthermore, there is a* triangle vertex *$v_\mathcal{T}$ for each triangle $\mathcal{T}$ in $\mathcal{G}$. For each triangle $\mathcal{T} \subseteq \mathcal{G}$ and each vertex $x \in \mathcal{V}(\mathcal{T})$, there are two edges*

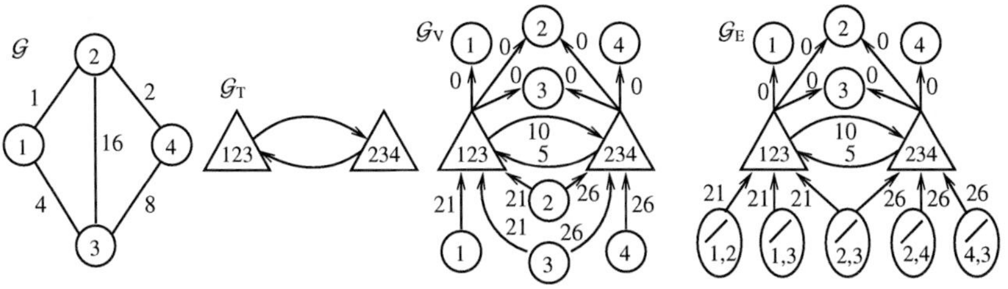

Figure 6.2: From left to right: a graph $\mathcal{G}$, the associated triangle graph $\mathcal{G}_{\mathrm{T}}$, the vertex-triangle-vertex graph $\mathcal{G}_{\mathrm{V}}$ with $\hat{w}_2$ edge weights and the edge-triangle-vertex graph $\mathcal{G}_{\mathrm{E}}$ with $\hat{w}_2$ edge weights. Note that the example graphs are planar only for the sake of legibility. In general, the graphs do not have to be planar.

$(v_{x\rightarrow}, v_{\mathcal{T}})$ and $(v_{\mathcal{T}}, v_{\rightarrow x})$ in $\mathcal{G}_{\mathrm{V}}$. For each two triangles $\mathcal{T}, \mathcal{T}' \subseteq \mathcal{G}$ with $|\mathcal{E}(\mathcal{T}) \cap \mathcal{E}(\mathcal{T}')| = 1$, there are two edges $(v_{\mathcal{T}}, v_{\mathcal{T}'})$ and $(v_{\mathcal{T}'}, v_{\mathcal{T}})$ in $\mathcal{G}_{\mathrm{V}}$.

Figure 6.2 shows an example of a vertex-triangle-vertex graph. An efficient algorithm for constructing $\mathcal{G}_{\mathrm{V}}$ is given in Algorithm 6.8.

By construction, a triangle path $\mathcal{P}$ from i to j in $\mathcal{G}$ directly corresponds to an ordinary path $\mathcal{P}_{\mathrm{V}}$ from the entry vertex $v_{i\rightarrow}$ to the exit vertex $v_{\rightarrow j}$ in $\mathcal{G}_{\mathrm{V}}$. I call $\mathcal{P}_{\mathrm{V}}$ an *entry-exit path*. In order to compute w_k *shortest* triangle paths using $\mathcal{G}_{\mathrm{V}}$, we need to define suitable edge weights. In the cases of w_2 and w_3, this is quite simple.

Definition 6.8 *Edge weights in $\mathcal{G}_{\mathrm{V}}$ are defined as follows, using $\mathcal{T}_a$ to denote the triangle associated with a triangle vertex a:*

$$\hat{w}_2(a,b) = \begin{cases} \sum_{e\in\mathcal{E}(\mathcal{T}_b)} w(e) & a \text{ is an entry vertex} \\ 0 & b \text{ is an exit vertex} \\ \sum_{e\in\mathcal{E}(\mathcal{T}_b)\setminus\mathcal{E}(\mathcal{T}_a)} w(e) & \text{otherwise} \ , \end{cases} \tag{6.23}$$

$$\hat{w}_3(a,b) = \begin{cases} 0 & b \text{ is an exit vertex} \\ \sum_{e\in\mathcal{E}(\mathcal{T}_b)} w(e) & \text{otherwise} \ . \end{cases} \tag{6.24}$$

I denote the length of a path $\mathcal{P}_{\mathrm{V}}$ according to the edge weights $\hat{w}_k$ in $\mathcal{G}_{\mathrm{V}}$:

$$\hat{w}_k(\mathcal{P}_{\mathrm{V}}) \stackrel{\text{def}}{=} \sum_{e\in_{\mathrm{M}}\mathcal{E}(\mathcal{P}_{\mathrm{V}})} \hat{w}_k(e) \ , \tag{6.25}$$

where $\mathcal{E}(\mathcal{P}_{\mathrm{V}})$ denotes the multiset of edges in $\mathcal{P}_{\mathrm{V}}$.

Proposition 6.9 *Let $\mathcal{P}$ be a triangle path in a graph $\mathcal{G}$, let $\mathcal{P}_{\mathrm{V}}$ be its corresponding entry-exit path in $\mathcal{G}_{\mathrm{V}}$, and let $k \in \{2,3\}$. Then $w_k(\mathcal{P}) = \hat{w}_k(\mathcal{P}_{\mathrm{V}})$.*

Algorithm 6.8 An efficient algorithm for constructing the vertex-triangle-vertex graph $\mathcal{G}_\mathrm{V}$. This algorithm is an extension of Algorithm 6.4.

Input: a graph $\mathcal{G}$
Output: the vertex-triangle-vertex graph $\mathcal{G}_\mathrm{V}$ of $\mathcal{G}$

Initialize $\mathcal{G}_\mathrm{V} := (\emptyset, \emptyset)$
for all $i \in \mathcal{V}(\mathcal{G})$ **do**
  Add entry and exit vertices $v_{i\rightarrow}$ and $v_{\rightarrow i}$ to $\mathcal{G}_\mathrm{V}$ (and store references from i to $v_{i\rightarrow}$ and $v_{\rightarrow i}$)
for all $e \in \mathcal{E}(\mathcal{G})$ **do**
  Initialize $\Delta(e) := \emptyset$ ▹ sequence of triangles containing edge e
for all $e \in \mathcal{E}(\mathcal{G})$ **do**
  for all $i \in \mathcal{V}(\mathcal{G})$ **do**
    if e and i form a triangle $\mathcal{T}$ in $\mathcal{G}$ **then**
      Add the triangle vertex $v_\mathcal{T}$ to $\mathcal{G}_\mathrm{V}$
      Connect $v_\mathcal{T}$ with the according entry and exit vertices
      Compute the weights of these new edges according to equation (6.23)
      for all $e' \in \mathcal{E}(\mathcal{T})$ **do**
        for all $v_{\mathcal{T}'} \in \Delta(e')$ **do**
          Add two edges connecting $v_\mathcal{T}$ to $v_{\mathcal{T}'}$ and vice versa
          Compute the weights of these new edges according to equation (6.23)
      for all $e' \in \mathcal{E}(\mathcal{T})$ **do**
        Insert $v_\mathcal{T}$ into $\Delta(e')$

Proof: The length $\hat{w}_k(\mathcal{P}_\mathrm{V})$ is a sum of edge weights over a multiset of edges in $\mathcal{G}$, which by construction equals $\mathcal{E}_k(\mathcal{P})$. Hence $\hat{w}_k(\mathcal{P}_\mathrm{V}) = \sum_{e \in_\mathrm{M} \mathcal{E}_k(\mathcal{P})} w(e) = w_k(\mathcal{P})$. □

Corollary 6.10 *Let $k \in \{2, 3\}$. $\hat{w}_k$ shortest entry-exit paths in $\mathcal{G}_\mathrm{V}$ correspond to w_k shortest triangle paths in $\mathcal{G}$.*

In the case of the w_1 length of triangle paths, it seems to be impossible to construct equally well suited weights in $\mathcal{G}_\mathrm{V}$ by non-local effects (cf. Example 6.5, edge e). In order to compute w_1 *shortest* triangle paths, however, it turns out that we do not need a new construction.

Theorem 6.11 *Let $\mathcal{P}$ be a triangle path from a vertex i to a vertex j. If $\mathcal{P}$ is a w_2 shortest triangle path from i to j, then it is also a w_1 shortest triangle path from i to j.*

The proof will be given in Section 6.4.4. By Corollary 6.10 and Theorem 6.11, in order to solve the w_k shortest triangle paths problem starting from a vertex x for $k \in \{1, 2, 3\}$, we can compute shortest entry-exit paths in $\mathcal{G}_\mathrm{V}$ starting from the entry vertex $v_{x\rightarrow}$ using, e. g. Dijkstra's algorithm (Appendix B.2). We have to use the following edge weights in $\mathcal{G}_\mathrm{V}$: $\hat{w}_2$ for $k \in \{1, 2\}$ and $\hat{w}_3$ for $k = 3$.

Algorithm 6.9 An efficient algorithm for constructing the edge-triangle-vertex graph $\mathcal{G}_{\mathrm{E}}$. This algorithm is a variant of Algorithm 6.8.

Input: a graph $\mathcal{G}$
Output: the edge-triangle-vertex graph $\mathcal{G}_{\mathrm{E}}$ of $\mathcal{G}$

Initialize $\mathcal{G}_{\mathrm{E}} := (\emptyset, \emptyset)$
for all $e \in \mathcal{E}(\mathcal{G})$ **do**
    Add the entry vertex $v_{e\rightarrow}$ to $\mathcal{G}_{\mathrm{E}}$ (and store a reference from e to $v_{e\rightarrow}$)
for all $i \in \mathcal{V}(\mathcal{G})$ **do**
    Add the exit vertex $v_{\rightarrow i}$ to $\mathcal{G}_{\mathrm{E}}$ (and store a reference from i to $v_{\rightarrow i}$)
for all $e \in \mathcal{E}(\mathcal{G})$ **do**
    Initialize $\Delta(e) := \emptyset$ ▹ sequence of triangles containing edge e
for all $e \in \mathcal{E}(\mathcal{G})$ **do**
    for all $i \in \mathcal{V}(\mathcal{G})$ **do**
        if e and i form a triangle $\mathcal{T}$ in $\mathcal{G}$ **then**
            Add the triangle vertex $v_{\mathcal{T}}$ to $\mathcal{G}_{\mathrm{E}}$
            Connect $v_{\mathcal{T}}$ with the according entry and exit vertices
            Compute the weights of these new edges according to equation (6.23)
            for all $e' \in \mathcal{E}(\mathcal{T})$ **do**
                for all $v_{\mathcal{T}'} \in \Delta(e')$ **do**
                    Add two edges connecting $v_{\mathcal{T}}$ to $v_{\mathcal{T}'}$ and vice versa
                    Compute the weights of these new edges according to equation (6.23)
            for all $e' \in \mathcal{E}(\mathcal{T})$ **do**
                Insert $v_{\mathcal{T}}$ into $\Delta(e')$

6.4.2 Triangle Paths Starting from Edges

Up to now, I considered triangle paths from one vertex to another. Alternatively, we can consider triangle paths from an edge to a vertex (or edge to edge or vertex to edge). The first variant is important for the selection of relative poses (Section 6.3).

The impact on the shortest triangle paths problem is very small, as the length of a triangle path only takes the triangles themselves into account. In order to compute a shortest triangle path from an edge to a vertex, however, the vertex-triangle-vertex graph $\mathcal{G}_{\mathrm{V}}$ has to be replaced by the *edge-triangle-vertex graph* $\mathcal{G}_{\mathrm{E}}$, which has an entry vertex $v_{e\rightarrow}$ for each edge $e \in \mathcal{E}(\mathcal{G})$ (and no other entry vertices). An example is given in Figure 6.2. Constructing $\mathcal{G}_{\mathrm{E}}$ is very similar to constructing $\mathcal{G}_{\mathrm{V}}$. For the sake of completeness, the full algorithm, which is a minor variation of Algorithm 6.8, is presented in Algorithm 6.9.

6.4.3 Direct Repetition of Triangles

In this section, I make a purely theoretical remark, essentially observing that forbidding the direct repetition of triangles does not actually restrict the problem class. The condition $|\mathcal{E}(\mathcal{T}_k) \cap \mathcal{E}(\mathcal{T}_{k+1})| = 1$ in Definition 6.1 could be relaxed to $\mathcal{E}(\mathcal{T}_k) \cap \mathcal{E}(\mathcal{T}_{k+1}) \neq \emptyset$, which would allow for identical consecutive triangles, i. e. direct repetitions. In the context of the shortest triangle paths problem, such “non-strict triangle paths” are irrelevant.

Proposition 6.12 *Let $\mathcal{P}$ be a triangle path and $k \in \{1,2,3\}$. If $\mathcal{P}$ is a w_k shortest triangle path, then $\mathcal{P}$ is also a w_k shortest non-strict triangle path.*

Proof: Obviously, each triangle path is also a non-strict triangle path. Each non-strict triangle path that is *not* a triangle path can be created from a triangle path by adding direct repetitions of triangles. Such additions cannot lead to a shorter (non-strict) triangle path. □

6.4.4 Proof of Theorem 6.11

Lemma 6.13 *Let $\mathcal{P}$ be a triangle path. Then we have $\mathcal{E}_1(\mathcal{P}) \subseteq_{\mathrm{M}} \mathcal{E}_2(\mathcal{P})$, $\mathcal{E}_1(\mathcal{P}) = \mathcal{U}(\mathcal{E}_2(\mathcal{P}))$, and $w_1(\mathcal{P}) \leq w_2(\mathcal{P})$.*

Proof: The first two expressions follow directly from Definition 6.4. As all the edge weights in $\mathcal{G}$ are non-negative, the third equation follows from the first one. □

Definition 6.14 *Let $\mathcal{P}$ be a triangle path and $k \in \{1,2,3\}$. Define new notation: $\mathcal{E}_k^+(\mathcal{P}) \stackrel{\text{def}}{=} \{\, e \in_{\mathrm{M}} \mathcal{E}_k(\mathcal{P}) \mid w(e) > 0 \,\}_{\mathrm{M}}$.*

Lemma 6.15 *Let $\mathcal{P}$ be a triangle path. Then we have $\mathcal{E}_1^+(\mathcal{P}) \subseteq_{\mathrm{M}} \mathcal{E}_2^+(\mathcal{P})$, $\mathcal{E}_1^+(\mathcal{P}) = \mathcal{U}(\mathcal{E}_2^+(\mathcal{P}))$ and $w_k(\mathcal{P}) = \sum_{e \in_{\mathrm{M}} \mathcal{E}_k^+(\mathcal{P})} w(e)$ for all $k \in \{1,2,3\}$.*

Proof: The first two equations follow from Lemma 6.13 and Definition 6.14 (the superscript “+” removes elements e with $w(e) = 0$ from all multisets). Third equation: by Definition 6.4, we have $w_k(\mathcal{P}) = \sum_{e \in_{\mathrm{M}} \mathcal{E}_k(\mathcal{P})} w(e)$, which equals $\sum_{e \in_{\mathrm{M}} \mathcal{E}_k^+(\mathcal{P})} w(e) + \sum_{e \in_{\mathrm{M}} \mathcal{E}_k(\mathcal{P}) \setminus_{\mathrm{M}} \mathcal{E}_k^+(\mathcal{P})} w(e)$. As all edges $e \in \mathcal{E}_k(\mathcal{P}) \setminus_{\mathrm{M}} \mathcal{E}_k^+(\mathcal{P})$ have weight $w(e) = 0$, we get $w_k(\mathcal{P}) = \sum_{e \in_{\mathrm{M}} \mathcal{E}_k^+(\mathcal{P})} w(e)$. □

Lemma 6.16 *Let $\mathcal{P}$ be a triangle path from a vertex i to a vertex j. If $w_2(\mathcal{P}) > w_1(\mathcal{P})$, then there is a triangle path $\mathcal{P}'$ from i to j with $\mathcal{E}_2^+(\mathcal{P}') \subsetneq_{\mathrm{M}} \mathcal{E}_2^+(\mathcal{P})$ and $w_2(\mathcal{P}') < w_2(\mathcal{P})$.*

Proof: Let $\mathcal{P} = (i, \mathcal{T}_1, \ldots, \mathcal{T}_n, j)$ be a triangle path from vertex i to vertex j with $w_2(\mathcal{P}) > w_1(\mathcal{P})$. By $\mathcal{E}_1^+(\mathcal{P}) \subseteq_{\mathrm{M}} \mathcal{E}_2^+(\mathcal{P})$ (Lemma 6.15), we get $\mathcal{E}_1^+(\mathcal{P}) \subsetneq_{\mathrm{M}} \mathcal{E}_2^+(\mathcal{P})$. As $\mathcal{E}_1^+(\mathcal{P}) = \mathcal{U}(\mathcal{E}_2^+(\mathcal{P}))$ (Lemma 6.15), this means that there are duplicate elements in $\mathcal{E}_2^+(\mathcal{P})$. Figure 6.1(b) shows an example of such a situation. Let e be a duplicate element in $\mathcal{E}_2^+(\mathcal{P})$. Let $k = \min_{e \in \mathcal{E}(\mathcal{T}_a)} a$ and $m = \max_{e \in \mathcal{E}(\mathcal{T}_a)} a$, i. e. the indices of the first and last triangle containing e. Then $e \notin \bigcap_{a=k}^{m} \mathcal{E}(\mathcal{T}_a)$. Otherwise e would be in $\mathcal{E}_2^+(\mathcal{P})$ only once (Definition 6.4). Hence there must be an l with $k < l < m$ and $e \notin \mathcal{E}(\mathcal{T}_l)$.

Remove triangles from $\mathcal{P}$ to get a new triangle path $\mathcal{P}' = (i, \mathcal{T}_1, \ldots, \mathcal{T}_k, \mathcal{T}_m, \ldots, \mathcal{T}_n, j)$. If $\mathcal{T}_k = \mathcal{T}_m$, we also have to remove $\mathcal{T}_m$: $\mathcal{P}' = (i, \mathcal{T}_1, \ldots, \mathcal{T}_k, \mathcal{T}_{m+1}, \ldots, \mathcal{T}_n, j)$. If additionally $m = n$,

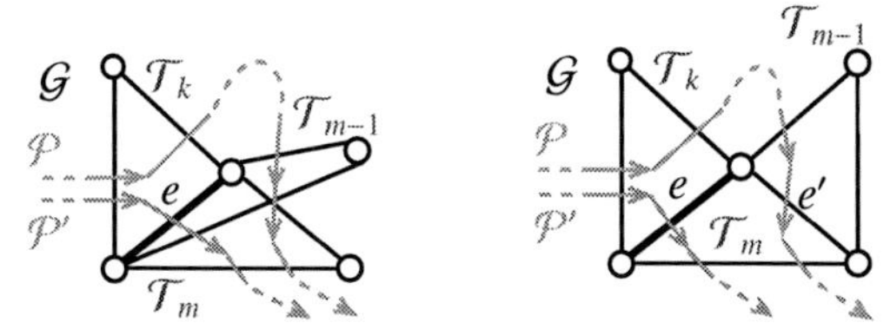

Figure 6.3: Left, right: cases 3a and 3b in the proof of Lemma 6.16.

the precise formulation is $\mathcal{P}' = (i, \mathcal{T}_1, \ldots, \mathcal{T}_k, j)$. In all cases, we have $\mathcal{E}_2^+(\mathcal{P}') \subseteq_M \mathcal{E}_2^+(\mathcal{P})$, as will be proven in the next paragraph. Also, by construction, $e \in \mathcal{E}_2^+(\mathcal{P}) \setminus_M \mathcal{E}_2^+(\mathcal{P}')$, i.e. e is in $\mathcal{E}_2^+(\mathcal{P}')$ at least once less than in $\mathcal{E}_2^+(\mathcal{P})$. Hence $\mathcal{E}_2^+(\mathcal{P}') \subsetneq_M \mathcal{E}_2^+(\mathcal{P})$ and $w_2(\mathcal{P}') < w_2(\mathcal{P})$.

While it is quite simple to see that $\mathcal{E}_2^+(\mathcal{P}') \subseteq_M \mathcal{E}_2^+(\mathcal{P})$, the formal proof will be a bit technically complicated. I will use the following new notation: $\tilde{\mathcal{E}}_2(\mathcal{P}) \stackrel{\text{def}}{=} \{\mathcal{E}(\mathcal{T}_1)\} \sqcup \{\, \mathcal{E}(\mathcal{T}_l) \setminus \mathcal{E}(\mathcal{T}_{l-1}) \mid 2 \leq l \leq n \,\}_M$. Obviously $\mathcal{E}_2(\mathcal{P}) = \bigsqcup \tilde{\mathcal{E}}_2(\mathcal{P})$ for any triangle path $\mathcal{P}$. We need three cases, as in the construction of $\mathcal{P}'$ (starting with the trivial cases):

1. $\mathcal{P}' = (i, \mathcal{T}_1, \ldots, \mathcal{T}_k, j)$:
   $\tilde{\mathcal{E}}_2(\mathcal{P}') \subseteq_M \tilde{\mathcal{E}}_2(\mathcal{P}) \Rightarrow \mathcal{E}_2(\mathcal{P}') \subseteq_M \mathcal{E}_2(\mathcal{P})$.

2. $\mathcal{P}' = (i, \mathcal{T}_1, \ldots, \mathcal{T}_k, \mathcal{T}_{m+1}, \ldots, \mathcal{T}_n, j)$ with $\mathcal{T}_k = \mathcal{T}_m$:
   $\Rightarrow \mathcal{E}(\mathcal{T}_{m+1}) \setminus \mathcal{E}(\mathcal{T}_k) = \mathcal{E}(\mathcal{T}_{m+1}) \setminus \mathcal{E}(\mathcal{T}_m) \Rightarrow \tilde{\mathcal{E}}_2(\mathcal{P}') \subseteq_M \tilde{\mathcal{E}}_2(\mathcal{P}) \Rightarrow \mathcal{E}_2(\mathcal{P}') \subseteq_M \mathcal{E}_2(\mathcal{P})$.

3. $\mathcal{P}' = (i, \mathcal{T}_1, \ldots, \mathcal{T}_k, \mathcal{T}_m, \ldots, \mathcal{T}_n, j)$ with $\mathcal{T}_k \neq \mathcal{T}_m$:
   While the previous two cases are trivial, this one is not, as the predecessor of $\mathcal{T}_m$ may have changed from $\mathcal{P}$ to $\mathcal{P}'$. We have $\tilde{\mathcal{E}}_2(\mathcal{P}') = \{\mathcal{E}(\mathcal{T}_1)\} \sqcup \{\, \mathcal{E}(\mathcal{T}_l) \setminus \mathcal{E}(\mathcal{T}_{l-1}) \mid 2 \leq l \leq k \vee m < l \leq n \,\}_M \sqcup \{\mathcal{E}(\mathcal{T}_m) \setminus \mathcal{E}(\mathcal{T}_k)\}$. Let $\{e'\} = \mathcal{E}(\mathcal{T}_m) \cap \mathcal{E}(\mathcal{T}_{m-1})$. We distinguish two cases:

   (a) $e' = e$ (see Figure 6.3 left):
   $\Rightarrow \mathcal{E}(\mathcal{T}_m) \cap \mathcal{E}(\mathcal{T}_k) = \mathcal{E}(\mathcal{T}_m) \cap \mathcal{E}(\mathcal{T}_{m-1}) \Rightarrow \mathcal{E}(\mathcal{T}_m) \setminus \mathcal{E}(\mathcal{T}_k) = \mathcal{E}(\mathcal{T}_m) \setminus \mathcal{E}(\mathcal{T}_{m-1}) \Rightarrow \tilde{\mathcal{E}}_2(\mathcal{P}') = \{\mathcal{E}(\mathcal{T}_1)\} \sqcup \{\, \mathcal{E}(\mathcal{T}_l) \setminus \mathcal{E}(\mathcal{T}_{l-1}) \mid 2 \leq l \leq k \vee m \leq l \leq n \,\}_M \subseteq_M \tilde{\mathcal{E}}_2(\mathcal{P}) \Rightarrow \mathcal{E}_2(\mathcal{P}') \subseteq_M \mathcal{E}_2(\mathcal{P})$.

   (b) $e' \neq e$ (see Figure 6.3 right):
   $\Rightarrow e' \notin \mathcal{E}(\mathcal{T}_k)$, as otherwise $\mathcal{T}_k = \mathcal{T}_m$. Hence there is a $k < h < m$ with $e' \in \mathcal{E}(\mathcal{T}_h) \setminus \mathcal{E}(\mathcal{T}_{h-1})$. Thus $e' \in \bigsqcup_{l=k+1}^{m-1} \mathcal{E}(\mathcal{T}_l) \setminus \mathcal{E}(\mathcal{T}_{l-1})$. As $e' \notin \mathcal{E}(\mathcal{T}_m) \setminus \mathcal{E}(\mathcal{T}_{m-1})$, we get $\mathcal{E}(\mathcal{T}_m) \subseteq_M \bigsqcup_{l=k+1}^{m} \mathcal{E}(\mathcal{T}_l) \setminus \mathcal{E}(\mathcal{T}_{l-1})$. Hence $\mathcal{E}(\mathcal{T}_m) \setminus \mathcal{E}(\mathcal{T}_k) \subseteq_M \mathcal{E}(\mathcal{T}_m) \subseteq_M \bigsqcup(\tilde{\mathcal{E}}_2(\mathcal{P}) \setminus_M \tilde{\mathcal{E}}_2(\mathcal{P}'))$ (*). We have $\tilde{\mathcal{E}}_2(\mathcal{P}) = (\tilde{\mathcal{E}}_2(\mathcal{P}) \setminus_M \tilde{\mathcal{E}}_2(\mathcal{P}')) \sqcup (\tilde{\mathcal{E}}_2(\mathcal{P}') \setminus_M \{\mathcal{E}(\mathcal{T}_m) \setminus \mathcal{E}(\mathcal{T}_k)\})$ and $\tilde{\mathcal{E}}_2(\mathcal{P}') = \{\mathcal{E}(\mathcal{T}_m) \setminus \mathcal{E}(\mathcal{T}_k)\} \sqcup (\tilde{\mathcal{E}}_2(\mathcal{P}') \setminus_M \{\mathcal{E}(\mathcal{T}_m) \setminus \mathcal{E}(\mathcal{T}_k)\})$. Finally $\tilde{\mathcal{E}}_2(\mathcal{P}') = \bigsqcup \tilde{\mathcal{E}}_2(\mathcal{P}') = (\mathcal{E}(\mathcal{T}_m) \setminus \mathcal{E}(\mathcal{T}_k)) \sqcup \bigsqcup(\tilde{\mathcal{E}}_2(\mathcal{P}') \setminus_M \{\mathcal{E}(\mathcal{T}_m) \setminus \mathcal{E}(\mathcal{T}_k)\}) \stackrel{\text{using (*)}}{\subseteq_M} \bigsqcup(\tilde{\mathcal{E}}_2(\mathcal{P}) \setminus_M \tilde{\mathcal{E}}_2(\mathcal{P}')) \sqcup \bigsqcup(\tilde{\mathcal{E}}_2(\mathcal{P}') \setminus_M \{\mathcal{E}(\mathcal{T}_m) \setminus \mathcal{E}(\mathcal{T}_k)\}) = \bigsqcup \tilde{\mathcal{E}}_2(\mathcal{P}) = \mathcal{E}_2(\mathcal{P})$.

In all cases, we have proven $\mathcal{E}_2(\mathcal{P}') \subseteq_M \mathcal{E}_2(\mathcal{P})$. Using Definition 6.14, we directly obtain $\mathcal{E}_2^+(\mathcal{P}') \subseteq_M \mathcal{E}_2^+(\mathcal{P})$. □

Corollary 6.17 *Let $\mathcal{P}$ be a triangle path from a vertex i to a vertex j. If $\mathcal{P}$ is a w_2 shortest triangle path, then $w_2(\mathcal{P}) = w_1(\mathcal{P})$.*

Proof: Let $\mathcal{P}$ be a w_2 shortest triangle path from i to j. By Lemma 6.16, this implies that $w_2(\mathcal{P}) \le w_1(\mathcal{P})$. Combined with $w_2(\mathcal{P}) \ge w_1(\mathcal{P})$ (Lemma 6.13), we get $w_2(\mathcal{P}) = w_1(\mathcal{P})$. □

Proof of Theorem 6.11: Let $\mathcal{P}$ be a w_2 shortest triangle path from a vertex i to a vertex j. Assume $\mathcal{P}$ is *not* a w_1 shortest triangle path from i to j. Then there is a w_1 shortest triangle path $\mathcal{P}'$ from i to j with $w_1(\mathcal{P}') < w_1(\mathcal{P})$. By Lemma 6.13, we have $w_1(\mathcal{P}') \le w_2(\mathcal{P}')$. By Corollary 6.17, we have $w_1(\mathcal{P}) = w_2(\mathcal{P})$. Two cases:

1. $w_1(\mathcal{P}') = w_2(\mathcal{P}')$:
   Then $w_2(\mathcal{P}') = w_1(\mathcal{P}') < w_1(\mathcal{P}) = w_2(\mathcal{P})$, i.e. $w_2(\mathcal{P}') < w_2(\mathcal{P})$. This contradicts $\mathcal{P}$ being a w_2 shortest triangle path from i to j.

2. $w_1(\mathcal{P}') < w_2(\mathcal{P}')$:
   By Lemma 6.16, there is a triangle path $\mathcal{P}''$ from i to j with $\mathcal{E}_2^+(\mathcal{P}'') \subsetneq_M \mathcal{E}_2^+(\mathcal{P}')$ and $w_2(\mathcal{P}'') < w_2(\mathcal{P}')$. (*) Again there are two cases:

   (a) There is an edge $e \in \mathcal{E}_2^+(\mathcal{P}')$ with $e \notin \mathcal{E}_2^+(\mathcal{P}'')$:
   Hence $e \in \mathcal{U}(\mathcal{E}_2^+(\mathcal{P}'))$ and $e \notin \mathcal{U}(\mathcal{E}_2^+(\mathcal{P}''))$. Together with $\mathcal{E}_2^+(\mathcal{P}'') \subsetneq_M \mathcal{E}_2^+(\mathcal{P}')$, we get $\mathcal{U}(\mathcal{E}_2^+(\mathcal{P}'')) \subsetneq \mathcal{U}(\mathcal{E}_2^+(\mathcal{P}'))$. Using Lemma 6.15, we get $\mathcal{E}_1^+(\mathcal{P}'') = \mathcal{U}(\mathcal{E}_2^+(\mathcal{P}'')) \subsetneq \mathcal{U}(\mathcal{E}_2^+(\mathcal{P}')) = \mathcal{E}_1^+(\mathcal{P}')$ and thus $w_1(\mathcal{P}'') < w_1(\mathcal{P}')$. This contradicts the fact that $\mathcal{P}'$ is a w_1 shortest triangle path from i to j.

   (b) Otherwise $\mathcal{U}(\mathcal{E}_2^+(\mathcal{P}'')) = \mathcal{U}(\mathcal{E}_2^+(\mathcal{P}'))$:
   Again, we distinguish two cases:

      i. $\mathcal{E}_1^+(\mathcal{P}'') \subsetneq_M \mathcal{E}_2^+(\mathcal{P}'')$:
      Then $w_1(\mathcal{P}'') < w_2(\mathcal{P}'')$. Apply the construction in the proof of Lemma 6.16 to $\mathcal{P}''$ to get a new triangle path $\mathcal{P}'''$ from i to j. Recursively continue at (*) after replacing $\mathcal{P}''$ by $\mathcal{P}'''$. Note that the recursion is eventually guaranteed to reach 2a or 2(b)ii, as $\mathcal{E}_2^+(\mathcal{P}''') \subsetneq \mathcal{E}_2^+(\mathcal{P}'')$ and $\mathcal{E}_2^+(\mathcal{P}'')$ is finite.

      ii. $\mathcal{E}_1^+(\mathcal{P}'') = \mathcal{E}_2^+(\mathcal{P}'')$:
      Then $w_1(\mathcal{P}'') = w_2(\mathcal{P}'')$. Using Lemma 6.15 and condition 2b, we get $\mathcal{E}_1^+(\mathcal{P}'') = \mathcal{U}(\mathcal{E}_2^+(\mathcal{P}'')) = \mathcal{U}(\mathcal{E}_2^+(\mathcal{P}')) = \mathcal{E}_1^+(\mathcal{P}')$ and hence $w_1(\mathcal{P}'') = w_1(\mathcal{P}')$. Combine known (in)equalities: $w_2(\mathcal{P}) = w_1(\mathcal{P}) > w_1(\mathcal{P}') = w_1(\mathcal{P}'') = w_2(\mathcal{P}'')$, i.e. $w_2(\mathcal{P}) > w_2(\mathcal{P}'')$. This contradicts the fact that $\mathcal{P}$ is a w_2 shortest triangle path from i to j. □

6.4.5 Time Complexity

In this section, I will analyze the running time complexities of the shortest triangle paths algorithms. The results are summarized in Table 6.1.

problem	time complexity
shortest triangle paths from a vertex or an edge to all vertices	$O(n^2m) \subseteq O(n^4)$
shortest triangle paths from all vertices to all vertices	$O(n^3m) \subseteq O(n^5)$
shortest triangle paths from all edges to all vertices	$O(n^2m^2) \subseteq O(n^6)$

Table 6.1: Running time complexities for solving various shortest triangle paths problems on a graph $\mathcal{G}$ with $n = |\mathcal{V}(\mathcal{G})|$ vertices and $m = |\mathcal{E}(\mathcal{G})|$ edges. The time required for constructing the auxiliary graphs $\mathcal{G}_V$ or $\mathcal{G}_E$, respectively, is included.

line	number of cycles of the for loop
2	m
4	n
6	m
8	m
9	n
14	3
15	$O(n)$ (as there are at most $O(n)$ triangles containing a given edge e)
16	3

Table 6.2: Number of cycles of the for loops in Algorithm 6.9.

First, we need to know the number of vertices and edges in $\mathcal{G}_V$. Let $n = |\mathcal{V}(\mathcal{G})|$ and $m = |\mathcal{E}(\mathcal{G})|$. Assume that $\mathcal{G}$ is not extremely sparse, i. e. $m \in \Omega(n)$. There are n entry vertices and n exit vertices. For each edge $e \in \mathcal{E}(\mathcal{G})$, there are at most $(n-2)$ triangles in $\mathcal{G}$. Hence $|\mathcal{V}(\mathcal{G}_V)| \in O(nm) \subseteq O(n^3)$. As mentioned before, there are at most $(n-2)$ triangles containing any fixed edge $e \in \mathcal{E}(\mathcal{G})$. All pairs of their associated triangle vertices in $\mathcal{G}_V$ are connected by two edges. Hence there are $O(n^2)$ edges in $\mathcal{G}_V$ for each $e \in \mathcal{E}(\mathcal{G})$. For each triangle vertex, there are six additional edges to entry and exit vertices. In total, we have $|\mathcal{E}(\mathcal{G}_V)| \in O(n^2m) \subseteq O(n^4)$. All of the above analysis also applies to the edge-triangle-vertex graph $\mathcal{G}_E$, except for the number of entry vertices, which is m instead of n.

Next, I will analyze the running time complexities of the Algorithms 6.8 and 6.9 for constructing $\mathcal{G}_V$ and $\mathcal{G}_E$, respectively. I will first analyze Algorithm 6.9 and then show that Algorithm 6.8 has the same time complexity. Except for the loops and the if statement, all remaining statements have a constant running time. The running time of the if statement in line 10 depends on the representation of the graph. In the case of an adjacency matrix, it is $O(1)$. In the case of adjacency lists, it consists of searching two lists with $O(n)$ elements. The number of cycles of the for loops are listed in Table 6.2. The total running time complexity of Algorithm 6.9 is hence dominated by the for loop in line 8 with the inner loops in the lines 9 and 15. In total, we get $O(n^2m) \subseteq O(n^4)$. As $\mathcal{G}_E$ contains $O(n^2m)$ edges, this can be considered very efficient. All of this also applies to Algorithm 6.8, except that the for loop in line 2 of Algorithm 6.9 is missing. The time complexity of Algorithm 6.8 is hence also $O(n^2m) \subseteq O(n^4)$.

The running time of Dijkstra's shortest paths algorithm (Appendix B.2) using ordinary heaps applied to $\mathcal{G}_V$ or $\mathcal{G}_E$ is $O((n^2m + nm)\log(nm)) = O(n^2m \log n) \subseteq O(n^4 \log n)$. From a theoretical point of view, the time complexity of Dijkstra's algorithm can be improved by using Fibonacci heaps. Thereby, the complexity is reduced by the factor $\log n$ to $O(n^2m) \subseteq O(n^4)$. Note that this is only $O(n)$ times the number of triangles. Also note that the time complexity of the Algorithms 6.8 and 6.9 for constructing $\mathcal{G}_\mathrm{V}$ and $\mathcal{G}_\mathrm{E}$, respectively, is also $O(n^2m) \subseteq O(n^4)$.

In order to compute shortest triangle paths between all pairs of vertices in $\mathcal{G}$, we can apply Dijkstra's algorithm to each entry vertex of $\mathcal{G}_\mathrm{V}$. The total running time is $O(n^3m) \subseteq O(n^5)$. Applying Dijkstra's algorithm to all entry vertices of $\mathcal{G}_\mathrm{E}$ to compute shortest triangle paths from all edges in $\mathcal{G}$ to all vertices has a running time of $O(n^2m^2) \subseteq O(n^6)$.

Note that I do *not* solve the all pairs shortest paths problem on $\mathcal{G}_\mathrm{V}$ or $\mathcal{G}_\mathrm{E}$. Applying the Floyd-Warshall algorithm on $\mathcal{G}_\mathrm{V}$ or $\mathcal{G}_\mathrm{E}$ has a time complexity of $O(n^3m^3) \subseteq O(n^9)$. Johnson's algorithm still requires a running time of $O(n^3m^2) \subseteq O(n^7)$. This is $O(m)$ times longer than computing all shortest entry-exit paths in $\mathcal{G}_\mathrm{V}$ as described above, and $O(n)$ times longer in the case of $\mathcal{G}_\mathrm{E}$. Despite explicitly modeling triangle paths from a vertex (or edge) to another vertex, this is the main advantage of having entry vertices in $\mathcal{G}_\mathrm{V}$ (and $\mathcal{G}_\mathrm{E}$).

6.5 Comparison to Vergés-Llahí et al.

In this section, I compare my shortest triangle paths algorithm and my multi-camera calibration method to the approach of Vergés-Llahí, Moldovan and Wada (2008) and Vergés-Llahí and Wada (2008).

Independently of me, Vergés-Llahí and Wada (2008) have developed an algorithm for the closely related shortest *triangle-connected paths* problem. Their triangle-connected paths are similar to my triangle paths, but more restrictive (there needs to be a path embedded within the triangle path). Note, however, that the actual computer vision problem that they treat does not require triangle-connected paths and can easily be generalized to triangle paths. Actually, (Vergés-Llahí and Wada, 2008, Fig. 3a) suggests that they effectively relax the triangle-connect paths restriction towards triangle paths in case of the first and last triangle. This should also work for the intermediate triangles.

Their main idea consists of constructing an auxiliary graph ($\mathcal{G}_\mathrm{V}$ without entry and exit vertices). They compute shortest triangle-connected paths between all vertices in $\mathcal{G}$ by solving the all pairs shortest paths problem on their auxiliary graph using the Floyd-Warshall algorithm or Johnson's algorithm. This is followed by a correction step and treatment of special cases. In contrast to that, I do not need any such "workarounds", as $\mathcal{G}_\mathrm{V}$ represents the original problem *exactly*. Furthermore, I have proven the correctness of my algorithm.

The approach of Vergés-Llahí and Wada has a running time of $O(n^3m^3) \subseteq O(n^9)$ using the Floyd-Warshall algorithm or $O(n^3m^2) \subseteq O(n^7)$ using Johnson's algorithm. (Their claim of a running time of $O(n^6)$ seems incorrect and is not supported by their argumentation.) As explained in Section 6.4.5, I only need $O(n^3m) \subseteq O(n^5)$. The same time complexity can be achieved for their shortest triangle-*connected* paths problem by adapting my entry vertices construction to their auxiliary graph and applying Dijkstra's algorithm to each entry vertex (in the case of non-negative edge weights).

My definition of the length of a triangle path differs from theirs. While they focus on the triangle-connected *path*, I take the triangles themselves into consideration and propose three alternative definitions. Their definition is well suited for their application, which only uses the edges on the path for the calibration. They require the constraint of having a *triangle-connected* path only to ensure that there are common point correspondences. This is valid if the correspondences are obtained from a video using a tracking algorithm, but not in the more general case of calibrating a multi-camera system.

In order to assess the quality of relative pose estimates, Vergés-Llahí, Moldovan and Wada (2008) use an unreliability measure for relative poses, which consists of an error residual and a constraint violation term. I avoid constraint violations by using the five point algorithm (Stewénius et al., 2006). Furthermore, opposed to their unreliability measure, my uncertainty measures provide a theoretical justification for the shortest triangle paths approach (Section 6.3).

For multi-camera calibration, Vergés-Llahí and Wada (2008) have to perform an explicit fusion of calibration results along several individual shortest triangle paths. I avoid this problem by letting triangle paths emerge from a common *edge* instead of a vertex (Section 6.3). This ensures that all triangle paths have a common edge and hence eliminates the need for a fusion step.

Finally, Vergés-Llahí and Wada choose the reference edge with minimum unreliability within a certain set of suitable edges. In contrast to this local criterion, which is applied independently of the shortest triangle-connected paths step, I choose the reference edge (and the whole set of relative poses used for calibration) according to a single, global, minimum uncertainty criterion (Section 6.3). Also, my method guarantees that a suitable reference edge actually *exists*.

6.6 Common Field of View Detection for Multi-Camera Calibration

In order to be able to extract point correspondences and estimate the relative pose of two cameras, they must have a *common field of view*, i. e. they must observe a common part of the scene. Otherwise, it is obviously impossible to extract valid correspondences and to estimate their relative pose. Hence, in such cases, there should not be an edge between the according cameras in the camera dependency graph. If we do not know which cameras have a common field of view, however, the calibration Algorithm 6.2 will simply create an edge for *all* camera pairs, leading to invalid edges with a wrong relative pose "estimate" in the case of camera pairs without a common field of view.

To a certain extent, the uncertainty-based selection of relative poses is able to avoid such invalid edges, as they typically have a high uncertainty (see experiments Section 7.3.2). In practice, however, the uncertainty of an invalid edge can sometimes be lower than the uncertainty of a valid edge. Obviously, this can mislead the uncertainty-based selection of relative poses. On the other hand, if camera pairs *without* a common field of view are *not* connected in the camera dependency graph, the uncertainty-based selection only has to handle the uncertainty caused by noisy correspondences and false matches (outliers). We can hence expect an improvement of the calibration results. In order to exploit this observation, I suggest detecting camera pairs without a common field of view while building the camera dependency graph (optional condition in line 5 of Algorithm 6.3).

Furthermore, if an ad hoc multi-camera system is set up in two or more visually separated rooms without manually specifying which camera is in which room, there will be very many invalid edges in the (complete) camera dependency graph. The calibration Algorithm 6.2 will hence try to jointly calibrate all cameras, which is impossible from the given input. More specifically, the *correct* camera dependency graph (i. e. *without* invalid edges) will consist of more than one triangle-connected component, each of which can only be calibrated up to a 3D similarity transformation (Section 6.1). If the camera dependency graph – *including* invalid edges – is triangle-connected, however, it will be wrongly calibrated up to a *single* similarity transformation. Despite that, the calibration algorithm will necessarily select at least several invalid edges causing serious errors in the calibration. Hence, in the case of cameras in two or more rooms, detecting camera pairs without a common field of view is required to decompose the camera dependency graph into subgraphs corresponding to the rooms.

In the Sections 6.6.1 through 6.6.3, I will present several measures for common field of view detection. In order to achieve a binary decision, a threshold is applied to one of these measures. Afterwards, I will give details on how common field of view detection can be used for multi-camera calibration, (a) in combination with uncertainty-based selection of relative poses (Section 6.6.4), and (b) to separate cameras in two or more rooms using an automatically determined threshold (Section 6.6.5). I want to thank Marcel Brückner for the collaboration in developing these methods (Brückner, Bajramovic and Denzler, 2009; Bajramovic, Brückner and Denzler, 2009).

6.6.1 Snavely's Criterion

The criterion of Snavely et al. (2008) is based on counting point correspondences. It is motivated by the fact that correct correspondences can only exist between images with a common field of view. In order for their approach to work, they require a reliable correspondence extraction method with a very low false positive rate.

Snavely et al. (2008) use the difference of Gaussian (DoG) detector (Section 3.1), the SIFT descriptor (Section 3.2), the Euclidean distance, and the two nearest neighbors matching with a stricter rejection threshold ($\theta_{2NN} = 0.6$) than suggest by Lowe (2004) ($\theta_{2NN} = 0.8$). Furthermore, they add an additional rejection mechanism. After constructing the set $\mathcal{J}'$ of candidate pairs as in the two nearest neighbor (2NN) matching, only uniquely matched pairs are selected instead of iteratively disregarding all ambiguously matched pairs *except* for the one which has just been selected by 2NN.

As there might still be a few – necessarily incorrect – correspondences between images *without* a common field of view, the number of correspondences is used as a measure. In order to classify an image pair as having a common field of view, a certain minimum number of correspondences is required.

6.6.2 Using Geometric Uncertainty-Measures for Common Field of View Detection

In the case of a wide baseline setup or ambiguities within the scene, the rejection of ambiguities used for Snavely's criterion (Section 6.6.1) tends to return only very few or no correspondences at all—despite a common field of view. In order to handle such difficult situations, a less strict rejection of ambiguities is required in the matching step (e. g. two nearest neighbor matching as described in Section 3.3). As this increases the false positive rate and leads to more (false) correspondences also in the case of images *without* a common field of view, simply counting correspondences is not very promising.

However, the correspondences between images *without* a common field of view can be expected to be very unstructured. Hence, I suggest assessing the set of correspondences between two images by means of a geometric measure based on the epipolar constraint, like e. g. my geometric uncertainty measures from Section 6.2. As argued above, the quality of correspondences between images with a common field of view can be expected to be higher than between unrelated images. Note that, for this approach, we have to assume that there is a translation between the two cameras (opposed to pure rotation about the optical center).

6.6.3 Probabilistic Uncertainty Measures Based on Soft Correspondences

Using a geometric uncertainty-measure (Section 6.6.2), the requirements posed on the matching step of the correspondence extraction are reduced compared to Snavely's criterion (Section 6.6.1). Going one step further, I suggest using point correspondence probabilities instead of hard matching decisions. After giving details on the correspondence probabilities, I will present a novel common field of view measure, which I have published in (Brückner, Bajramovic and Denzler, 2009). This measure has been specifically developed for the purpose of common field of view detection. The main idea consists of assessing how peaked the probability distributions are.

Point Correspondence Probabilities

If two points are matched incorrectly, e. g. due to ambiguities in the image, the resulting point correspondence $(\boldsymbol{p}_1, \boldsymbol{p}_2)$ is useless. Probabilistic point correspondences, as suggested by Domke and Aloimonos (2006a) for relative pose estimation, on the other hand, provide a way of avoiding hard matching decisions, retaining much more information. Instead of using a set of point pairs, the correspondence information between two images is described by conditional probability distributions $p(\boldsymbol{p}_2 \mid \boldsymbol{p}_1)$. I adopt this idea to the problem of detecting images with a common field of view.

Due to their invariance properties (Lowe, 2004; Mikolajczyk and Schmid, 2005), I use SIFT descriptors instead of Gabor filters to construct the conditional probability distributions $p(\boldsymbol{p}_2 \mid \boldsymbol{p}_1)$. In each image, I extract a set of interest points $C_1 = \{\boldsymbol{p}_{1,1}, \ldots, \boldsymbol{p}_{1,m_1}\}$ and $C_2 = \{\boldsymbol{p}_{2,1}, \ldots, \boldsymbol{p}_{2,m_2}\}$, respectively, using the DoG detector (Section 3.1) and compute the SIFT descriptor $\mathbf{des}(\boldsymbol{p}_k)$ (Section 3.2) for each point $\boldsymbol{p}_k \in C_k$ $(k = 1, 2)$. I model $p(\boldsymbol{p}_2 \mid \boldsymbol{p}_1)$ with $\boldsymbol{p}_1 \in C_1$

and $\boldsymbol{p}_2 \in C_2$ using the exponential distribution and the Euclidean distances between pairs of SIFT descriptors as follows:

$$p(\boldsymbol{p}_{2,j} \mid \boldsymbol{p}_{1,i}) \propto \exp\left(-\frac{d_{ij}}{\lambda}\right) , \tag{6.26}$$

where λ is the inverse scale parameter of the exponential distribution and

$$d_{ij} \stackrel{\text{def}}{=} \operatorname{dist}(\mathbf{des}(\boldsymbol{p}_{1,i}), \mathbf{des}(\boldsymbol{p}_{2,j})) \tag{6.27}$$

denotes the Euclidean distances between descriptors (as in equation (3.7)). Note that I only use the second index for points $\boldsymbol{p}_{1,i}$ and $\boldsymbol{p}_{2,j}$ when I need them to refer to d_{ij}.

Inspired by the good performance of Snavely's method (cf. experiments in Section 7.4.2), I construct an alternative distribution

$$p(\boldsymbol{p}_{2,j} \mid \boldsymbol{p}_{1,i}) \propto \exp\left(-\frac{d'_{ij}}{\lambda}\right) , \tag{6.28}$$

$$\text{with } d'_{ij} \stackrel{\text{def}}{=} \begin{cases} \dfrac{d_{ij} - d_{\mathrm{NN},2}(i)}{d_{\mathrm{NN},2}(i)} & \text{if } d_{\mathrm{NN},2}(i) \neq 0 \\ 0 & \text{if } d_{\mathrm{NN},2}(i) = 0 \wedge d_{ij} = d_{\mathrm{NN},2}(i) \\ \infty & \text{if } d_{\mathrm{NN},2}(i) = 0 \wedge d_{ij} \neq d_{\mathrm{NN},2}(i) \end{cases} . \tag{6.29}$$

by incorporating the distance to the nearest neighbor

$$d_{\mathrm{NN},2}(i) \stackrel{\text{def}}{=} \min_{j \in \mathcal{I}_2} d_{ij} \tag{6.30}$$

of the point $\boldsymbol{p}_{1,i}$, where $\mathcal{I}_2 = \{1, \ldots, m_2\}$ denotes the set of indices in C_2. Note that this variant is similar to the two nearest neighbors rejection method. If the distance to the second nearest neighbor is large compared to the distance to the first nearest neighbor, there will be a single high peak in the distribution.

Finally, each of the resulting conditional probability distributions $p(\boldsymbol{p}_2 \mid \boldsymbol{p}_1)$ have to be normalized such that the following condition holds for all $\boldsymbol{p}_1 \in C_1$:

$$\sum_{\boldsymbol{p}_2 \in C_2} p(\boldsymbol{p}_2 \mid \boldsymbol{p}_1) = 1 . \tag{6.31}$$

Since every point in an image can only have a single corresponding point in the second image, I enforce $|C_1| = |C_2| = m$ by selecting exactly m points from each of the two point sets C_1 and C_2. After sorting the pairs $C_1 \times C_2$ according to $p(\boldsymbol{p}_2 \mid \boldsymbol{p}_1)$, I independently select the m best points (i. e. with highest probability) from C_1 and C_2. For a more formal description, let the relation "better", denoted by $\succ$, be defined on C_1 and C_2, respectively, as follows:

$$\begin{aligned} \boldsymbol{p}_1 \succ \boldsymbol{p}'_1 \quad &\Leftrightarrow \quad \max_{\boldsymbol{p}_2 \in C_2} p(\boldsymbol{p}_2 \mid \boldsymbol{p}_1) > \max_{\boldsymbol{p}_2 \in C_2} p(\boldsymbol{p}_2 \mid \boldsymbol{p}'_1) \qquad \text{for} \quad \boldsymbol{p}_1, \boldsymbol{p}'_1 \in C_1 , \\ \boldsymbol{p}_2 \succ \boldsymbol{p}'_2 \quad &\Leftrightarrow \quad \max_{\boldsymbol{p}_1 \in C_1} p(\boldsymbol{p}_2 \mid \boldsymbol{p}_1) > \max_{\boldsymbol{p}_1 \in C_1} p(\boldsymbol{p}'_2 \mid \boldsymbol{p}_1) \qquad \text{for} \quad \boldsymbol{p}_2, \boldsymbol{p}'_2 \in C_2 . \end{aligned} \tag{6.32}$$

According to these strict partial orders, I (independently) select the best m points from C_1 and C_2. Afterwards, in the case of the second distribution (equation (6.28)), the conditional probabilities need to be recomputed using the reduced point sets, as the nearest neighbors may have changed. An obvious upper bound for the value m is $\min(|C_1|, |C_2|)$, but smaller values can give better results (cf. experiments in Section 7.4.1).

Probabilistic Uncertainty Measures

If two images share a common field of view, it is likely that the conditional probability distributions $p(\boldsymbol{p}_2 \mid \boldsymbol{p}_1)$ will have some clear peaks, as the distances to a few descriptors are very low. On the other hand, the conditional probability distributions $p(\boldsymbol{p}_2 \mid \boldsymbol{p}_1)$ of two images showing two different scenes can be expected to tend towards uniform distributions, since most descriptors differ significantly. Hence, I propose using the normalized joint entropy as a common field of view measure:

$$H(C_1, C_2) \stackrel{\text{def}}{=} -\frac{1}{|C_1| \cdot |C_2|} \sum_{\boldsymbol{p}_1 \in C_1} \sum_{\boldsymbol{p}_2 \in C_2} p(\boldsymbol{p}_2, \boldsymbol{p}_1) \log\big(p(\boldsymbol{p}_2, \boldsymbol{p}_1)\big) , \tag{6.33}$$

$$\text{with } p(\boldsymbol{p}_2, \boldsymbol{p}_1) = p(\boldsymbol{p}_2 \mid \boldsymbol{p}_1)\, p(\boldsymbol{p}_1) , \tag{6.34}$$

where $p(\boldsymbol{p}_1)$ is a uniform distribution if no prior information is available. The joint entropy is maximized if all conditional probability distributions $p(\boldsymbol{p}_2 \mid \boldsymbol{p}_1)$ are uniform. In case of the second model in equation (6.28), it is minimized if every interest point in the first image has a unique corresponding point with an identical descriptor in the second image. In case of equation (6.26), the minimum is only reached if, additionally, the non-corresponding descriptors have infinite distance.

6.6.4 Combination with Uncertainty-Based Selection of Relative Poses

As explained above in Section 6.6, we can expect improved multi-camera calibration results if camera pairs without a common field of view are not connected in the camera dependency graph $\mathcal{G}_R$. We can use common field of view detection to automatically determine which camera pairs should be connected in $\mathcal{G}_R$ (optional condition in line 5 of Algorithm 6.3).

The combination of common field of view detection and uncertainty-based selection of relative poses can also be interpreted as follows. Suppose that we begin by constructing the complete camera dependency graph (including invalid edges). Common field of view detection removes an edges if its uncertainty (according to, e. g. the specialized common field of view measure from Section 6.6.3) lies above a certain threshold. This constitutes a *local* criterion applied to each edge *individually*. The selection of relative poses (Section 6.3), on the other hand, solves a *global* optimization problem minimizing the *total* uncertainty of *all* selected edges. Combining both methods can hence be interpreted as first removing particularly bad edges and selecting a subset with minimum total uncertainty from the remaining edges. Note that we can – but do not have to – use different uncertainty measures for the two steps.

Note that the common field of view detection might exclude more edges from the camera dependency graph than necessary (false negatives), thus possibly forcing the uncertainty-based selection to revert to suboptimal triangle paths using the remaining edges. Furthermore, if a (correct) triangle-connected component is (incorrectly) separated by the common field of view detection, there will be an additional ambiguity in the resulting calibration (i. e. one additional unknown 3D similarity transformation). I will hence investigate experimentally, how various common field of view detection thresholds influence the multi-camera calibration (see Section 7.5.1).

6.6.5 Separating Cameras in Two or More Rooms

In the case of cameras in two or more separate rooms, choosing a good threshold for common field of view detection is crucial. If the number of rooms is known, however, a suitable threshold can be chosen automatically such that the camera dependency graph can be separated into the appropriate number of subgraphs. I propose two methods of separating the graph. Both of them iteratively remove edges according to a decreasing common field of view threshold, starting with the complete camera dependency graph.

The first method marks the graph as separated if the number of *connected components* (Appendix B.1) in the graph equals the number of rooms. This approach is motivated by the fact that a (correct) edge in the camera dependency graph implies that the cameras have a common field of view and hence cannot be in two different (visually separated) rooms.

The second method uses the number of *triangle-connected components* (Section 6.1) instead. If a pair of cameras is no longer part of any triangle, this method aborts, signaling a failure. This alternative approach is motivated by the fact that calibration is possible up to one similarity transformation *per triangle connected component.* From a graph theoretical point of view, the graph will decompose into two triangle-connected components earlier on in the process of removing one edge after the other than it will decompose into two connected components. Due to the failure condition, the probability of producing an incorrect separation is reduced. However, as experimental results show (Section 7.5.2), the probability of producing *any* separation at all is rather low, too. Nevertheless, *if* this method produces a separation, it can be considered more reliable than in the case of the first method.

In a correctly separated graph, each component can be calibrated individually. This means that we can reinsert all edges within each component before computing its calibration. For the calibration, we can apply the uncertainty-based selection of relative poses as usual. Optionally, we can also combine it with another common field of view detection as described in Section 6.6.4. Note that the common field of view threshold used at that point may (a) be chosen independently for each component and (b) differ from the one used in the separation step. Hence, assuming the separation of rooms is correct, the calibration results are *not* influenced by the separation step (compared to manually specifying which camera is in which room).

Chapter 7

Experiments

In this chapter, I will present an extensive experimental evaluation of the methods described in this dissertation. Section 7.1 will assess the benefit of using partial rotation knowledge for intrinsic rotational self-calibration. Section 7.2 will compare established methods for estimating the relative pose of two cameras and assess the associated minor contributions. Additionally, Section 7.2.3 will analyze my uncertainty measures on relative pose estimates. Section 7.3 will be dedicated to multi-camera self-calibration using uncertainty-based selection of relative poses. Section 7.4 will analyze the new method for detecting camera pairs with a common field of view. Section 7.5 will evaluate the combination of common field of view detection and uncertainty-based multi-camera calibration. Furthermore, Section 7.5.2 will show that common field of view detection is well suited for automatically separating cameras in different rooms if there are no identical objects in different rooms. A proof-of-concept application using a multi-camera system to track an object in 3D will be presented in Section 7.6.

7.1 Rotational Self-Calibration with Partial Rotation Knowledge

In this part of the experiments, I will analyze the influence of partial rotation knowledge on rotational self-calibration (Chapter 5). Using simulated data, I will first show that additional rotation knowledge reduces the influence of noise—compared to the standard linear and non-linear algorithms. Afterwards, I will present results for real data using various hardware setups. These experiments are similar to the ones I have published in (Bajramovic and Denzler, 2007). The main differences are that I (a) use more appropriate hardware and (b) investigate further possible sources for systematic errors.

Simulation

For the first simulation (RS1), I use a virtual pinhole camera with the following intrinsic parameters:

$$K^{(GT)} = \begin{pmatrix} 100 & 0 & 150 \\ 0 & 100 & 100 \\ 0 & 0 & 1 \end{pmatrix} , \tag{7.1}$$

where the superscript $^{(GT)}$ denotes ground truth. These values are of course unknown to the self-calibration algorithms. Point correspondences are generated by projecting 100 3D points into the camera twice—before and after rotating the camera about its X or Y axis. Each resulting 2D point is modified by uniformly distributed, additive noise in the range $[-\phi/2, \phi/2] \times [-\phi/2, \phi/2]$. I systematically perform experiments for different values of the noise parameter ϕ. If one of the resulting 2D points of a corresponding pair lies outside of the image area $[0, 300] \times [0, 200]$, the pair is removed. The 3D points are randomly generated by a uniform distribution on the cuboid $[-15000, 15000] \times [-10000, 10000] \times [-10000, 10000]$ (in pixel units). As an alternative, more difficult situation (RS2), I use the following intrinsic parameteres

$$K^{(GT)} = \begin{pmatrix} 400 & 0 & 150 \\ 0 & 400 & 100 \\ 0 & 0 & 1 \end{pmatrix} . \tag{7.2}$$

As this reduces the aperture angle of the camera, I increase the number of 3D points to 2000.

I perform a series of ten (relative) rotations about the Y axis followed by another ten rotations about the X axis. The rotation angle is 10° for each rotation. The initial configuration for the first sequence of rotations is $\boldsymbol{R} = \mathrm{Rod}((0, -25°, 0)^T)$, and $\boldsymbol{R} = \mathrm{Rod}((0, 0, -25°)^T)$ for the second one.

I measure the error of the normalized self-calibration result $\boldsymbol{K}'$ (Section 5.1.3) by computing the Frobenius norm of the difference between $\boldsymbol{K}'$ and the normalized ground truth data $\boldsymbol{K}'^{(GT)}$:

$$e_K \stackrel{\text{def}}{=} \left\| \boldsymbol{K}' - \boldsymbol{K}'^{(GT)} \right\|_2 . \tag{7.3}$$

The normalized ground truth data $\boldsymbol{K}'^{(GT)}$ is computed using $\boldsymbol{K}'^{(GT)} = \boldsymbol{T}\boldsymbol{K}^{(GT)}$ (cf. equation (5.22)), where $\boldsymbol{T}$ is defined in Section 5.1.3. Additionally, I use the relative error in the focal length

$$e_f \stackrel{\text{def}}{=} \frac{\left| f_x - f_x^{(GT)} \right|}{2 f_x^{(GT)}} + \frac{\left| f_y - f_y^{(GT)} \right|}{2 f_y^{(GT)}} . \tag{7.4}$$

If the self-calibration fails, e. g. because ω is not positive definite, I set both error measures to infinity. Each experiment is repeated 100 times with identical parameters. In the plots, I will display the median error over the 100 repetitions.

Figure 7.1(a) shows the results of the simulation in the simple situation RS1. You can clearly see the improvements gained by using partial rotation knowledge. As expected, a greater amount of rotation knowledge leads to better results. The linear algorithm is outperformed by the non-linear ones, and additional rotation knowledge further improves the results.

However, there are clusters in the plots: "common axes", "common axes + known angles up to scale" and "common rotations" perform almost equally well. The same is the case for "known axes" and "known axes + known angles up to scale". In this experiment, knowing rotation angles up to scale does *not* further improve self-calibration. However, there is a pronounced difference between "common axes", "known axes" and completely "known rotations". Knowing only "common axes" is already better than "unknown rotations", although this is clearly visible only for high noise levels. Note that these results are consistent with the hierarchy in Figure 5.1.

The results for the difficult situation RS2 are shown in Figure 7.1(c). In this case, the absolute errors are much larger than in the simple situation RS1. As far as the ranking of the algorithms is concerned, however, the main impression is quite similar except for a few interesting differences. The most striking ones are the large improvement gained by completely "known rotations" and the bad behavior of the nonlinear method with "unknown rotations". Furthermore, "known axes + known angles up to scale" perform worse than "known axes". The experiments on real data with ground truth initialization of the optimization (Figure 7.4(c)) suggest that this is probably due to convergence problems or a bad local minimum.

The results for the zero skew variants of the algorithms are shown in the Figures 7.1(b) and 7.1(d). The first important observation is that the error is reduced further. However, the improvement gained by (correctly) assuming zero skew is different for the various algorithms. As the better algorithms seem to gain less, the differences between the results for the various types of partial rotation knowledge are much smaller, but still visible. The case of completely "known rotations" distinguishes surprisingly well from the rest.

Real Data

For the experiments with real hardware, I use a Sony DFW-VL500 progressive scan firewire camera at a resolution of 320×240 and alternatively an AVT Pike progressive scan firewire camera at a resolution of 1388×1038. The respective camera is mounted onto a Directed Perception PTU-46-17.5 pan-tilt unit with a nodal adapter such that the tilt axis is identical to the X axis of the camera coordinate system, and the pan axis for tilt setting 0 is identical to the Y axis. The nodal adapter allows the camera to be mounted with its optical center in the center of rotation. Note, however, that the position of the optical center of the camera is not known precisely. The center of rotation is hence only approximately in the optical center.

The pan-tilt unit performs two rotation subsequences similar to the setup in the simulation. I record one sequence with 10° rotations and another one with 5° rotations. Each sequence is repeated ten times with a randomly modified initial pan-tilt configuration. Example images are given in Figure 7.2.

To get point correspondences, I track up to 200 points using KLT tracking (Appendix D.6). All points which could be tracked from the beginning to the end of each 5° or 10° subsequence, respectively, are used as point correspondences.

A ground truth estimate of the camera parameters is gained using Zhang's method (see Appendix D.5), which is based on a planar calibration pattern. I use the implementation from the Friedrich Schiller University of Jena (Süße and Ortmann, 2003; Süße et al., 2006). For the experiments with zero skew assumption, the skew of the Zhang estimate is set to zero. In order to

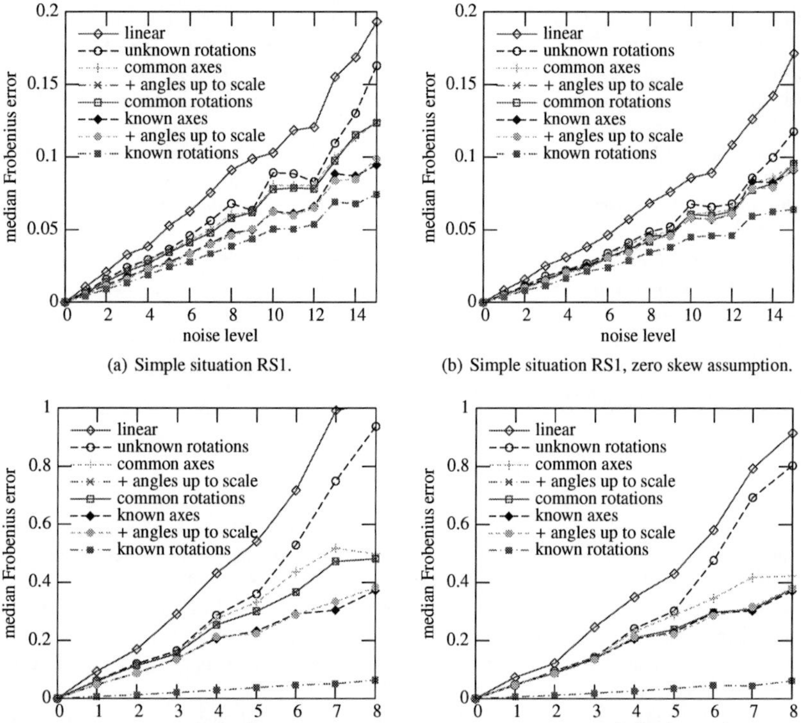

(a) Simple situation RS1.

(b) Simple situation RS1, zero skew assumption.

(c) Difficult situation RS2.

(d) Difficult situation RS2, zero skew assumption.

Figure 7.1: Median of Frobenius error e_K for various noise levels ϕ in the simulations RS1 and RS2 without and with the zero skew assumption. Note the different scales of the axes.

(a) Horizontal subsequence (rotation about the Y axis).

(b) Vertical subsequence (rotation about the X axis).

Figure 7.2: Example images of the data used for rotational self-calibration.

visualize the results for the ten repetitions of each sequence, I use box plots (see Appendix A.8).

As lens distortions are known to cause a systematic error in rotational self-calibration (Tordoff and Murray, 2004), I optionally correct the radial distortion of the images before performing KLT tracking in order to simulate a distortion-free camera. For this task, I use the MultiCamera-Calibration tool from the Christian-Albrechts-Universität zu Kiel (Schiller, 2009; Schiller et al., 2008), which uses Zhang's method (Appendix D.5) and a nonlinear refinement step to calibrate the pinhole and distortion models (cf. Appendices D.1 and D.2).

The results for the relative error in the focal length are given in the Figures 7.3–7.5. The according results for the Frobenius error are given in the Figures E.1–E.3. Except for minor details, they show the same effects and lead to the same conclusions.

In all situations, the nonlinear self-calibration method using completely "known rotations" achieves very good results. All other algorithms, however, are highly sensitive to violations of the following two model assumptions: pure rotation about the optical center and a distortion-free camera. In order to fulfill the first assumption, I use the nodal adapter. By comparing the Figures 7.3(b) and 7.4(a), you can see that, as expected, the errors are even larger without the nodal adapter. Interestingly, however, in the case of completely "known rotations", the results are very good even in spite of the severely violated assumption.

The second assumption is fulfilled by correcting the radial distortion of the input images as described above. Figures 7.5(a) and 7.5(b) show that the calibration error is greatly reduced in this situation (compare to Figures 7.3(a) and 7.3(b)). This shows that distortion correction is very important for rotational self-calibration—even in the case of a camera with seemingly low

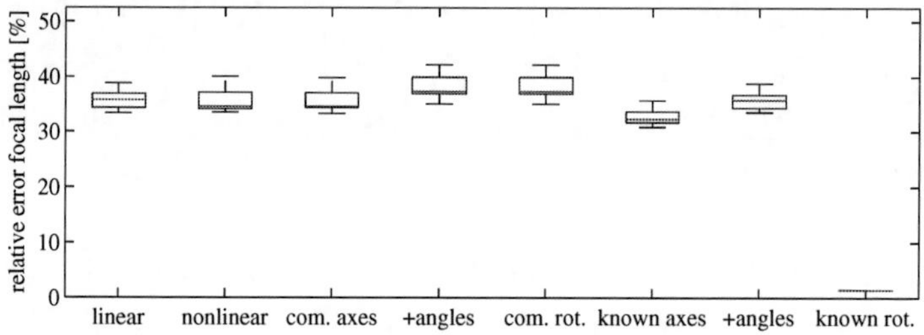

(a) 5° sequence, no zero skew assumption.

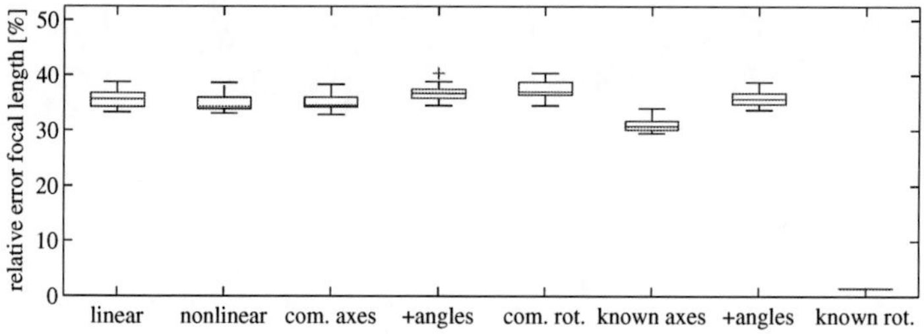

(b) 5° sequence, zero skew assumption.

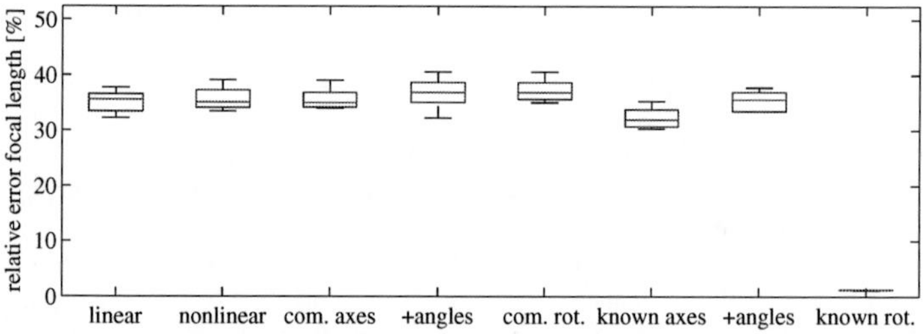

(c) 10° sequence, zero skew assumption.

Figure 7.3: Main results of rotational self-calibration with real data: box plots (Appendix A.8) showing the relative error in the focal length e_f for the 5° and 10° sequences using the Sony camera, with and without the zero skew assumption. In all cases, only full rotation knowledge gives good results.

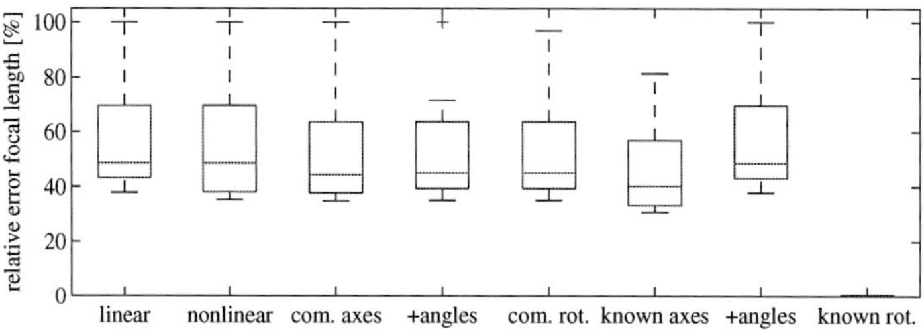

(a) 5° sequence, without nodal adapter, zero skew assumption. This setup severely violates the assumption that the optical center of the camera coincides with the rotation center. Note the changed scale of the error axis.

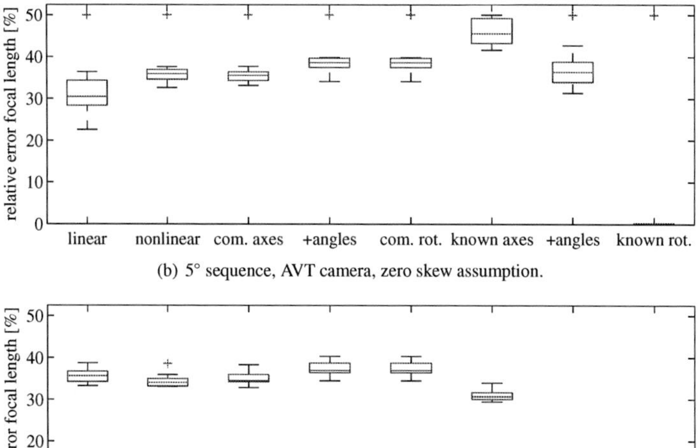

(b) 5° sequence, AVT camera, zero skew assumption.

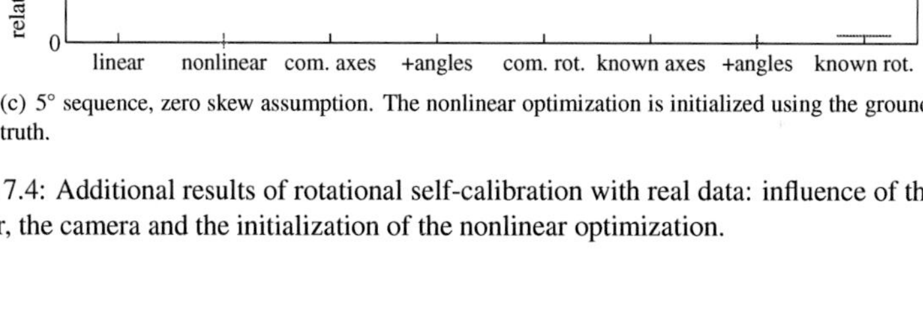

(c) 5° sequence, zero skew assumption. The nonlinear optimization is initialized using the ground truth.

Figure 7.4: Additional results of rotational self-calibration with real data: influence of the nodal adapter, the camera and the initialization of the nonlinear optimization.

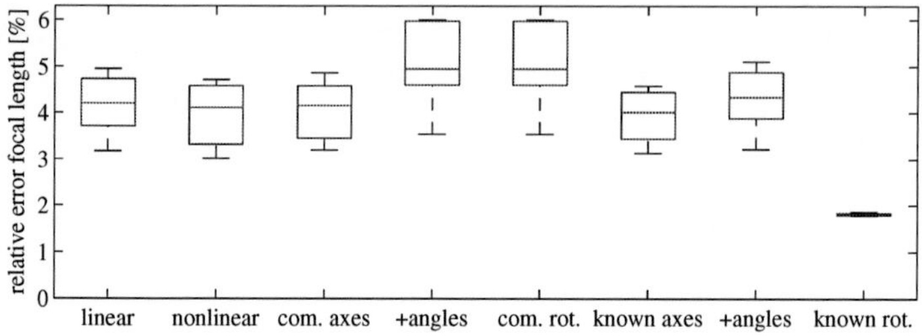

(a) 5° sequence, no zero skew assumption, radial distortion correction. The results without radial distortion correction are given in Figure 7.3(a). Note the changed scale of the error axis.

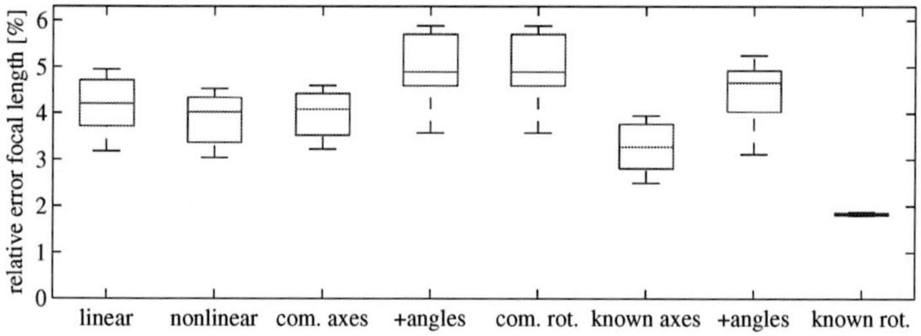

(b) 5° sequence, zero skew assumption, radial distortion correction. The results without radial distortion correction are given in Figure 7.3(b). Note the changed scale of the error axis.

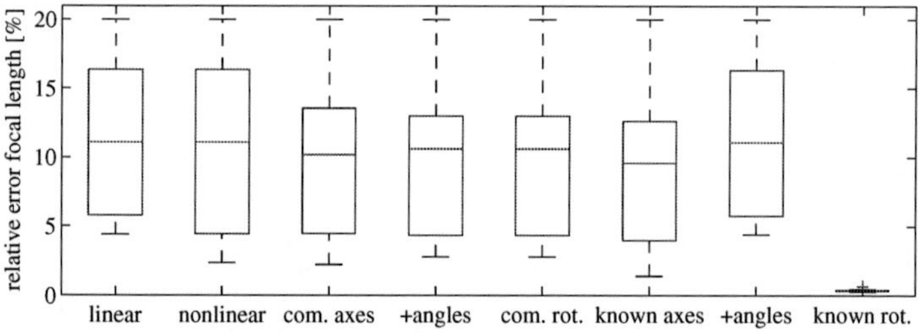

(c) 5° sequence, without nodal adapter, zero skew assumption, radial distortion correction. This setup severely violates the assumption that the optical center of the camera coincides with the rotation center. The results without radial distortion correction are given in Figure 7.4(a). Note the changed scale of the error axis.

Figure 7.5: Results of rotational self-calibration with real data *after correcting the radial distortion*: box plots (Appendix A.8) showing the relative error in the focal length e_f for the 5° sequences using the Sony camera, with and without the zero skew assumption, mounted with and without the nodal adapter.

distortion (see Figure 1.1). As using pattern-based calibration to correct radial distortion before applying a self-calibration method does not make any sense in practice, there is ongoing work aimed at integrating radial distortion estimation into rotation self-calibration with partial rotation knowledge.

Observing the details, you can also see that

1. The effect that only completely "known rotations" give good results, is independent of the camera (compare Figures 7.3(b) and 7.4(b)).

2. In contrast to the simulation, the results show only a minor improvement in some cases of partial rotation knowledge. This may be due to a rather low noise level.

3. The zero skew assumption has no pronounced influence on the calibration error (compare Figures 7.3(a) and 7.3(b) as well as 7.5(a) and 7.5(b)).

4. Neither does rotating by 10° instead of 5° (compare Figures 7.3(b) and 7.3(c)).

5. As convergence problems might cause errors, I additionally initialize the optimization using the ground truth calibration. Comparing Figures 7.3(b) and 7.4(c), you can see that most results are almost unaffected by this change. Only in the case of "known axes + known angles up to scale", the optimization results seriously depend on the initialization.

6. Correcting the radial distortion of the input images before performing the radial distortion reveals the source of the systematic error (compare Figures 7.5(a) and 7.3(a) as well as 7.5(b) and 7.3(b)). Note, however, that there is still some systematic error if the camera is not rotated about its optical center (compare Figures 7.5(c), 7.5(b) and 7.4(a)).

7. Interestingly, the lowest error is achieved using known rotations, correction of radial distortion but rotation, which is *not* about the optical center (Figure 7.5(c)). However, the variation of the focal length estimated by the pattern based calibration (which is used as ground truth) is up to a few percent. The precision of the focal length error can hence *not* be trusted to be below 2%.

Summary and Conclusions

On simulated data, I showed that using partial rotation knowledge reduces the influence of noise on the results of rotational self-calibration. The more knowledge we have about the rotations, the better we can expect the self-calibration results to be. Especially the case of completely known rotations leads to a pronounced improvement.

In the case of real data, completely "known rotations" gave very good results, whereas no or only partial rotation knowledge led to a systematic error caused by radial distortion. Correcting the distortion before performing the self-calibration leads to much better results in these cases. However, an improvement of the calibration results in the case of *partial* rotation knowledge could not be observed on real data.

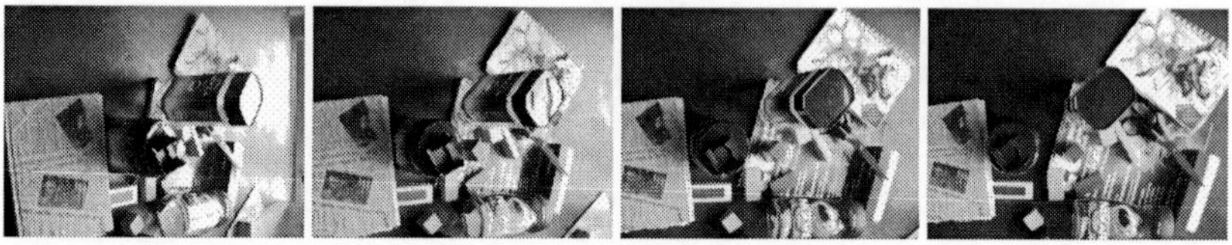

(a) Setup "sphere", images 1, 4, 7 and 10.

(b) Setup "forward", images 1, 2, 3 and 4.

Figure 7.6: Example images of the setups "sphere" and "forward" used for the relative pose estimation experiments.

7.2 Estimation of Relative Poses and Their Uncertainties

In this part of the experiments, I will evaluate and compare the relative pose estimation algorithms (Chapter 4) and analyze the correlation between the error in the relative pose estimates and the uncertainty measures presented in Section 6.2. In Section 7.2.1, I will evaluate the basic algorithms for estimating the essential matrix (Section 4.2) on simulated data. Afterwards I will analyze and compare the *robust* relative pose estimation algorithms on simulated and real data (Section 7.2.2). I want to thank Marcel Brückner for the collaboration on an earlier version of these experiments (Brückner, Bajramovic and Denzler, 2008). Finally, I will present the correlation between the relative pose estimates and the uncertainty measures on real data (Section 7.2.3).

In the simulation, the ground truth for the relative pose $\left(\boldsymbol{R}_{\text{rel}}^{(\text{GT})}, \boldsymbol{t}_{\text{rel}}^{(\text{GT})}\right)$, is known by construction. In order to get reliable ground truth in the experiment on real data, I mount a Sony DFW-VL500 camera onto a Stäubli RX90 robot arm with known hand-eye-transformation and take images of a static scene from several camera poses. I record two special sequences. In the sequence "sphere", the camera is placed on a sphere looking to its center taking 11 images, such that there is mostly sideways motion and rotation. In the sequence "forward", the camera moves forward taking 5 images. Example images are given in Figure 7.6.

Additionally, I use the same setups (S1–S5) as in the multi-camera self-calibration experiments in Section 7.3 (see Figures 7.18 and 7.19). Note, however, that there are some camera pairs in the setups S2–S5 which do not have a common field of view. Hence their relative poses cannot be estimated and will usually result in a very high error. I will present results with and without prior correction of radial distortion as described in Section 7.1.

I use two different error measures to compare the estimate of the relative pose $(\boldsymbol{R}_{\text{rel}}, \boldsymbol{t}_{\text{rel}}^{*})$, where $\boldsymbol{t}_{\text{rel}}^{*}$ is known up to positive scale, to the ground truth $\left(\boldsymbol{R}_{\text{rel}}^{(\text{GT})}, \boldsymbol{t}_{\text{rel}}^{(\text{GT})}\right)$:

- Given the unknown positive scale of $\boldsymbol{t}^*_{\text{rel}}$, the translation error e_{T} is defined as the angle (in degree, $0 \leq e_{\text{T}} \leq 180$) between the ground truth translation $\boldsymbol{t}^{(\text{GT})}_{\text{rel}}$ and the estimate $\boldsymbol{t}^*_{\text{rel}}$:

$$e_{\text{T}} \stackrel{\text{def}}{=} \frac{180}{\pi} \cdot \left| \arccos \left(\frac{\boldsymbol{t}^{*\,\text{T}}_{\text{rel}} \boldsymbol{t}^{(\text{GT})}_{\text{rel}}}{\|\boldsymbol{t}^*_{\text{rel}}\| \cdot \|\boldsymbol{t}^{(\text{GT})}_{\text{rel}}\|} \right) \right| . \tag{7.5}$$

- The rotation error e_{R} is the rotation angle (in degree, $0 \leq e_{\text{R}} \leq 180$) of the relative rotation $\boldsymbol{R} = \boldsymbol{R}^{(\text{GT})}_{\text{rel}} \boldsymbol{R}^{\text{T}}_{\text{rel}}$ between the ground truth $\boldsymbol{R}^{(\text{GT})}_{\text{rel}}$ and the estimate $\boldsymbol{R}_{\text{rel}}$. Details on how to compute the rotation angle of $\boldsymbol{R}$ are given in Appendix A.2.1.

All simulation experiments are repeated 500 times each. All experiments on real data are repeated 20 times. Finally, the medians of e_{T} and e_{R} over all repetitions are computed. In the evaluation, I focus on the median translation error as the rotation error is much lower and gives structurally very similar results. Some results for the median rotation error are included in the appendix, Figures E.4 and E.5.

7.2.1 Comparison of Basic Algorithms for Estimating the Essential Matrix

In this part of the experiments, I evaluate the basic algorithms for estimating the essential matrix (Section 4.2) on simulated data as in (Brückner, Bajramovic and Denzler, 2008). In order to apply the error measures defined above, I extract the relative pose from the essential matrix *without* using the cheirality constraint. Due to the resulting fourfold ambiguity, I modify the error measures as follows:

- As the translation is known only up to *arbitrary* scale, I use the following variant e'_{T} of the translation error e_{T}:

$$e'_{\text{T}} \stackrel{\text{def}}{=} \frac{180}{\pi} \cdot \left| \arccos \left(\frac{\left|\boldsymbol{t}^{*\,\text{T}}_{\text{rel}} \boldsymbol{t}^{(\text{GT})}_{\text{rel}}\right|}{\|\boldsymbol{t}^*_{\text{rel}}\| \cdot \|\boldsymbol{t}^{(\text{GT})}_{\text{rel}}\|} \right) \right| . \tag{7.6}$$

  The maximum of this error is 90 degree.

- The ambiguity resulting in two solutions for $\boldsymbol{R}_{\text{rel}}$ is resolved by computing the rotation error e_{R} for both solutions and taking the smaller one as the rotation error e'_{R}.

The simulation consists of two virtual pinhole cameras $(\boldsymbol{K}, \boldsymbol{I}, \boldsymbol{0})$ and $(\boldsymbol{K}, \boldsymbol{R}^{(\text{GT})}_{\text{rel}}, \boldsymbol{t}^{(\text{GT})}_{\text{rel}})$ with an image size of 640×480 and intrinsic parameters

$$\boldsymbol{K} = \begin{pmatrix} 500 & 0 & 320 \\ 0 & 500 & 240 \\ 0 & 0 & 1 \end{pmatrix} . \tag{7.7}$$

The scene consists of random 3D points uniformly distributed in a cuboid (distance from first camera 1, depth 2, width and height 0.85). These 3D points are projected into the cameras. Noise

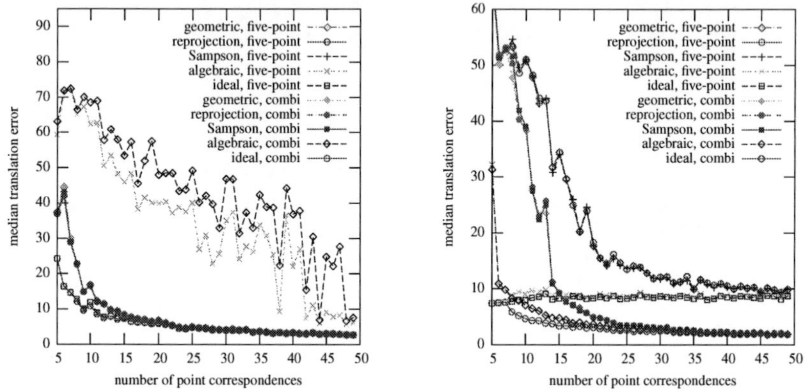

(a) Sideways motion. The plots for "euclidean", "reprojection", "Sampson" and their "combi" variants are almost identical, as are "ideal" and "ideal, combi".

(b) Forward motion. The plots for "euclidean", "reprojection" and "Sampson" are almost identical, as are their "combi" variants.

Figure 7.7: Comparison of error measures for automatic selection of the best solution applied to the five-point algorithm. Median translation error for varying number of point correspondences m. The Plots "ideal" show the minimum error among all solutions without automatic selection.

is simulated by adding random values uniformly distributed in $[-\phi/2, \phi/2]$ to all coordinates. I choose $\phi = 3$ for all experiments.

First, I analyze the performance of the automatic selection of the best solution applied to the five-point algorithm (Section 4.2.7). Figure 7.7(a) shows the results for sideways motion ($\boldsymbol{t}_{\text{rel}}^{(\text{GT})} = (0.1, 0, 0)^{\text{T}}, \boldsymbol{R}_{\text{rel}}^{(\text{GT})} = \boldsymbol{I}$). It also contains the error of the ideal selection which is computed by comparing all essential matrices to the ground truth. The automatic selection works equally well with all error measures except for the algebraic one. Given enough points, the results almost reach the ideal selection.

In the case of forward motion ($\boldsymbol{t}_{\text{rel}}^{(\text{GT})} = (0, 0, -0.1)^{\text{T}}, \boldsymbol{R}_{\text{rel}}^{(\text{GT})} = \boldsymbol{I}$), the algebraic error is best (Figure 7.7(b)). Given enough points, the other error measures also give good results. For few points, however, the selection does not work well.

To summarize, if there is no prior knowledge about the translation, the Sampson or geometric error measure are the most reasonable choices. The reprojection error also works well, but is computationally much more expensive.

The next experiment compares the various estimation algorithms. In contrast to the results presented by Stewénius et al. (2006) and Nistér (2004), I apply automatic selection using the Sampson error measure for the five-point and seven-point algorithms, which gives a more realistic comparison. Figure 7.8 shows the results for sideways and forward motion. For sideways motion, the five-point algorithm with automatic selection still gives superior results. For forward motion, however, the eight-point algorithm is best. Surprisingly, in this case, the eight-point

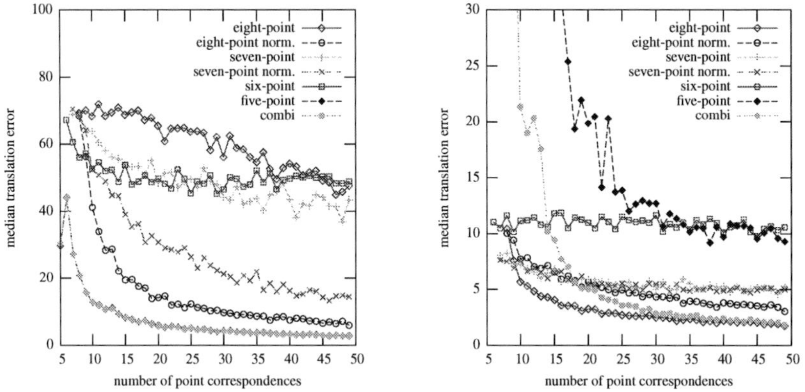

(a) Sideways motion. The plots for "five-point" and "combi" are almost identical.

(b) Forward motion. The plots for "seven-point" and "seven-point norm." are mostly identical.

Figure 7.8: Comparison of algorithms with Sampson error for automatic selection. Median translation error for varying number of point correspondences m.

algorithm with data normalization is *worse* than without normalization (opposed to sideways motion).

Given this situation, I add a combination "combi" of the five-point and the *un*normalized eight-point algorithms to the comparison (Section 4.2.8). For sideways motion (Figures 7.7(a) and 7.8(a)), the results of the combination are almost identical to the five-point results (except for selection using the algebraic error). For forward motion (Figures 7.7(b) and 7.8(b)), the automatic selection works better than the five-point algorithm alone, but still needs enough points to produce good results. Then, however, the combination reaches the results of the unnormalized eight-point algorithm, which is the best single algorithm in this situation.

In summary the simulation results is that my combination approach using the Sampson error measure for automatic selection is the best choice for outlier-free data without prior knowledge about the translation.

7.2.2 Evaluation of Robust Relative Pose Estimation Algorithms

In contrast to the previous section, I will now evaluate the *robust* relative pose estimation algorithms. Instead of taking the essential matrix as the result of the estimation, I will consider the extraction of the relative pose using the cheirality constraint as part of the estimation algorithms.

First, I will use the simulated data described in Section 7.2.1 to analyze the influence of certain parameters (Figures 7.9 and 7.10) and compare the algorithms and some variants (Figures 7.11 and 7.12(a)) at varying proportions of outliers. Afterwards, I will use real data to repeat

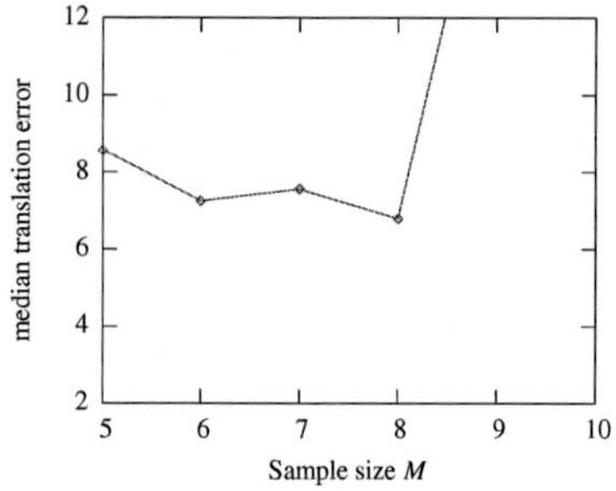

(a) RANSAC, sample size M.

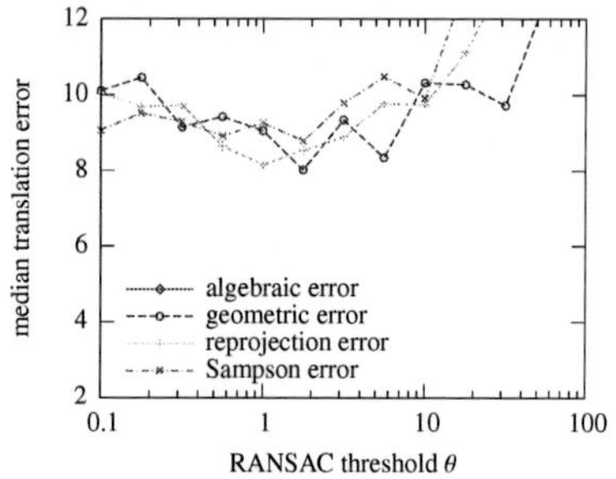

(b) RANSAC, threshold θ.

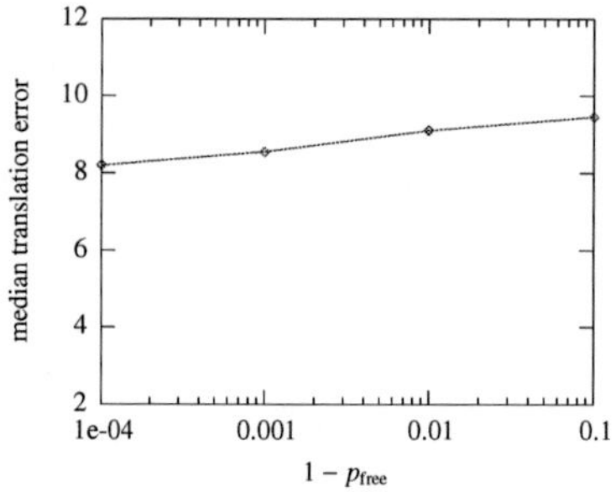

(c) RANSAC, probability p_{free}.

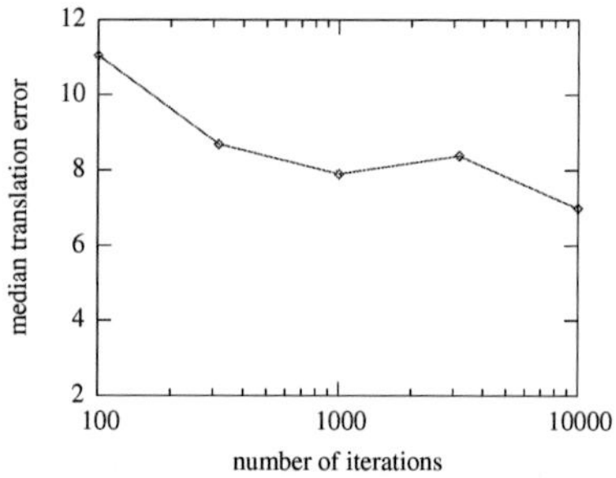

(d) Non-adaptive RANSAC, number of iterations N.

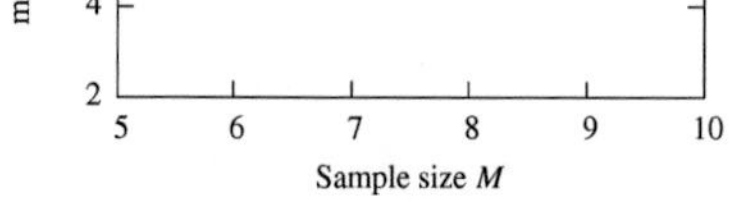

(e) Cauchy, sample size M.

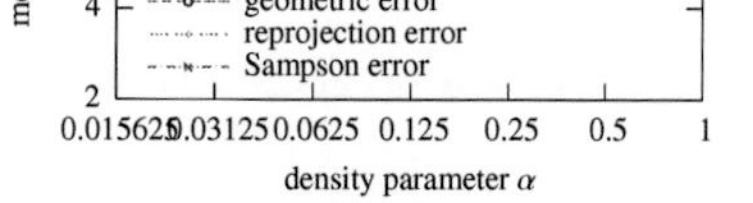

(f) Cauchy, density parameter α.

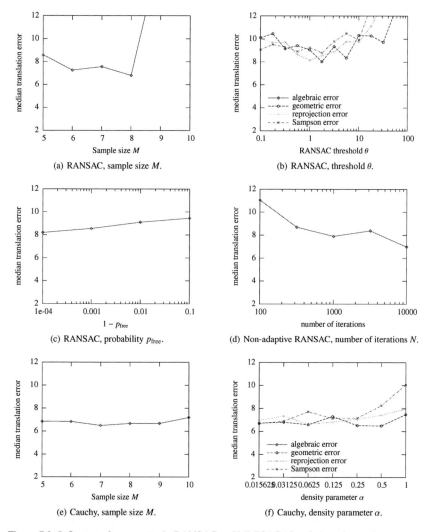

Figure 7.9: Influence of parameters in RANSAC and MLESAC (Cauchy) on the median translation error. There are 30% outliers in the correspondences.

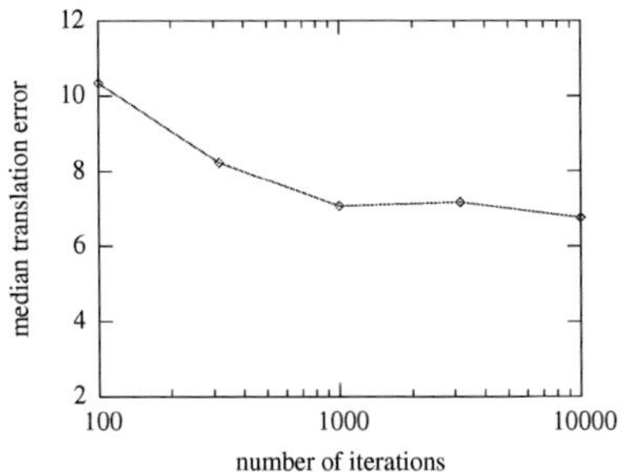

(a) Cauchy, number of iterations N.

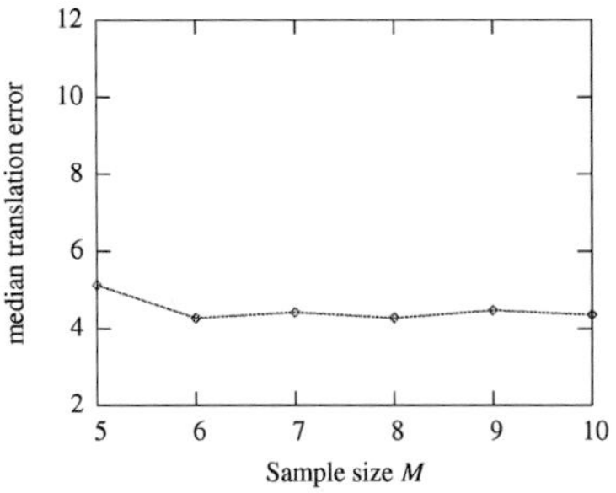

(b) Blake-Zisserman, sample size M.

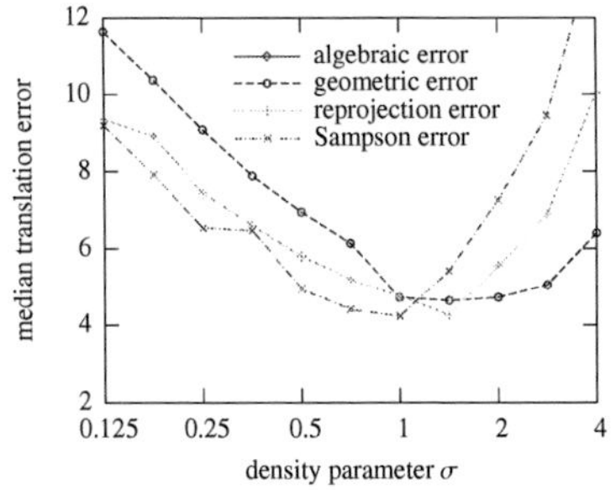

(c) Blake-Zisserman, density parameter σ.

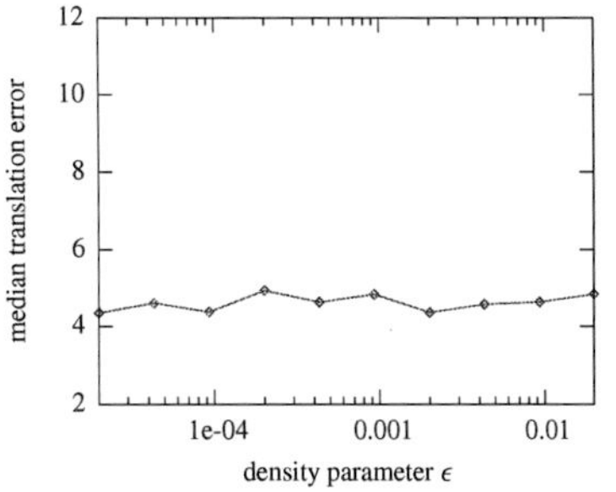

(d) Blake-Zisserman, density parameter ϵ.

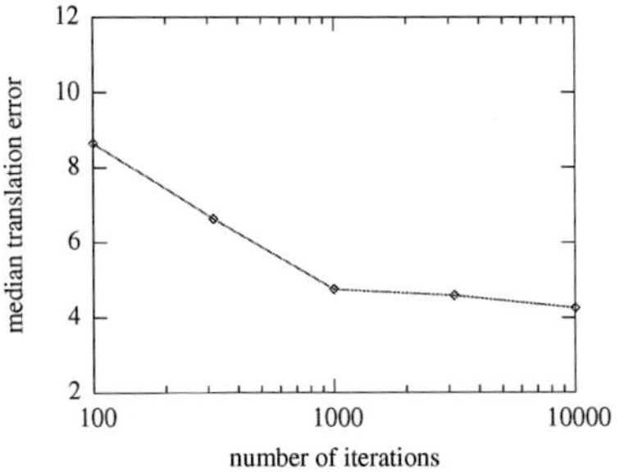

(e) Blake-Zisserman, number of iterations N.

Figure 7.10: Influence of parameters in MLESAC (Cauchy, Blake-Zisserman) on the median translation error. There are 30% outliers in the correspondences.

the parameter analysis and compare the most relevant algorithms again.

I investigate the RANSAC algorithm (Section 4.3.1) with and without the adaptation of the number of iterations N (referred to as “RANSAC” and “RANSAC non-adaptive”, respectively), as well as the MLESAC algorithm (Section 4.3.2) using the Cauchy and the Blake-Zisserman model (referred to as “MLESAC Cauchy” and “MLESAC Blake-Zisserman”, respectively). Furthermore I assess the influence of the epipolar distance measure (Section 4.2.7) and the combination of the five-point and eight-point algorithms (Section 4.3.1).

Parameters Analysis on Simulated Data

The simulation setup is similar to the one in Section 7.2.1, but with a different camera setup: $\boldsymbol{t}_{\mathrm{rel}}^{(\mathrm{GT})} = (0.1, 0, 0.1)^{\mathrm{T}}$ and $\boldsymbol{R}_{\mathrm{rel}}^{(\mathrm{GT})} = \mathrm{Rod}((0, 0.01, 0)^{\mathrm{T}})$. Furthermore, I generate outliers by replacing a proportion p_{out} of the point correspondences by randomly generated points within the image areas.

The analysis of the parameters is *not* intended to find the globally best values, but to (a) find reasonably good values and (b) identify, how sensitive the choice of each parameter is. Resulting from a manual "optimization", I use the following values in the simulation unless specified otherwise:

- RANSAC: geometric epipolar distance measure (equation (4.36)), $\theta = 2$,
  - Adaptive RANSAC: $p_{\mathrm{free}} = 0.999$, $M = 5$,
  - Non-adaptive RANSAC: $N = 3000$,
- MLESAC: Sampson epipolar distance measure (equation (4.39)), $N = 3000$, $M = 5$,
  - Cauchy distribution: $\alpha = 0.125$,
  - Blake-Zisserman distribution: $\sigma = 0.7$, $\epsilon = 0.004$.

The results of the parameter analysis on simulated data are shown in the Figures 7.9 and 7.10. The most critical values are the RANSAC threshold θ (Figure 7.9(b)) and the density parameters α (Figure 7.9(f)) and σ (Figure 7.10(c)). Both must be assumed to depend on the data, especially on the noise level.

Furthermore note that these parameters depend on the choice of the epipolar distance measure. In the case of the RANSAC algorithm, the geometric measure appears to be the best one (Figure 7.9(b)). The reprojection measure gives comparable results, but is computationally much more expensive. The results of the algebraic measure show a very high error.

The number of iterations N (Figures 7.9(d), 7.10(a), and 7.10(e)) is also important, but its influence on the results is quite simple: the more iterations, the lower the error. For $N \to \infty$, we may (probably) assume that the error converges to a certain value, which is probably not much lower than for $N = 10000$. In the case of the adaptive RANSAC algorithm, the parameters p_{free} (Figure 7.9(c)) and M (Figure 7.9(a)) indirectly control the number of iterations. While increasing p_{free} directly increases the number of iterations, a large sample size M also reduces the chance of finding an outlier-free sample and hence has a negative effect on the results.

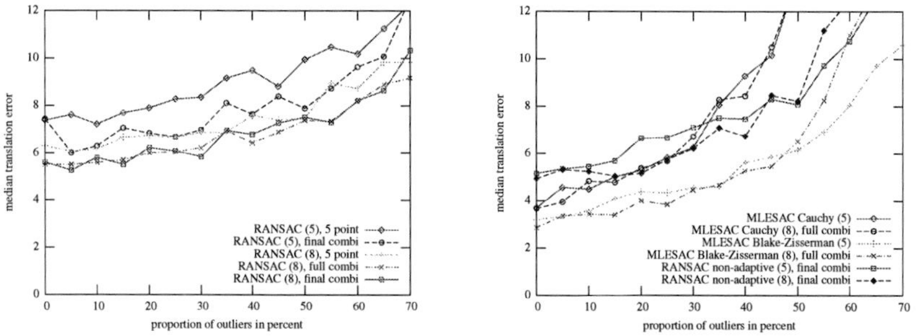

(a) Adaptive RANSAC. (b) Non-adaptive RANSAC and MLESAC.

Figure 7.11: Comparison of sample sizes M (in parentheses) and basic algorithms versus combination methods in robust relative pose estimation algorithms showing the median translation error on data with a varying proportion of outliers p_{out}.

Comparison of Methods on Simulated Data

The comparison of the basic relative pose estimation algorithms (Section 7.2.1) showed that the five-point algorithm is clearly superior in general. However, in the case of forward motion, the eight-point algorithm is better. As explained in Section 4.3.1, there are two possibilities of combining the five-point and the eight-point algorithms in the context of RANSAC. On the one hand, I use a combination of the five-point and the eight-point algorithm ("full combination", abbreviated "full combi" in the plots). On the other hand, I use only the five-point algorithm to generate hypotheses and the combination of the five-point and the eight-point algorithms for the final estimation ("final combination", abbreviated "final combi" in the plots). The "full combination" approach can also be applied to MLESAC. Lacking a set of inliers (like the best support set), however, the "final combination" is not an option.

Figure 7.11 compares these combination possibilities to the pure five-point variant on data with a varying proportion of outliers. In the case of the adaptive RANSAC algorithm (Figure 7.11(a)), a fair comparison of the various variants is only possible if the sample sizes M are equal. For $M = 5$ and $M = 8$, the "final combination" is clearly superior to using the five-point algorithm alone. In the case of $M = 8$, we can also use the "full combination" approach. When using only a sample size $M = 5$, however, the results are clearly worse, as the number of iterations is greatly reduced compared to $M = 8$.

In contrast to that, M has no influence on the number of iterations of the non-adaptive RANSAC and the MLESAC algorithms. Accordingly, the influence of M on the results is not very pronounced (Figures 7.9(e) and 7.10(b)). I hence compare the five-point algorithm using a sample size $M = 5$ and the "final combination" with $M = 8$ (Figure 7.11(b)). In the case of MLESAC with the Cauchy model, there is no clear difference. In the cases of non-adaptive RANSAC and MLESAC with the Blake-Zisserman model, the "full combination" is better for

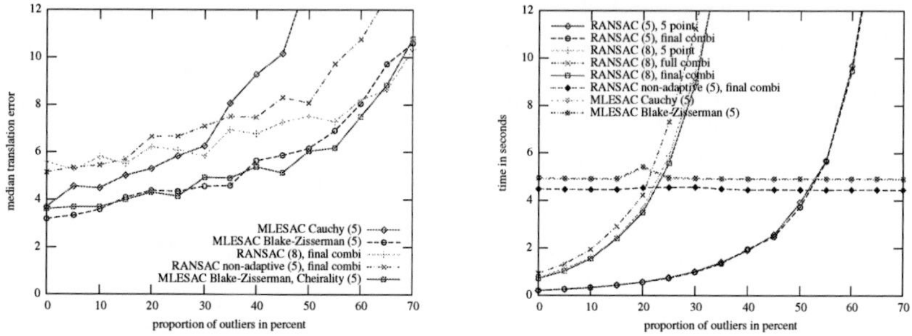

(a) Median translation error.

(b) Mean computation time.

Figure 7.12: Main comparison of robust relative pose estimation algorithms on data with a varying proportion of outliers p_{out}. The sample size is given in parentheses.

low to moderate outlier proportions, whereas $M = 5$ is superior for high outlier proportions. The problem in the latter case is that the probability of randomly selecting eight instead of only five inlier point correspondences is quite low. Increasing the number of iterations might lead to an advantage of the "full combination" with $M = 8$ compared to the five-point algorithm with $M = 5$ also in the case of a high outlier proportion.

Finally, a comparison of the best variants of the RANSAC and the MLESAC algorithms is given in Figure 7.12(a). MLESAC using the Blake-Zisserman model clearly gives the best results. The Cauchy model is quite good on data with a low proportion of outliers, but very bad in the case of many outliers. The adaptive and non-adaptive variants of RANSAC are comparably good. In the case of a high proportion of outliers, the adaptation leads to very many iterations N and produces better results than non-adaptive RANSAC with $N = 3000$.

Figure 7.12(a) also shows the results of the MLESAC algorithm using the Blake-Zisserman model with integrated cheirality constraint (Algorithm 4.6). The new method works very well and is about as good as the MLESAC algorithm using the Blake-Zisserman model without integrated cheirality (Algorithm 4.5). This shows that resolving the four-fold ambiguity during the MLESAC iterations is optional. Given the fact that the variant with integrated cheirality requires about 140 times more computation time, checking cheirality after the MLESAC iterations is clearly preferable.

Figure 7.12(b) shows that there are severe differences in the computational costs of the methods. Adaptive RANSAC is very efficient in the case of a low outlier proportion, but suffers from an exponentially growing running time as the proportion of outliers increases. Using a sample size $M > 5$ increases this effect further. Non-adaptive RANSAC and MLESAC (with $N = 3000$), on the other hand, are much more expensive than adaptive RANSAC if the proportion of outliers is low. In the case of MLESAC using the Blake-Zisserman model, the additional costs are rewarded by better results.

Analysis of Parameters on Real Data

In order to verify the analysis of the parameters on simulated data, I perform similar experiments on real data. In order to get reliable ground truth for the relative poses, I mount a Sony DFW-VL500 camera onto a Stäubli RX90 robot arm with known hand-eye-transformation and take images of a static scene from several camera poses. I use the setups S1 and S4 of the multi-camera self-calibration experiments in Section 7.3 (see Figures 7.18 and 7.19). Note that there are some camera pairs in the setup S4 which do not have a common field of view. Hence their relative poses cannot be estimated correctly and will usually result in a very high error. I will present results with and without prior correction of radial distortion as described in Section 7.1.

I assume the intrinsic pinhole parameters to be known. Alternatively, my rotational self-calibration method could be applied (Chapter 5). In order to get point correspondences as input for the multi-camera self-calibration, I use the difference of Gaussian interest point detector (Section 3.1), the SIFT descriptor (Section 3.2) and two nearest neighbor matching (Section 3.3) with $m = 100$.

For the evaluation, I estimate the relative poses of all camera pairs within each setup and repeat each estimation 20 times. The plots in the Figures 7.13, 7.14 and 7.15 show the median translation error over all camera pairs and repetitions. I use the same parameter values as in the simulation unless specified otherwise.

You can clearly see that prior correction of radial distortion can greatly reduce the translation error, especially on setup S4. In the case of undistorted images, the experiments on real data mostly confirm the findings from the simulation concerning the influence of the parameters. Note that while the parameter values used in the simulation are not optimal for the setups S1 and S4, there is only little room for improvement.

Comparison of Methods on Real Data

Figure 7.16 shows a comparison of the robust relative pose estimation algorithms. Apart from the main comparison based on a combined evaluation of the setups S1–S5, I also include results for the special setups "sphere" and "forward". Individual results for the setups S1–S5 are given in Figure E.6.

The results for the special setups "sphere" and "forward" (Figures 7.16(a)–7.16(d)) show that the five-point algorithm gives very good results for general motion *as well as* forward motion. These results suggest that a combination of the five-point and the eight-point algorithm is probably not necessary in practice—opposed to the simulation results in Figure 7.7(b). Interestingly, the results on images with distortion correction are *worse* than on the original distorted images. These are the only results in this dissertation showing this behavior. A possible reason could be errors in the hand-eye-transformation of the robot arm which leads to a minor error in the ground truth. In the case of the "forward" setup, the five-point algorithm might even benefit from the distortion in the sense that it partly compensates the problem with forward motion visible in the simulation experiments (see Figure 7.7(b)).

The combined comparison on the setups S1–S5 clearly shows that the MLESAC algorithm with the Blake-Zisserman model gives the best results. On images with corrected distortion, the

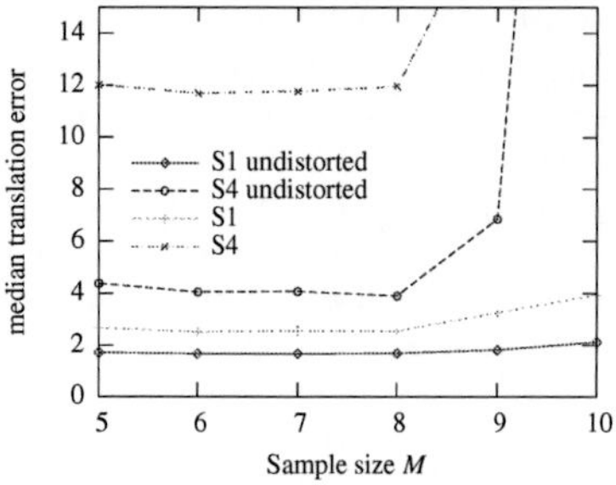

(a) RANSAC, sample size M.

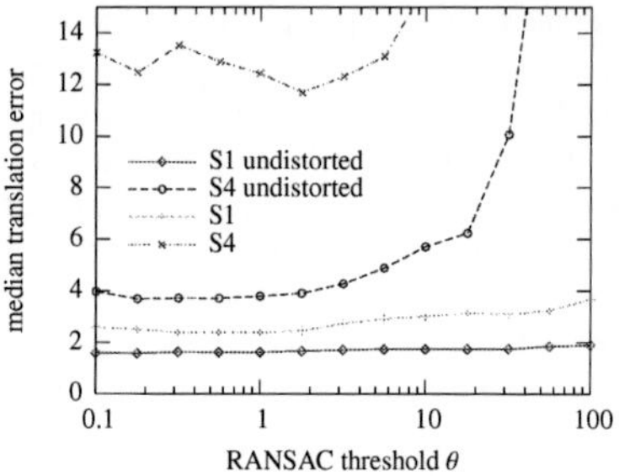

(b) RANSAC, threshold θ.

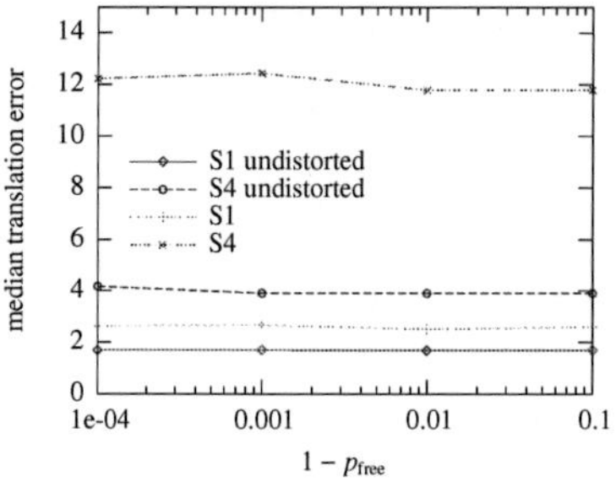

(c) RANSAC, probability p_{free}.

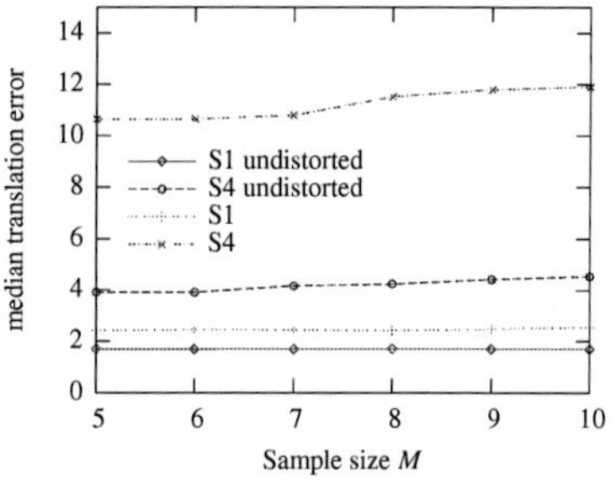

(d) Non-adaptive RANSAC, sample size M.

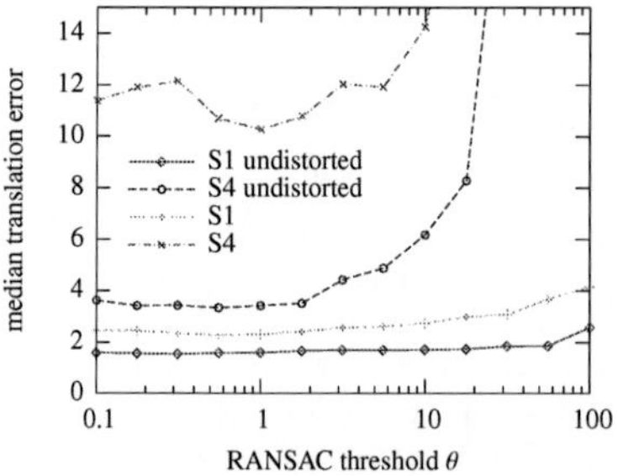

(e) Non-adaptive RANSAC, threshold θ.

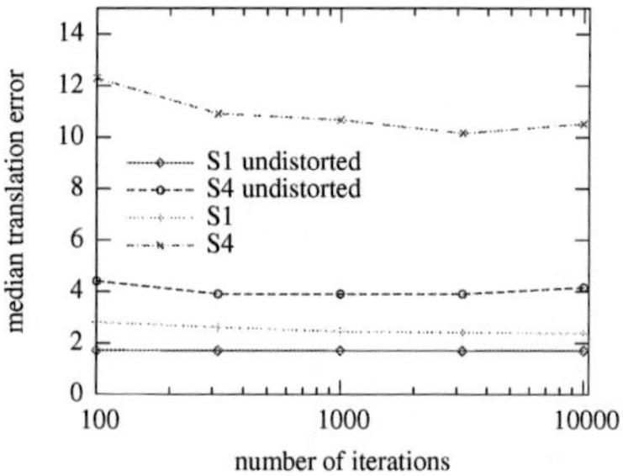

(f) Non-adaptive RANSAC, number of iterations N.

Figure 7.13: Influence of parameters in RANSAC on the median translation error for the setups S1 and S4 with ("undistorted") and without correction of radial distortion.

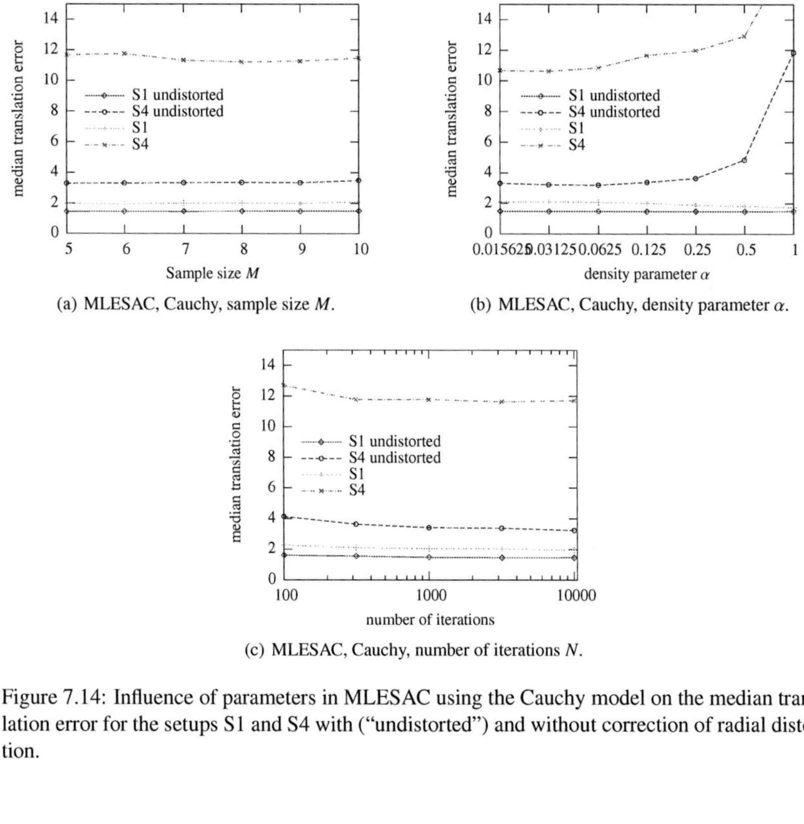

(a) MLESAC, Cauchy, sample size M.

(b) MLESAC, Cauchy, density parameter α.

(c) MLESAC, Cauchy, number of iterations N.

Figure 7.14: Influence of parameters in MLESAC using the Cauchy model on the median translation error for the setups S1 and S4 with ("undistorted") and without correction of radial distortion.

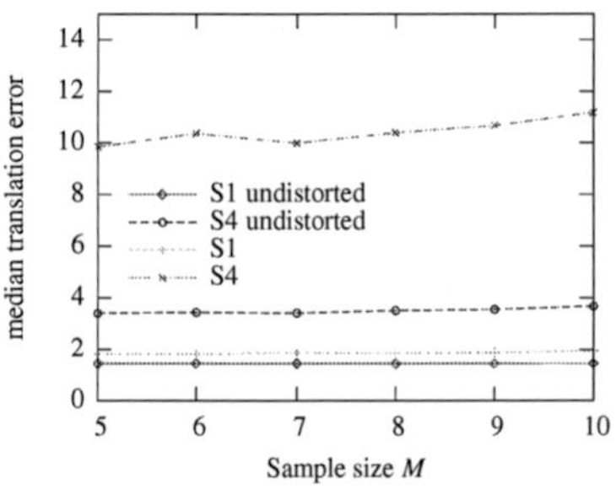

(a) MLESAC, Blake-Zisserman, sample size M.

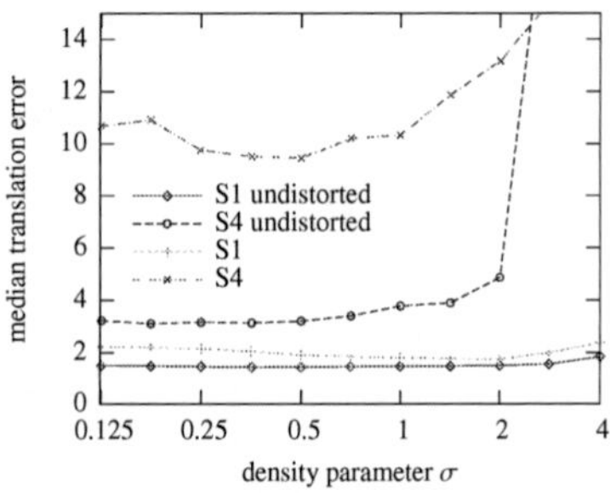

(b) MLESAC, Blake-Zisserman, density parameter σ.

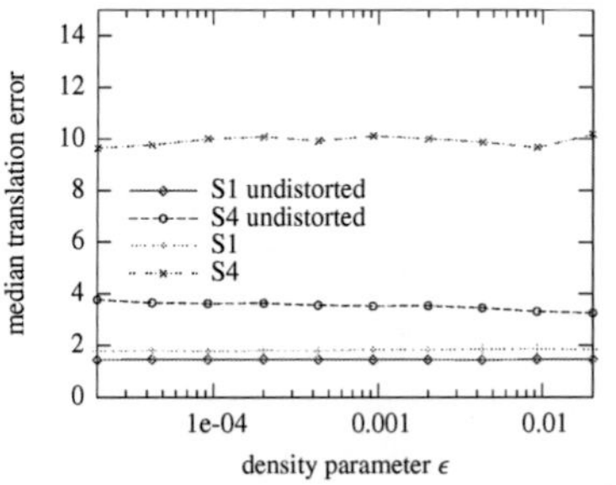

(c) MLESAC, Blake-Zisserman, density parameter ϵ.

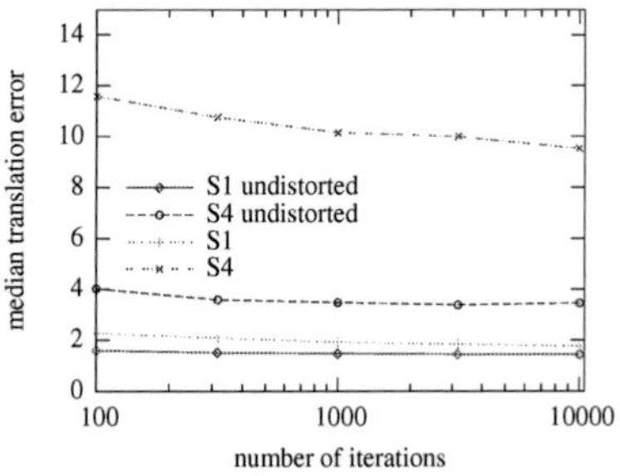

(d) MLESAC, Blake-Zisserman, number of iterations N.

Figure 7.15: Influence of parameters in MLESAC using the Blake-Zisserman model on the median translation error for the setups S1 and S4 with ("undistorted") and without correction of radial distortion.

results improve greatly and the Cauchy model is as good as the Blake-Zisserman model. In all cases, the RANSAC algorithm is inferior to the MLESAC algorithm. These results are consistent with the simulation experiments.

7.2.3 Correlation of the Uncertainty Measures with the Error in Relative Pose Estimates

In order to assess the uncertainty measures, I present the linear Pearson as well as the nonlinear Spearman correlation of the translation error and each uncertainty measure in Figure 7.17. The rank-based Spearman correlation has the advantage that it does not only respond to a linear dependency. Figure 7.17(a) shows that there is a high correlation between the translation error and each uncertainty measure, except for the smoothed information measure using the Cauchy model. Even though the Spearman correlation of the smoothed information measure is much better than the Pearson correlation, this measure is clearly inferior to the information and the entropy. The latter gives good results in all plots and can be considered to be the best uncertainty measure (as far as the correlation is concerned). On data without distortion correction, however, the information measure can have a higher correlation. The Blake-Zisserman model is clearly superior to the Cauchy model.

An interesting effect is that the correlation is *lower* on data with lower translation errors. This can be observed by comparing (a) the results with and without distortion correction and (b) setup S1 to the combined evaluation (cf. Figures 7.16 and E.6). This indicates that the uncertainty measures are good at detecting situations with very inconsistent data (high proportion of outliers), but less useful in assessing the precision of a relative pose estimate.

7.3 Multi-Camera Self-Calibration

In this part of the experiments, I will evaluate the (extrinsic) multi-camera self-calibration method presented in Chapter 6. After analyzing the parameters in Section 7.3.1, I will present a comparison of self-calibration results using each one of my three uncertainty measures and also random uncertainty values for the selection of relative poses. As an alternative to the random selection caused by the random uncertainties, I will consider naive deterministic selection based on breadth first search (BFS). As the approximation of the uncertainty measures is based on the extended MLESAC algorithm (Section 6.2.1), I will not use the RANSAC algorithm for multi-camera self-calibration. Furthermore, given the results in the previous section, I will only use the Blake-Zisserman model (equations (6.8) and (4.49)) and the five-point algorithm (Section 4.2.4).

In order to get reliable ground truth of the camera poses, I mount a Sony DFW-VL500 camera onto a Stäubli RX90 robot arm with known hand-eye-transformation and take images of a static scene from several camera poses, which effectively form a multi-camera system. Example images of the five sequences S1–S5 are given in the Figures 7.18 and 7.19. I make these multi-camera self-calibration test setups publically available (Bajramovic, 2010). Note that some camera pairs in the setups S2–S5 do not have a common field of view, which poses an additional

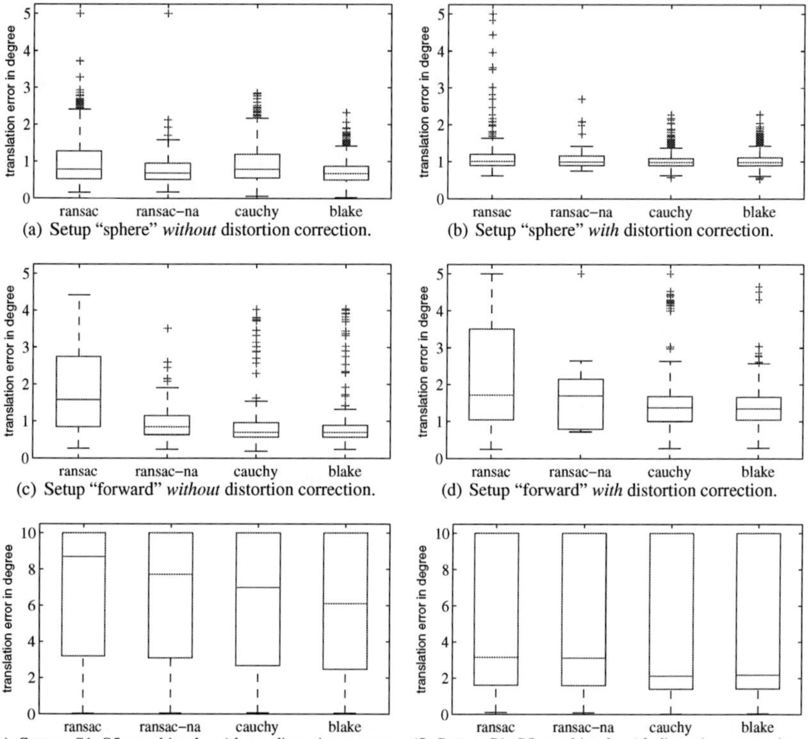

(a) Setup "sphere" *without* distortion correction.
(b) Setup "sphere" *with* distortion correction.
(c) Setup "forward" *without* distortion correction.
(d) Setup "forward" *with* distortion correction.
(e) Setups S1–S5 combined, *without* distortion correction.
(f) Setups S1–S5 combined, *with* distortion correction.

Figure 7.16: Comparison of robust relative pose estimation algorithms on real data with and without correction of radial distortion using the setups "sphere", "forward" and S1–S5 combined. The box plots (Appendix A.8) show results for RANSAC ("ransac"), non-adaptive RANSAC ("ransac-na"), MLESAC using the Cauchy model ("cauchy") and MLESAC using the Blake-Zisserman model ("blake"). Note that the error values are truncated at the upper limit of the respective Y axis to emphasize the relevant details. Also note that the sequences S2–S5 do *not* provide a common field of view for all camera pairs. The upper quartile of the translation error is between 70° and 90° in these cases, the maximum is 90°. Individual results for the setups S1–S5 are given in Figure E.6.

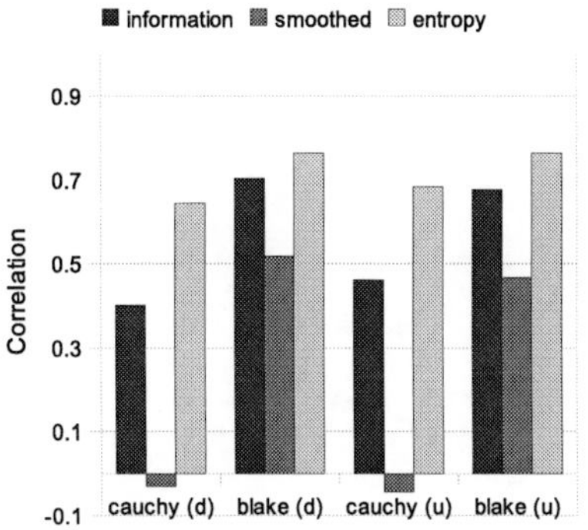

(a) Setups S1–S5 combined, linear Pearson correlation coefficient.

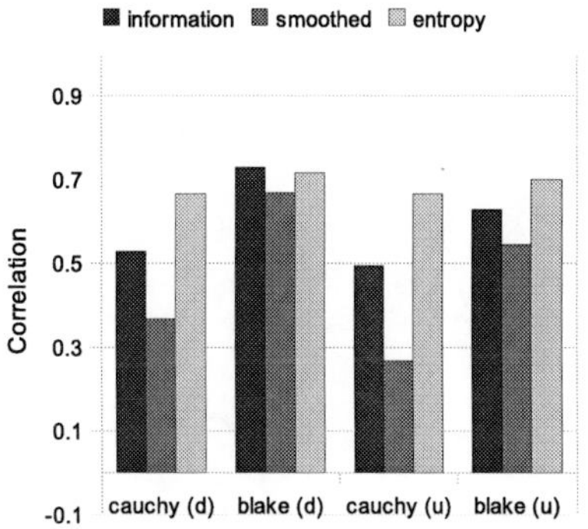

(b) Setups S1–S5 combined, Spearman correlation coefficient.

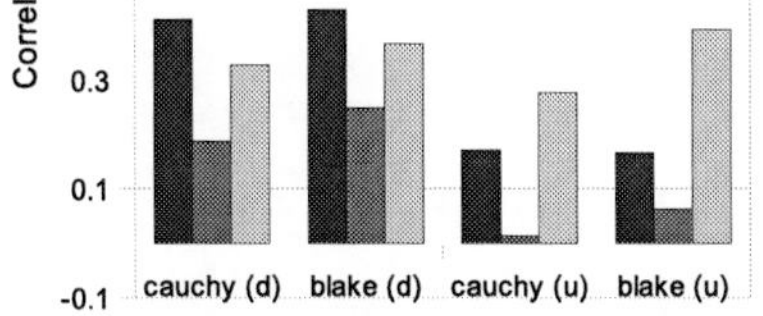

(c) Setup S1, linear Pearson correlation coefficient.

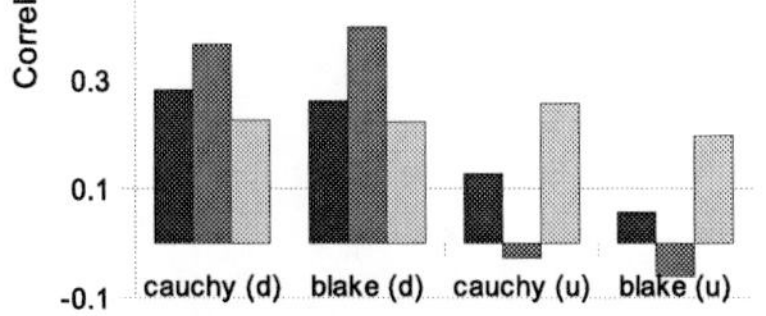

(d) Setup S1, Spearman correlation coefficient.

Figure 7.17: Correlation between the translation error and the uncertainty measures on real data with "(u)" and without "(d)" correction of radial distortion using the setups S1 and S1–S5 combined.

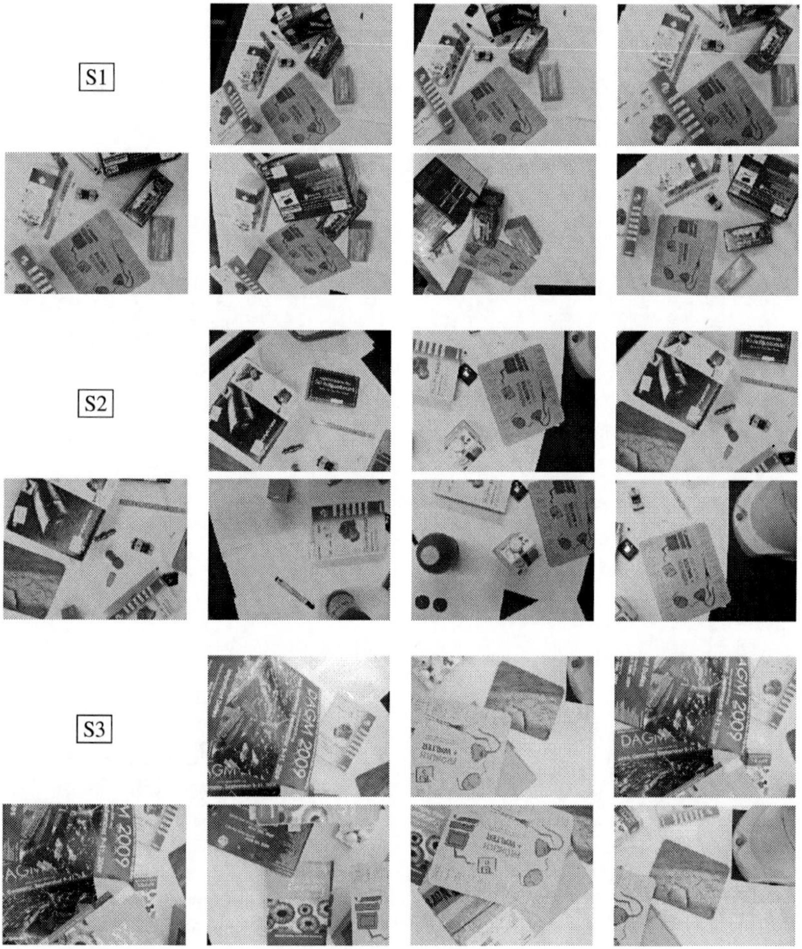

Figure 7.18: Example images of the first three setups S1–S3 used for the multi-camera self-calibration experiments. Only in setup S1 *all* camera pairs share a common field of view.

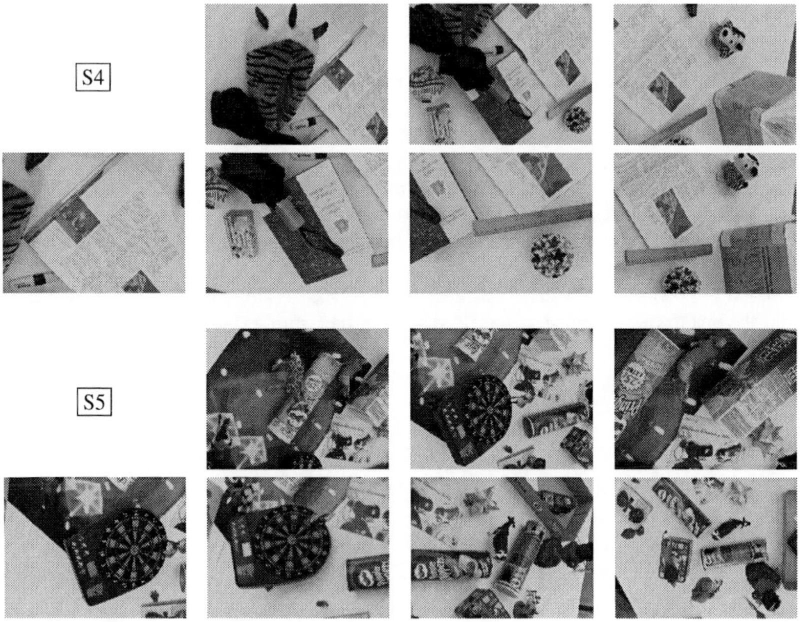

Figure 7.19: Example images of setups S4 and S5 used for the multi-camera self-calibration experiments.

difficulty for the calibration. I will present results with and without prior correction of radial distortion as described in Section 7.1.

I assume the intrinsic pinhole parameters to be known. Alternatively, my rotational self-calibration method could be applied (Chapter 5). In order to get point correspondences as input for the multi-camera self-calibration, I use the difference of Gaussian interest point detector (Section 3.1), the SIFT descriptor (Section 3.2) and two nearest neighbor matching (Section 3.3) with $m = 100$ (as in the previous section).

Error Measures

I evaluate (a) the median and (b) the mean Euclidean distance between the estimated camera positions and the according ground truth. The main difference between the two measures is the sensitivity to outliers. In case the calibration is good except for a single camera, the median error will be low, but the mean error will be considerably higher. From an application point of view, a low median error may be sufficient even if not all cameras are well calibrated (cf. multi-camera tracking results in Figure 7.33). Nevertheless, a low mean error is, of course, generally more desirable. As the calibration algorithms are randomized, I repeat each experiment 20 times and present the median of the results (i. e. the median of the median or the median of the mean position error).

In order to compute the distances between a multi-camera calibration estimate and the ground truth, the unknown 3D similarity transformation of the estimate has to be compensated. This can be achieved by registering the estimated camera positions $(\boldsymbol{c}_i)_{1\leq i\leq n}$ and the ground truth $(\boldsymbol{c}_i^{(\mathrm{GT})})_{1\leq i\leq n}$ with respect to a 3D similarity transformation. The camera position $\boldsymbol{c}_i$ can be computed from the camera pose $(\boldsymbol{R}_i, \boldsymbol{t}_i)$ as follows:

$$\boldsymbol{c}_i = -\boldsymbol{R}_i^{\mathrm{T}} \boldsymbol{t}_i \ . \tag{7.8}$$

Mathematically, we need to solve the following equation system:

$$\boldsymbol{c}_i^{(\mathrm{GT})} = \alpha_{\mathrm{reg}} \boldsymbol{R}_{\mathrm{reg}} \boldsymbol{c}_i + \boldsymbol{t}_{\mathrm{reg}} \quad \text{for} \quad 1 \leq i \leq n \ , \tag{7.9}$$

where α_{reg}, $\boldsymbol{R}_{\mathrm{reg}}$ and $\boldsymbol{t}_{\mathrm{reg}}$ denote the scale factor, rotation and translation of the 3D similarity transformation, respectively. As these equations only hold for a perfect calibration, a least squares approach is more useful for measuring the multi-camera calibration error:

$$\operatorname*{argmin}_{\alpha_{\mathrm{reg}}, \boldsymbol{R}_{\mathrm{reg}}, \boldsymbol{t}_{\mathrm{reg}}} \sum_{i=1}^{n} \left\| \alpha_{\mathrm{reg}} \boldsymbol{R}_{\mathrm{reg}} \boldsymbol{c}_i + \boldsymbol{t}_{\mathrm{reg}} - \boldsymbol{c}_i^{(\mathrm{GT})} \right\|^2 \ . \tag{7.10}$$

I use the closed form solution to this problem presented by Horn (1987). It is based on the following three facts:

1. The translation $\boldsymbol{t}_{\mathrm{reg}}$ is the difference between the centroid of the ground truth camera positions and the rotated and scaled centroid of the estimated camera positions.

2. The scale α_{reg} is the ratio of the root-mean-square deviations of the camera positions (estimated or ground truth, respectively) from their respective centroids.

3. The rotation $\boldsymbol{R}_{\text{reg}}$, represented as a unit quaternion, is the eigenvector corresponding to the largest eigenvalue of a certain symmetric 4×4 data matrix.

I use the resulting estimate $(\alpha_{\text{reg}}, \boldsymbol{R}_{\text{reg}}, \boldsymbol{t}_{\text{reg}})$ of the similarity transformation to measure the mean error of the camera positions:

$$\frac{1}{n} \sum_{i=1}^{n} \left\| \alpha_{\text{reg}} \boldsymbol{R}_{\text{reg}} \boldsymbol{c}_i + \boldsymbol{t}_{\text{reg}} - \boldsymbol{c}_i^{(\text{GT})} \right\| . \tag{7.11}$$

If the calibration of a few cameras is totally wrong, they pose outliers to the least squares problem in equation (7.10) and accordingly have a severe influence on the estimated similarity transformation. In order to compute the median error of the camera positions, however, it is important that the best half of the cameras is well registered, while the others may be disregarded. I hence use a randomized least median of squares (LMedS) estimator (Zhang et al., 1995) to estimate the similarity transformation in this case. It is very similar to the RANSAC algorithm (see Section 4.3.1), but uses the median of the squared errors

$$\operatorname*{med}_{1 \leq i \leq n} \left\| \alpha_{\text{reg}} \boldsymbol{R}_{\text{reg}} \boldsymbol{c}_i + \boldsymbol{t}_{\text{reg}} - \boldsymbol{c}_i^{(\text{GT})} \right\|^2 \tag{7.12}$$

instead of the size of the best support set. Accordingly, it does not require a threshold parameter, but does not support an adaptation of the number of iterations and is limited to dealing with an outlier proportion of 50%.

7.3.1 Analysis of Parameters

Figure 7.20 shows the results of the parameter analysis focussing on the mean position error. Some of the parameters have already been evaluated in the context of relative pose estimation and are re-evaluated here with regard to multi-camera self-calibration. For the sake of legibility, I only use the setups S1 and S4.

The influence of the parameters σ and ϵ of the Blake-Zisserman model are similar to the results in Section 7.2.2. The additional parameter ϕ of the extended probabilistic model (equation (6.8)) gives good results when set to zero, which is equivalent to using the simpler model (equation (4.47)), or to 0.5 as suggested by Engels and Nistér (2005). Setting the number of MLESAC iterations N to 3000 seems to be sufficient. The influence of the resolution of the approximation function ψ is somewhat chaotic, but values around 100 seem to give good results. The smoothing parameter γ of the smoothed information does not seem to have any pronounced influence on the calibration error.

7.3.2 Comparison of Uncertainty-Based Relative Pose Selection with Naive Selection and Random Edge Weights

In Figure 7.21, I present a combined evaluation of the setups S1–S5. Individual results for each setup are given in the Figures E.7 and E.8. The most obvious observation is that my uncertainty

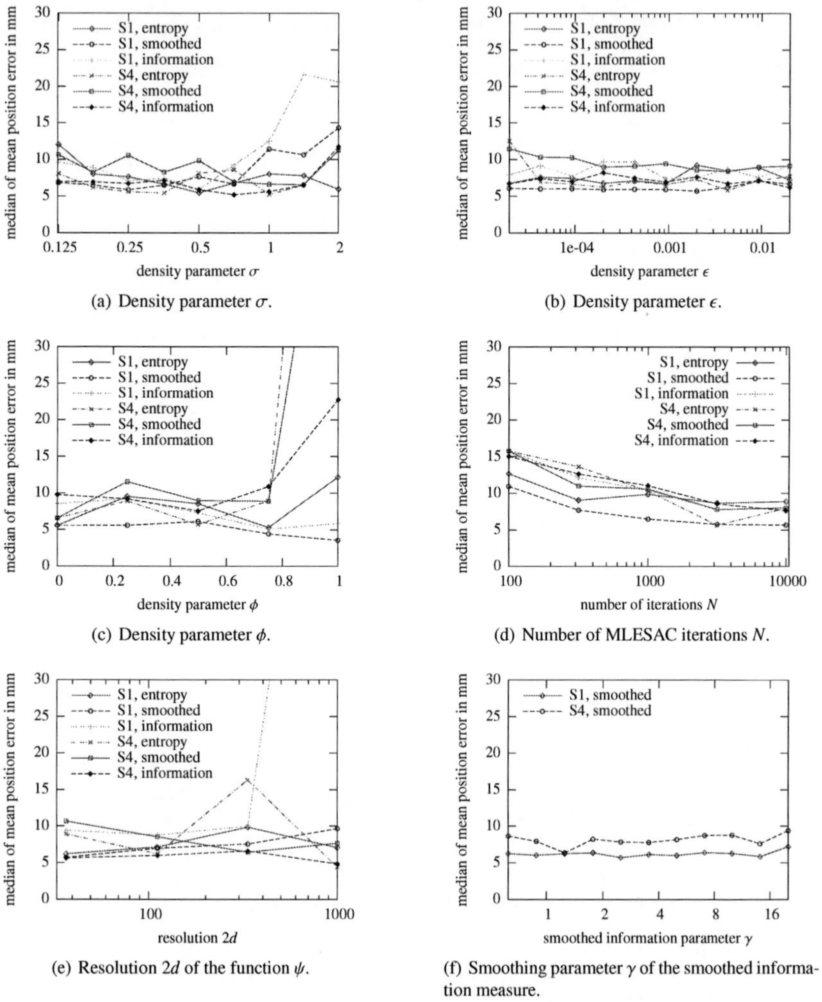

(a) Density parameter σ.

(b) Density parameter ϵ.

(c) Density parameter ϕ.

(d) Number of MLESAC iterations N.

(e) Resolution $2d$ of the function ψ.

(f) Smoothing parameter γ of the smoothed information measure.

Figure 7.20: Influence of parameters in MLESAC using the extended Blake-Zisserman model and also of parameters of the approximation of the uncertainty measures on the median of the mean position error of the multi-camera calibration for the setups S1 and S4 after correction of radial distortion.

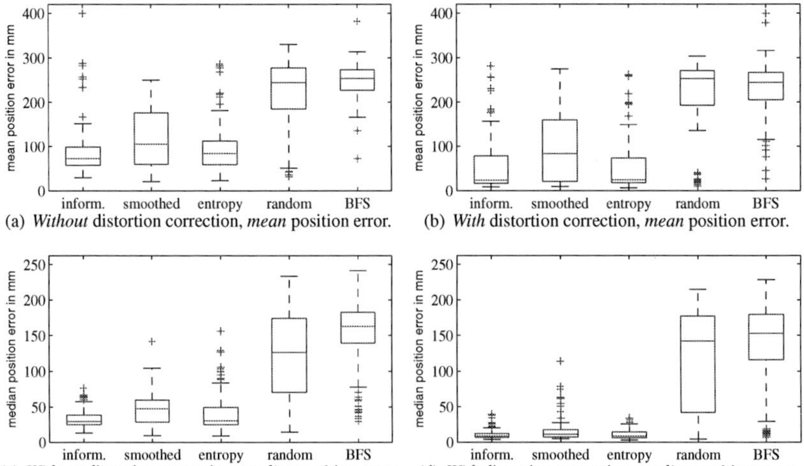

(a) *Without* distortion correction, *mean* position error.
(b) *With* distortion correction, *mean* position error.
(c) *Without* distortion correction, *median* position error.
(d) *With* distortion correction, *median* position error.

Figure 7.21: Uncertainty based selection of relative poses for multi-camera self-calibration using the information, the smoothed information or the entropy uncertainty measure compared to selection using random uncertainty values and also naive selection via breadth first search (BFS). The box plots (Appendix A.8) show *combined* results for the setups S1–S5. Separate results for each sequence are given in the Appendix, Figures E.7 and E.8. A more detailled plot showing only the results of the information, the smoothed information and the entropy measure is given in Figure E.9.

based selection of relative poses (Section 6.3) clearly outperforms the naive selection based on breadth first search (BFS). Furthermore, comparing the uncertainty measures shows that (a) all three measure are clearly better than using random edge weights for the selection and (b) that the information and entropy give comparably good results, while the smoothed information measure seems to be less reliable.

As in the relative pose estimation experiments (Section 7.2), the results are greatly improved by correcting the radial distortion. Comparing the mean and the median error indicates that not all cameras are well calibrated in all cases, especially in setup S2 (Figures E.7(d) and E.8(d)). If all camera pairs have a common field of view, the improvement gained by uncertainty based selection of relative poses is less pronounced (Figures E.7(b) and E.8(b)). If the radial distortion is *not* corrected, random edge weights can even outperform the entropy measure (which is the worst one in this case, see Figures E.7(a) and E.8(a)).

7.3.3 Comparison of Point Correspondence Algorithms

In this section, I present a comparison of the interest point detectors, the descriptors and the matching algorithms described in Chapter 3. As in the publication (Bajramovic, Koch and Denzler, 2009), I use the detectors and descriptors implementation of Mikolajczyk et al. (2005); Mikolajczyk and Schmid (2005). For the DoG-SIFT combination, I alternatively also use the SIFT++ implementation of Vedaldi (2007). I want to thank Michael Koch for the collaboration on an earlier version of these experiments (Bajramovic, Koch and Denzler, 2009).

I only present results for the setup S1, as the other, more difficult setups could not be evaluated. This is probably caused by the singular value decomposition in the five-point algorithm, which does not seem to converge and runs infinitely (or at least much, much longer than usually) in some cases with "bad" correspondences. The precise cause and nature of the problem are currently unknown and left for future research, as the comparison of point correspondence algorithms is only a minor part of this dissertation.

Figure 7.22 gives a comparison of the matching algorithms. The nearest neighbor matching outperforms the other two methods. However, in the case of data without correction of radial distortion and considering the median position error (Figure 7.22(c)), the 2NN matching gives slightly better results. Based on earlier results, which focused on that situation (Bajramovic, Koch and Denzler, 2009), the 2NN matching is used in all other experiments in this dissertation.

The comparison of the point detectors and descriptors is given in the Figures 7.23 and E.10. The low-dimensional descriptors, moment invariants (mom) and steerable filters (jla), are clearly not as good as the higher-dimensional ones, SIFT and GLOH. The performance of the point detectors varies without a clear winner. The affine region extension of the Harris-Laplace and the Hessian-Laplace detectors do not show an improvement. The performance of the difference of Gaussian (DoG) detector and the SIFT descriptor depends on the implementation. The SIFT++ implementation is clearly better. Based on these results, the SIFT++ implementation of the DoG-SIFT combination (with 2NN matching) is used in all other experiments in this dissertation.

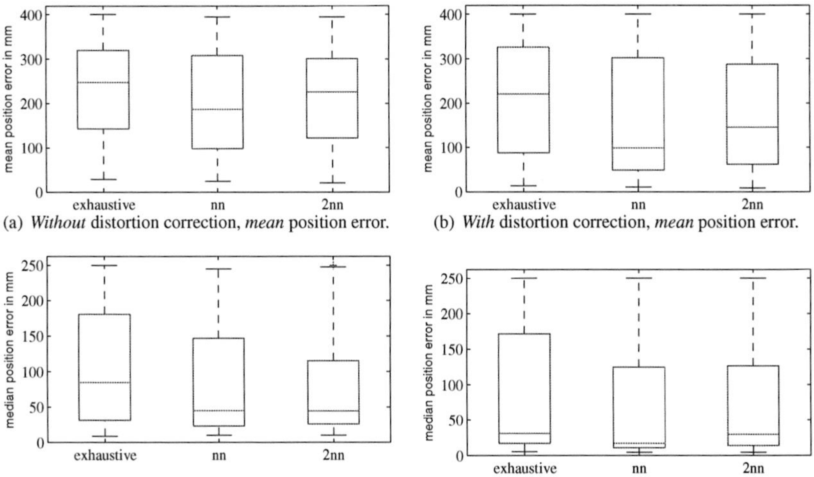

(a) *Without* distortion correction, *mean* position error.

(b) *With* distortion correction, *mean* position error.

(c) *Without* distortion correction, *median* position error.

(d) *With* distortion correction, *median* position error.

Figure 7.22: Comparison of matching algorithms jointly evaluated for all detector and descriptor combinations on the setup S1. The entropy measure is used for the uncertainty-based selection of relative poses.

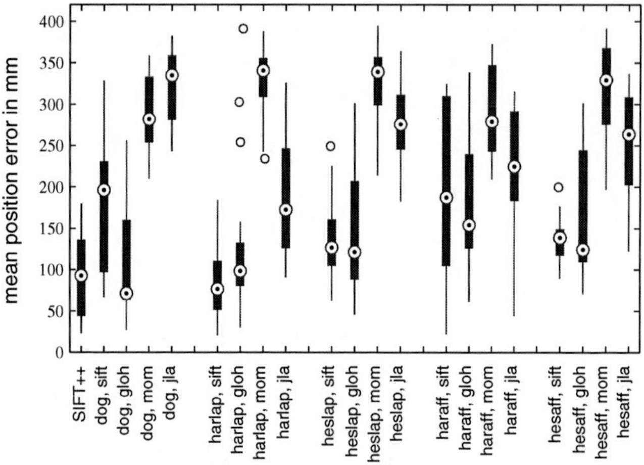

(a) *Without* distortion correction.

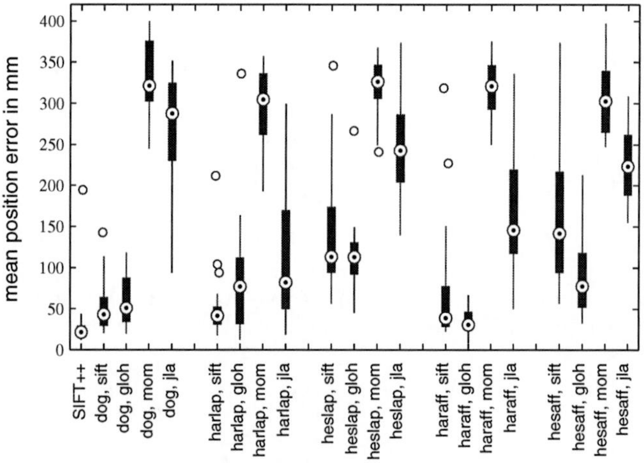

(b) *With* distortion correction.

Figure 7.23: Mean camera position errors of multi-camera self-calibration using point correspondences extracted by different point detectors and descriptors with 2NN matching on the setup S1. The entropy measure is used for the uncertainty-based selection of relative poses. The median errors are presented in Figure E.10.

7.4 Common Field of View Detection

In this part of the experiments, I will evaluate how good the novel probabilistic dissimilarity measures (Section 6.6.3) and also the novel "geometric" uncertainty measures (Section 6.2) perform at the task of common field of view detection. I want to thank Marcel Brückner for the collaboration on these experiments (Brückner, Bajramovic and Denzler, 2009). We use two Sony DFW-VL500 cameras, each mounted on top of a Directed Perception PTU-46-17.5 pan-tilt unit. While one camera carries out a pan movement and records 25 images, the other one records 9 images in a tilt sequence. In the experiment `desk1`, the baseline between the cameras is rather small and the scene does not have many ambiguities. Example images of this sequence are shown in Figure 7.24. For the experiment `desk2`, we choose a wide baseline and place different ambiguities (identical objects) in the scene. An impression of this sequence is given in Figure 7.24. The task for each of these two sequences consists of finding image pairs between the two cameras with a common field of view. Only about one quarter of the image pairs share a common field of view.

We perform a third experiment called `robo` with a camera mounted onto a robot arm, which we use to record 14 images showing different parts of the surrounding room. Example images of this sequence are shown in Figure 7.24. As this sequence is recorded using a single camera as opposed to two pan-tilt cameras, the task consists of finding image pairs with a common field of view considering all possible pairs (except for pairs of identical images).

Ground truth is obtained by manually marking polygons of common fields of view in all image pairs. An image pair is considered having a common field of view if the area of the respective polygon in each image covers at least ten percent of the total image area.

We compute Receiver Operator Characteristic (ROC) curves for each individual experiment as well as jointly for all three scenes (denoted `all`) using common thresholds. For the sake of clarity, however, we condense most of the ROC curves into a single value by computing the area under the curve. In the first part of the evaluation, we analyze the influence of the parameters m and λ of the probabilistic measures by plotting the ROC areas for varying parameter values. In the second part, we present a comparison of the individual methods using ROC curves as well as a bar chart showing ROC areas. In the plots, we use the following terms to refer to the individual methods:

- "Snavely": the criterion described in Section 6.6.1 using a two nearest neighbors rejection threshold $\theta_{2NN} = 0.6$,
- "geometric information/entropy/smoothed NN/2NN": respectively, the geometric information, entropy or smoothed information measure (Section 6.6.2) using nearest neighbor or two nearest neighbors matching using the default rejection threshold $\theta_{2NN} = 0.8$ to extract $m = 50$ correspondences (Section 3.3),
- "probabilistic (NN)": the probabilistic measure (Section 6.6.3, equation (6.26)) and its nearest neighbor variant (equation (6.28)).

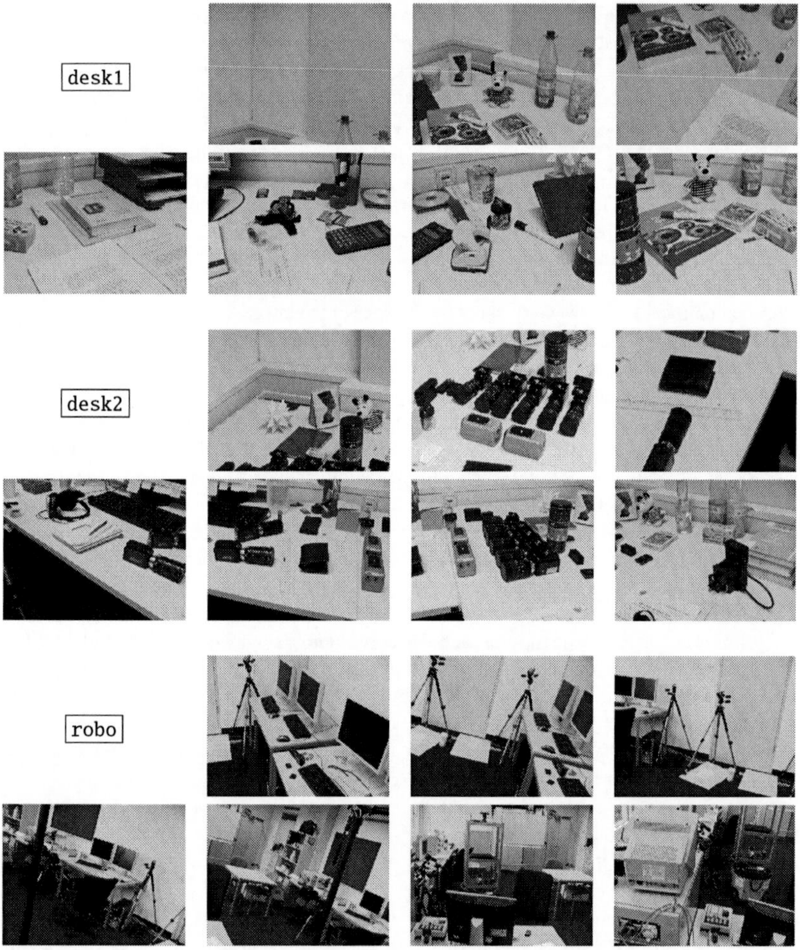

Figure 7.24: Example images of the test data for common field of view detection. In the cases of desk1 and desk2, the top rows show images from the tilt sequences and the bottom rows images from the pan sequences, respectively.

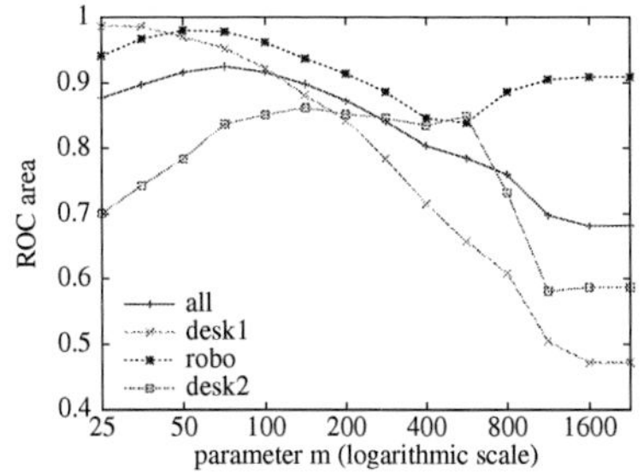

(a) Parameter *m* of the "probabilistic" method.

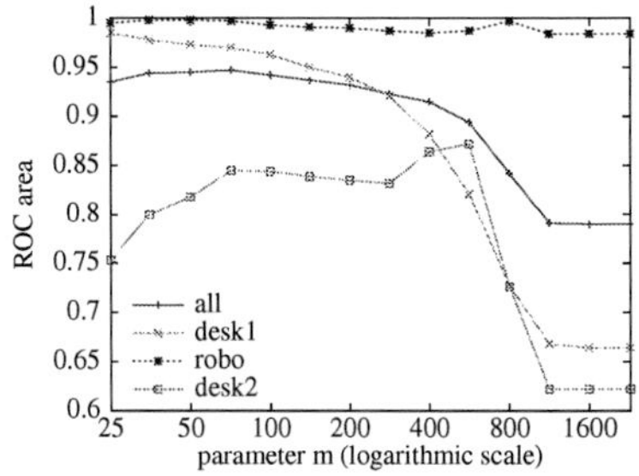

(b) Parameter *m* of the "probabilistic NN" method.

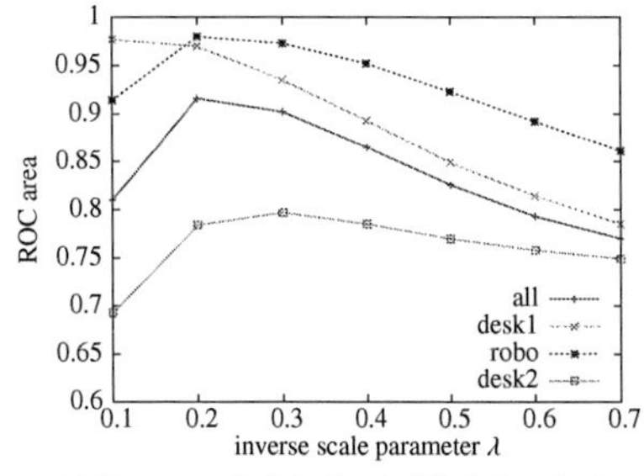

(c) Parameter λ of the "probabilistic" method.

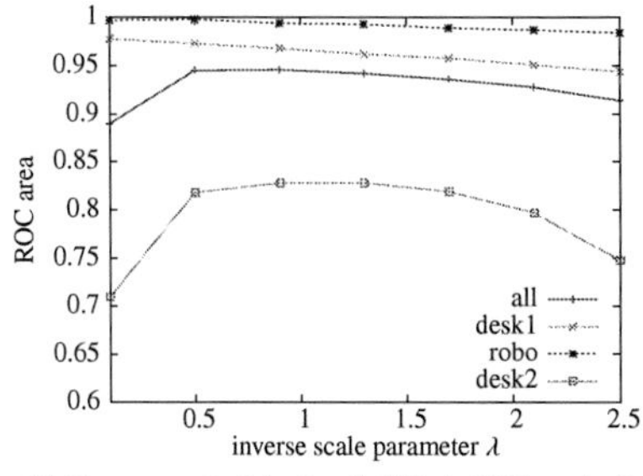

(d) Parameter λ of the "probabilistic NN" method.

Figure 7.25: Analysis of the parameters m and λ of the probabilistic common field of view measures using the areas and the ROC curves.

7.4.1 Analysis of Parameters of the Probabilistic Uncertainty Measures

Figures 7.25(a) and 7.25(b) show the ROC areas for different values of the parameter m (see Section 6.6.3), starting with $m = 25$ and increasing by a factor of $\sqrt{2}$. In both cases, the best overall result is achieved by a value of $m = 71$, which we use in all other experiments. Interestingly, the best result on the `desk2` sequence using "probabilistic NN" is achieved by setting $m = 500$.

Another parameter we investigate is the inverse scale parameter λ in the exponential distribution in the equations (6.26) and (6.28) used by the "probabilistic" and the "probabilistic NN" methods. Figures 7.25(c) and 7.25(d) show the resulting ROC areas using various values for λ. In the case of "probabilistic", the best results are achieved at $\lambda = 0.2$. The method "probabilistic NN" performs best using $\lambda = 0.5$. We use these values in all subsequent experiments.

Note that in the case of "probabilistic NN", the choice of the parameters m and λ is not very critical, since greater values lead to only slightly worse results.

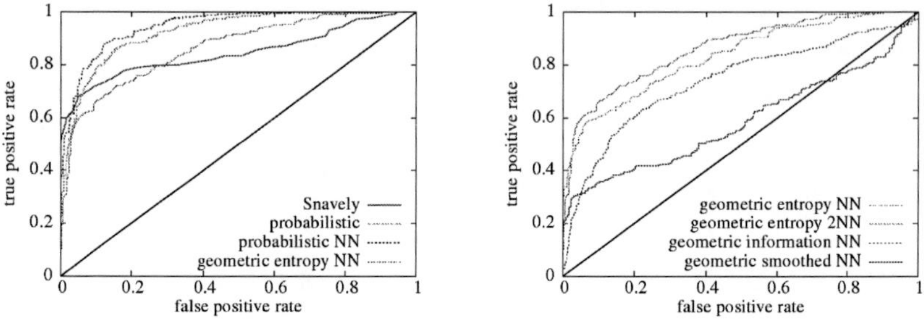

(a) Main comparison.

(b) Further methods.

Figure 7.26: ROC plot comparing the various common field of view detection methods jointly on all three sequences.

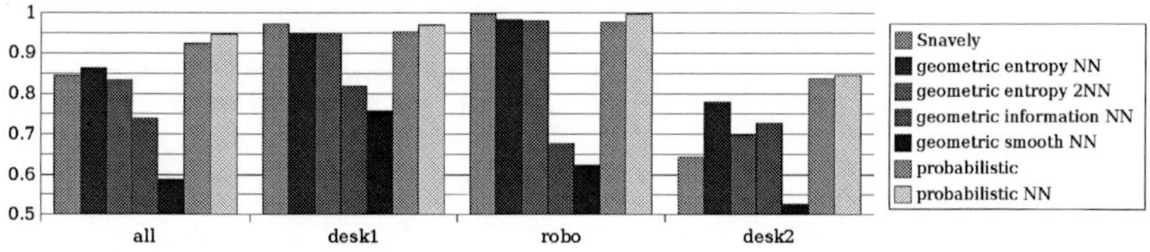

Figure 7.27: Comparison of the ROC areas of all methods evaluated jointly on all three sequences and also individually on each single one.

7.4.2 Comparison of Methods

Figure 7.26 shows the results of all three experiments combined in one ROC plot for each method. At very low false positive rates, "Snavely" shows the best performance, closely followed by "probabilistic NN" and "probabilistic". However, starting at slightly higher false positive rates, "probabilistic NN" and "probabilistic" achieve a higher true positive rate. "Probabilistic NN" clearly shows the best overall performance.

Only at high false positive rates, "geometric entropy NN" reaches higher true positive rates than "Snavely". Within the group of geometric measures, "geometric entropy NN" gives the best results. The variant using the two nearest neighbors rejection during correspondence matching ("geometric entropy 2NN") performs slightly worse. This indicates that strict rejection of ambiguities during the matching process is disadvantageous for the geometric measures. The remaining two measures, "geometric information NN" and "geometric smoothed NN", perform worse than the entropy measure. "Geometric smoothed NN" produces acceptable results only at low false positive rates.

Figure 7.27 shows the ROC area results of all methods evaluated on each of the three sequences as well as jointly on all sequences. In case of the two easier sequences, `desk1` and robo, the methods “Snavely” and “probabilistic NN” perform almost identically. On the difficult sequence desk2, however, our methods “probabilistic NN”, “probabilistic” and “geometric entropy NN” perform much better than “Snavely”. The best overall results are achieved by “probabilistic NN”.

The good results of the probabilistic dissimilarity measures confirm the hypothesis that avoiding hard matching decisions leads to improved common field of view detection. The observation that “probabilistic NN” outperforms “probabilistic” is consistent with Lowe's observation, that absolute SIFT descriptor distances are inferior to a comparison of the first and second nearest neighbor (Lowe, 2004). Somewhat surprisingly, the geometric methods were not able to outperform the results of the “Snavely” method.

7.5 Common Field of View Detection and Multi-Camera Calibration

In this section, I will present experiments on the combination of the uncertainty-based selection of relative poses and common field of view detection as well as the separation of rooms prior to calibration. I want to thank Marcel Brückner for the collaboration on an earlier version of these experiments on data without radial distortion correction (Bajramovic, Brückner and Denzler, 2009).

7.5.1 Combination with Uncertainty-Based Selection of Relative Poses

First I investigate how common field of view detection affects the accuracy of the multi camera calibration. Common field of view detection uses a threshold on the common field of view measure (Section 6.6) to remove individual edges from the complete camera dependency graph. Note that the lower the threshold is, the more edges are removed from the graph. The maximum threshold hence corresponds to the complete camera dependency graph.

Decreasing the threshold only has an effect on the graph if the new threshold leads to the removal of at least one additional edge. Hence, there is a finite set of relevant thresholds (which of course depends on the input). All of them are evaluated in the following experiments.

The experiments are performed on the same data as in Section 7.3 using the same registration of the calibration estimate with the ground truth and the same error measure.

For the common field of view computation, I set $\lambda = 0.5$ and $m = 71$ (cf. Section 7.4.1). For relative pose and uncertainty estimation, I use the parameters $\sigma = 0.25$, $\epsilon = 0.002$ and $\phi = 0.5$, perform 3000 sampling iterations, and use a resolution of 100×100 for ψ. Each calibration is repeated 20 times.

I use three alternative edge weights for the uncertainty-based selection of relative poses: the epipolar geometry based entropy measure defined in equation (6.5) (“geometric entropy”), the common field of view measure defined in equation (6.33) (“probabilistic NN”), and random values (“random”). Note that the measure “geometric entropy” has been simply referred to as “entropy” in Section 7.3. As the measure “probabilistic NN” is also an entropy, I use the new

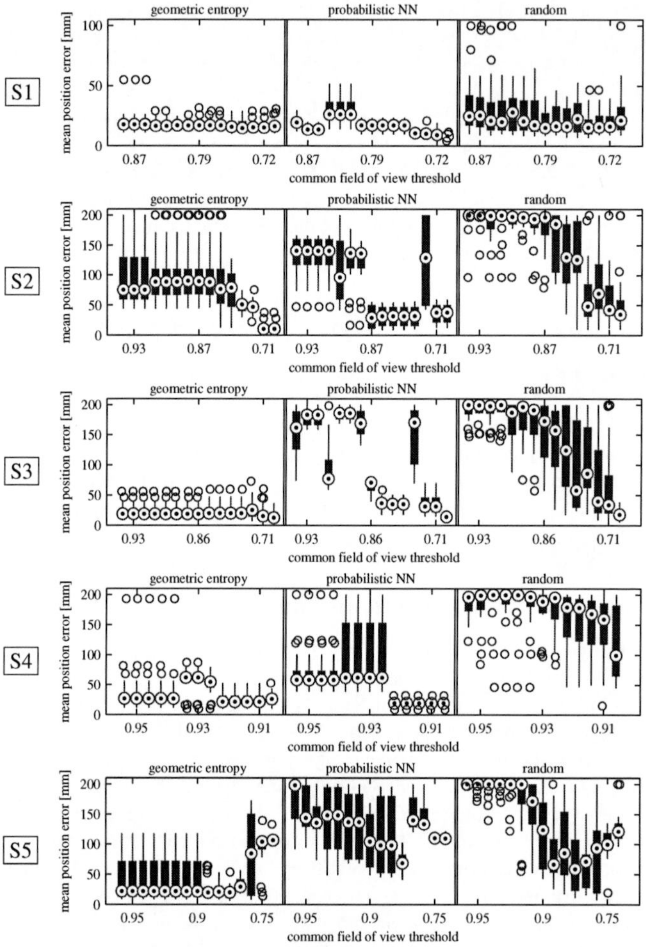

Figure 7.28: Combination of common field of view detection and uncertainty based selection of relative poses, results for the setups S1, S2, S3, S4 and S5 (from top to bottom) with correction of radial distortion. For each of the three edge weights "geometric entropy" (left), "probabilistic NN" (middle), and "random" (right), the mean position errors (in millimeters) are presented using box plots (Appendix A.8) depending on different field of view thresholds. Note that smaller thresholds lead to fewer remaining edges in the camera dependency graph. For the sake of legibility, only 15 thresholds are shown (including the minimum and maximum).

name "geometric entropy" to avoid confusion.

I calibrate each setup using the camera dependency graphs resulting from common field of view detection with every possible threshold—provided that the resulting graph is triangle connected. The results on images with and without radial distortion correction are presented in the Figures 7.28 and E.11.

Prior common field of view detection is able to improve the results for each setup and each type of edge weights. Note, however, that the improvement can be very small in the case of the "geometric entropy" weights, as these often already give good results without common field of view detection. Note also that it is not easy to predict how many edges need to be removed – or which threshold needs to be chosen – in order to reach a improvement of the results. In the case of random edge weights, the improvements are very pronounced. This is not surprising, as more and more invalid edges are removed, which can otherwise only be avoided by chance. However, as far as the absolute results using the best threshold are concerned, the "geometric entropy" edge weights and – most of the time – also the "probabilistic NN" edge weights are much better than "random" edge weights. This shows that common field of view detection alone is not enough and should be combined with uncertainty-based selection of relative poses. If all camera pairs of a setup share a common field of view, removing edges from the graph only has a minor impact on the results, as can be seen in Figure 7.28, setup S1.

To summarize the results: common field of view detection improves uncertainty-based multi camera calibration. However, it is not trivial to choose the best common field of view threshold. The impact of common field of view detection depends on the uncertainty measure and, as expected, is most pronounced in the case of random values. The best overall results are obtained by combining common field of view detection with uncertainty-based relative pose selection using the "geometric entropy" measure.

7.5.2 Separating Cameras in Different Rooms

As explained in Section 6.6.4, a correct separation of the camera dependency graph into subgraphs is required if the cameras are positioned in different rooms without specifying which camera is in which room. As in (Bajramovic, Brückner and Denzler, 2009), I simulate such a situation by combining the images of two or three setups. Note that the setups S1, S2 and S3 contain identical objects, which poses a serious problem. I nevertheless include these combinations in the experiments to demonstrate the limitations of the method.

For these experiments, I use pairs and triples of these setups to verify whether the common field of view detection is able to separate the graph into two or three subgraphs, respectively. For each pair and triple of setups, Figure 7.29 shows the resulting ranges of suitable thresholds of the connected components method ("components") and the triangle connected components method ("triangle"). All pairs and triples of setups, which do not contain identical objects, are correctly separated. As argued in Section 6.6.4, the threshold can be *automatically* chosen if the number of rooms is known. The fact that there is a certain range of suitable thresholds indicates that the separation is quite robust, as removing a few more edges than necessary still produces the same separation. Also note that the threshold range of the correctly separated triples is the intersection of the threshold ranges of the three pairs consisting of these setups.

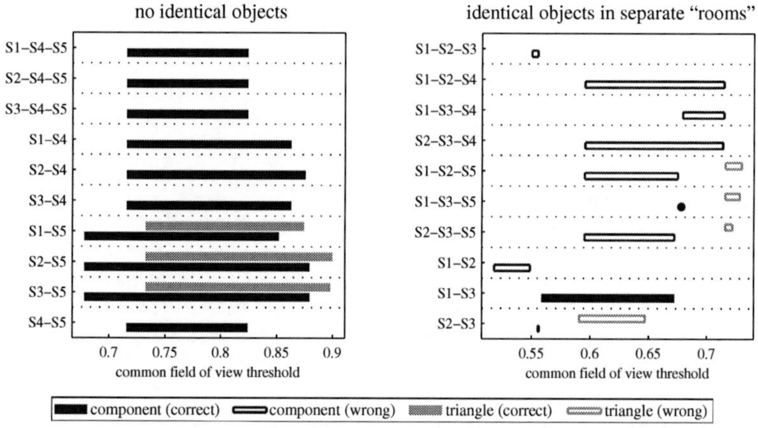

Figure 7.29: Ranges of thresholds which separate the cameras into two or three groups, respectively. For each pair and triple of setups, the connected "component" and "triangle" connected component criterion are displayed for data with radial distortion correction. If there is no bar, the method was not able to separate the setups. An unfilled bar indicates that the separation is *not* correct. Note that wrong separations only occur in pathological situations, which contain identical objects in separate rooms (right figure).

If at least two out of the three setups S1, S2 and S3, which contain identical objects, are combined, the separation does not work correctly in most cases. Somewhat surprisingly, the pairs S1–S3 and S2–S3 and the triple S1–S3-S5 are nevertheless separated correctly. While the influence of radial distortion correction on the room separation results is very limited in general, in the case of rooms containing identical objects, it is more relevant (compare Figures 7.29 and E.12).

The triangle connected components criterion appears to be inferior to the connected components criterion. The latter separates the graph as soon as it decomposes into two connected components and hence always produces a result for at least one threshold. The former method, however, requires the graph to decompose into two triangle connected components, which consist of at least three cameras each. Hence, it is possible that this criterion does not produce any separation.

As explained in Section 6.6.4, the common field of view detection threshold used for the separation has no influence on the subsequent calibration as long as the separation is correct. As each subgraph is calibrated on its own, the common field of view threshold used for *calibration* can be chosen independently for each subgraph. The according calibration results have been presented in Section 7.5.1.

7.6 A Multi-Camera Object Tracking System

As an application example of multi-camera self-calibration, I present a multi-camera object tracking system, which reconstructs the motion path of an object. After introducing the main ideas, I will present algorithmic and technical details in Section 7.6.1. Finally, I will present experimental results in Section 7.6.2.

After setting up the multi-camera system, I apply my self-calibration method (as in the experiments in Section 7.3). After this initialization, the system tracks an object in the image sequences of each camera individually. Given the resulting positions $\boldsymbol{p}_{i,t}$ of the object's center for each camera i, which can observe the object at a given point in time t, the 3D position $\boldsymbol{q}_t$ of the object is reconstructed (if there are at least two such points $\boldsymbol{p}_{i,t}$). The sequence $(\boldsymbol{q}_t)_{t\geq 0}$ gives the motion path of the object.

Note that the 3D reconstruction requires the points $(\boldsymbol{p}_{i,t})_i$ to correspond for each t. In the case of "small" objects, which only cover a small part of the image areas, the object's center points found in multiple cameras can often be assumed to correspond approximately—but in general not exactly (neither in theory nor in practice).

7.6.1 Details

Object Tracking by Object Detection

As this demonstration focuses on the 3D reconstruction of the motion path, the tracking task is simplified by using an easily detectable object (a pink ball, see Figure 7.30) and solving the tracking task by detecting the object independently in each frame and camera.

Figure 7.30: One example image from each camera of the multi-camera object tracking demonstration videos recorded at (roughly) the same point in time. The pink ball is the easily detectable object of interest. Images recorded at a different point in time without the object being visible are used for the multi-camera self-calibration. The setup of the multi-camera system is shown in Figure 7.31.

Aiming at a simple proof-of-concept implementation using data recorded in a controlled environment, the object is simply detected as follows:

1. Convert the image to the HSV color space (Gonzalez and Woods, 2002).

2. A pixel with color $(h, s, v)^{\mathrm{T}}$ is considered to (probably) belong to the pink ball if $h \geq 210 \wedge s \geq 100 \wedge v \geq 240$ (assuming pixel values in the range $[0, 255]$).

3. Detect all 8-connected components and their bounding boxes (Gonzalez and Woods, 2002). In order to suppress noise and minor background clutter, if a region contains less than 100 object pixels or if its bounding box is less than 10 pixels wide or high, it is discarded.

4. The largest remaining region is the result of the detection process. If there is no region at all, the object is considered not to be (fully) visible.

5. The center of gravity of the object pixels within the resulting region is used as the object's center.

6. If the center of gravity is less than 20 pixels from the image border, the object is considered not to be fully visible. This step ensures that only a completely visible ball is detected. Otherwise, the center of gravity is usually very different from the center of the ball.

On-line Reconstruction of the Motion Path

In order to reconstruct the motion path, I formulate the following optimization problem, which penalizes large motion between two subsequent frames:

$$\hat{\boldsymbol{q}}_t = \underset{\boldsymbol{q}_t}{\operatorname{argmin}} \sum_{i \in \mathcal{I}_t} \rho(d(\boldsymbol{p}_{i,t}, \boldsymbol{K}_i(\boldsymbol{R}_i \boldsymbol{q}_t + \boldsymbol{t}_i)) + \lambda \underbrace{\|\boldsymbol{q}_t - \hat{\boldsymbol{q}}_{t-1}\|^2}_{\text{penalization}} , \tag{7.13}$$

where $\mathcal{I}_t$ denotes the set of image indices for which the object has been detected at time t, $d(\cdot, \cdot)$ denotes the Euclidean distance of points in homogeneous coordinates, λ denotes the weight of the penalization term and ρ denotes the robust Pseudo-Huber error function

$$\rho(x) = 2b^2 \left(\sqrt{1 + \frac{x^2}{b^2}} - 1 \right) . \tag{7.14}$$

This function approximates x^2 for $x < b$ (inliers) and $|x|$ for $x \geq b$ (outliers), but has the beneficial property that it is twice continuously differentiable. The outlier threshold b is a parameter of the function.

In the subsequent experiments, I will use the weight $\lambda = 100$ and set the outlier threshold parameter of the robust error function to $b = 1$ (see equation (7.14)). Both values have been found to be a good choice by experimental evaluation. If the 3D reconstruction $\hat{\boldsymbol{q}}_{t-1}$ for the previous frame is not available, either because $t = 0$ or because the object was only detected in at most one image at $t - 1$, the penalization term is not used (set $\lambda = 0$).

In order to solve this optimization problem for each t, I first find an initial estimate for the 3D point and subsequently apply the second-order trust-region method described in Appendix C.1. If the object has been visible in at least two cameras in the previous frame $t - 1$, I use $\hat{\boldsymbol{q}}_{t-1}$ as an initial estimate for $\boldsymbol{q}_t$. Otherwise, I triangulate the 3D point $\boldsymbol{q}_t$ given the point correspondences as described in Appendix D.4. As a special case, if the object has only been detected in at most one image in the current frame t, there will not be any reconstruction $\hat{\boldsymbol{q}}_t$.

The second-order trust-region method requires the gradient and the Hessian of the objective function. In order to compute these derivatives, I first exploit the linearity of the derivation operator

$$\begin{aligned} &\frac{\partial}{\partial x} \left(\sum_{i \in \mathcal{I}_t} \rho(d(\boldsymbol{p}_{i,t}, \boldsymbol{K}_i(\boldsymbol{R}_i \boldsymbol{q}_t + \boldsymbol{t}_i)) + \lambda \|\boldsymbol{q}_t - \boldsymbol{q}_{t-1}\|^2 \right) \\ &= \sum_{i \in \mathcal{I}_t} \frac{\partial}{\partial x} \rho(d(\boldsymbol{p}_{i,t}, \boldsymbol{K}_i(\boldsymbol{R}_i \boldsymbol{q}_t + \boldsymbol{t}_i)) + \lambda \frac{\partial}{\partial x} \|\boldsymbol{q}_t - \boldsymbol{q}_{t-1}\|^2 , \end{aligned} \tag{7.15}$$

where x denotes any component of $\boldsymbol{q}_t$, and then use Maple™ to compute symbolic expressions (and generate C code) for the remaining derivatives. I use the very same approach for the Hessian matrix.

Figure 7.31: The setup of the multi-camera system used for the multi-camera tracking experiments.

Technical Details

In principle, the reconstruction of the motion path described above works on-line. As this application example is only intended to demonstrate the usefulness and also the quality of the multi-camera self-calibration, the proof-of-concept implementation first records roughly synchronized videos from the cameras and subsequently processes the data. Note, however, that the system only uses information that would also be available to an on-line system.

For the recording process, each of the six Sony DFW-VL500 cameras is connected to its own computer. Figure 7.31 shows the setup of the multi-camera system. The videos are roughly synchronized by starting the recording process at each computer at a fixed time. The computers' clocks are synchronized via the network time protocol.At a framerate of 15 frames per second, the resulting videos are synchronized up to roughly one frame (i. e. 67 ms). By using timestamps, this could be reduced to at most half a frame, but the simple synchronization has proven to suffice for the demonstration.

In order to self-calibrate the multi-camera system, I use one image from each camera taken before (or after) the object is visible in the scene. I assume the intrinsic pinhole parameters to be known. Alternatively, my rotational self-calibration method could be applied (Chapter 5). Furthermore, I correct the radial distortion of the images as mentioned in Section 7.1. The multi-camera self-calibration is performed using the MLESAC algorithm with the Blake-Zisserman model and the entropy uncertainty measure for relative pose selection (as in the experiments in Section 7.3).

7.6.2 Results

I evaluate the multi-camera tracking application on two different sequences. In both cases, the object has been moved such that there are roughly 90° angles and two depth levels in the 3D motion path. In the first sequence, there is one occlusion caused by a person walking through the scene. In the second sequence, the object is often observed only by two or three cameras. Around the middle of the sequence, the object can only be observed by one or no camera, which makes it impossible to reconstruct the 3D positions of the object.

Figures 7.32 and 7.33 show the reconstructed 3D motion paths of both sequences along with the multi-camera calibrations, the detected 2D motion paths of each camera, according reprojections of the reconstructed 3D motion path and the resulting reprojection errors. The reconstructed motions paths are very plausible showing roughly 90° turns and also two depth levels. In detail, however, the reconstructed motions paths are clearly not perfect. There are several sources for these errors:

- The multi-camera calibration is probably not perfect. Especially camera 4 in sequence 2 does not seem to be well calibrated.
- The simple object detection method can cause quite heavy noise in the detected object centers.
- Errors in the synchronization of the cameras of up to 67 ms lead to systematic errors in the detected object positions.

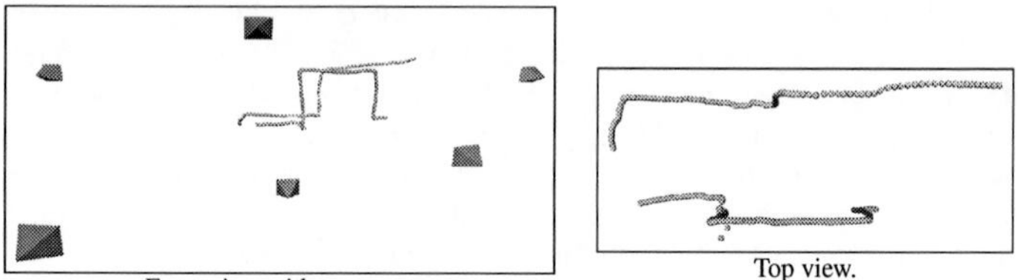

Front view with cameras. Top view.

(a) Reconstructed motion path and multi-camera calibration. The cameras are visualized as pyramids. The spheres represent the motion path of the pink ball. The color of the ball is faded over time such that the most recent position has the highest saturation. The reconstructed motion path clearly shows the roughly 90° changes of the motion direction (front view) and the two depth levels (top view).

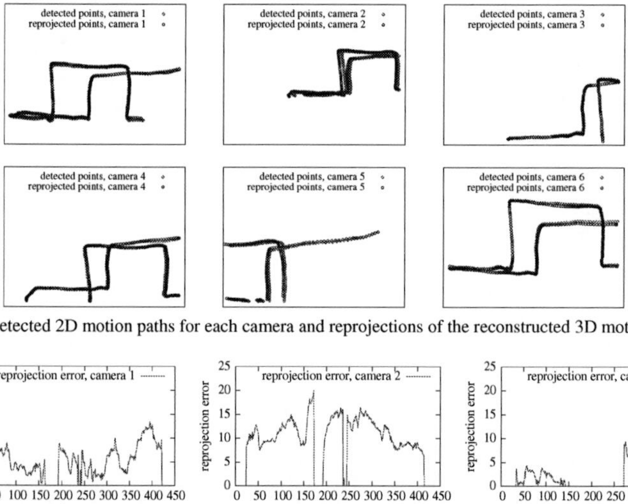

(b) Detected 2D motion paths for each camera and reprojections of the reconstructed 3D motion path.

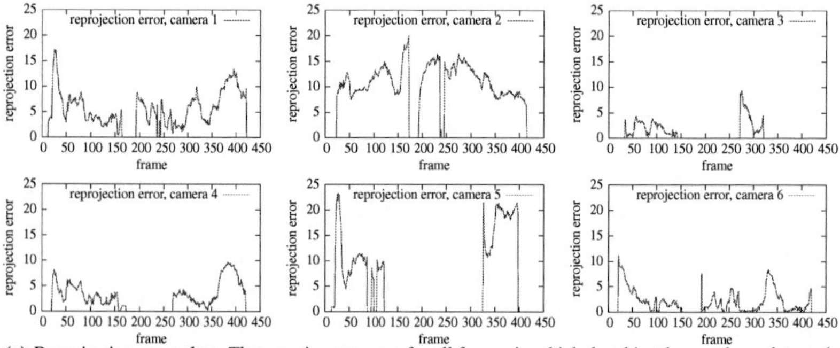

(c) Reprojection error plots. The error is set to zero for all frames in which the object has not been detected.

Figure 7.32: Reconstructed 3D motion path, detected and reprojected 2D motion paths, as well as reprojection errors for sequence 1.

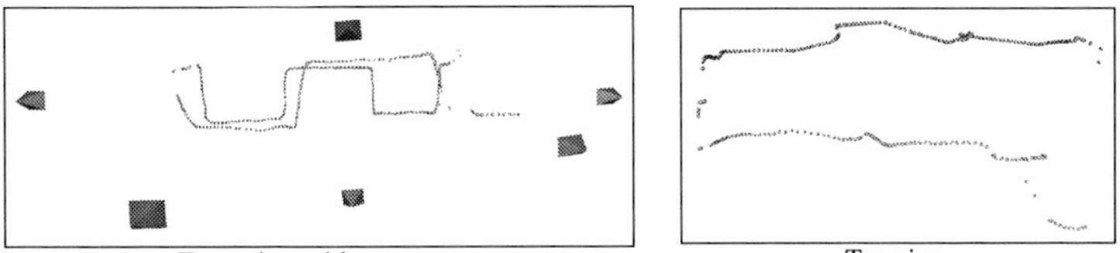

Front view with cameras. Top view.

(a) Reconstructed motion path and multi-camera calibration. The cameras are visualized as pyramids. The spheres represent the motion path of the pink ball. The color of the ball is faded over time such that the most recent position has the highest saturation. The reconstructed motion path clearly shows the roughly 90° changes of the motion direction (front view) and the two depth levels (top view). Note, however, that the beginning of the sequence is not well reconstructed.

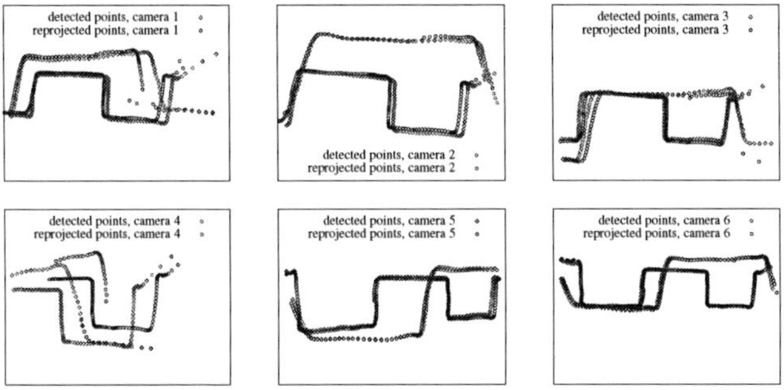

(b) Detected 2D motion paths for each camera and reprojections of the reconstructed 3D motion path.

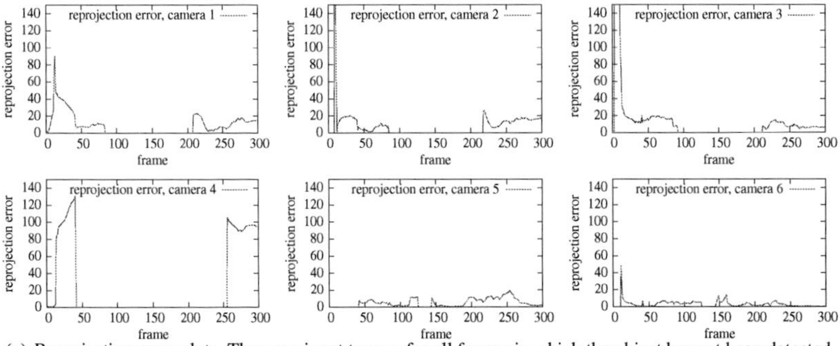

(c) Reprojection error plots. The error is set to zero for all frames in which the object has not been detected.

Figure 7.33: Reconstructed 3D motion path, detected and reprojected 2D motion paths, as well as reprojection errors for sequence 2. Note that camera 4 always has a very high reprojection error. This indicates that camera 4 is probably not well calibrated.

Chapter 8

Summary, Discussion and Future Work

In this final chapter, I will give a summary of this dissertation followed by a discussion of the results and ideas for future work.

8.1 Summary

In this dissertation, a multi-camera self-calibration method has been developed, which neither requires a calibration object nor any user interaction. Chapter 1 described the problem, its difficulty and relevance. An overview of existing approaches was given in Chapter 2. Established techniques for extracting point correspondences and estimating the relative pose of two cameras were described in the Chapters 3 and 4 along with some minor contributions. Chapter 5 was dedicated to intrinsic self-calibration of a rotating camera. The main contribution of this chapter consisted of algorithms for exploiting (partial) prior knowledge of the camera rotations. These methods are applicable to cameras mounted onto pan-tilt units.

The central contributions of this dissertation were presented in Chapter 6. As a whole, it described an extrinsic multi-camera calibration method, which only requires a single image from each camera along with its intrinsic parameters. It contains the following contributions:

- Three novel measures of the uncertainty of a relative pose estimate were presented along with a method for approximating them (Section 6.2).
- A criterion for selecting relative poses for extrinsic multi-camera self-calibration was formulated as a discrete optimization problem aiming to minimize the total uncertainty (Section 6.2).
- An efficient algorithm for solving the equivalent problem of finding shortest (i. e. minimum weight) triangle paths in a suitable graph was developed and its correctness has been proven (Section 6.4). This constitutes the main theoretical contribution of this dissertation.
- The precise differences between these contributions and the work by Vergés-Llahí et al. were analyzed (Section 6.5).

- As a complementary, supportive technique, a method for detecting camera pairs with a common field of view was developed and combined with the uncertainty-based selection of relative poses (Section 6.6).

Chapter 7 presented an extensive experimental evaluation of the methods described in this dissertation. In addition to evaluating all methods on real data with known ground truth, some details were analyzed using simulated data. A proof-of-concept 3D tracking system demonstrated the practical applicability of the self-calibration method. The appendix provided several basics and specific techniques from other fields as well as supplemental experimental evaluations.

8.2 Discussion of Experimental Results

Section 7.1 assessed the benefit of using partial rotation knowledge for intrinsic rotational self-calibration. The results on simulated data showed that using partial rotation knowledge reduces the influence of noise on the rotational self-calibration results. As in the simulation, completely known rotations also gave the best results on real data. However, the difference to all other cases of partial rotation knowledge is large—in contrast to the simulation results. Further analysis showed that this is due to severe systematic errors caused by radial distortion. Interestingly, the distortions do not seem to have a relevant influence in the case of using completely known rotations.

Section 7.2 compared established methods for estimating the relative pose of two cameras and assessed the associated minor contributions. As a consequence, the MLESAC algorithm based on the five-point algorithm and the Blake-Zisserman model was used for all subsequent experiments. Additionally, Section 7.2.3 analyzed my uncertainty measures on relative pose estimates. These experiments showed that my uncertainty measures are correlated with the error of the relative pose estimates. However, they also revealed that the correlation is rather low in the case of easy data. In other words, the uncertainty measures are good at distinguishing between good and bad relative pose estimates, but less reliable in the case of good versus very good estimates.

Section 7.3 was dedicated to multi-camera self-calibration using uncertainty-based selection of relative poses. The evaluation clearly showed that the uncertainty-based selection outperforms random and naive selection of relative poses. However, the difference between the mean and the median error revealed that not all cameras are always well calibrated. In practice, however, it often suffices if most cameras are well calibrated, as demonstrated by the proof-of-concept multi-camera object tracking application presented in Section 7.6.

Section 7.4 analyzed the new method for detecting camera pairs with a common field of view. It showed that the dedicated probabilistic methods clearly outperform the uncertainty measures on relative pose estimates and also an established technique (Snavely's method). They are particularly good in situations with ambiguities and a wide baseline. This indicates that soft point correspondences have the potential of outperforming classical point correspondences by avoiding hard decisions in ambiguous situations.

Section 7.5 evaluated the combination of common field of view detection and uncertainty-based multi-camera calibration. When using the entropy uncertainty measure, the combination gave an important improvement in one out of five setups only. On the other hand, random selection of relative poses clearly benefits from common field of view detection. Together these results show that the global criterion of the uncertainty-based selection of relative poses is very good and clearly better than the local common field of view criterion combined with random selection. However, the results of the global criterion can in some cases be improved by the local common field of view detection criterion. This may be due to the uncertainty measure sometimes failing to correctly distinguish between good and bad relative pose estimates. Furthermore, Section 7.5.2 showed that common field of view detection is well suited for automatically separating cameras in different rooms if there are no identical objects in different rooms.

The proof-of-concept multi-camera object tracking application presented in Section 7.6 demonstrated that the results of my multi-camera self-calibration method are well suited for reconstructing the 3D motion path of a moving object. However, it also revealed that there is still room for further improvement of the self-calibration method.

8.3 Future Work

The methods and results presented in this dissertation suggest several different opportunities for minor and also major future work. Rotational self-calibration is seriously flawed if the camera suffers from radial distortion. Even though completely known rotations seem to compensate for this problem, it appears desirable to integrate the estimation of radial distortion into rotational self-calibration with partial rotation knowledge. We have very recently described such a method showing results comparable to those in Section 7.1 (Brückner, Bajramovic and Denzler, 2011). The difference is that radial distortion is estimated as part of rotational self-calibration and *not* as a preliminary step based on a calibration pattern.

Furthermore, approximately known rotations could be exploited by formulating rotational self-calibration as an MAP estimation problem integrating the approximate prior knowledge. Certain additional constraints on rotations, like restrictions on the range of valid angles, could be integrated in the same way.

While my experiments on multi-camera self-calibration show that my uncertainty measures are well suited for uncertainty-based selection of relative poses, there are some aspects which are not satisfactory, yet. On the one hand, the approximate marginalization and discretization is not very elegant from a theoretical point of view. Using numeric integration e. g., might be an alternative. Recent attempts to approximate the uncertainty measures using a numeric integration library failed, however, indicating that this is not a simple problem.

Furthermore, the precision of the uncertainty measures in distinguishing between good and very good relative pose estimates is currently limited. Improving this aspect has the potential to further increase the precision of multi-camera self-calibration. Possible approaches are solving the problem mentioned in the previous paragraph and/or employing a more sophisticated sampling strategy like the one proposed by Goshen and Shimshoni (2006) to increase the "resolution" close to the optimum.

Each triangle of relative poses must be geometrically consistent (Läbe and Förstner, 2006). This aspect could be integrated into my multi-camera self-calibration method as an additional uncertainty measure (on triangles instead of individual relative poses). A cost function on triangles could be easily added to the shortest triangle path algorithm.

The way triangles are currently handled (scale estimation and concatenation of relative poses) could also be changed. One alternative would be to perform a 3D reconstruction for each camera pair and register the resulting 3D points as briefly described in Section 7.3. A similar approach has been described by Vergés-Llahí and Wada (2008). This alternative has the benefit of being able to handle collinear camera positions and might have the potential for higher accuracy. However, it requires knowing correspondences between more than two images (multi-correspondences).

Instead of restricting the uncertainty-based selection to subgraphs of shortest triangle paths as presented in Section 6.3, we could allow for arbitrary triangle-connected subgraphs spanning the whole camera dependency graph and select the one with minimum total uncertainty. The difference between these two possibilities is very similar to the difference between a minimum shortest paths tree and a minimum spanning tree. Using subgraphs of shortest triangle paths has the advantage that any error propagation possibly caused by concatenating relative poses is limited as triangle paths with fewer edges are usually preferred (depending on the edge weights). On the other hand, the alternative described in this paragraph might be able to select a subset of relative poses with a lower total uncertainty. Note, however, that a different optimization algorithm than the one described in Section 6.4 would be needed for this alternative.

The combination of common field of view detection and uncertainty-based selection of relative poses described in Section 6.6.4 is only a first step demonstrating that the two techniques can support each other. Additional work on finding a good threshold for common field of view detection in this context or even a more direct integration is necessary.

The experiments showed that sometimes not all cameras are well calibrated (Sections 7.3 and 7.6). While it is clearly desirable to improve the method in order to avoid such cases, this might not be possible in general due to the difficulty of the problem. In any case, additional information quantifying the reliability of the calibration of each camera would clearly be beneficial to the user. One possible approach could be using the total uncertainty of a shortest triangle path from the reference camera pair to each camera. Of course the suitability of this proposed measure still needs to be evaluated.

A classical approach for improving the accuracy of a 3D reconstruction and/or multi-camera calibration is known as bundle adjustment (Triggs et al., 1999). It should be investigated to which extent bundle adjustment can improve the precision of the calibration estimated by my multi-camera self-calibration method. While some work on this issue has been done already (Philips, 2009), the results are inconclusive and a more thorough evaluation is needed.

Most 3D computer vision techniques rely on point correspondences. Especially in a wide-baseline setup, however, state-of-the-art techniques have severe difficulties or even fail miserably (Figure 1.2). Apart from occlusions, the main problem arises from ambiguities of the interest point descriptors. As demonstrated by the common field of view measures and e. g. by Domke and Aloimonos (2006b), soft point correspondences (correspondence probabilities) might be a promising way of handling these ambiguities instead of making a hard, error prone decision early on in the pipeline. One possibility for integrating soft correspondences into the relative pose and uncertainty estimation methods presented in this dissertation may be to sample hard correspondences from the correspondence distribution as part of a new variant of the MLESAC algortihm.

Appendix A

Mathematical Background

In this part of the appendix, I briefly present some mathematical concepts, which are relevant to this dissertation: homogeneous coordinates, representations of 3D rotations, three different matrix decompositions, and methods for computing the roots of polynomials.

A.1 Homogeneous Coordinates

Homogeneous coordinates are commonly used in 3D computer vision. Probably the simplest approach is to think of homogeneous coordinates as a tool to elegantly express equality of vectors up to scale. While this is not the only advantage of homogeneous coordinates, it is – arguably – the most important and also the most obvious one.

For the sake of simplicity, I will first describe 2D homogeneous coordinates followed by a brief formal definition for the general n dimensional case. The main idea is to represent a 2D point by a vector in $\mathbb{R}^3$. Let

$$\begin{pmatrix} u \\ v \end{pmatrix} \in \mathbb{R}^2 \tag{A.1}$$

be a point in *Euclidean coordinates*. In homogeneous coordinates, it is represented by

$$\begin{pmatrix} u \\ v \\ 1 \end{pmatrix} \in \mathbb{P}^2 \tag{A.2}$$

or, more generally, by any

$$\begin{pmatrix} wu \\ wv \\ w \end{pmatrix} \in \mathbb{P}^2 \quad \text{with} \quad w \neq 0 \ , \tag{A.3}$$

where $\mathbb{P}^2$ denotes the set of 2D homogeneous points, which is also known as the *projective plane*.

Accordingly, given a point in homogeneous coordinates

$$\begin{pmatrix} u \\ v \\ w \end{pmatrix} \in \mathbb{P}^2 , \tag{A.4}$$

its Euclidean coordinates are

$$\begin{pmatrix} u/w \\ v/w \end{pmatrix} \in \mathbb{R}^2 \tag{A.5}$$

if $w \neq 0$. Otherwise, the point lies on the *line at infinity* and has no Euclidean representation. While this may appear to be a problem, it is actually the second most important advantage of homogeneous coordinates: the ability to express points at infinity as a direction vector.

Formally, the projective space $\mathbb{P}^n$ is defined as the quotient space of $\mathbb{R}^{n+1} \setminus \{\mathbf{0}\}$, i. e. the set of all equivalence classes, with respect to the equivalence relation $\cong$:

$$\mathbb{P}^n \stackrel{\text{def}}{=} (\mathbb{R}^{n+1} \setminus \{\mathbf{0}\})/_{\cong} . \tag{A.6}$$

The equivalence relation $\cong$ is defined as

$$\boldsymbol{p} \cong \boldsymbol{q} \Leftrightarrow \exists \lambda \in \mathbb{R} \setminus \{0\} : \boldsymbol{p} = \lambda \boldsymbol{q} \quad \text{for } \boldsymbol{p}, \boldsymbol{q} \in \mathbb{R}^{n+1} . \tag{A.7}$$

A point in homogeneous coordinates is formally an equivalence class, i. e. a set of vectors. Nevertheless, elements of $\mathbb{P}^n$ are represented by vectors in $\mathbb{R}^{n+1}$. e. g. it is common to write $(2, 3, 7)^\mathrm{T} \in \mathbb{P}^2$ instead of $[(2, 3, 7)^\mathrm{T}]_{\cong} \in \mathbb{P}^2$. Due to this simplification, using $=$ to denote equality in $\mathbb{P}^n$ leads to ambiguous notation. Instead, I will always use the symbol $\cong$ as in the following example:

$$\begin{pmatrix} 2 \\ 3 \\ 7 \end{pmatrix} \cong \begin{pmatrix} 4 \\ 6 \\ 14 \end{pmatrix} . \tag{A.8}$$

This can either be interpreted as equality in $\mathbb{P}^2$ or as equality up to scale in $\mathbb{R}^3$. In most situations, both interpretations are valid.

Despite points, lines can also be easily represented in homogeneous coordinates. In Euclidean coordinates, a line $\mathcal{L}$ can be defined by the following equation:

$$\begin{pmatrix} u \\ v \end{pmatrix} \in \mathcal{L} \quad \Leftrightarrow \quad au + bv + c = 0 , \tag{A.9}$$

where a, b, c are the parameters of the line. Written in vector form, we have

$$(a, b, c) \begin{pmatrix} u \\ v \\ 1 \end{pmatrix} = 0 \tag{A.10}$$

or equivalently

$$(a, b, c)\begin{pmatrix} wu \\ wv \\ w \end{pmatrix} = 0 \quad \text{for any } w \neq 0 \ . \tag{A.11}$$

Hence, a vector $\boldsymbol{l} \in \mathbb{P}^n$ represents a line $\mathcal{L}$ in the following sense:

$$\boldsymbol{p} \in \mathcal{L} \quad \Leftrightarrow \quad \boldsymbol{l}^{\mathrm{T}}\boldsymbol{p} = 0 \qquad \text{for } \boldsymbol{p} \in \mathbb{P}^n \ . \tag{A.12}$$

Note that calling elements of $\mathbb{P}^n$ vectors is not strictly correct, as $\mathbb{P}^n$ is not a vector space. It is quite common to do so, nevertheless.

A.2 Representation of 3D Rotations

There are several ways of representing rotations. After giving a short overview of some important representations with a focus on the three dimensional case (Section A.2), I will explain rotation vectors and the axis-angle representation (Section A.2.1) in more detail. Additionally, I will show how a special concatenation of three rotations influences the rotation axis of the second rotation (Section A.2.2).

Overview

Probably the best-known representation of an n-dimensional rotation is a *special orthogonal* $n \times n$ *matrix* $\boldsymbol{R}$, also simply known as a *rotation matrix* (Ma et al., 2004, Section 2.3):

Definition A.1 (rotation matrix) *A matrix* $\boldsymbol{R} \in \mathbb{R}^{n \times n}$ *is called* orthogonal matrix *iff* $\boldsymbol{R}\boldsymbol{R}^T = \boldsymbol{R}^T\boldsymbol{R} = \boldsymbol{I}$, *where* $\boldsymbol{I}$ *is the identity matrix. An orthogonal matrix* $\boldsymbol{R} \in \mathbb{R}^{n \times n}$ *is called* special orthogonal matrix *or* rotation matrix *iff* $\det(\boldsymbol{R}) = 1$.

Given a vector $\boldsymbol{x} \in \mathbb{R}^n$, its image under the rotation is given by the linear mapping

$$\boldsymbol{x} \rightarrow \boldsymbol{R}\boldsymbol{x} \ . \tag{A.13}$$

Three dimensional rotations can be represented by fewer than nine parameters (Ma et al., 2004, Section 2.3). A quite natural approach is to specify the *rotation axis* $\boldsymbol{v} \in \mathbb{R}^3$ with $||\boldsymbol{v}|| = 1$ and the *rotation angle* $\alpha \in \mathbb{R}$. To get a minimal representation, axis and angle can be encoded in one vector by setting $\boldsymbol{w} = \alpha\boldsymbol{v}$. This is known as *canonical exponential coordinates for rotations* or simply the *rotation vector*.

Euler angles are a further possibility for a minimal representation. They specify the angles of three consecutive rotations about three fixed axes, e. g. the Z, Y and X axes. However, this representation has a singularity known as the *gimbal lock*, which makes it less attractive for computer vision. A further, very popular representation uses a *unit quaternion*, which has four parameters.

A.2.1 Rotation Vector and Axis-Angle

A vector $\boldsymbol{w} \in \mathbb{R}^3$ can be used to represent a 3D rotation $\boldsymbol{R}$ as follows (Ma et al., 2004, Section 2.3), (Hartley and Zisserman, 2003, Appendix A4.3.2):

$$\boldsymbol{R} = \exp(\boldsymbol{w}) \ . \tag{A.14}$$

This representation $\boldsymbol{w}$ is known as the *rotation vector* (or *canonical exponential coordinates*). The matrix-valued exponential function can be more conveniently evaluated using *Rodrigues' formula*:

$$\exp(\boldsymbol{w}) = \mathrm{Rod}(\boldsymbol{w}) \stackrel{\text{def}}{=} \boldsymbol{I} + \frac{[\boldsymbol{w}]_\times}{||\boldsymbol{w}||} \sin(||\boldsymbol{w}||) + \frac{([\boldsymbol{w}]_\times)^2}{||\boldsymbol{w}||^2}(1 - \cos(||\boldsymbol{w}||)) \ , \tag{A.15}$$

where

$$[\boldsymbol{w}]_\times \stackrel{\text{def}}{=} \begin{pmatrix} 0 & -w_3 & w_2 \\ w_3 & 0 & -w_1 \\ -w_2 & w_1 & 0 \end{pmatrix} \quad \text{for} \quad \boldsymbol{w} = \begin{pmatrix} w_1 \\ w_2 \\ w_3 \end{pmatrix} \tag{A.16}$$

denotes the *skew symmetric matrix* of $\boldsymbol{w}$.

The closely related axis-angle representation separates the rotation axis $\boldsymbol{v} \in \mathbb{R}^3$ with $||\boldsymbol{v}|| = 1$ and the rotation angle $\alpha \in \mathbb{R}$. The according rotation vector is hence

$$\boldsymbol{w} = \alpha \boldsymbol{v} \ . \tag{A.17}$$

I denote the according rotation matrix by

$$\mathrm{Rod}(\boldsymbol{v}, \alpha) \stackrel{\text{def}}{=} \mathrm{Rod}(\alpha \boldsymbol{v}) \ . \tag{A.18}$$

In this case, Rodrigues' formula can be written in the following simpler form:

$$\mathrm{Rod}(\boldsymbol{v}, \alpha) = \boldsymbol{I} + [\boldsymbol{v}]_\times \sin(\alpha) + ([\boldsymbol{v}]_\times)^2(1 - \cos(\alpha)) \tag{A.19}$$

Conversion from Rotation Matrix to Axis-Angle and Rotation Vector

Each rotation matrix can be represented by a rotation vector $\boldsymbol{w}$ or a rotation axis $\boldsymbol{v}$ and an angle α (Ma et al., 2004, Theorem 2.8), even though the representation is not unique (e. g. the angle is periodic). Given a rotation matrix $\boldsymbol{R}$, the axis $\boldsymbol{v}$ and the angle α can be computed as follows (Ma et al., 2004, proof of Theorem 2.8). First, compute the angle

$$\alpha = \arccos\left(\frac{\mathrm{trace}(\boldsymbol{R}) - 1}{2}\right) \ . \tag{A.20}$$

For the axis, distinguish the following cases:

- If α is not a multiple of π (i. e. $\sin(\alpha) \neq 0$):

$$v = \frac{1}{2\sin(\alpha)} \begin{pmatrix} r_{32} - r_{23} \\ r_{13} - r_{31} \\ r_{21} - r_{12} \end{pmatrix} . \tag{A.21}$$

- If $\sin(\alpha) = 0 \wedge \cos(\alpha) = 1$, $\boldsymbol{R}$ is the identity. Set $\boldsymbol{v} = 0$.
- Otherwise ($\sin(\alpha) = 0 \wedge \cos(\alpha) = -1$), first determine the entries of $\boldsymbol{v}$ up to signs:

$$v = \frac{1}{\sqrt{2}} \begin{pmatrix} \pm\sqrt{r_{11} + 1} \\ \pm\sqrt{r_{22} + 1} \\ \pm\sqrt{r_{33} + 1} \end{pmatrix} . \tag{A.22}$$

As the overall sign of $\boldsymbol{v} = (v_1, v_2, v_3)^{\mathrm{T}}$ is arbitrary, choose the sign of one non-zero entry and compute the remaining signs accordingly:

  - If $v_1 \neq 0$:

$$\begin{aligned} \mathrm{sign}(v_1) &= 1 \\ \mathrm{sign}(v_2) &= \mathrm{sign}(r_{12}) \\ \mathrm{sign}(v_3) &= \mathrm{sign}(r_{13}) \ . \end{aligned} \tag{A.23}$$

  - If $v_1 = 0 \neq v_2$:

$$\begin{aligned} \mathrm{sign}(v_2) &= 1 \\ \mathrm{sign}(v_3) &= \mathrm{sign}(r_{23}) \ . \end{aligned} \tag{A.24}$$

  - If $v_1 = v_2 = 0 \neq v_3$:

$$\mathrm{sign}(v_3) = 1 \ . \tag{A.25}$$

Note that $\boldsymbol{v} = \boldsymbol{0}$ is impossible in this case ($\boldsymbol{R}$ would be the identity, see the previous case). Also note that this case is not constructively handled by Ma et al. (2004), but it is easy to see that the formulas are correct by looking at $\mathrm{Rod}(\boldsymbol{v}, \alpha)$.

In order to compute the rotation vector given a rotation matrix, simply combine the above results according to equation (A.17).

A.2.2 Rotating the Rotation Axis

In the section, I will present a simple proposition and corollary regarding a special concatenation of three rotations, which can be interpreted as rotating the axis of a single rotation. Probably, the resulting two equations are known in the literature. Lacking a suitable reference, however, I will present my own proofs.

Proposition A.2 *Let $\boldsymbol{R}$ be a rotation matrix and $\boldsymbol{w} \in \mathbb{R}^3$ be a rotation vector. Then the following equation holds:*

$$\boldsymbol{R}\mathrm{Rod}(\boldsymbol{w})\boldsymbol{R}^{\mathrm{T}} = \mathrm{Rod}(\boldsymbol{R}\boldsymbol{w}) \ . \tag{A.26}$$

Proof: The following Maple™ code proves the equation:

```
with(LinearAlgebra);
Rod2 := proc (v, a) local x, y, z; x := v[1]; y := v[2]; z := v[3]; \
  Matrix([[cos(a)+x*x*(1-cos(a)), x*y*(1-cos(a))-z*sin(a),           \
    y*sin(a)+x*z*(1-cos(a))],                                          \
  [z*sin(a)+x*y*(1-cos(a)), cos(a)+y*y*(1-cos(a)),                     \
    -x*sin(a)+y*z*(1-cos(a))],                                         \
  [-y*sin(a)+x*z*(1-cos(a)), x*sin(a)+y*z*(1-cos(a)),                  \
  cos(a)+z*z*(1-cos(a))]]) end proc;
Norm2 := proc (v) sqrt(v[1]^2+v[2]^2+v[3]^2) end proc;
Rod1 := proc (w) local a, v; a := Norm2(w, 2); v := Multiply(w, 1/a); \
  Rod2(v, a) end proc;
R := Rod1(<rx, ry, rz>);
simplify(MatrixAdd(Multiply(Multiply(R, Rod2(<x,y,z>,a)), Transpose(R)), \
  Multiply(Rod2(Multiply(R, <x,y,z>),a),-1)));
```

In the code, Rod1 and Rod2 correspond to the one and two parameter variants of Rod. The last command symbolically (!) evaluates to zero and thus proves the equation. □

Corollary A.3 *Let $\boldsymbol{R}$ be a rotation matrix, $\boldsymbol{v} \in \mathbb{R}^3$ with $\|\boldsymbol{v}\| = 1$ be a rotation axis, and $\alpha \in \mathbb{R}$ be an angle. Then the following equation holds:*

$$\boldsymbol{R}\mathrm{Rod}(\boldsymbol{v}, \alpha)\boldsymbol{R}^{\mathrm{T}} = \mathrm{Rod}(\boldsymbol{R}\boldsymbol{v}, \alpha) \ . \tag{A.27}$$

Proof:

$$\boldsymbol{R}\mathrm{Rod}(\boldsymbol{v}, \alpha)\boldsymbol{R}^{\mathrm{T}} = \boldsymbol{R}\mathrm{Rod}(\alpha\boldsymbol{v})\boldsymbol{R}^{\mathrm{T}} \underset{\text{Proposition}}{=} \mathrm{Rod}(\boldsymbol{R}(\alpha\boldsymbol{v})) = \mathrm{Rod}(\alpha\boldsymbol{R}\boldsymbol{v}) \underset{\|\boldsymbol{R}\boldsymbol{v}\|=1}{=} \mathrm{Rod}(\boldsymbol{R}\boldsymbol{v}, \alpha) \ . \tag{A.28}$$

The condition $\|\boldsymbol{R}\boldsymbol{v}\| = 1$ is fulfilled, because $\|\boldsymbol{v}\| = 1$ and $\boldsymbol{R}$ is a rotation matrix. □

A.3 Singular Value Decomposition

The *singular value decomposition* is a numerical tool that can be used for several different tasks. In this section, I will briefly describe the decomposition and certain applications, which are needed in this dissertation. For further details, the reader is referred to the literature (Gill et al., 1998, Section 5.6), (Press et al., 1994, Section 2.6), (Hartley and Zisserman, 2003, Appendix A4.4), (Trucco and Verri, 1998, Appendix A.6). Note that I will not discuss how the singular value decomposition can actually be computed. A nontrivial numerical algorithm is required for this task (Press et al., 1994, Section 2.6). In practice, however, we can simply use a library function.

Let $\boldsymbol{A} \in \mathbb{R}^{m\times n}$ with $m \geq n$ be a matrix. Its singular value decomposition is

$$\boldsymbol{A} = \boldsymbol{U}\mathrm{diag}_{m\times n}(\boldsymbol{s})\boldsymbol{V}^{\mathrm{T}} \ , \tag{A.29}$$

where $\boldsymbol{U} \in \mathbb{R}^{m\times m}$ and $\boldsymbol{V} \in \mathbb{R}^{n\times n}$ are rotation matrices (see Definition A.1), $\boldsymbol{s} \in \mathbb{R}^n$ is a vector containing the nonnegative singular values, and $\mathrm{diag}_{m\times n}(\cdot)$ denotes an $m \times n$ diagonal matrix. The singular values in the vector $\boldsymbol{s} = (s_1, \ldots, s_n)$ are required to be in descending order, i. e. $s_1 \geq \ldots \geq s_n \geq 0$. As the size of the diagonal matrix is usually clear from the context, I write diag instead of $\mathrm{diag}_{m\times n}$. Note that computing the singular value decomposition has a time complexity of $O(n^3)$.

Enforcing Singular Values

Suppose we have computed an estimate $\boldsymbol{A}$ for a matrix $\boldsymbol{A}_{\mathrm{ideal}}$. Further suppose that the matrix $\boldsymbol{A}_{\mathrm{ideal}}$ has to fulfill constraints, which can be expressed in terms of its singular values. The singular value decomposition can be used to compute an approximation to $\boldsymbol{A}$ that has certain singular values (Trucco and Verri, 1998, Appendix A.6). Let $\boldsymbol{A} = \boldsymbol{U}\mathrm{diag}(\boldsymbol{s})\boldsymbol{V}^{\mathrm{T}}$ be the singular valued decomposition of the matrix $\boldsymbol{A}$. Then the approximation $\boldsymbol{A}'$ with minimal Frobenius distance to $\boldsymbol{A}$ having singular values $\boldsymbol{s}'$ is given by

$$\boldsymbol{A}' = \boldsymbol{U}\mathrm{diag}(\boldsymbol{s}')\boldsymbol{V}^{\mathrm{T}} \ . \tag{A.30}$$

Rank Enforcement

Let the rank of the matrix $\boldsymbol{A}$ be $r = \mathrm{rank}(\boldsymbol{A})$. By enforcing that the smallest singular values are zero, i. e.

$$\boldsymbol{s}' = (s_1, \ldots, s_{r'}, 0, \ldots, 0)^{\mathrm{T}} \ , \tag{A.31}$$

we can compute an approximation $\boldsymbol{A}'$ to $\boldsymbol{A}$ with a certain rank $r' \leq r$.

Orthogonalization

Orthogonalization is a further application of enforcing singular values. Given a square matrix $\boldsymbol{A}$, we compute a rotation matrix $\boldsymbol{R}$ as an approximation with minimal Frobenius distance as follows:

$$\boldsymbol{R} = \boldsymbol{U}\mathrm{diag}(1, \ldots, 1)\boldsymbol{V}^{\mathrm{T}} \ . \tag{A.32}$$

Null Space

Let the rank of the matrix $\boldsymbol{A}$ be $r = \text{rank}(\boldsymbol{A})$. Then its (right) null space has dimension $(n - r)$. The (right) *null space* of a matrix $\boldsymbol{A}$ consists of all vectors $\boldsymbol{x}$ such that

$$\boldsymbol{A}\boldsymbol{x} = \boldsymbol{0} \ . \tag{A.33}$$

An orthonormal basis of that null space is given by the last $(n - r)$ columns of $\boldsymbol{V}$.

Now suppose that the rank of $\boldsymbol{A}$ is actually larger than r (e. g. because it was computed from noisy data), but we nevertheless want to compute an approximation to the null space with $(n - r)$ dimensions. This is typically the case if, from a theoretical point of view, $\boldsymbol{A}$ must have rank r, but actually has higher rank due to noise. The procedure described above gives a least squares approximation with respect to the result being an orthonormal system. In the one dimensional case (i. e. $n-r = 1$) this means "with respect to $\|\boldsymbol{x}\| = 1$" (Trucco and Verri, 1998, Appendix A.6). You can also think of this procedure as first enforcing that the rank of $\boldsymbol{A}$ is r and then taking the last $(n - r)$ columns of $\boldsymbol{V}$ (which is unaffected by the rank enforcement).

A.4 Cholesky Decomposition

The *Cholesky decomposition* is a specialized decomposition of symmetric, positive definite matrices. In this section, I will briefly describe the decomposition and show how it can be applied to solve suitable inhomogeneous equation systems. For further details, the reader is referred to the literature (Gill et al., 1998, Section 4.9.2), (Conn et al., 2000, Section 4.3.3). Note that I will not discuss how the Cholesky decomposition can actually be computed. In practice, we can simply use a library function.

Let $\boldsymbol{A} \in \mathbb{R}^{n \times n}$ be a symmetric (i. e. $\boldsymbol{A} = \boldsymbol{A}^{\mathrm{T}}$), positive definite (i. e. $\forall \boldsymbol{v} \neq 0 : \boldsymbol{v}^{\mathrm{T}}\boldsymbol{A}\boldsymbol{v} > 0$) matrix. Its Cholesky decomposition is defined as follows:

$$\boldsymbol{A} = \boldsymbol{L}\boldsymbol{L}^{\mathrm{T}} \ , \tag{A.34}$$

where $\boldsymbol{L} = (l_{ij})_{1 \leq i,j \leq n}$ denotes a quadratic lower triangle matrix, i. e. $l_{ij} = 0$ for all $i < j$. The matrix $\boldsymbol{L}$ is called *Cholesky factor*. Note, however, that some authors define the Cholesky factor as $\boldsymbol{L}^{\mathrm{T}}$ instead of $\boldsymbol{L}$. The decomposition is unique up to the signs of the columns of $\boldsymbol{L}$. Computing the Cholesky decomposition has a time complexity of $O(n^3)$.

Test for Positive Definiteness

The Cholesky decomposition can be used to test whether a given symmetric matrix $\boldsymbol{A}$ is positive definite. If $\boldsymbol{A}$ is not positive definite, the Cholesky decomposition is not defined and the decomposition algorithm will fail. Accordingly, if the decomposition succeeds, $\boldsymbol{A}$ is positive definite.

Solving an Inhomogeneous Equation System

The Cholesky decomposition can be used to solve a homogeneous equation system

$$\boldsymbol{A}\boldsymbol{x} = \boldsymbol{b} \tag{A.35}$$

if the matrix $\boldsymbol{A}$ is symmetric and suchpositive definite (Gill et al., 1998, Section 4.3.3). First, compute the Cholesky decomposition as in equation (A.34). Then we have

$$\boldsymbol{L}\boldsymbol{L}^{\mathrm{T}}\boldsymbol{x} = \boldsymbol{b} \ . \tag{A.36}$$

Using the definition

$$\boldsymbol{c} \overset{\text{def}}{=} \boldsymbol{L}^{\mathrm{T}}\boldsymbol{x} \ , \tag{A.37}$$

we get

$$\boldsymbol{L}\boldsymbol{c} = \boldsymbol{b} \ . \tag{A.38}$$

As $\boldsymbol{L}$ is a lower triangle matrix, $\boldsymbol{c}$ can be computed line by line starting with the first one (Gill et al., 1998, Section 4.2.2). Afterwards, we use equation (A.37) to compute $\boldsymbol{x}$ line by line starting with the last one.

A.5 Eigenvalues, Eigenvectors, and Eigendecomposition

Eigenvalues and eigenvectors are a quite broad mathematical topic. In this section, however, I will only introduce concepts relevant to this dissertation. For further information, the reader is referred to the literature (Strang, 1993, Chapter 6), (Press et al., 1994, Chapter 11), (Golub and van Loan, 1996, Chapter 7). In particular, I will not discuss how eigenvalues and eigenvectors can be computed. Note that there are dedicated algorithms for certain special cases, like symmetric matrices, or for computing only the smallest eigenvalue. In practice, there are library functions for most cases, which can be easily used.

Let $\boldsymbol{A} \in \mathbb{R}^{n \times n}$ be a square matrix. Consider the following equation:

$$\boldsymbol{A}\boldsymbol{v} = \lambda\boldsymbol{v} \ . \tag{A.39}$$

Any solution $\lambda \in \mathbb{C}, \boldsymbol{v} \in \mathbb{C}^n \setminus \{\boldsymbol{0}\}$ to that equation is called an *eigenpair*. It consists of the *eigenvalue* λ and the *eigenvector* $\boldsymbol{v}$. If the matrix $\boldsymbol{A}$ is symmetric, all eigenvalues and eigenvectors are real. Note that most eigenvalue and eigenvector problems have a time complexity of $O(n^3)$.

Enforcing Eigenvalues

Enforcing eigenvalues is quite similar to enforcing singular values (see above). For this task, we need the *eigendecomposition* of a square matrix $\boldsymbol{A}$, which is also known as matrix diagonalization (Strang, 1993, Section 6.2). It is defined as follows:

$$\boldsymbol{A} = \boldsymbol{Q}\mathrm{diag}(\lambda_1, \ldots, \lambda_n)\boldsymbol{Q}^{-1} \ , \tag{A.40}$$

where the columns of the matrix $\boldsymbol{Q}$ are the eigenvectors of $\boldsymbol{A}$. Note that the eigendecomposition is not necessarily defined. This is the case if there are not enough linearly independent eigenvectors. If $\boldsymbol{A}$ is real and symmetric or has exactly n distinct eigenvalues, however, the eigendecomposition is guaranteed to exist. Also note that if $\boldsymbol{A}$ is not real and symmetric, the eigenvalues and the matrix $\boldsymbol{Q}$ are in general complex.

In order to enforce that a given square matrix $\boldsymbol{A}$ has the eigenvalues $\lambda'_1, \ldots, \lambda'_n$, we replace it by the matrix

$$\boldsymbol{A}' = \boldsymbol{Q}\operatorname{diag}(\lambda'_1, \ldots, \lambda'_n)\boldsymbol{Q}^{-1} \ . \tag{A.41}$$

A.6 Companion Matrix

In this section, I will present a method for computing the roots of a single univariate polynomial

$$f : x \to \sum_{i=0}^{n} m_i x^i \ , \tag{A.42}$$

where $m_i \in \mathbb{C}$ for $0 \leq i \leq n$ and $m_n \neq 0$. A value $x \in \mathbb{C}$ is called a *root* of f iff $f(x) = 0$. The companion matrix of f is defined as (Cox et al., 2005, Chapter 3, Exercise 11)

$$\boldsymbol{C}_f \stackrel{\text{def}}{=} (c_{jk})_{1 \leq j,k \leq n} \quad \text{with } c_{jk} \stackrel{\text{def}}{=} \begin{cases} -m_{n-k}/m_n & \text{if } j = 1 \\ 1 & \text{if } j > 1 \wedge j = k+1 \\ 0 & \text{otherwise} \ , \end{cases} \tag{A.43}$$

which can also be written as

$$\boldsymbol{C}_f = \begin{pmatrix} -m_{n-1}/m_n & -m_{n-2}/m_n & \ldots & -m_1/m_n & -m_0/m_n \\ 1 & & & & 0 \\ & 1 & & & 0 \\ & & \ddots & & \vdots \\ & & & 1 & 0 \end{pmatrix} . \tag{A.44}$$

The eigenvalues of $\boldsymbol{C}_f$ are identical with the roots of f in $\mathbb{C}$ (Cox et al., 2005, Chapter 2, Corollary 4.6). Note that Cox et al. (2005) define the companion matrix as $\boldsymbol{C}_f^{\mathrm{T}}$ even though they state that $\boldsymbol{C}_f$ is more common. As the eigenvalues of $\boldsymbol{C}_f$ and $\boldsymbol{C}_f^{\mathrm{T}}$ are identical, this difference is irrelevant in this context.

Obviously, the same method can be used to find the (complex) roots of a polynomial with coefficients $m_i \in \mathbb{R}, 0 \leq i \leq n$. The real-valued roots of f can also be determined, as they equal the real-valued eigenvalues of $\boldsymbol{C}_f$.

A.7 Gröbner Bases

Gröbner bases are a non-trivial mathematical tool from the area of computer algebra. They are useful for computing the common roots of a set of multivariate polynomials. In this dissertation, they are used as part of the five-point algorithm (Section 4.2.4). As the theory of Gröbner bases is somewhat complicated and actually not needed in order to implement or basically understand the five-point algorithm, I will only very briefly present the main idea. For further details, the reader is referred to the literature, e. g. (Weispfenning and Becker, 1998; Cox et al., 2005).

The common roots of a set of *univariate* polynomials equal the roots of their greatest common divisor, i. e. a single polynomial. Hence, by computing the greatest common divisor (using, e. g. the efficient Euclidean algorithm), the problem of finding the common roots of a set of polynomials can be reduced to finding the roots of a single polynomial. In the case of multivariate polynomials, however, a reduction to a single polynomial is in general not possible. In a way, (reduced) Gröbner bases are the multivariate generalization of the greatest common divisor.

A Gröbner basis is a set of multivariate polynomials, which is defined with respect to the original set of multivariate polynomials and a so called term order, which can be chosen quite arbitrarily. The actual definition of a Gröbner basis is rather complicated and not needed for a rough description. Their most important property is that the polynomials in the Gröbner basis have the same common roots as the original set.

Given a set of multivariate polynomials, the Buchberger algorithm can be used to compute a Gröbner basis. In general, however, this algorithm has a high time complexity. In special situations, however, there are more efficient alternatives. In the case of the five-point algorithm, e. g. a Gauss-Jordan elimination of a suitably defined coefficient matrix suffices (see Section 4.2.4).

Once a Gröbner basis with respect to a suitable term order has been computed, it can be used to find the common roots of the original set of polynomials. This can be accomplished, e. g. by constructing the action matrix of a certain linear mapping. The eigenvectors of this matrix equal the common roots of the original polynomial system.

A.8 Box Plots

A box plot (Figure A.1), as proposed by Tukey (1977), compactly visualizes the distribution of univariate data. It consists of a (blue) box depicting the lower quartile (i. e. the 0.25 quantile $q_{0.25}$) and the upper quartile (i. e. the 0.75 quantile $q_{0.75}$). The box is divided by a (red) line representing the median (i. e. the 0.5 quantile $q_{0.5}$). The spread of the data outside of the range between the lower and upper quartiles (i. e. outside of the box) is indicated by two lines and circles for outliers as follows. A line is drawn from the bottom of the box to the extreme data point below the lower quartile but with a maximum distance of $1.5r_{\text{iq}}$ from the lower quartile, where $r_{\text{iq}} = q_{0.75} - q_{0.25}$ denotes the interquartile range (i. e. the height of the box). An according line is drawn above the box. Data points outside of the range $[q_{0.25} - r_{\text{iq}}, q_{0.75} + r_{\text{iq}}]$ (covered by the box and the lines) are considered to be outliers. They are visualized by (red) crosses. An annotated example is given in Figure A.1, left.

There is also a more compact variant of box plots, which is useful for arranging many box plots next to each other. Instead of the box, there is a (blue) narrow bar. The median is indicated by a (blue) circle containing a (black) dot. Outliers are visualized by small (blue) circles. An annotated example is given in Figure A.1, right.

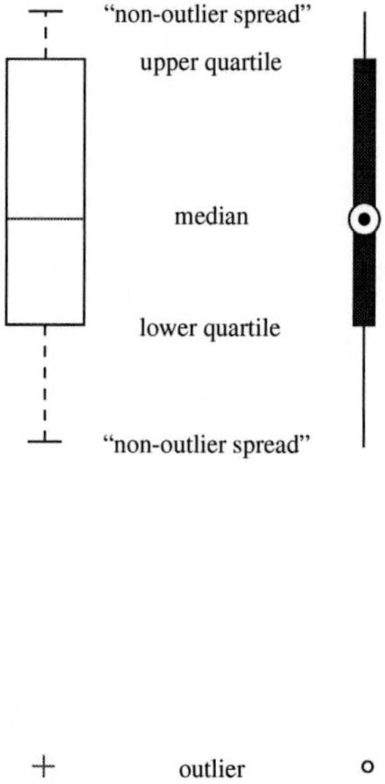

Figure A.1: Examples of box plots in normal (left) and compact style (right) visualizing the same data.

Appendix B

Graph Algorithms

In this appendix, I will describe two well known graph algorithms, which are used in Chapter 6: breadth first search and Dijkstra's shortest paths algorithm. I will only give a brief description of the algorithms, assuming familiarity with basic graph theoretic concepts (like vertices, edges, paths, etc.). For further details or a general introduction, the reader is referred to the literature (Cormen et al., 2001; Sedgewick, 1988). Note that I will formulate all algorithms for directed graphs $\mathcal{G} = (\mathcal{V}(\mathcal{G}), \mathcal{E}(\mathcal{G}))$, where $\mathcal{V}(\mathcal{G})$ denotes the vertices and $\mathcal{E}(\mathcal{G})$ the edges of $\mathcal{G}$. An undirected graph can simply be interpreted as a bidirectional graph.

B.1 Breadth First Search and Connected Components

Breadth first search (BFS) (Cormen et al., 2001, Section 22.2), (Sedgewick, 1988, Chapter 29) is an algorithm for traversing a graph, i. e. visiting all of its vertices by moving along its edges. It uses a simple data structure called *queue* (Cormen et al., 2001, Section 10.1), (Sedgewick, 1988, Chapter 3), which supports the following operations:

1. Create an empty queue.
2. Check if the queue is empty.
3. Insert an element at the back of the queue (`insert`).
4. Retrieve and remove the element at the front of the queue (`get`), i. e. the oldest (remaining) element inserted by the `insert` operation.

Pseudocode for breadth first search is given in Algorithm B.1.

In case of a bidirectional (or undirected) graph, breadth first search can be used to detect the connected components (Cormen et al., 2001, Appendix B.4), (Sedgewick, 1988, Chapter 30). A *connected compontent* consists of all vertices, which are pairwisely connected by a path, i. e. a sequence of subsequently adjacent vertices. Algorithm B.1 (optionally) assigns a component ID to each vertex and counts the connected components. Two vertices are in the same connected component iff there component IDs are equal. A graph is called *connected* iff it has at most one connected component. Obviously, this property is also checked by Algorithm B.1.

Algorithm B.1 Breadth first search and (optional) detection of connected components.

Input: a graph $\mathcal{G}$ (for detecting connected components, $\mathcal{G}$ must be bidirectional)
Ensure: each vertex is visited allowing for optional additional processing
Output: the number of connected components i ▹ only for connected components
Output: a connected component ID $c(v)$ for each vertex v ▹ only for connected components
Set $i := 0$ ▹ only for connected components
Create an empty queue Q
for all vertices $v \in \mathcal{V}(\mathcal{G})$ **do**
    Set $t(v) :=$ false ▹ mark v as "untouched"
for all vertices $v \in \mathcal{V}(\mathcal{G})$ **do**
    if not $t(v)$ **then** ▹ v has not yet been "touched" by the algorithm
        $i := i + 1$ ▹ start a new component ▹ only for connected components
        `Insert` v into the queue Q and set $t(v) =$ true
        while the queue Q is not empty **do**
            `Get` the element u from the front of the queue Q
            Set $c(u) = i$ ▹ u is in component number i ▹ only for connected components
            Optionally perform any operations in the event of "visiting the vertex u"
            for all $(u, w) \in \mathcal{E}(\mathcal{G})$ **do** ▹ for all adjacent vertices w
                if not $t(w)$ **then** ▹ w has not yet been "touched" by the algorithm
                    `insert` w into the queue Q and set $t(w) =$ true

B.2 Dijkstra's Shortest Paths Algorithm

Dijkstra's algorithm (Cormen et al., 2001, Section 24.3), (Sedgewick, 1988, Chapter 31) solves the *single source shortest paths problem* in a non-negatively edge-weighted, directed graph $\mathcal{G}$. Such a graph has a function $w : \mathcal{E}(\mathcal{G}) \to [0, \infty[$, which specifies the edges weights (or "lengths"). Let $\mathcal{P} = (v_1, \ldots, v_k)$ with $(v_i, v_{i+1}) \in \mathcal{E}(\mathcal{G})$ for all $1 \le i < k$ be a path from v_1 to v_k in $\mathcal{G}$. The *length* (or more generally *cost*) $w(\mathcal{P})$ of the path $\mathcal{P}$ is defined as the sum of the weights of all its edges:

$$w(\mathcal{P}) \stackrel{\text{def}}{=} \sum_{i=1}^{k-1} w(v_i, v_{i+1}) \ . \tag{B.1}$$

The single source shortest paths problem consists of finding a shortest path from a given start vertex s to each other vertex t. A path $\mathcal{P}$ from s to t is called a *shortest path* (or minimum cost path) iff there is no other path $\mathcal{P}'$ from s to t with shorter length (lower cost), i. e. $w(\mathcal{P}') < w(\mathcal{P})$.

Dijkstra's algorithm for solving the single source shortest paths problem is presented in Algorithm B.2. It uses a data structure called *priority queue* (Cormen et al., 2001, Section 6.5), (Sedgewick, 1988, Chapter 11), which supports the following operations:

1. Create a priority queue from a set $\mathcal{V}$ with weights $d : \mathcal{V} \to \mathbb{R}$.

2. Check if the priority queue is empty.

Algorithm B.2 Dijkstra's shortest paths algorithm.

Input: a graph $\mathcal{G}$ with non-negative edge weights $w : \mathcal{E}(\mathcal{G}) \to [0, \infty[$
Input: a start vertex $s \in \mathcal{V}(\mathcal{G})$
Output: for each $v \in \mathcal{V}(\mathcal{G})$: the length $d(v)$ of a shortest path from s to v
Output: for each $v \in \mathcal{V}(\mathcal{G})$: the predecessor $p(v)$ within the computed shortest path from s to v

```
for all vertices v ∈ V(G) do
    Set u(v) := true                                   ▷ mark v as undone
    if v = s then                                      ▷ initialize the distance d(v) of v from s
        Set d(v) := 0
    else
        Set d(v) := ∞
Create the priority queue Q from V(G) with weights d
p(s) := nil                                            ▷ s has no predecessor
while Q is not empty do
    Extract the minimum element v from Q
    Set u(v) := false                                  ▷ we are done with v
    for all (v, v′) ∈ E(G) do                          ▷ for all adjacent vertices v′
        if u(v′) then                                  ▷ is v′ undone?
            if d(v) + w(v, v′) < d(v′) then            ▷ found a shorter path to v′?
                Set d(v′) := d(v) + w(v, v′)           ▷ update the distance
                Set p(v′) := v                         ▷ update the predecessor
                Update the weight of v′ to d(v′) in Q  ▷ update the priority queue
```

3. Retrieve and remove the element v with minimum weight $d(v)$ within the priority queue (`extract`).

4. Change the weight $d(v)$ of an element v of the priority queue (`update`).

There are several possibilities for implementing a priority queue. The practically most relevant implementation (in the context of Dijkstra's algorithm) uses a so called heap (Cormen et al., 2001, Section 6.1), (Sedgewick, 1988, Chapter 11). This leads to a total running time of Dijkstra's algorithm of $O((n + m) \log n)$, where $n = |\mathcal{V}(\mathcal{G})|$ and $m = |\mathcal{E}(\mathcal{G})|$. Theoretically, using a Fibonacci heap (Cormen et al., 2001, Chapter 20) instead of a heap improves the running time to $O(n \log n + m)$ (Cormen et al., 2001, Section 24.3). In practice, however, the constant overhead of Fibonacci heaps is so huge, that the heap variant of Dijkstra's algorithm is more efficient.

Appendix C

Nonlinear Optimization Algorithms

In this chapter, I will present two nonlinear optimization algorithms: a trust-region algorithm (Section C.1) and the Levenberg-Marquardt algorithm (Section C.2). In both cases, the task is to minimize an *objective function*

$$f : \mathbb{R}^d \to \mathbb{R} \ , \tag{C.1}$$

which is required to be twice continuously differentiable. Expressed in a formula, we want to solve

$$\operatorname*{argmin}_{\boldsymbol{x} \in \mathbb{R}^d} f(\boldsymbol{x}) \ . \tag{C.2}$$

Both algorithms iteratively compute a sequence of points $\left(\boldsymbol{x}^{(k)}\right)_{k \geq 0}$. The upper index k denotes the iteration. We require that the sequence $\left(f(\boldsymbol{x}^{(k)})\right)_{k \geq 0}$ decreases monotonically, i. e.

$$f\left(\boldsymbol{x}^{(k+1)}\right) \leq f\left(\boldsymbol{x}^{(k)}\right) \quad \text{for all } k \geq 0 \ . \tag{C.3}$$

If the sequence $\left(\boldsymbol{x}^{(k)}\right)_{k \geq 0}$ converges, its limit is the result of the algorithm. Indeed, under certain mild conditions, both algorithms can be proved to converge to a local minimum of the objective function. Which local minimum is found, however, depends on the initialization $\boldsymbol{x}^{(0)}$. There is, in general, no guarantee that it will be the global minimum. For further details and the actual proofs, the reader is referred to the literature (Conn et al., 2000; Nocedal and Wright, 1999).

The term *trust-region method* refers to a whole class of nonlinear optimization algorithms. The main aspect is that they operate within a so called *trust-region*, which is typically defined as a hypersphere around the current point $\boldsymbol{x}^{(k)}$ with a certain *trust-region radius* $\Delta^{(k)}$. Further details will be given in Section C.1. Note that the Levenberg-Marquardt algorithm can also be interpreted as a trust-region method (see Section C.2). Hence, I will first describe the idea behind trust-region methods and present one specific, explicit trust-region algorithm, before I present the Levenberg-Marquardt algorithm—even though the latter is older than the modern trust-region concept and also simpler than the trust-region algorithm in Section C.1.

C.1 A Trust-Region Algorithm

In this section, I will present one specific, explicit trust-region algorithm. I have already used this algorithm in my diploma thesis. This section is hence mostly a translation of (Bajramovic, 2004, Section 2.2). A thorough introduction to trust regions methods is given by Conn et al. (2000). A brief one can, e. g. be found in (Nocedal and Wright, 1999; Alt, 2002).

C.1.1 Main Idea

I will begin by giving an overview of how the points $\boldsymbol{x}^{(k)}$ are computed. At each iteration k, we use a model

$$m^{(k)} : \mathbb{R}^d \to \mathbb{R} \ , \tag{C.4}$$

to approximate the objective function f within the so called *trust-region*

$$\mathcal{B}^{(k)} = \left\{ \boldsymbol{x} \in \mathbb{R}^d \;\middle|\; \left\|\boldsymbol{x} - \boldsymbol{x}^{(k)}\right\| \le \Delta^{(k)} \right\} \ , \tag{C.5}$$

where $\|\cdot\|$ denotes the Euclidean norm in $\mathbb{R}^d$ and $\Delta^{(k)} > 0$ is the current *trust-region radius*.

Starting at the point $\boldsymbol{x}^{(k)}$, we compute a *step* $\boldsymbol{s}^{(k)}$ with respect to

$$\boldsymbol{x}^{(k)} + \boldsymbol{s}^{(k)} \in \mathcal{B}^{(k)} \ , \tag{C.6}$$

or equivalently,

$$\|\boldsymbol{s}^{(k)}\| \le \Delta^{(k)} \ . \tag{C.7}$$

The idea is that $\boldsymbol{x}^{(k)} + \boldsymbol{s}^{(k)}$ should be the global minimum of the model $m^{(k)}$ within the trust-region, i. e.

$$\boldsymbol{s}^{(k)} = \underset{\|\boldsymbol{s}\| \le \Delta^k}{\operatorname{argmin}}\, m^{(k)}\left(\boldsymbol{x}^{(k)} + \boldsymbol{s}\right) \ . \tag{C.8}$$

This optimization problem is known as the *trust-region subproblem*. In order for the algorithm to converge, however, each step $\boldsymbol{s}^{(k)}$ only needs to *sufficiently reduce* the model $m^{(k)}$. For a definition of "sufficiently reduce" and the according theory, please refer to (Conn et al., 2000, Chapter 6). In Section C.1.6, I will present a suitable method for computing such steps, i. e. for (approximately) solving the trust-region subproblem.

After computing $\boldsymbol{s}^{(k)}$, we assess its quality by comparing the reduction of the objective function f and the reduction of the model $m^{(k)}$. Details will be given in Section C.1.2. If the quality is sufficient, we accept the step, i. e. we set

$$\boldsymbol{x}^{(k+1)} = \boldsymbol{x}^{(k)} + \boldsymbol{s}^{(k)} \ , \tag{C.9}$$

and keep or increase the trust-region radius. Otherwise, the step is rejected, i. e.

$$\boldsymbol{x}^{(k+1)} = \boldsymbol{x}^{(k)} \ , \tag{C.10}$$

and the trust-region radius is reduced, as the model $m^{(k)}$ obviously does not approximate the objective function f well within the old trust-region.

C.1.2 Model and Trust-Region Radius

In this section, I will begin filling in the details of the above generic procedure. I will use a quadratic model of the objective function as Conn et al. (2000, Section 6.1):

$$m^{(k)}\left(\boldsymbol{x}^{(k)}+\boldsymbol{s}\right)=f\left(\boldsymbol{x}^{(k)}\right)+\left(\boldsymbol{g}^{(k)}\right)^{\mathrm{T}}\cdot\boldsymbol{s}+\frac{1}{2}\cdot\boldsymbol{s}^{\mathrm{T}}\cdot\boldsymbol{H}^{(k)}\cdot\boldsymbol{s}\ , \tag{C.11}$$

where

$$\boldsymbol{g}^{(k)}=\nabla f\left(\boldsymbol{x}^{(k)}\right) \tag{C.12}$$

denotes the gradient of the objective function f at the point $\boldsymbol{x}^{(k)}$ and $\boldsymbol{H}^{(k)}$ is a symmetric $d\times d$ matrix, which is required to approximate the Hessian $\nabla^2 f\left(\boldsymbol{x}^{(k)}\right)$. I choose to use the Hessian itself, i. e.

$$\boldsymbol{H}^{(k)}=\nabla^2 f\left(\boldsymbol{x}^{(k)}\right)\ . \tag{C.13}$$

Due to this choice, the model $m^{(k)}$ is the second-order Taylor expansion of f at the point $\boldsymbol{x}^{(k)}$. It is hence a good local approximation of the objective function f at that point. This *local* property motivates the restriction that each step has to be within a trust-region around $\boldsymbol{x}^{(k)}$.

There are simple heuristics for choosing the initial trust-region radius $\Delta^{(0)}$ (Conn et al., 2000, Section 17.2). They are summarized in the following equation:

$$\Delta^{(0)}_{\text{ideal}}\stackrel{\text{def}}{=}\begin{cases}\dfrac{\left\|\boldsymbol{g}^{(0)}\right\|^2}{\left|(\boldsymbol{g}^{(0)})^{\mathrm{T}}\cdot\boldsymbol{H}^{(0)}\cdot\boldsymbol{g}^{(0)}\right|} & \text{if } \left(\boldsymbol{g}^{(0)}\right)^{\mathrm{T}}\cdot\boldsymbol{H}^{(0)}\cdot\boldsymbol{g}^{(0)}\neq 0 \text{ and } \left\|\boldsymbol{g}^{(0)}\right\|^2\neq 0\\ \frac{1}{10}\cdot\left\|\boldsymbol{g}^{(0)}\right\| & \text{if } \left(\boldsymbol{g}^{(0)}\right)^{\mathrm{T}}\cdot\boldsymbol{H}^{(0)}\cdot\boldsymbol{g}^{(0)}=0 \text{ and } \left\|\boldsymbol{g}^{(0)}\right\|^2\neq 0\\ 1 & \text{if } \left\|\boldsymbol{g}^{(0)}\right\|^2=0\ .\end{cases} \tag{C.14}$$

According to (Conn et al., 2000, Section 17.4.4), if the objective function is influenced by noise, the initial trust-region radius should not be chosen too small:

$$\Delta^{(0)}=\max\left(\Delta^{(0)}_{\text{ideal}},\Delta_{\min}\right)\ , \tag{C.15}$$

where $\Delta_{\min}$ is a lower bound, which should be chosen with respect to the noise level.

In order to assess the quality of a step $\boldsymbol{s}^{(k)}$, according to (Conn et al., 2000, Section 6.1), we compare the reduction of the model $m^{(k)}$ to the reduction of the objective function f at the point $\boldsymbol{x}^{(k)}+\boldsymbol{s}^{(k)}$ using the ratio

$$\rho^{(k)}\stackrel{\text{def}}{=}\frac{f\left(\boldsymbol{x}^{(k)}\right)-f\left(\boldsymbol{x}^{(k)}+\boldsymbol{s}^{(k)}\right)}{m^{(k)}\left(\boldsymbol{x}^{(k)}\right)-m^{(k)}\left(\boldsymbol{x}^{(k)}+\boldsymbol{s}^{(k)}\right)}\ . \tag{C.16}$$

The greater the reduction of f (numerator) is relative to the reduction of the model $m^{(k)}$ (denominator), the larger $\rho^{(k)}$ will be. Hence, $\rho^{(k)}$ is a measure for the quality of the step $\boldsymbol{s}^{(k)}$, and also assesses how well the model $m^{(k)}$ approximates f within the trust-region $\mathcal{B}^{(k)}$.

If the step $\boldsymbol{s}^{(k)}$ is good, i. e. if $\rho^{(k)}\geq\eta_1$, we accept it according to equation (C.9). The value $0<\eta_1<1$ is a quality parameter (Conn et al. (2000, Section 17.1) suggest $\eta_1=0.05$). On the other hand, if the step is bad, i. e. $\rho^{(k)}<\eta_1$, it is rejected according to equation (C.10).

The reduction ratio $\rho^{(k)}$ is also used to compute the new trust-region radius $\Delta^{(k+1)}$. If the model $m^{(k)}$ approximates the objective function f either (a) badly, (b) well, or (c) very well within the trust-region $\mathcal{B}^{(k)}$, the trust-region radius is (a) decreased, (b) kept, or (c) increased, respectively. We use the following equation for this adaptation (Conn et al., 2000, Section 17.1):

$$\Delta^{(k+1)} = \begin{cases} \max\left(\mu_1 \cdot \left\|\boldsymbol{s}^{(k)}\right\|, \Delta^{(k)}\right) & \text{if } \rho^{(k)} \geq \eta_2 \\ \Delta^{(k)} & \text{if } \eta_1 \leq \rho^{(k)} < \eta_2 \\ \mu_2 \cdot \left\|\boldsymbol{s}^{(k)}\right\| & \text{if } \rho^{(k)} < \eta_1 \ , \end{cases} \tag{C.17}$$

where η_2 denotes another quality parameter with $\eta_1 \leq \eta_2 < 1$. The parameters μ_1 and μ_2 with $0 < \mu_2 < 1 \leq \mu_1$ control how fast the trust-region radius is increased or decreased, respectively. Conn et al. (2000, Section 17.1) suggest using the following values:

$$\eta_2 = 0.9, \quad \mu_1 = 2.5, \quad \mu_2 = 0.25 \ . \tag{C.18}$$

According to equation (C.7), we have $\left\|\boldsymbol{s}^{(k)}\right\| \leq \Delta^{(k)}$. Hence, it is guaranteed that the trust-region radius is actually decreased in the third case of equation (C.17).

C.1.3 Numerical Aspects

In this section, I will describe how some numerical aspects of the trust-region algorithm can be improved according to Conn et al. (2000, Section 17.4). Equation (C.11) can be written as follows:

$$m^{(k)}\left(\boldsymbol{x}^{(k)} + \boldsymbol{s}\right) = f\left(\boldsymbol{x}^{(k)}\right) + \psi^{(k)}(\boldsymbol{s}) \tag{C.19}$$

with

$$\psi^{(k)}(\boldsymbol{s}) \overset{\text{def}}{=} \left(\boldsymbol{g}^{(k)}\right)^{\mathrm{T}} \cdot \boldsymbol{s} + \frac{1}{2} \cdot (\boldsymbol{s})^{\mathrm{T}} \cdot \boldsymbol{H}^{(k)} \cdot \boldsymbol{s} \ . \tag{C.20}$$

By substituting $\boldsymbol{s} = \boldsymbol{0}$ into equation (C.11), we get

$$m^{(k)}\left(\boldsymbol{x}^{(k)}\right) = f\left(\boldsymbol{x}^{(k)}\right) \ . \tag{C.21}$$

Now, the denominator of equation (C.16) can be written as (Conn et al., 2000, Section 17.4.1)

$$m^{(k)}\left(\boldsymbol{x}^{(k)}\right) - m^{(k)}\left(\boldsymbol{x}^{(k)} + \boldsymbol{s}^{(k)}\right) = f\left(\boldsymbol{x}^{(k)}\right) - \left(f\left(\boldsymbol{x}^{(k)}\right) + \psi^{(k)}\left(\boldsymbol{s}^{(k)}\right)\right) = -\psi^{(k)}\left(\boldsymbol{s}^{(k)}\right) \ . \tag{C.22}$$

According to Conn et al. (2000, Section 17.4.1), the last expression is numerically more stable, as cancellation effects are avoided. We get the following equation for the reduction ratio:

$$\rho^{(k)} = \frac{f\left(\boldsymbol{x}^{(k)}\right) - f\left(\boldsymbol{x}^{(k)} + \boldsymbol{s}^{(k)}\right)}{-\psi^{(k)}\left(\boldsymbol{s}^{(k)}\right)} = \frac{f\left(\boldsymbol{x}^{(k)} + \boldsymbol{s}^{(k)}\right) - f\left(\boldsymbol{x}^{(k)}\right)}{\psi^{(k)}\left(\boldsymbol{s}^{(k)}\right)} \ . \tag{C.23}$$

Cancellation effects can also occur in the numerator of equation (C.23). Especially in the vicinity of a local minimum, the difference is often much smaller than the two values of the objective function. However, it is impossible to find a generally better formula. Conn et al.

(2000, Section 17.4.2) hence suggest setting $\rho^{(k)} = 1$ if the absolute values of the numerator and the denominator of equation (C.23) are below a small multiple of the relative machine precision ϵ_{M}. The following formula summarizes the procedure

$$\rho^{(k)} = \begin{cases} 1 & \text{if } \left| f\left(\boldsymbol{x}^{(k)} + \boldsymbol{s}^{(k)}\right) - f\left(\boldsymbol{x}^{(k)}\right) \right| \le \epsilon_\rho \\ & \text{and } \left| \psi^{(k)}\left(\boldsymbol{s}^{(k)}\right) \right| \le \epsilon_\rho \\ \dfrac{f\left(\boldsymbol{x}^{(k)} + \boldsymbol{s}^{(k)}\right) - f\left(\boldsymbol{x}^{(k)}\right)}{\psi^{(k)}\left(\boldsymbol{s}^{(k)}\right)} & \text{otherwise,} \end{cases} \tag{C.24}$$

where $\epsilon_\rho > 0$ denotes a parameter, which should be chosen as a small multiple of the relative machine precision ϵ_{M}. The latter is defined as follows:

$$\epsilon_{\mathrm{M}} \stackrel{\text{def}}{=} \min\{\, \epsilon > 0 \mid 1 + \epsilon > 1 \,\} \; . \tag{C.25}$$

Note that it is crucial that this formula is evaluated using the floating point arithmetics of the according computer. In $\mathbb{R}$, ϵ_{M} is undefined.

C.1.4 Termination

When applying the trust-region algorithm, we need the iteration to terminate eventually. However, according to (Conn et al., 2000, Section 17.4.3.1), this is a difficult problem. I will subsequently describe a certain subset of their termination criteria, which I have chosen to use.

A necessary condition for a (local) minimum of f is that the gradient of f vanishes. Hence, the iteration can be terminated if the norm of the gradient is below a threshold $\epsilon_{\mathrm{g}} > 0$:

$$\left\| \nabla f\left(\boldsymbol{x}^{(k)}\right) \right\| \le \epsilon_{\mathrm{g}} \; . \tag{C.26}$$

As the gradient depends on the scale of f, the threshold ϵ_{g} should be chosen relative to that as follows

$$\epsilon_{\mathrm{g}} = \epsilon_{\mathrm{r}} \cdot \left\| \nabla f\left(\boldsymbol{x}_{\mathrm{typ}}\right) \right\| \; , \tag{C.27}$$

where $\boldsymbol{x}_{\mathrm{typ}}$ denotes a "typical" value of $\boldsymbol{x}$ and $\epsilon_{\mathrm{r}} > 0$ is a termination parameter.

According to Section C.1.3, the computation of $\rho^{(k)}$ can be influenced by numerical problems, especially if the trust-region radius $\Delta^{(k)}$ becomes small, which is typically the case close to a minimum. Hence, the algorithm should be terminated as soon as the trust-region radius $\Delta^{(k)}$ is too small according to the inequality

$$\Delta^{(k)} \le \epsilon_\Delta \cdot \left\| \boldsymbol{x}^{(k)} \right\| \; . \tag{C.28}$$

The parameter $\epsilon_\Delta > 0$ should be chosen with the same order of magnitude as the relative machine precision ϵ_{M}.

For numerical reasons, the algorithm should also be terminated if the points $\boldsymbol{x}^{(k)}$ and $\boldsymbol{x}^{(k)} + \boldsymbol{s}^{(k)}$ are numerically nearly indistinguishable, which is detected by the condition

$$\left| \left[\boldsymbol{s}^{(k)} \right]_i \right| < \epsilon_{\mathrm{M}} \cdot \left| \left[\boldsymbol{x}^{(k)} \right]_i \right| \quad \text{for all } 1 \le i \le d \text{ with } \left| \left[\boldsymbol{x}^{(k)} \right]_i \right| \ne 0 \; , \tag{C.29}$$

where $[\cdot]_i$ denotes the ith entry of a vector.

Algorithm C.1 A trust-region algorithm.

Input: initial solution $\boldsymbol{x}^{(0)}$
Input: typical value of $\boldsymbol{x}$: $\boldsymbol{x}_{\text{typ}}$
Parameter: quality parameters η_1, η_2 with $0 < \eta_1 \leq \eta_2 < 1$ (e. g. $\eta_1 = 0.05$, $\eta_2 = 0.9$)
Parameter: adaptation parameters μ_1, μ_2 with $0 < \mu_2 < 1 \leq \mu_1$ (e. g. $\mu_1 = 2.5$, $\mu_2 = 0.25$)
Parameter: (termination) parameters $\epsilon_\rho, \epsilon_{\text{r}}, \epsilon_\Delta$
Parameter: minimum initial trust-region radius $\Delta_{\min}$

Initialize $k := 0$
Compute $\nabla f(\boldsymbol{x}_{\text{typ}})$
Compute ϵ_{g} according to equation (C.27)
Compute $f(\boldsymbol{x}^{(0)})$, $\boldsymbol{g}^{(0)} := \nabla f(\boldsymbol{x}^{(0)})$ and $\boldsymbol{H}^{(0)} := \nabla^2 f(\boldsymbol{x}^{(0)})$
Compute the initial trust-region radius $\Delta^{(0)}$ according to equation (C.15)
while none of the termination criteria (C.26) and (C.28) holds **do**
    Compute the step $\boldsymbol{s}^{(k)}$ by solving the trust-region subproblem (e. g. using Algorithm C.2)
    if the termination criterion (C.29) holds **then**
        terminate
    Compute $f(\boldsymbol{x}^{(k)} + \boldsymbol{s}^{(k)})$
    Compute the reduction ratio $\rho^{(k)}$ according to equation (C.24)
    if $\rho^{(k)} \geq \eta_1$ **then**
        Set $\boldsymbol{x}^{(k+1)} := \boldsymbol{x}^{(k)} + \boldsymbol{s}^{(k)}$
        Set $f(\boldsymbol{x}^{(k+1)}) := f(\boldsymbol{x}^{(k)} + \boldsymbol{s}^{(k)})$
        Compute $\boldsymbol{g}^{(k+1)} := \nabla f(\boldsymbol{x}^{(k+1)})$ and $\boldsymbol{H}^{(k+1)} := \nabla^2 f(\boldsymbol{x}^{(k+1)})$
    else
        Set $\boldsymbol{x}^{(k+1)} := \boldsymbol{x}^{(k)}$
        Set $f(\boldsymbol{x}^{(k+1)}) := f(\boldsymbol{x}^{(k)})$, $\boldsymbol{g}^{(k+1)} := \boldsymbol{g}^{(k)}$, and $\boldsymbol{H}^{(k+1)} := \boldsymbol{H}^{(k)}$
    Compute the new trust-region radius $\Delta^{(k+1)}$ according to equation (C.17)
    Set $k := k + 1$

C.1.5 The Algorithm

Even though I have not yet explained how the trust-region subproblem can be solved, the main trust-region algorithm can already be summarized in Algorithm C.1. An algorithm for solving the subproblem will be presented in Section C.1.6.

The running time of the trust-region algorithm is dominated by the time needed for solving the trust-region subproblem (see Section C.1.6) and for computing $f(\boldsymbol{x})$, $\boldsymbol{g}^{(k)}$, and $\boldsymbol{H}^{(k)}$. Often, computing the Hessian $\boldsymbol{H}^{(k)}$ will take at least $\Omega(d^2)$ time. In case of a diagonal (approximation of the) Hessian, $\Omega(d)$ may suffice. The same holds for the memory requirement.

C.1.6 Solving the Trust-Region Subproblem

Conn et al. (2000, Chapter 7) describe several approaches for (approximatively) solving the trust-region subproblem. I have chosen the variant in (Conn et al., 2000, Section 7.3), which I will describe in this section. Note that this method is well suited for low-dimensional problems. For large values of the dimension d, however, the time complexity of the algorithm is too high and another method should be used (Conn et al., 2000, Chapter 7).

I will formulate the trust-region subproblem in terms of the function $\psi^{(k)}$. By equation (C.20), we have

$$\operatorname*{argmin}_{\|s\|\leq\Delta^{(k)}} m^{(k)}\left(\boldsymbol{x}^{(k)}+\boldsymbol{s}\right)=\operatorname*{argmin}_{\|s\|\leq\Delta^{(k)}} \psi^{(k)}(\boldsymbol{s}) \ . \tag{C.30}$$

The following proposition gives a necessary condition for the exact solutions of the trust-region subproblem.

Proposition C.1 *Let $\boldsymbol{s}_M$ be the global minimum of the function $\psi^{(k)}(\boldsymbol{s})$ with respect to $\|s\| \leq \Delta^{(k)}$. Define*

$$\boldsymbol{H}^{(k)}(\lambda) \stackrel{\text{def}}{=} \boldsymbol{H}^{(k)} + \lambda \cdot \boldsymbol{I} \ , \tag{C.31}$$

where $\boldsymbol{I}$ denotes the identity matrix. Then $\lambda_M \geq 0$ exists such that

1. $\boldsymbol{H}^{(k)}(\lambda_M) \cdot \boldsymbol{s}_M = -\boldsymbol{g}^{(k)}$,
2. $\boldsymbol{H}^{(k)}(\lambda_M)$ *is positive semi-definite*
3. $\lambda_M \cdot \left(\|\boldsymbol{s}_M\| - \Delta^{(k)}\right) = 0.$

If $\boldsymbol{H}^{(k)}(\lambda_M)$ positive definite, the vector $\boldsymbol{s}_M$ is unique.

Proof: See (Conn et al., 2000, Corollary 7.2.2). □

I will subsequently present an algorithm for (approximatively) solving the trust-region subproblem based on this proposition. If λ_M is known, $\boldsymbol{s}_M$ can simply be computed as the solution of property 1. Hence, I will focus on finding a suitable value λ.

Equation (C.31) can be interpreted as a regularization of the Hessian $\boldsymbol{H}^{(k)}$. If the matrix $\boldsymbol{H}^{(k)}(\lambda)$ is positive definite, it defines a modified quadratic model with a unique global minimum. The idea is to find such a regularization that the minimum is within the trust-region.

According to Conn et al. (2000, Section 7.3.1), the inequality $\lambda \geq -\lambda_{\min}$ (or $\lambda > -\lambda_{\min}$, respectively) needs to hold in order for $\boldsymbol{H}^{(k)}(\lambda)$ to be positive semi-definite (or positive definite, respectively). The value $\lambda_{\min}$ denotes the smallest eigenvalue of the Hessian $\boldsymbol{H}^{(k)}$, i. e. the smallest solution $\tilde{\lambda}$ to

$$\boldsymbol{H}^{(k)} \cdot \boldsymbol{v} = \tilde{\lambda} \cdot \boldsymbol{v} \quad \text{with} \quad \boldsymbol{v} \in \mathbb{R}^d \setminus \{\boldsymbol{0}\} \ . \tag{C.32}$$

As $\boldsymbol{H}^{(k)}$ is symmetric, this eigenproblem has d real-valued eigenvalues (Conn et al., 2000, Section 2.2). Hence, the smallest eigenvalue $\lambda_{\min}$ is well-defined.

If $\boldsymbol{H}^{(k)}$ is positive definite, we set $\lambda_0 = 0$. Then $\boldsymbol{H}^{(k)}(\lambda_0)$ is obviously also positive definite and the properties 2 and 3 in Proposition C.1 hold for λ_0. Hence, we can compute the unique solution $\boldsymbol{s}_0$ to the equation

$$\boldsymbol{H}^{(k)}(\lambda_0) \cdot \boldsymbol{s}_0 = -\boldsymbol{g}^{(k)} \ . \tag{C.33}$$

This equation can be solved using the Cholesky decomposition (see Appendix A.4). Note that the Cholesky decomposition can also be used to test whether a symmetric matrix is positive definite.

If $||s_0|| \leq \Delta^{(k)}$ holds, $s^{(k)} = s_0$ is the solution of the trust-region subproblem. Otherwise, λ_0 is inappropriate.

On the other hand, if $H^{(k)}$ is not positive definite, we set $\lambda_0 = -\lambda^+_{\min}$, where $\lambda^+_{\min}$ denotes a value slightly smaller than $\lambda_{\min}$. If $\lambda_{\min} < 0$, we have $\lambda_0 > -\lambda_{\min}$ and hence $H^{(k)}(\lambda_0)$ is positive definite. Again, we compute s_0 as the unique solution to equation (C.33). If $\lambda_0 \neq 0$, according to property 3 of Proposition C.1, we need the equation $||s_0|| - \Delta^{(k)} = 0$ to hold. If it does, $s^{(k)} = s_0$ is a solution of the trust-region subproblem. Otherwise, λ_0 is inappropriate.

If we have not found a solution yet, we define

$$s(\lambda) \stackrel{\text{def}}{=} -\left(H^{(k)}(\lambda)\right)^{-1} \cdot g^{(k)} \tag{C.34}$$

for $\lambda > -\lambda_{\min}$. By $\lambda > -\lambda_{\min}$, $H^{(k)}(\lambda)$ is positive definite and invertible. The vector $s(\lambda)$ is hence well-defined. Because of property 3 of Proposition C.1, we compute λ as a root of

$$||s(\lambda)|| - \Delta^{(k)} = 0 \ . \tag{C.35}$$

According to Conn et al. (2000), equation (C.35) is not well suited for using the Newton method. They propose using

$$\phi(\lambda) = 0 \tag{C.36}$$

with

$$\phi(\lambda) \stackrel{\text{def}}{=} \frac{1}{||s(\lambda)||} - \frac{1}{\Delta^{(k)}} \tag{C.37}$$

instead. As $\Delta^{(k)} > 0$ holds, the equations (C.35) and (C.36) are equivalent.

According to Conn et al. (2000, Section 7.3.3), starting with a value $\lambda_0 > -\lambda_{\min}$, the Newton method iteratively computes values λ_j as follows:

$$\lambda_{j+1} = \lambda_j - \frac{\phi(\lambda_j)}{\nabla\phi(\lambda_j)} \ . \tag{C.38}$$

According to (Conn et al., 2000, Lemma 7.3.1), if $g^{(k)} \neq 0$, we have

$$\nabla\phi(\lambda) = \frac{(s(\lambda))^{\mathrm{T}} \cdot \left(H^{(k)}(\lambda)\right)^{-1} \cdot s(\lambda)}{||s(\lambda)||^3} \ . \tag{C.39}$$

The condition $g^{(k)} \neq 0$ holds as the trust-region method would have already been terminated otherwise.

As $H^{(k)}(\lambda)$ is positive definite, the Cholesky decomposition (Appendix A.4)

$$H^{(k)}(\lambda) = L \cdot L^{\mathrm{T}} \tag{C.40}$$

is defined, where L denotes a quadratic lower triangle matrix. Hence, we have

$$\begin{aligned}(s(\lambda))^{\mathrm{T}} \cdot \left(H^{(k)}(\lambda)\right)^{-1} \cdot s(\lambda) &= (s(\lambda))^{\mathrm{T}} \cdot L^{-\mathrm{T}} \cdot L^{-1} \cdot s(\lambda) \\ &= \left(L^{-1} \cdot s(\lambda)\right)^{\mathrm{T}} \cdot L^{-1} \cdot s(\lambda) \\ &= ||y||^2 \end{aligned} \tag{C.41}$$

with

$$y \overset{\text{def}}{=} \boldsymbol{L}^{-1} \cdot \boldsymbol{s}(\lambda) \ . \tag{C.42}$$

This definition can be reformulated as

$$\boldsymbol{L} \cdot \boldsymbol{y} = \boldsymbol{s}(\lambda) \ . \tag{C.43}$$

In order to perform a step of the Newton method, according to equation (C.38), we need to compute the following value

$$\begin{aligned} -\frac{\phi(\lambda)}{\nabla\phi(\lambda)} &= \left(\frac{1}{\Delta^{(k)}} - \frac{1}{\|\boldsymbol{s}(\lambda)\|}\right) \cdot \frac{\|\boldsymbol{s}(\lambda)\|^3}{\|\boldsymbol{y}\|^2} \\ &= \frac{\|\boldsymbol{s}(\lambda)\| - \Delta^{(k)}}{\|\boldsymbol{s}(\lambda)\| \cdot \Delta^{(k)}} \cdot \frac{\|\boldsymbol{s}(\lambda)\|^3}{\|\boldsymbol{y}\|^2} \\ &= \frac{\|\boldsymbol{s}(\lambda)\| - \Delta^{(k)}}{\Delta^{(k)}} \cdot \frac{\|\boldsymbol{s}(\lambda)\|^2}{\|\boldsymbol{y}\|^2} \ . \end{aligned} \tag{C.44}$$

This allows us to formulate an explicit description for computing a step of the Newton method:

1. Compute $\boldsymbol{L}$ via Cholesky decomposition such that $\boldsymbol{H}^{(k)}(\lambda_j) = \boldsymbol{L} \cdot \boldsymbol{L}^{\mathrm{T}}$ holds.
2. Solve $\boldsymbol{L} \cdot \boldsymbol{L}^{\mathrm{T}} \cdot \boldsymbol{s}(\lambda_j) = -\boldsymbol{g}^{(k)}$ for $\boldsymbol{s}(\lambda_j)$.
3. Solve $\boldsymbol{L} \cdot \boldsymbol{y} = \boldsymbol{s}(\lambda_j)$ for $\boldsymbol{y}$.
4. Compute λ_{j+1} according to the equations (C.38) and (C.44).

According to Conn et al. (2000, Section 7.3.11), the Newton method can be started at λ_0 if $\|\boldsymbol{s}_0\| > \Delta^{(k)}$ holds. In this case, the Newton iteration can be terminated if

$$\left|\|\boldsymbol{s}(\lambda_j)\| - \Delta^{(k)}\right| \leq \kappa \cdot \Delta^{(k)} \tag{C.45}$$

holds (Conn et al., 2000, Section 7.3.10), where $0 < \kappa < 1$ denotes a parameter. The description in (Conn et al., 2000, Section 7.3.10) leads to the suggestion $\kappa = 0.1$. Note that this termination criterion does allow for solutions slightly outside of the trust-region, which is admitted as an approximate solution of the trust-region subproblem. Let $\lambda^{(k)}$ be the result of the Newton method. Then $\boldsymbol{s}^{(k)} = \boldsymbol{s}(\lambda^{(k)})$ is the (approximate) solution of the trust-region problem.

If $\|\boldsymbol{s}_0\| < \Delta^{(k)}$ holds and $\boldsymbol{s}_0$ is not already a solution of the trust-region subproblem, we could also use the Newton method. However, due to certain complications in this case, Conn et al. (2000, Section 7.3.11) suggest the following procedure. Compute an eigenvector $\boldsymbol{v}$ to the eigenvalue $\lambda_{\min}$. By definition, we have

$$\left(\boldsymbol{H}^{(k)} - \lambda_{\min} \cdot \boldsymbol{E}\right) \cdot \boldsymbol{v} = \boldsymbol{0} \ . \tag{C.46}$$

By equation (C.31), this leads to

$$\boldsymbol{H}^{(k)}(-\lambda_{\min}) \cdot \beta \cdot \boldsymbol{v} = \boldsymbol{0} \quad \text{for all } \beta \in \mathbb{R} \ . \tag{C.47}$$

By the equation $\lambda_0 = -\lambda^+_{\min} \approx -\lambda_{\min}$, we get

$$\boldsymbol{H}^{(k)}(\lambda_0) \cdot \beta \cdot \boldsymbol{v} \approx \boldsymbol{0} \quad \text{for all } \beta \in \mathbb{R} \ . \tag{C.48}$$

As $\boldsymbol{s}_0$ solves equation (C.33), we further have

$$\boldsymbol{H}^{(k)}(\lambda_0) \cdot (\boldsymbol{s}_0 + \beta \cdot \boldsymbol{v}) \approx -\boldsymbol{g}^{(k)} \quad \text{for all } \beta \in \mathbb{R} \ . \tag{C.49}$$

In order to solve the trust-region problem, due to property 3 of Proposition C.1, we use the roots β_1 and β_2 of the following quadratic equation

$$||\boldsymbol{s}_0 + \beta \cdot \boldsymbol{v}|| - \Delta^{(k)} = 0 \ . \tag{C.50}$$

That this actually is a quadratic equation will become clear later. Amongst the two possible steps $\boldsymbol{s}_0 + \beta_1 \cdot \boldsymbol{v}$ and $\boldsymbol{s}_0 + \beta_2 \cdot \boldsymbol{v}$, we choose the one that reduces the model the most as the (approximate) solution of the trust-region subproblem:

$$\boldsymbol{s}^{(k)} = \boldsymbol{s}_0 + \beta_0 \cdot \boldsymbol{v} \quad \text{with} \quad \beta_0 \stackrel{\text{def}}{=} \operatorname*{argmin}_{\beta \in \{\beta_1, \beta_2\}} \psi(\boldsymbol{s}_0 + \beta \cdot \boldsymbol{v}) \ . \tag{C.51}$$

In order to compute the roots β_1 and β_2, we reformulate equation (C.50):

$$||\boldsymbol{s}_0 + \beta \boldsymbol{v}||^2 = \left(\Delta^{(k)}\right)^2 \ . \tag{C.52}$$

We further have

$$\begin{aligned}
0 &= ||\boldsymbol{s}_0 + \beta \boldsymbol{v}||^2 - \left(\Delta^{(k)}\right)^2 \\
&= \left(\sum_{i=1}^{d} ([\boldsymbol{s}_0]_i + \beta \cdot [\boldsymbol{v}]_i)^2\right) - \left(\Delta^{(k)}\right)^2 \\
&= \left(\sum_{i=1}^{d} \left([\boldsymbol{s}_0]_i^2 + 2 \cdot [\boldsymbol{s}_0]_i \cdot [\boldsymbol{v}]_i \cdot \beta + [\boldsymbol{v}]_i^2 \cdot \beta^2\right)\right) - \left(\Delta^{(k)}\right)^2 \\
&= \left(\sum_{i=1}^{d} [\boldsymbol{v}]_i^2\right) \cdot \beta^2 + \left(2 \cdot \sum_{i=1}^{d} [\boldsymbol{s}_0]_i \cdot [\boldsymbol{v}]_i\right) \cdot \beta + \left(\sum_{i=1}^{d} [\boldsymbol{s}_0]_i^2\right) - \left(\Delta^{(k)}\right)^2 \\
&= ||\boldsymbol{v}||^2 \cdot \beta^2 + 2 \cdot \boldsymbol{s}_0^{\mathrm{T}} \cdot \boldsymbol{v} \cdot \beta + ||\boldsymbol{s}_0||^2 - \left(\Delta^{(k)}\right)^2 \ .
\end{aligned} \tag{C.53}$$

This equation can easily be solved for the two roots in closed form. The inequality $||\boldsymbol{s}_0|| < \Delta^{(k)}$ ensures that the equation actually has two real solutions.

The complete algorithm for solving the trust-region subproblem is summarized in Algorithm C.2. For details on computing the Cholesky decomposition, the smallest eigenvalue and an according eigenvector, please refer to Appendix A.4 and A.5 and the literature mention there. Note that these numeric standard problems are implemented in software libraries, which can be readily used.

The time complexity of a Newton iteration (lines 21 through 26 of Algorithm C.2) is dominated by computing the Cholesky decomposition. Assuming that the Newton iteration terminates after a fixed maximum number of iterations, the running time of the whole Algorithm C.2 is dominated by the time needed to compute the Cholesky decomposition, the smallest eigenvalue and an according eigenvector (by solving a linear equation system). All of these problems have a time complexity of $O(d^3)$ (see Appendix A.4 and A.5).

C.2 Levenberg-Marquardt

Even though it is historically older, the Levenberg-Marquardt method can be interpreted as a second-order trust-region algorithm with the following modifications compared to Section C.1 (Nocedal and Wright, 1999):

- The Hessian matrix is (usually) approximated by the squared Jacobian matrix of a certain function.
- There is no *explicit* trust-region radius. Instead, there is a regularization parameter $\lambda^{(k)}$.
- The regularization is used to heuristically solve the trust-region subproblem.
- A simplified, "inverse" variant of equation (C.17) is used to adapt $\lambda^{(k)}$ (instead of $\Delta^{(k)}$).

I will present the details in the remainder of this section. For the Levenberg-Marquardt algorithm, we assume that the objective function has the following form:

$$f(\boldsymbol{x}) = \sum_{i=1}^{e} \rho(r_i(\boldsymbol{x})) \tag{C.54}$$

where

$$\boldsymbol{r} : \mathbb{R}^d \to \mathbb{R}^e : \boldsymbol{x} \to (r_1(\boldsymbol{x}), \ldots, r_e(\boldsymbol{x}))^{\mathrm{T}} \quad \text{with} \quad r_i : \mathbb{R}^d \to \mathbb{R} \tag{C.55}$$

is the residual function and $\rho : \mathbb{R} \to \mathbb{R}$ is an error function. Both need to be twice continuously differentiable. Given this special form, the gradient and the Hessian are

$$\nabla f(\boldsymbol{x}) = \sum_{i=1}^{e} \rho'(r_i(\boldsymbol{x}))\nabla r_i(\boldsymbol{x}) \tag{C.56}$$

$$\nabla^2 f(\boldsymbol{x}) = \sum_{i=1}^{e} \rho''(r_i(\boldsymbol{x}))\nabla r_i(\boldsymbol{x})\,(\nabla r_i(\boldsymbol{x}))^{\mathrm{T}} + \sum_{i=1}^{e} \rho'(r_i(\boldsymbol{x}))\nabla^2 r_i(\boldsymbol{x}) \ , \tag{C.57}$$

where ρ' and ρ'' denote the first and second derivatives of ρ, respectively. A first-order Taylor approximation of $\boldsymbol{r}$ leads to $\nabla^2 r_i(\boldsymbol{x}) \approx \boldsymbol{0}$ and we get the following approximation of the Hessian:

$$\nabla^2 f(\boldsymbol{x}) \approx \sum_{i=1}^{e} \rho''(r_i(\boldsymbol{x}))\nabla r_i(\boldsymbol{x})\,(\nabla r_i(\boldsymbol{x}))^{\mathrm{T}} \ . \tag{C.58}$$

Algorithm C.2 An algorithm for (approximately) solving the trust-region subproblem.

Input: the gradient $g^{(k)}$ and the Hessian $H^{(k)}$

Output: (approximate) solution $s^{(k)}$ of the trust-region subproblem

Parameter: ϵ_λ with $\epsilon_\lambda > 0$ and ϵ_λ very small

1: Try to compute the Cholesky factor L_0 of the Hessian such that $H^{(k)} = L_0 \cdot L_0^T$ holds
2: **if** the Cholesky decomposition succeeded **then**   ▷ i. e. $H^{(k)}$ is positive definite
3:      Set $\lambda_0 := 0$
4:      Set $H^{(k)}(\lambda_0) := H^{(k)}$
5: **else**
6:      Compute the smallest eigenvalue $\lambda_{\min}$ of the Hessian $H^{(k)}$
7:      Set $\lambda_0 := -\lambda_{\min} \cdot (1 + \epsilon_\lambda)$
8:      Compute $H^{(k)}(\lambda_0) := H^{(k)} + \lambda_0 \cdot E$
9: Compute the Cholesky factor L_0 such that $H^{(k)}(\lambda_0) = L_0 \cdot L_0^T$ holds
10: Solve $L_0 \cdot L_0^T \cdot s_0^{(k)} = -g^{(k)}$ for $s_0^{(k)}$
11: **if** $\left\| s_0^{(k)} \right\| \leq \Delta^{(k)}$ **then**
12:      **if** $\lambda_0 = 0$ or $\left\| s_0^{(k)} \right\| = \Delta^{(k)}$ **then**
13:          Set $s^{(k)} := s_0^{(k)}$
14:      **else**
15:          Compute an according eigenvector v of the eigenvalue $\lambda_{\min}$
16:          Compute the solution β of $\left\| s_0^{(k)} + \beta \cdot v \right\| = \Delta^{(k)}$ with minimum value $\psi^{(k)}(s_0^{(k)} + \beta \cdot v)$
17:          Set $s^{(k)} := s_0^{(k)} + \beta \cdot v$
18: **else**
19:      Set $j := 0$
20:      **while** $\left| \left\| s_j^{(k)} \right\| - \Delta^{(k)} \right| > \kappa \cdot \Delta^{(k)}$ **do**   ▷ Newton method
21:          Set $j := j + 1$
22:          Solve $L_{j-1} \cdot y_j = s_{j-1}^{(k)}$ for y_j
23:          Set $\lambda_j := \lambda_{j-1} + \dfrac{\left\| s_{j-1}^{(k)} \right\| - \Delta^{(k)}}{\Delta^{(k)}} \cdot \dfrac{\left\| s_{j-1}^{(k)} \right\|^2}{\left\| y_j \right\|^2}$
24:          Compute $H^{(k)}(\lambda_j) := H^{(k)} + \lambda_j \cdot E$
25:          Compute the Cholesky factor L_j such that $H^{(k)}(\lambda_j) = L_j \cdot L_j^T$
26:          Solve $L_j \cdot L_j^T \cdot s_j^{(k)} = -g^{(k)}$ for $s_j^{(k)}$
27:      Set $s^{(k)} := s_j^{(k)}$

Note that this approximation of the Hessian may be considered as being optional.

In the important special case of a least squares problem (i. e. $\rho(x) = x^2/2$), we have $\rho'(x) = x$ and $\rho''(x) = 1$ and the approximation of the Hessian can be considered to be good. The gradient and the Hessian can now be compactly expressed by using the Jacobian $\boldsymbol{J}$ of $\boldsymbol{r}$:

$$\nabla f(\boldsymbol{x}) = \sum_{i=1}^{e} r_i(\boldsymbol{x}) \nabla r_i(\boldsymbol{x}) = \boldsymbol{J}^{\mathrm{T}} \boldsymbol{r}(\boldsymbol{x}) \quad \text{with} \quad \boldsymbol{J} \stackrel{\text{def}}{=} \nabla \boldsymbol{r}(\boldsymbol{x}) \tag{C.59}$$

$$\nabla^2 f(\boldsymbol{x}) \approx \sum_{i=1}^{e} \nabla r_i(\boldsymbol{x}) \left(\nabla r_i(\boldsymbol{x})\right)^{\mathrm{T}} = \boldsymbol{J}\boldsymbol{J}^{\mathrm{T}} \tag{C.60}$$

Note that I define the gradient as a column vector. For the sake of consistency, I accordingly define the Jacobian matrix such that the gradients of the component functions r_i are the *columns* of the Jacobian matrix (i. e. the Jacobian of a function $\mathbb{R}^d \to \mathbb{R}$ equals its gradient).

The Levenberg-Marquardt algorithm uses a parameter λ as in Proposition C.1 to solve the trust-region subproblem given in equation (C.8). However, instead of explicitly representing the trust-region radius $\Delta^{(k)}$ and finding an according value $\lambda^{(k)}$, we store and adapt the regularization parameter $\lambda^{(k)}$ directly.

The trust-region logic is mostly unchanged. If a step $\boldsymbol{s}^{(k)}$ is good, it is accepted. Otherwise it is rejected. Instead of adapting the trust-region radius, however, we adapt the regularization parameter $\lambda^{(k)}$. The details are a bit simpler than in Section C.1. Every step reducing the objective function is accepted (i. e. $\eta_1 = 0$). In each such case, the trust-region radius is increased by decreasing $\lambda^{(k)}$ (i. e. roughly speaking, $\eta_2 = 0$ in equation (C.17)). On the other hand, if a step increases the objective function, it is rejected and $\lambda^{(k)}$ is increased. The adaptation is hence simply

$$\lambda^{(k+1)} = \begin{cases} \lambda^{(k)}/\mu_1 & \text{if } f\left(\boldsymbol{x}^{(k)} + \boldsymbol{s}^{(k)}\right) < f\left(\boldsymbol{x}^{(k)}\right) \\ \lambda^{(k)}/\mu_2 & \text{otherwise} \ , \end{cases} \tag{C.61}$$

where μ_1 and μ_2 effectively have the same role as in equation (C.17), but are typically set to

$$\mu_1 = 10 \quad \text{and} \quad \mu_2 = 0.1 \ . \tag{C.62}$$

Solving the trust-region subproblem is very simple, as we already have the value $\lambda = \lambda^{(k)}$. Hence all we have to do is solve a linear equation system (as in the lines 9 and 10 in Algorithm C.2). Note that the heuristically adapted value $\lambda^{(k)}$ does not necessarily give a positive definite matrix $\boldsymbol{H}^{(k)}\left(\lambda^{(k)}\right)$. If this requirement is not fulfilled, we can simply consider the step unsuccessful and increase $\lambda^{(k)}$.

Except for the trust-region radius, the same stopping conditions as in Section C.1 can be used. It is, however, more common to directly specify ϵ_g instead of using equation (C.27). The complete procedure is summarized in Algorithm C.3. Its time complexity is identical to that of the trust-region algorithm in Section C.1

Algorithm C.3 The Levenberg-Marquardt algorithm.

Input: initial solution $\boldsymbol{x}^{(0)}$
Parameter: adaptation parameters μ_1, μ_2 with $0 < \mu_2 < 1 \leq \mu_1$ (e. g. $\mu_1 = 10, \mu_2 = 0.1$)
Parameter: termination parameter ϵ_g ▹ alternatively use equation (C.27)
Parameter: initial regularization parameter $\lambda^{(0)}$ (e. g. $\lambda^{(0)} = 1$)

Initialize $k := 0$
Compute $f(\boldsymbol{x}^{(0)})$, $\boldsymbol{g}^{(0)}$, and $\boldsymbol{H}^{(0)}$ according to the equations (C.56) and (C.58)
while the termination criterion (C.26) does not hold **do**
    Compute the Cholesky factor $\boldsymbol{L}$ such that $\boldsymbol{H}^{(k)}(\lambda^{(k)}) = \boldsymbol{L} \cdot \boldsymbol{L}^{\mathrm{T}}$ holds
    Solve $\boldsymbol{L} \cdot \boldsymbol{L}^{\mathrm{T}} \cdot \boldsymbol{s}^{(k)} = -\boldsymbol{g}^{(k)}$ for $\boldsymbol{s}^{(k)}$
    if the termination criterion (C.29) holds **then**
        terminate
    Compute $f(\boldsymbol{x}^{(k)} + \boldsymbol{s}^{(k)})$
    if $f(\boldsymbol{x}^{(k)} + \boldsymbol{s}^{(k)}) < f(\boldsymbol{x}^{(k)})$ **then**
        Set $\boldsymbol{x}^{(k+1)} := \boldsymbol{x}^{(k)} + \boldsymbol{s}^{(k)}$
        Set $f(\boldsymbol{x}^{(k+1)}) := f(\boldsymbol{x}^{(k)} + \boldsymbol{s}^{(k)})$
        Compute $\boldsymbol{g}^{(k+1)}$ and $\boldsymbol{H}^{(k+1)}$ according to the equations (C.56) and (C.58)
        Decrease the regularization parameter: $\lambda^{(k+1)} := \lambda^{(k)} / \mu_1$
    else
        Set $\boldsymbol{x}^{(k+1)} := \boldsymbol{x}^{(k)}$
        Set $f(\boldsymbol{x}^{(k+1)}) := f(\boldsymbol{x}^{(k)})$, $\boldsymbol{g}^{(k+1)} := \boldsymbol{g}^{(k)}$, and $\boldsymbol{H}^{(k+1)} := \boldsymbol{H}^{(k)}$
        Increase the regularization parameter: $\lambda^{(k+1)} := \lambda^{(k)} / \mu_2$
    Set $k := k + 1$

Appendix D

3D Computer Vision Background

In this appendix, I will *briefly* introduce some basic 3D computer vision concepts, which are used in this thesis. For a general introduction to the topic or additional details, the reader is referred to the literature. The textbook of Trucco and Verri (1998) provides a comparatively simple introduction, whereas Hartley and Zisserman (2003) cover the topic more broadly and more thoroughly. Some additional aspects are covered by Ma et al. (2004).

D.1 Pinhole Camera Model and Coordinate Systems

In this section, I will describe the standard *pinhole camera* model, which is also known as *perspective projection*. Even though modern cameras have sophisticated lens systems, the pinhole model is a good approximation of their imaging geometry. The most important deviation from this model is caused by radial distortion, which will be treated in Section D.2.

The pinhole camera model is a function, which maps a 3D point to the 2D location of its image in the picture. The core of the pinhole camera model is a central projection of the 3D space onto the image plane:

$$\begin{pmatrix} x \\ y \\ z \end{pmatrix} \to \frac{f}{z} \begin{pmatrix} x \\ y \end{pmatrix} , \tag{D.1}$$

where f denotes the focal length. Expressing the 2D image point in homogeneous coordinates (Appendix A.1) allows writing this non-linear function in a seemingly linear form:

$$\begin{pmatrix} x \\ y \\ z \end{pmatrix} \to \begin{pmatrix} fx/z \\ fy/z \\ 1 \end{pmatrix} \cong \begin{pmatrix} fx \\ fy \\ z \end{pmatrix} = \begin{pmatrix} f & 0 & 0 \\ 0 & f & 0 \\ 0 & 0 & 1 \end{pmatrix} \begin{pmatrix} x \\ y \\ z \end{pmatrix} . \tag{D.2}$$

In addition to this projection, the 2D point has to be transformed into the pixel coordinate system. The whole mapping can be expressed as follows:

$$\boldsymbol{p} \cong \boldsymbol{K} \boldsymbol{q}_{\mathrm{C}} , \tag{D.3}$$

where $q_C \in \mathbb{R}^3$ denotes a 3D point in the camera coordinate system, $p \in \mathbb{P}^2$ is the imaged point in homogeneous 2D pixel coordinates, and K is the camera calibration matrix

$$K \stackrel{\text{def}}{=} \begin{pmatrix} f_x & s & o_x \\ 0 & f_y & o_y \\ 0 & 0 & 1 \end{pmatrix} , \tag{D.4}$$

where f_x and f_y are the effective focal lengths, s is the skew parameter, and $(o_x, o_y)^T$ is the principal point. While these so called *intrinsic camera parameters* do have a geometric meaning, in the context of this thesis, it is enough to think of a pinhole camera as a matrix K. Note that equation (D.3) relates Euclidean 3D coordinates and homogeneous 2D coordinates. More precisely, the result of the multiplication is interpreted as a member of $\mathbb{P}^2$. It is this "trick" that allows expressing the non-linear central projection of the pinhole camera model as a "linear" mapping.

In order to be able to express 3D points in a coordinate system which is independent of the camera, a separate world coordinate system is used. The rigid transformation of a 3D point from world coordinates $q \in \mathbb{R}^3$ to camera coordinates $q_C \in \mathbb{R}^3$ is expressed as follows:

$$q_C = Rq + t , \tag{D.5}$$

where R is a 3D rotation matrix defining the orientation of the camera and $t \in \mathbb{R}^3$ is a translation vector. Together, (R, t) are called the *pose* of the camera and are also known as the *extrinsic camera parameters*. The vector t is the origin of the world coordinate system expressed in the *camera* coordinate system. Accordingly, $-R^T t$ is the origin of the camera coordinate system, which is also called the *optical center* or the *projection center* of the camera, expressed in world coordinates.

The 2D image p of a 3D point q in world coordinates can now be expressed as:

$$p \cong K(Rq + t) . \tag{D.6}$$

Hence, a pinhole camera can be represented by the tuple (K, R, t) or, more compactly, by a single 3×4 projection matrix:

$$C = K(R|t) . \tag{D.7}$$

The mapping can then be expressed as

$$p \cong C\tilde{q} , \tag{D.8}$$

where $\tilde{q} \in \mathbb{P}^3$ denotes q in homogeneous coordinates (add the entry 1 to the vector).

D.2 Radial Distortion

Even though the pinhole model provides a good approximation of the imaging geometry of modern cameras, a more precise approximation can be achieved by incorporating *radial distortion* into the camera model (Hartley and Zisserman, 2003, Section 7.4), (Heikkilä and Silvén, 1997; Schiller et al., 2008). For an example of images with obvious radial distortion, see Figure 1.1(d) and compare to Figure 1.1(f).

There are several different models for radial distortion in the literature. Most auhors use a distortion function of the following form

$$\begin{pmatrix} x \\ y \end{pmatrix} \to \left(1 + \sum_{i=1}^{n} \kappa_i r^i\right) \begin{pmatrix} x \\ y \end{pmatrix} \quad \text{with} \quad r = \sqrt{x^2 + y^2} \; . \tag{D.9}$$

The various models differ (a) in the subset of parameters $(\kappa_i)_{1 \leq i \leq n}$, which are actually used (the others are set to zero), and (b) whether the distortion is applied "forwards" or "backwards". Note that equation (D.9) assumes that the center of radial distortion is the coordinate origin (i. e. the optical axis is the center of radial distortion in 3D). This can easily be extended to allow for a different center of radial distortion.

The distortion model should be integrated into the pinhole model in between the actual projection and the transformation into the pixel coordinate system:

$$\boldsymbol{p} \cong \underbrace{\begin{pmatrix} f_x/f & s/f & o_x \\ 0 & f_y/f & o_y \\ 0 & 0 & 1 \end{pmatrix}}_{\stackrel{\text{def}}{=} \boldsymbol{L}} \boldsymbol{d} \left(\underbrace{\begin{pmatrix} f & 0 & 0 \\ 0 & f & 0 \\ 0 & 0 & 1 \end{pmatrix}}_{\stackrel{\text{def}}{=} \boldsymbol{K}_f} \boldsymbol{q}_C \right) , \tag{D.10}$$

where $\boldsymbol{d}$ denotes the radial distortion function (see below).

The task of *correcting radial distortion* consists of computing a new image from a given one such that the pinhole model is valid for the new image. For that we need a mapping from the actual image points $\boldsymbol{p}$ to undistorted image points $\boldsymbol{p}_u$, which satisfy the pinhole camera model

$$\boldsymbol{p}_u \cong \boldsymbol{K} \boldsymbol{q}_C \; . \tag{D.11}$$

In order to find such points, solve equation (D.10) for $\boldsymbol{q}_C$ (up to scale):

$$\boldsymbol{q}_C \cong \boldsymbol{K}_f^{-1} \boldsymbol{d}^{-1} \left(\boldsymbol{L}^{-1} \boldsymbol{p} \right) \; . \tag{D.12}$$

Undistorted image points can hence be computed as follows:

$$\boldsymbol{p}_u \cong \boldsymbol{K} \boldsymbol{K}_f^{-1} \boldsymbol{d}^{-1} \left(\boldsymbol{L}^{-1} \boldsymbol{p} \right) \; . \tag{D.13}$$

In order to avoid the need for inverting $\boldsymbol{d}$, we can use an inverse model. For practical situations, the following one usually suffices (cf. equation (D.9)):

$$\boldsymbol{d}^{-1} \begin{pmatrix} u \\ v \\ w \end{pmatrix} \cong \begin{pmatrix} (1 + \kappa_1 r^2 + \kappa_2 r^4) u \\ (1 + \kappa_1 r^2 + \kappa_2 r^4) v \\ w \end{pmatrix} \quad \text{with} \quad r^2 = \frac{u^2}{w^2} + \frac{v^2}{w^2} \; . \tag{D.14}$$

Given equation (D.14) and $\boldsymbol{K}_\mathrm{f}^{-1} = \mathrm{diag}(1/f, 1/f, 1)$, equation (D.12) can be written in a simpler, equivalent form:

$$\boldsymbol{q}_\mathrm{C} \cong \boldsymbol{d}'^{-1}\left(\boldsymbol{K}^{-1}\boldsymbol{p}\right) , \tag{D.15}$$

where $\boldsymbol{d}'^{-1}$ is defined as in equation (D.14), but with parameters κ_1' and κ_2' instead of κ_1 and κ_2. They are related as follows: $\kappa_1' = f^2\kappa_1$ and $\kappa_2' = f^4\kappa_2$. For radial distortion correction, we can accordingly use the following simpler formulation instead of equation (D.13):

$$\boldsymbol{p}_\mathrm{u} \cong \boldsymbol{K}\boldsymbol{d}'^{-1}\left(\boldsymbol{K}^{-1}\boldsymbol{p}\right) . \tag{D.16}$$

D.3 Epipolar Geometry

The *epipolar geometry* describes the relative imaging geometry of two cameras. Let $\boldsymbol{q}$ be a 3D point in world coordinates and let $(\boldsymbol{K}_i, \boldsymbol{R}_i, \boldsymbol{t}_i)$ with $i = 1, 2$ be two pinhole cameras. Let $\boldsymbol{p}_i = \boldsymbol{K}_i(\boldsymbol{R}_i\boldsymbol{q} + \boldsymbol{t}_i)$ be the images of $\boldsymbol{q}$. The points $\boldsymbol{p}_1$ and $\boldsymbol{p}_2$ are said to *correspond*. Their combination $(\boldsymbol{p}_1, \boldsymbol{p}_2)$ is called a *point correspondence*.

Relative Pose

The *relative pose* $(\boldsymbol{R}_\mathrm{rel}, \boldsymbol{t}_\mathrm{rel})$ expresses the rigid transformation between the two camera coordinate systems such that

$$\boldsymbol{q}_{\mathrm{C},2} = \boldsymbol{R}_\mathrm{rel}\boldsymbol{q}_{\mathrm{C},1} + \boldsymbol{t}_\mathrm{rel} , \tag{D.17}$$

where

$$\boldsymbol{q}_{\mathrm{C},i} = \boldsymbol{R}_i\boldsymbol{q} + \boldsymbol{t}_i, \quad i = 1, 2 \tag{D.18}$$

denotes the 3D point $\boldsymbol{q}$ in the ith camera coordinate system. The relative pose can hence be computed as follows:

$$\begin{aligned} \boldsymbol{R}_\mathrm{rel} &= \boldsymbol{R}_2\boldsymbol{R}_1^\mathrm{T} , \\ \boldsymbol{t}_\mathrm{rel} &= \boldsymbol{t}_2 - \boldsymbol{R}_\mathrm{rel}\boldsymbol{t}_1 . \end{aligned} \tag{D.19}$$

In the special situation $\boldsymbol{R}_1 = \boldsymbol{I}$, $\boldsymbol{t}_1 = \boldsymbol{0}$, where $\boldsymbol{I}$ denotes the identity matrix, we have $\boldsymbol{R}_\mathrm{rel} = \boldsymbol{R}_2$ and $\boldsymbol{t}_\mathrm{rel} = \boldsymbol{t}_2$.

Fundamental Matrix

The *fundamental matrix* $\boldsymbol{F}$ relates two corresponding points $\boldsymbol{p}_1, \boldsymbol{p}_2$ (in homogeneous coordinates) as follows:

$$\boldsymbol{p}_1^\mathrm{T}\boldsymbol{F}\boldsymbol{p}_2 = 0 . \tag{D.20}$$

This equation is known as the *epipolar constraint* (expressed in image coordinates, cf. equation (D.23)). It can be interpreted as follows. Given a point $\boldsymbol{p}_2$, the corresponding point $\boldsymbol{p}_1$ must lie of the *epipolar line* $\boldsymbol{F}\boldsymbol{p}_2$. Note that $\boldsymbol{F}\boldsymbol{p}_2$ is a homogeneously represented 2D line (see Appendix A.1).

If point correspondences are known, the epipolar constraint can be used to estimate the fundamental matrix *without* any further knowledge about the cameras. The eight-point and the seven-point algorithms can be used for that task (see Sections 4.2.1 and 4.2.2).

The fundamental matrix can be computed in terms of the calibration matrices $\boldsymbol{K}_i$ and the relative pose $(\boldsymbol{R}_{\text{rel}}, \boldsymbol{t}_{\text{rel}})$ of the cameras:

$$\boldsymbol{F} \cong \boldsymbol{K}_1^{-\mathrm{T}} [\boldsymbol{t}_{\text{rel}}]_\times \boldsymbol{R}_{\text{rel}} \boldsymbol{K}_2^{-1} \ , \tag{D.21}$$

where $[\boldsymbol{t}]_\times$ denotes the *skew symmetric matrix* of the vector $\boldsymbol{t}$ (see equation (A.16)) and $\cong$ expresses equality up to scale also for matrices (cf. equation (A.6)).

Essential Matrix

The epipolar geometry can also be encoded in the *essential matrix* $\boldsymbol{E}$. It expresses the epipolar constraint in terms of *camera normalized coordinates*. Given an image point $\boldsymbol{p}$ and the calibration matrix $\boldsymbol{K}$, the camera normalized coordinates of $\boldsymbol{p}$ are

$$\hat{\boldsymbol{p}} \overset{\text{def}}{\cong} \boldsymbol{K}^{-1}\boldsymbol{p} \ . \tag{D.22}$$

Interpreted as a vector in $\mathbb{R}^3$, $\hat{\boldsymbol{p}}$ defines a ray in the camera coordinate system, which emanates from the optical center $(0,0,0)^\mathrm{T}$ and passes through the 3D point $\boldsymbol{q}_\mathrm{C}$. This can be expressed compactly in the formula $\hat{\boldsymbol{p}} \cong \boldsymbol{q}_\mathrm{C}$.

Using camera normalized coordinates, the epipolar constraint becomes

$$\hat{\boldsymbol{p}}_1^\mathrm{T} \boldsymbol{E} \hat{\boldsymbol{p}}_2 = 0 \ . \tag{D.23}$$

Opposed to the fundamental matrix, the essential matrix

$$\boldsymbol{E} \cong [\boldsymbol{t}_{\text{rel}}]_\times \boldsymbol{R}_{\text{rel}} \tag{D.24}$$

does not depend on the intrinsic parameters of the cameras. The relation to the fundamental matrix is

$$\boldsymbol{F} \cong \boldsymbol{K}_2^{-\mathrm{T}} \boldsymbol{E} \boldsymbol{K}_1^{-1} \ . \tag{D.25}$$

D.4 Triangulation

The problem of (multi-camera) *triangulation* consists of reconstructing the 3D point $\boldsymbol{q}$ given its images $\boldsymbol{p}_i$ with $1 \le i \le n$ taken by $n \ge 2$ cameras from different locations (i. e. $\boldsymbol{t}_{\text{rel}} \neq \boldsymbol{0}$ for all camera pairs). I will present a linear algorithm for the case of known intrinsic parameters and known poses of the cameras (Hartley and Zisserman, 2003, Section 12.2). More sophisticated triangulation algorithms, which are beneficial in cases with less knowledge, can be found in the literature (Kanatani et al., 2008; Hartley and Sturm, 1997; Hartley and Zisserman, 2003).

If the poses are only known up to a (common) rigid or similarity transformation, the reconstruction will also be known up to the same transformation. Hence, in the case of $n = 2$ cameras, their relative pose suffices. The calibration will then be represented in the camera coordinate system of the first camera, which is usually set to $(\boldsymbol{I}, \boldsymbol{0})$. If the scale of the relative pose is unknown, the reconstructed point $\boldsymbol{q}$ will share the same unknown scale factor.

In this section, the 3D point $\boldsymbol{q}$ is expressed in homogeneous coordinates $\tilde{\boldsymbol{q}} \in \mathbb{P}^3$. In addition to producing very compact equations, this allows to reconstruct vanishing points, which lie on the plane at infinity. Let the n cameras be $\boldsymbol{C}_i = \boldsymbol{K}_i(\boldsymbol{R}_i|\boldsymbol{t}_i)$ for $1 \leq i \leq n$.

The cross product is used to circumvent the unknown scale factor in equation (D.8):

$$\boldsymbol{p}_i \times \boldsymbol{C}_i\tilde{\boldsymbol{q}} = 0 \ . \tag{D.26}$$

This can be written as three scalar equations, two of which are linearly independent:

$$\begin{aligned} u_i\boldsymbol{c}_{i,3}^{\mathrm{T}}\tilde{\boldsymbol{q}} - w_i\boldsymbol{c}_{i,1}^{\mathrm{T}}\tilde{\boldsymbol{q}} &= 0 \\ v_i\boldsymbol{c}_{i,3}^{\mathrm{T}}\tilde{\boldsymbol{q}} - w_i\boldsymbol{c}_{i,2}^{\mathrm{T}}\tilde{\boldsymbol{q}} &= 0 \\ u_i\boldsymbol{c}_{i,2}^{\mathrm{T}}\tilde{\boldsymbol{q}} - v_i\boldsymbol{c}_{i,1}^{\mathrm{T}}\tilde{\boldsymbol{q}} &= 0 \end{aligned} \tag{D.27}$$

where $\boldsymbol{c}_{i,j}^{\mathrm{T}}$ denotes the jth row of $\boldsymbol{C}_i$ and $\boldsymbol{p}_i = (u_i, v_i, w_i)^{\mathrm{T}}$. The first two equations can be written compactly as follows:

$$\boldsymbol{A}_i\tilde{\boldsymbol{q}} = \boldsymbol{0} \ , \tag{D.28}$$

where

$$\boldsymbol{A}_i = \begin{pmatrix} u_i\boldsymbol{c}_{i,3}^{\mathrm{T}} - w_i\boldsymbol{c}_{i,1}^{\mathrm{T}} \\ v_i\boldsymbol{c}_{i,3}^{\mathrm{T}} - w_i\boldsymbol{c}_{i,2}^{\mathrm{T}} \end{pmatrix} = \begin{pmatrix} u_ic_{i,31} - w_ic_{i,11} & u_ic_{i,32} - w_ic_{i,12} & u_ic_{i,33} - w_ic_{i,13} & u_ic_{i,34} - w_ic_{i,14} \\ v_ic_{i,31} - w_ic_{i,21} & v_ic_{i,32} - w_ic_{i,22} & v_ic_{i,33} - w_ic_{i,23} & u_ic_{i,34} - w_ic_{i,24} \end{pmatrix} \tag{D.29}$$

and $c_{i,jk}$ denotes the entries of $\boldsymbol{C}_i = (c_{i,jk})_{jk}$. Given $n \geq 2$ cameras and image points, the matrices $\boldsymbol{A}_i$ can be stacked giving the following equation system:

$$\boldsymbol{A}\tilde{\boldsymbol{q}} = \boldsymbol{0} \ . \tag{D.30}$$

Ideally, the matrix $\boldsymbol{A}$ has rank defect one and hence equation (D.30) can be solved via singular value decomposition (see Appendix A.3). In practice, due to noise in the image points $\boldsymbol{p}_i$, $\boldsymbol{A}$ will often have full rank. In this case, the least squares approximation to $\tilde{\boldsymbol{q}}$ with respect to $\|\tilde{\boldsymbol{q}}\| = 1$ is computed in the very same way (using the smallest singular value instead of the zero singular value as explained in Appendix A.3).

D.5 Pattern-Based Calibration

Zhang (1999) describes a method for calibrating a camera (intrinsic and extrinsic parameters) given at least three images of a planar calibration pattern as shown in Figure D.1. The world coordinate system is chosen such that the calibration pattern is in the XY plane and also such that the coordinates of reliably detectable points are known in (metric) world coordinates. Points $\boldsymbol{q} = (q_1, q_2, q_3)$ on the calibration pattern hence have Z coordinate $q_3 = 0$ and the following equation holds (cf. equation (D.6)):

$$\boldsymbol{p} \cong \boldsymbol{K}(\boldsymbol{R} \mid \boldsymbol{t})\tilde{\boldsymbol{q}} = \underbrace{\boldsymbol{K}\begin{pmatrix}\boldsymbol{r}_1 & \boldsymbol{r}_2 & \boldsymbol{t}\end{pmatrix}}_{\stackrel{\text{def}}{\cong}\boldsymbol{H}} \tilde{\boldsymbol{q}}_{2\text{D}} \; , \tag{D.31}$$

where $\tilde{\boldsymbol{q}} = (q_1, q_2, q_3, 1)$ denotes the homogeneous representation of $\boldsymbol{q}$, $\boldsymbol{R} = \begin{pmatrix}\boldsymbol{r}_1^{\mathrm{T}} & \boldsymbol{r}_2^{\mathrm{T}} & \boldsymbol{r}_3^{\mathrm{T}}\end{pmatrix}$, $\boldsymbol{q}_{2\text{D}} = (q_1, q_2)^{\mathrm{T}}$, and accordingly $\tilde{\boldsymbol{q}}_{2\text{D}} = (q_1, q_2, 1)^{\mathrm{T}}$. The important observation is that this map is a homography, which I denote by $\boldsymbol{H}$.

Given correspondences between known points $\boldsymbol{q}_{2\text{D}}$ on the calibration pattern and their images $\boldsymbol{p}$ (in one of the images), we can estimate the homography $\boldsymbol{H}$ as described in Section 5.1.1. The method for establishing such correspondences of course depends on the calibration pattern (Figure D.1). The centers of the black boxes are detected by fitting rectangles using the approach of Süße and Ortmann (2003) and computing the intersection of the two diagonals. The calibration pattern has been designed such that it is rotationally unambiguous and hence suitable for global point matching based on the Hungarian method as proposed by Süße et al. (2006). For the purpose of this dissertation, however, the correspondences could also be established manually (even though this might be less accurate).

Defining $\boldsymbol{H} = \begin{pmatrix}\boldsymbol{h}_1^{\mathrm{T}} & \boldsymbol{h}_2^{\mathrm{T}} & \boldsymbol{h}_3^{\mathrm{T}}\end{pmatrix}$, we can write the defining equation of the homography $\boldsymbol{H}$ as follows:

$$\begin{pmatrix}\boldsymbol{h}_1^{\mathrm{T}} & \boldsymbol{h}_2^{\mathrm{T}} & \boldsymbol{h}_3^{\mathrm{T}}\end{pmatrix} \cong \boldsymbol{K}\begin{pmatrix}\boldsymbol{r}_1 & \boldsymbol{r}_2 & \boldsymbol{t}\end{pmatrix} \; . \tag{D.32}$$

As $\boldsymbol{r}_1$ and $\boldsymbol{r}_2$ are orthonormal, we get the following two constraints:

$$\boldsymbol{h}_1^{\mathrm{T}} \underbrace{\boldsymbol{K}^{-\mathrm{T}}\boldsymbol{K}^{-1}}_{\stackrel{\text{def}}{=}\omega} \boldsymbol{h}_2 = 0 \tag{D.33}$$

$$\boldsymbol{h}_1^{\mathrm{T}}\boldsymbol{K}^{-\mathrm{T}}\boldsymbol{K}^{-1}\boldsymbol{h}_1 = \boldsymbol{h}_2^{\mathrm{T}}\boldsymbol{K}^{-\mathrm{T}}\boldsymbol{K}^{-1}\boldsymbol{h}_2 \; , \tag{D.34}$$

which can be interpreted as constraints on the image of the absolute conic (IAC) ω. Given at least three homographies $\boldsymbol{H}$ estimated from images taken from different viewpoints, these constraints can be used to estimate ω and hence $\boldsymbol{K}$.

The above constraints can be written as the following linear equation system:

$$\begin{pmatrix}\boldsymbol{v}_{12}^{\mathrm{T}} \\ \boldsymbol{v}_{11}^{\mathrm{T}} - \boldsymbol{v}_{22}^{\mathrm{T}}\end{pmatrix} \boldsymbol{b} = \boldsymbol{0} \; , \tag{D.35}$$

Figure D.1: Three images of the calibration pattern used for Zhang's calibration method captured from three different viewpoints (i. e. camera poses). The centers of the black squares are used to establish correspondences.

where $\boldsymbol{b}$ is defined as in equation (5.18) and

$$\boldsymbol{v}_{ij} = (h_{i1}h_{j1}, h_{i1}h_{j2} + h_{i2}h_{j1}, h_{i2}h_{j2}, h_{i3}h_{j1} + h_{i1}h_{j3}, h_{i3}h_{j2} + h_{i2}h_{j3}, h_{i3}h_{j3})^{\mathrm{T}} \tag{D.36}$$

with $\boldsymbol{H} = (h_{ij})_{1\leq i,j\leq 3}$. Given more than one homography $\boldsymbol{H}$, we can stack these equation systems in the form

$$\boldsymbol{B}\boldsymbol{b} = \boldsymbol{0} \ . \tag{D.37}$$

Given at least three homographies $\boldsymbol{H}$ estimated from images taken from different viewpoints, the matrix $\boldsymbol{B}$ has rank defect one (in theory). The singular value decomposition $\boldsymbol{B} = \boldsymbol{U}\mathrm{diag}(\boldsymbol{s})\boldsymbol{V}^{\mathrm{T}}$ can hence be used to solve for $\boldsymbol{b}$ up to scale by taking the last column of $\boldsymbol{V}$ (cf. Section A.3). On noisy data, this gives a least squares approximation.

Finally, we can rearrange the entries of $\boldsymbol{b}$ to get $\boldsymbol{\omega}$. The intrinsic parameters $\boldsymbol{K}$ can be extracted from $\boldsymbol{\omega}$ as described in Section 5.1.2. Note, however, that the homographies used there are very different from the ones described here. Only the computation of $\boldsymbol{K}$ from $\boldsymbol{\omega}$ is identical.

In order to compute the extrinsic camera parameters (of each image), we use equation (D.32) to get:

$$\boldsymbol{r}_1 = \lambda \boldsymbol{K}^{-1}\boldsymbol{h}_1 \tag{D.38}$$

$$\boldsymbol{r}_2 = \lambda \boldsymbol{K}^{-1}\boldsymbol{h}_2 \tag{D.39}$$

$$\boldsymbol{r}_3 = \boldsymbol{r}_1 \times \boldsymbol{r}_2 \tag{D.40}$$

$$\boldsymbol{t} = \lambda \boldsymbol{K}^{-1}\boldsymbol{h}_3 \tag{D.41}$$

$$\lambda \stackrel{\text{def}}{=} \frac{1}{\|\boldsymbol{K}^{-1}\boldsymbol{h}_1\|} = \frac{1}{\|\boldsymbol{K}^{-1}\boldsymbol{h}_2\|} \ . \tag{D.42}$$

Due to noise, the resulting $\boldsymbol{R}$ is in general not a rotation matrix. It should hence be orthogonalized as described in Section A.3. Optionally, the estimate produced by the algebraic approach can be refined by nonlinear optimization.

D.6 KLT Tracking

The *Kanade-Lucas-Tomasi (KLT) tracker* is a template-based point tracker (Lucas and Kanade, 1981; Shi and Tomasi, 1994; Bergen et al., 1992; Baker and Matthews, 2004). Its purpose is to track feature points in a video sequence and can hence be used to establish point correspondences. I use the variant and implementation described by Kähler (2009b, Section 3.1). As tracking is not in the focus of this dissertation, I will only present the main idea and mention certain improvements and approximations.

Given a reference image I_0 and a (small) patch defined by a set of pixel locations $\mathcal{P}$ in I_0, the tracking task is to find the new locations $\boldsymbol{\mu}(\boldsymbol{p}, \boldsymbol{v}_t)$ for all points $\boldsymbol{p} \in \mathcal{P}$ and all images I_t with $t > 0$, where $\boldsymbol{\mu}$ is the common motion model with parameters $\boldsymbol{v}_t$. Given this formulation, we need to estimate $\boldsymbol{v}_t$ for all $t > 0$.

The main assumption of the KLT tracker is that changes in the image are only caused by motion, i. e. the gray values of the points in $\mathcal{P}$ do not change. This is known as the *brightness constancy assumption* and can be formally expressed as follows:

$$I_t(\boldsymbol{\mu}(\boldsymbol{p}, \boldsymbol{v}_t)) = I_0(\boldsymbol{p}) \quad \text{for all } \boldsymbol{p} \in \mathcal{P} \text{ and all } t > 0 \ . \tag{D.43}$$

The expression $I_t(\boldsymbol{p})$ denotes the gray value of the pixel at position $\boldsymbol{p}$ in the image I_t. If the location $\boldsymbol{p}$ is not on the pixel grid, $I_t(\boldsymbol{p})$ is approximated by using, e. g. bilinear interpolation (Gonzalez and Woods, 2002).

There are several possible choices for the motion model $\boldsymbol{\mu}$. I use the affine model

$$\boldsymbol{\mu}(\boldsymbol{p}, \boldsymbol{v}_t) = \begin{pmatrix} v_{t,3} & v_{t,4} \\ v_{t,5} & v_{t,6} \end{pmatrix} \boldsymbol{p} + \begin{pmatrix} v_{t,1} \\ v_{t,2} \end{pmatrix} \quad \text{with} \quad \boldsymbol{v} = (v_{t,1}, \ldots, v_{t,6})^{\mathrm{T}} \ . \tag{D.44}$$

Note that, in this context, the points $\boldsymbol{p}$ are in Euclidean coordinates (i. e. $\boldsymbol{p} \in \mathbb{R}^2$). This motion model is assumed to be valid within a small region (e. g. a 15×15 image patch).

As there is always noise in the images, which violates the brightness constancy assumption, the task of finding suitable motion parameters is formulated as a nonlinear optimization problem with the following objective function:

$$f(\boldsymbol{v}_t) = \sum_{\boldsymbol{p} \in \mathcal{P}} (r_{\boldsymbol{p}}(\boldsymbol{v}_t))^2 \quad \text{with} \quad r_{\boldsymbol{p}}(\boldsymbol{v}_t) = I_t(\boldsymbol{\mu}(\boldsymbol{p}, \boldsymbol{v}_t)) - I_0(\boldsymbol{p}) \ . \tag{D.45}$$

Kähler (2009b, Section 3.1) uses the Levenberg-Marquardt algorithm (see Appendix C.2) to minimize this objective function. The optimization is performed for each $t > 0$, initialized by the result $\boldsymbol{v}_{t-1}$ for the previous image. Note that we need the derivatives of the images in order to compute the derivatives of f, which are needed for the optimization. In practice, the image derivatives are approximated by using, e. g. the Sobel filter (Gonzalez and Woods, 2002).

Point Correspondences

In order to find a set of point correspondences, Kähler (2009b) detects a set of reference points $\mathcal{R}$ using the corner detector of Shi and Tomasi (1994), which is very similar to the Harris detector described in Section 3.1. For each reference point $\boldsymbol{p}_\mathrm{R} \in \mathcal{R}$, all pixel locations within the $n \times n$ neighborhood (with $n = 15$, e. g.) of $\boldsymbol{p}_\mathrm{R}$ define the point set $\mathcal{P}(\boldsymbol{p}_\mathrm{R})$. Each point set $\mathcal{P}(\boldsymbol{p}_\mathrm{R})$ is tracked individually resulting in motion parameters $\boldsymbol{v}_t(\boldsymbol{p}_\mathrm{R})$. For each reference point $\boldsymbol{p}_\mathrm{R} \in \mathcal{R}$, which can be tracked successfully from I_0 to a certain image I_t (usually with $t \gg 1$), the correspondence $(\boldsymbol{p}_\mathrm{R}, \boldsymbol{\mu}(\boldsymbol{p}_\mathrm{R}, \boldsymbol{v}_t(\boldsymbol{p}_\mathrm{R})))$ is established.

Improvements and Approximations

In order to improve the numerical stability of the KLT tracker, the image points are normalized. The actual method used by Kähler (2009b) is a simplified variant of the one described in Section 5.1.1. There is no translation and the points are anisotropically scaled such that both coordinates are in the range $[0, 1]$.

In order to speed up the nonlinear optimization and to increase the chance of converging to the correct minimum, a Gaussian resolution hierarchy is used (Lindeberg, 1994; Gonzalez and Woods, 2002). The optimization is first performed at a low resolution and subsequently at increasingly higher resolutions, each time initialized with the motion parameters resulting from the previous resolution. More precisely, at the first five resolution levels, only the translation parameters $(v_{t,1}, v_{t,2})$ are optimized, followed by two levels optimizing all six parameters.

In order to further speed up the tracking, a compositional approach (Baker and Matthews, 2004) combined with the Hager approximation (Hager and Belhumeur, 1998) is used to approximately compute the derivatives during the optimization.

Appendix E

Additional Experimental Results

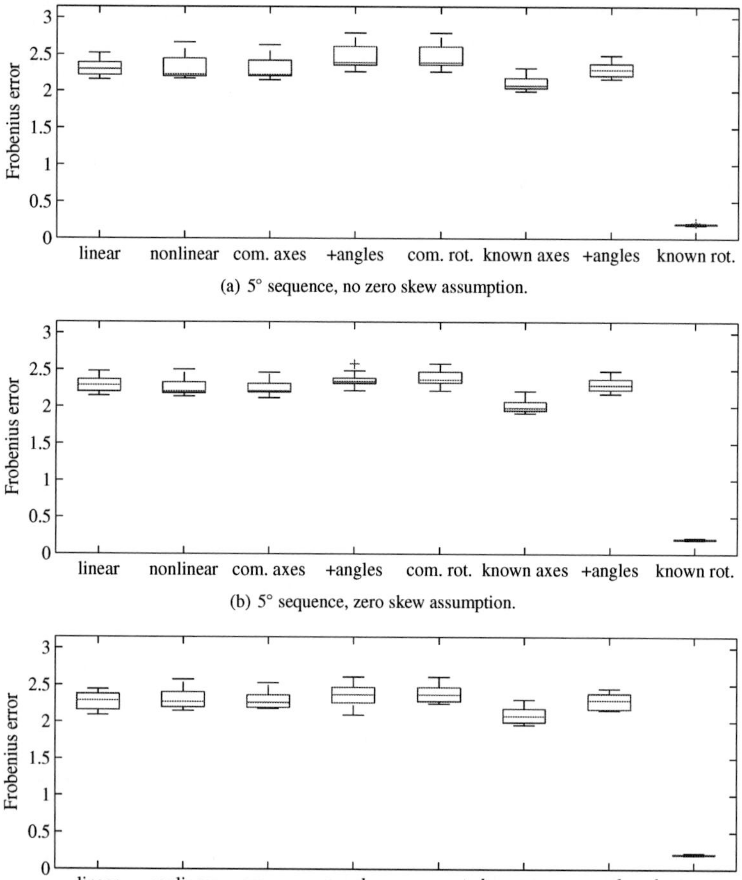

(a) 5° sequence, no zero skew assumption.

(b) 5° sequence, zero skew assumption.

(c) 10° sequence, zero skew assumption.

Figure E.1: Main results of rotational self-calibration with real data using the Frobenius error e_K instead of e_f as in Figure 7.3.

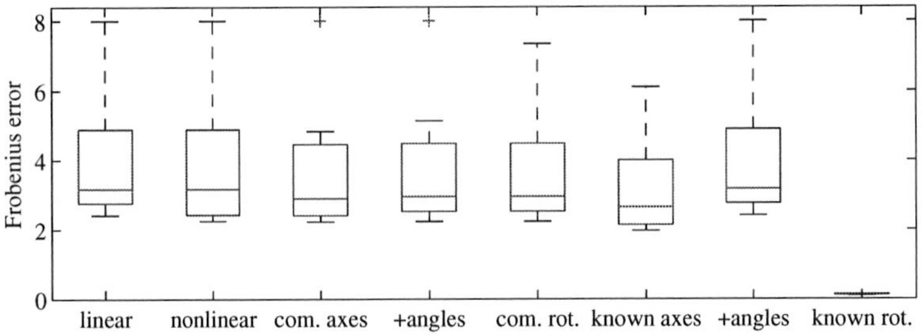

(a) 5° sequence, without nodal adapter, zero skew assumption. This setup severely violates the assumption that the optical center of the camera coincides with the rotation center. Note the changed scale of the error axis.

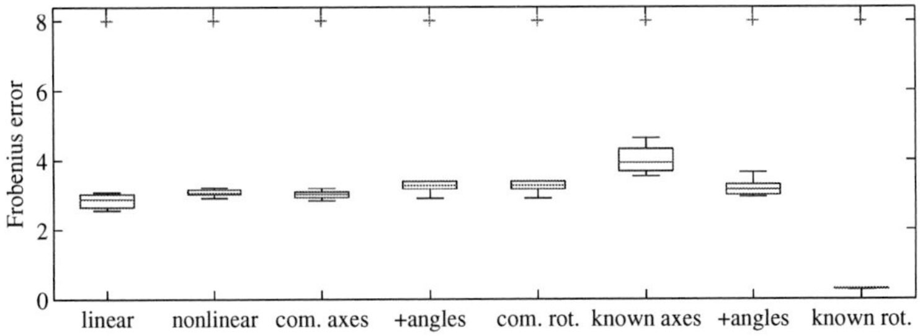

(b) 5° sequence, AVT camera, zero skew assumption. Note the changed scale of the error axis.

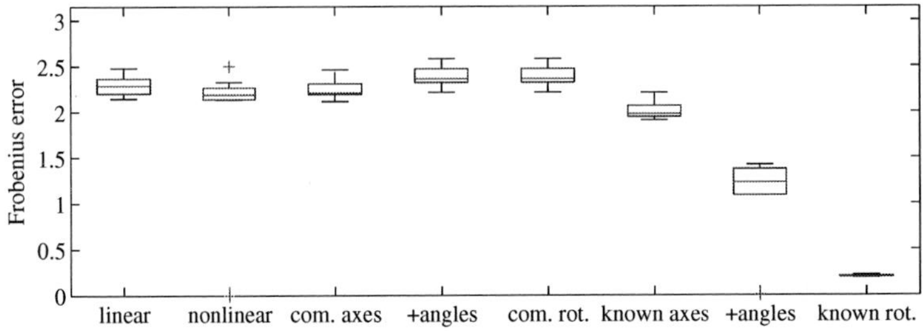

(c) 5° sequence, zero skew assumption. The nonlinear optimization has been initialized with the ground truth.

Figure E.2: Additional results of rotational self-calibration with real data using the Frobenius error e_{K} instead of e_{f} as in Figure 7.4.

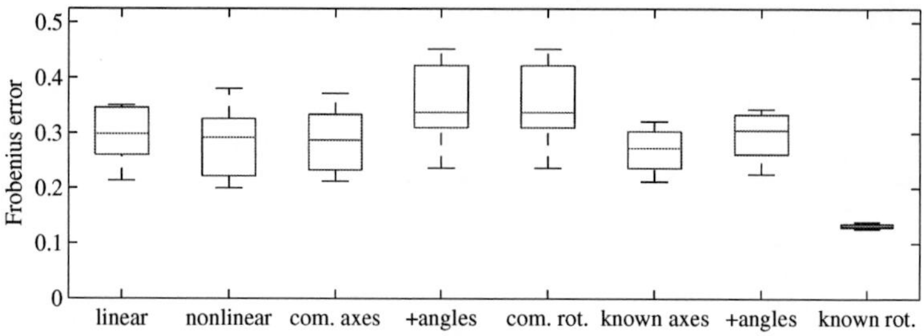

(a) 5° sequence, no zero skew assumption, radial distortion correction. The results without radial distortion correction are given in Figure E.1(a). Note the changed scale of the error axis.

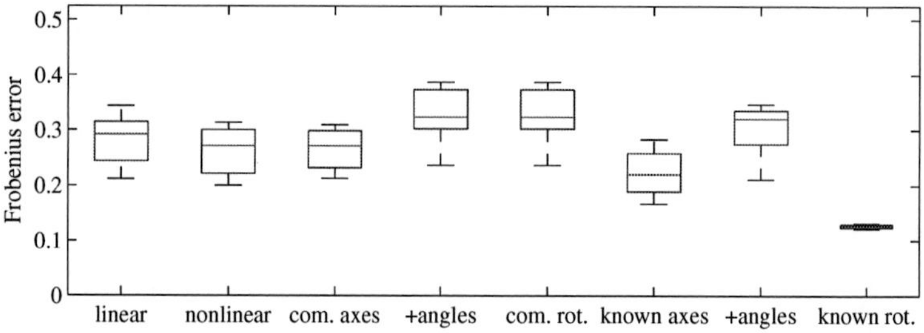

(b) 5° sequence, zero skew assumption, radial distortion correction. The results without radial distortion correction are given in Figure E.1(b). Note the changed scale of the error axis.

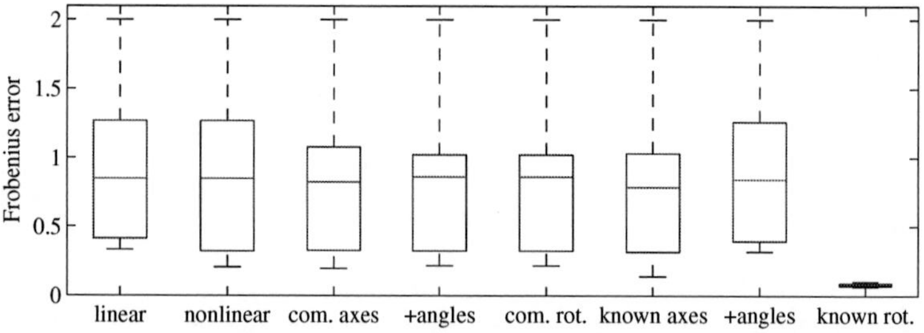

(c) 5° sequence, without nodal adapter, zero skew assumption, radial distortion correction. This setup severely violates the assumption that the optical center of the camera coincides with the rotation center. The results without radial distortion correction are given in Figure E.2(a). Note the changed scale of the error axis.

Figure E.3: Additional results of rotational self-calibration with real data using the Frobenius error e_{K} instead of e_{f} as in Figure 7.5.

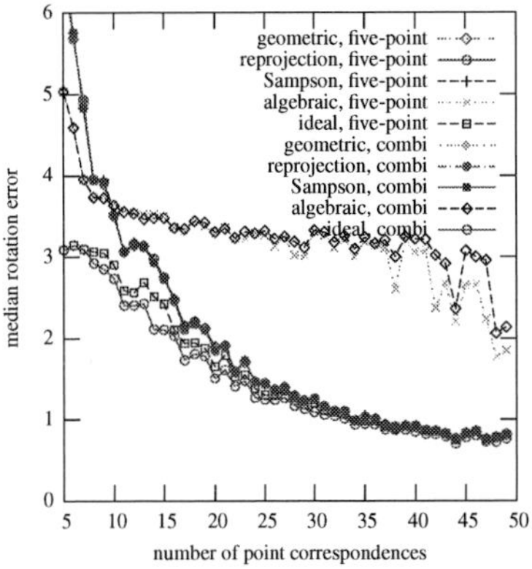

(a) Forward motion. The plots for "euclidean", "reprojection" and "Sampson" are almost identical, as are their "combi" variants.

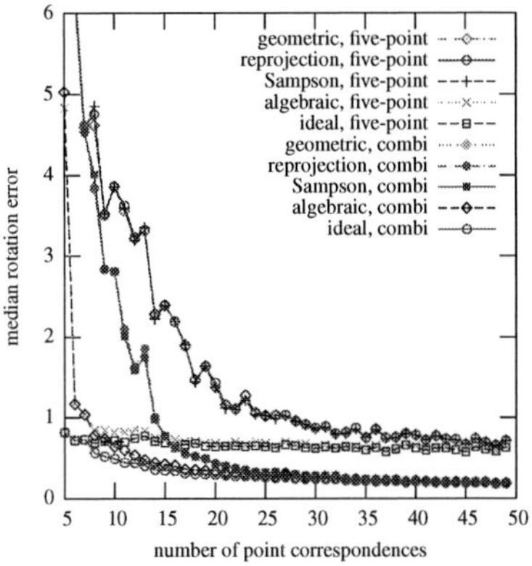

(b) Sideways motion. The plots for "euclidean", "reprojection", "Sampson" and their "combi" variants are almost identical, as are "ideal" and "ideal, combi".

Figure E.4: Comparison of error measures for automatic selection of the best solution in the five point algorithm. Median rotation error for varying number of point correspondences m. The plots "ideal" show the minimum error among all solutions without automatic selection.

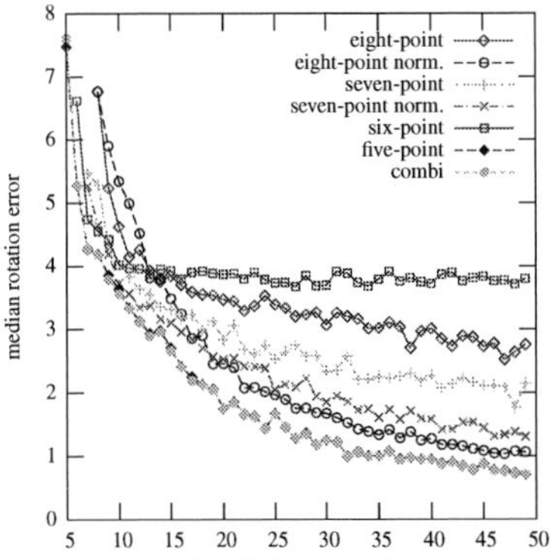

(a) Sideways motion. The plots for "5 point" and "combi" are almost identical.

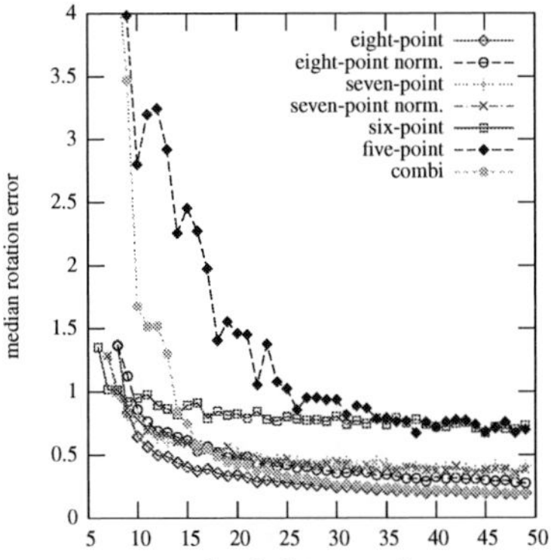

(b) Forward motion. The plots for "7 point" and "7 point norm." are mostly identical.

Figure E.5: Comparison of essential matrix estimation algorithms. Median rotation error for varying number of point correspondences m.

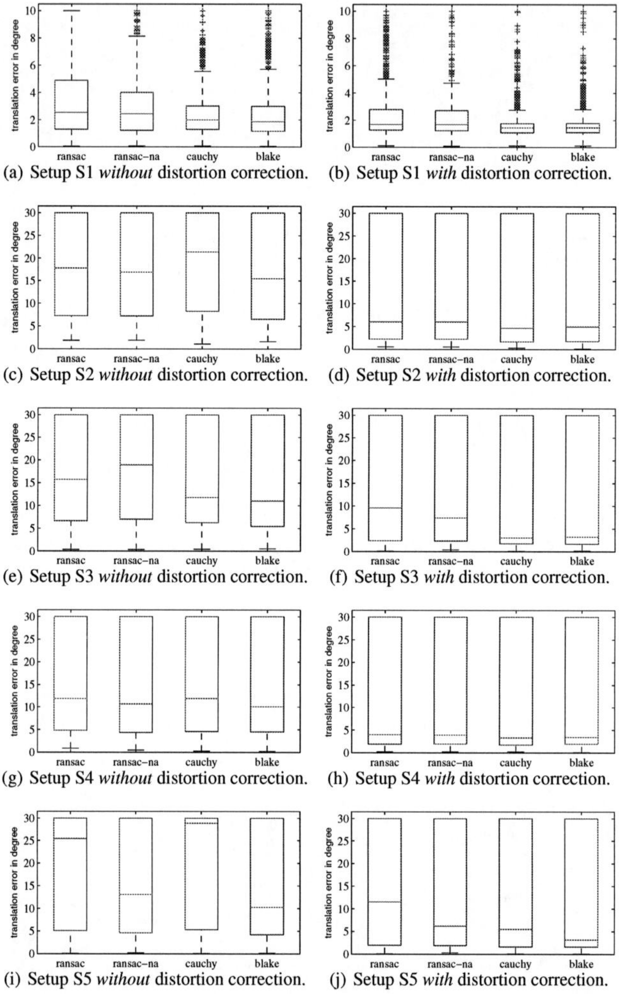

(a) Setup S1 *without* distortion correction. (b) Setup S1 *with* distortion correction.

(c) Setup S2 *without* distortion correction. (d) Setup S2 *with* distortion correction.

(e) Setup S3 *without* distortion correction. (f) Setup S3 *with* distortion correction.

(g) Setup S4 *without* distortion correction. (h) Setup S4 *with* distortion correction.

(i) Setup S5 *without* distortion correction. (j) Setup S5 *with* distortion correction.

Figure E.6: Comparison of robust relative pose estimation algorithms, individual results for the setups S1–S5 (cf. Figure 7.16. Note that the error values are truncated at the upper limit of the respective Y axis to emphasize the relevant details. Also note that the squences S2–S5 do *not* provide a common field of view for all camera pairs. The upper quartile of the translation error is between 70° and 90° in these cases, the maximum is 90°.

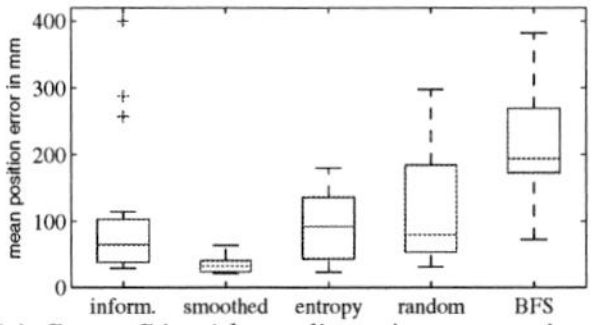

(a) Setup S1 *without* distortion correction.

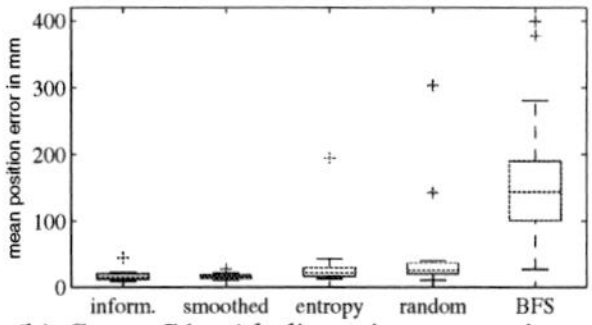

(b) Setup S1 *with* distortion correction.

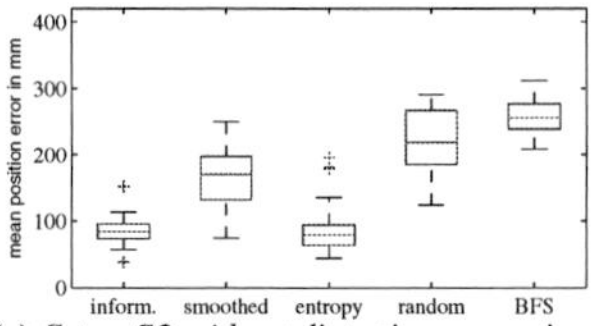

(c) Setup S2 *without* distortion correction.

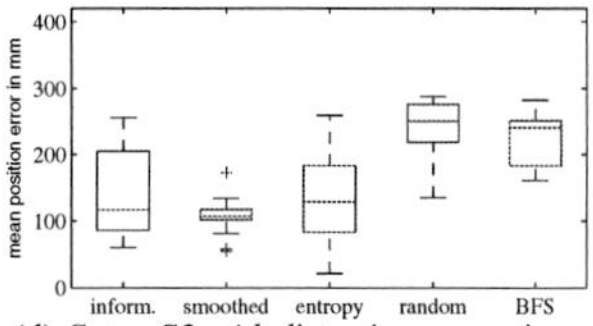

(d) Setup S2 *with* distortion correction.

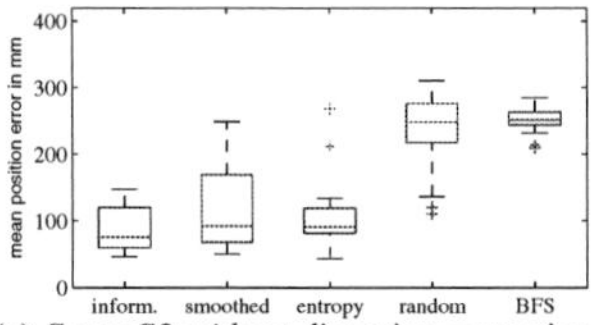

(e) Setup S3 *without* distortion correction.

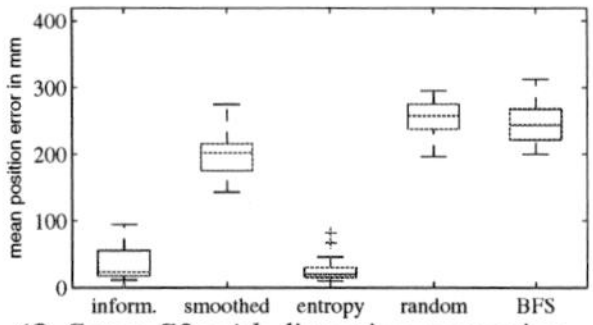

(f) Setup S3 *with* distortion correction.

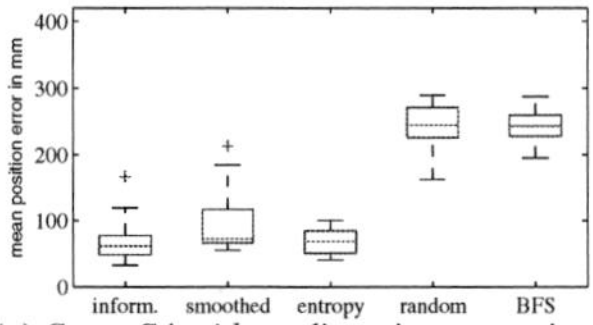

(g) Setup S4 *without* distortion correction.

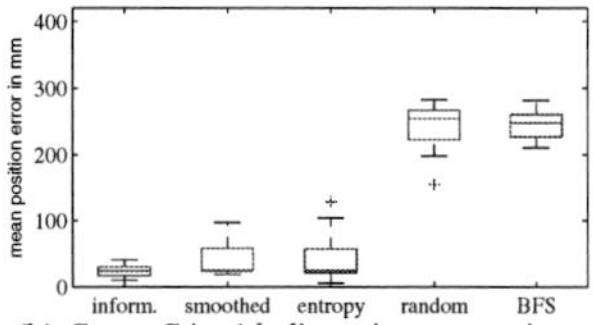

(h) Setup S4 *with* distortion correction.

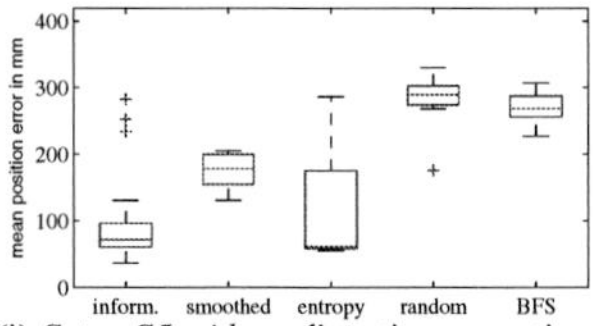

(i) Setup S5 *without* distortion correction.

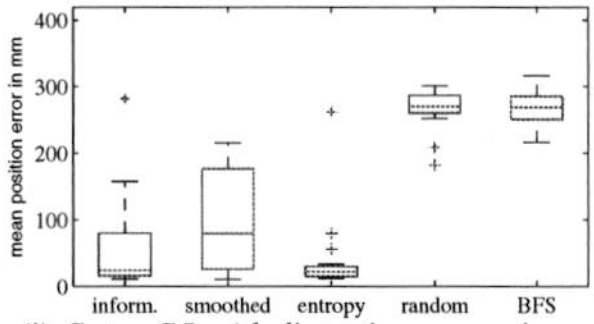

(j) Setup S5 *with* distortion correction.

Figure E.7: Uncertainty based selection of relative poses for multi-camera self-calibration using the information, the smoothed information or the entropy uncertainty measure compared to selection using random uncertainty values and also naive selection via breadth first search (BFS). The left side shows the *mean* position error in millimeters without correction of radial distortion, the right side with correction.

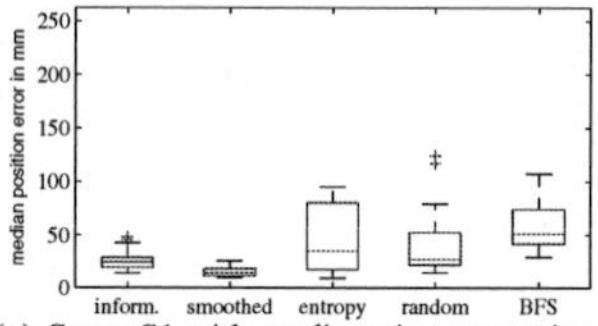

(a) Setup S1 without distortion correction.

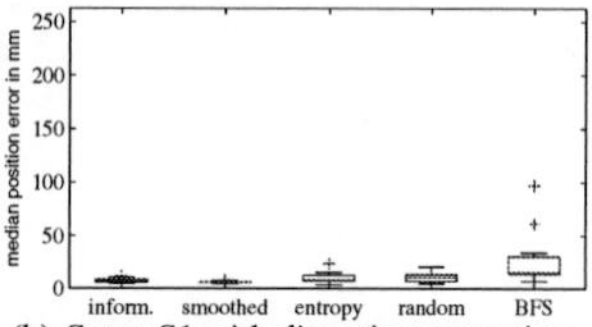

(b) Setup S1 with distortion correction.

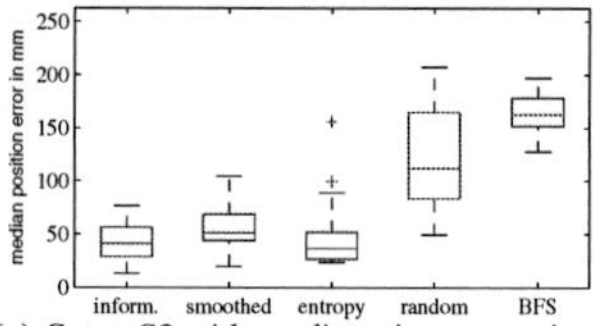

(c) Setup S2 without distortion correction.

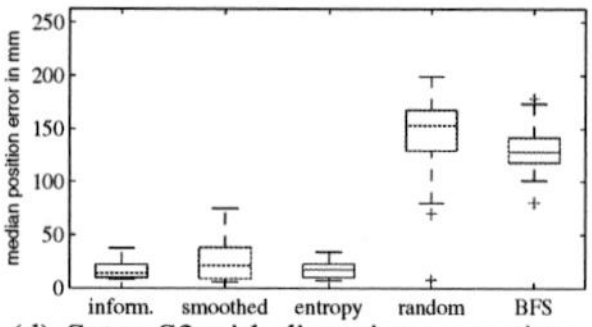

(d) Setup S2 with distortion correction.

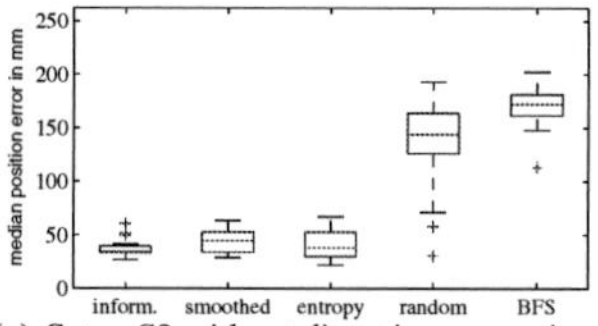

(e) Setup S3 without distortion correction.

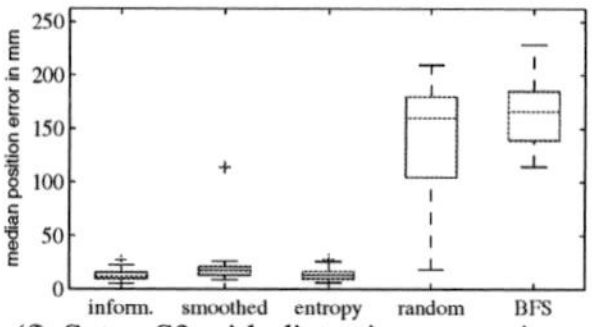

(f) Setup S3 with distortion correction.

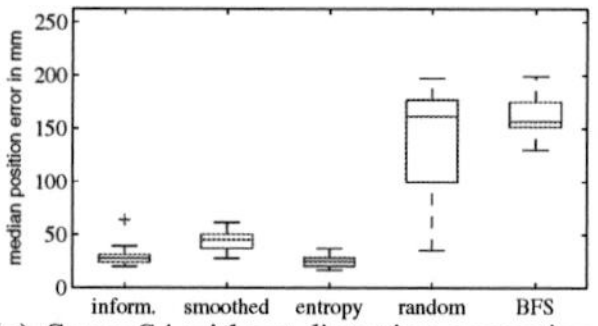

(g) Setup S4 without distortion correction.

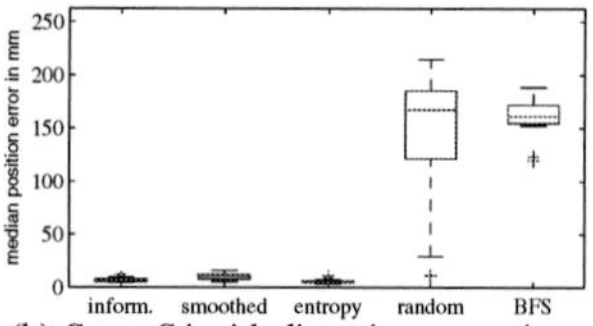

(h) Setup S4 with distortion correction.

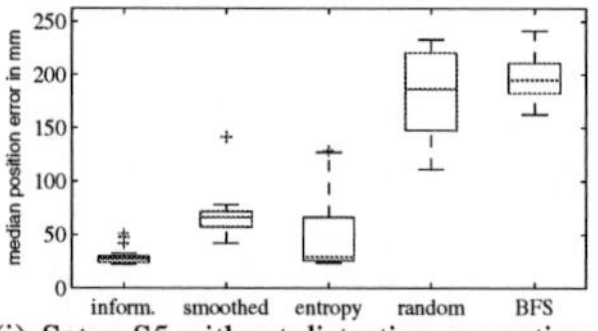

(i) Setup S5 without distortion correction.

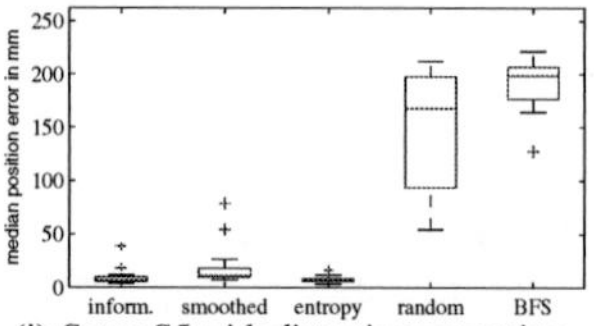

(j) Setup S5 with distortion correction.

Figure E.8: Uncertainty based selection of relative poses for multi-camera self-calibration using the information, the smoothed information or the entropy uncertainty measure compared to selection using random uncertainty values and also naive selection via breadth first search (BFS). The left side shows the *median* position error in millimeters without correction of radial distortion, the right side with correction.

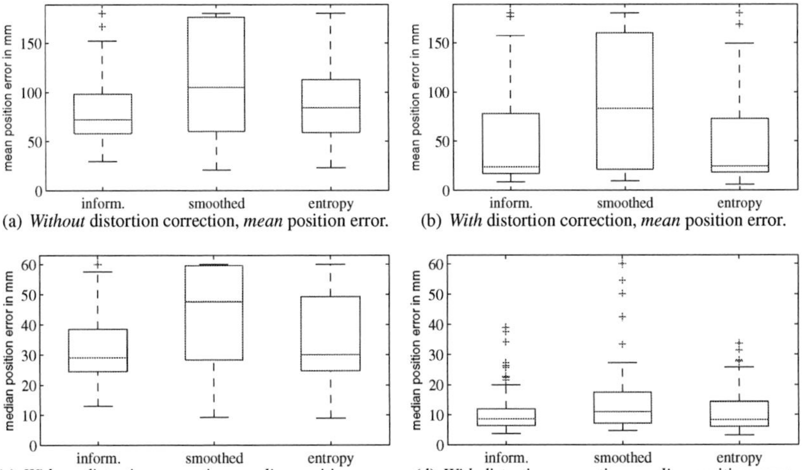

(a) *Without* distortion correction, *mean* position error.

(b) *With* distortion correction, *mean* position error.

(c) *Without* distortion correction, *median* position error.

(d) *With* distortion correction, *median* position error.

Figure E.9: More detailled version of Figure 7.21 showing only the results of the information, the smoothed information and the entropy measure for the setups S1–S5 (combined evaluation).

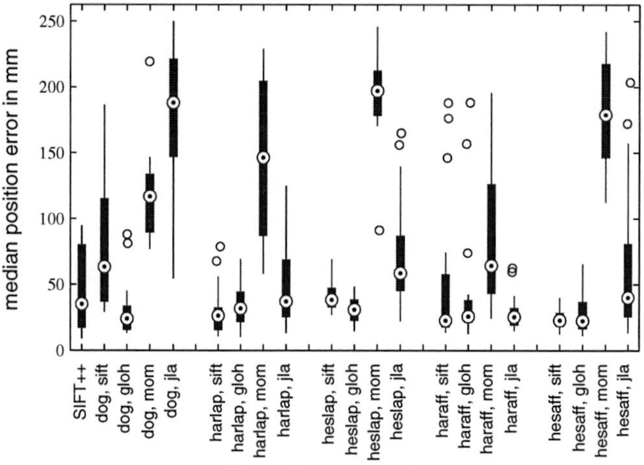

(a) *Without* distortion correction.

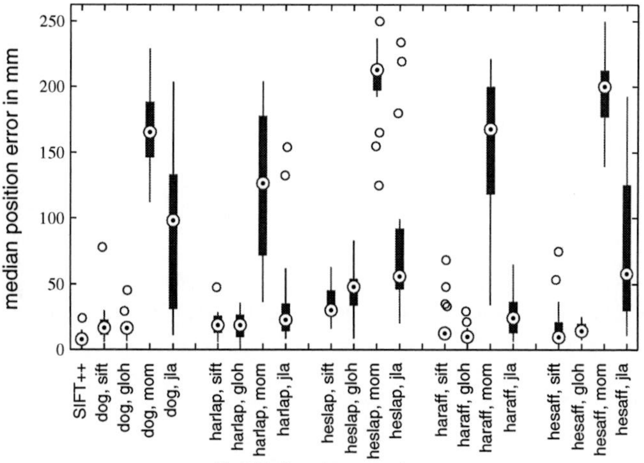

(b) *With* distortion correction.

Figure E.10: *Median* camera position errors of multi-camera self-calibration using point correspondences extracted by different point detectors and descriptors with 2NN matching on the setup S1. The entropy measure is used for the uncertainty-based selection of relative poses.

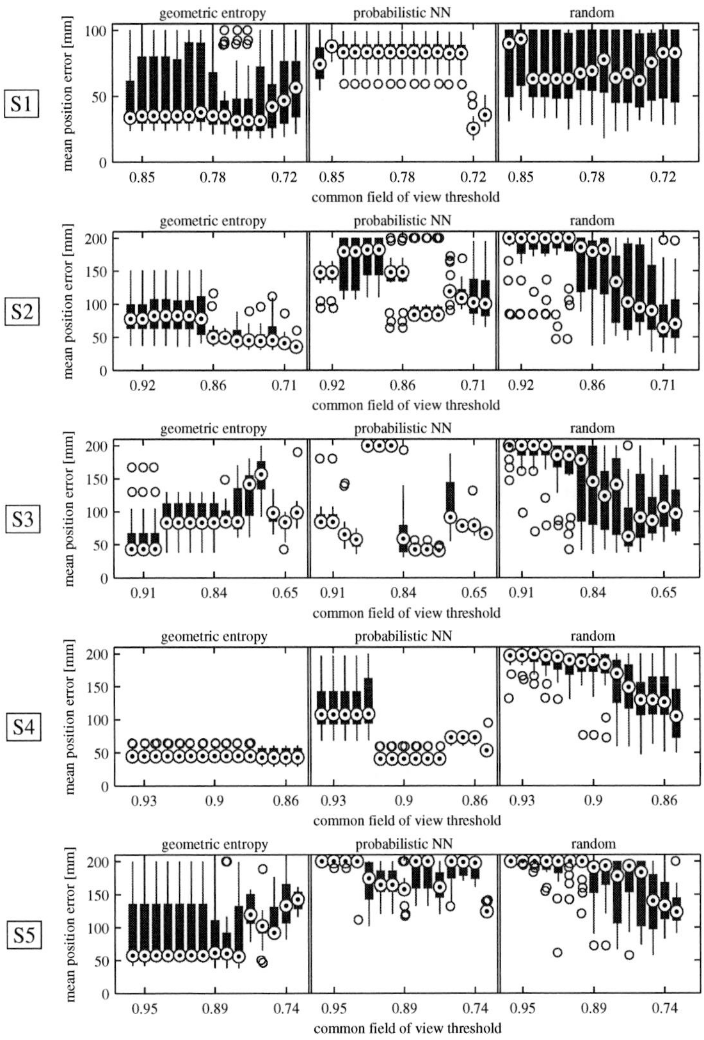

Figure E.11: Combination of common field of view detection and uncertainty based selection of relative poses as in Figure 7.28, but without radial distortion correction.

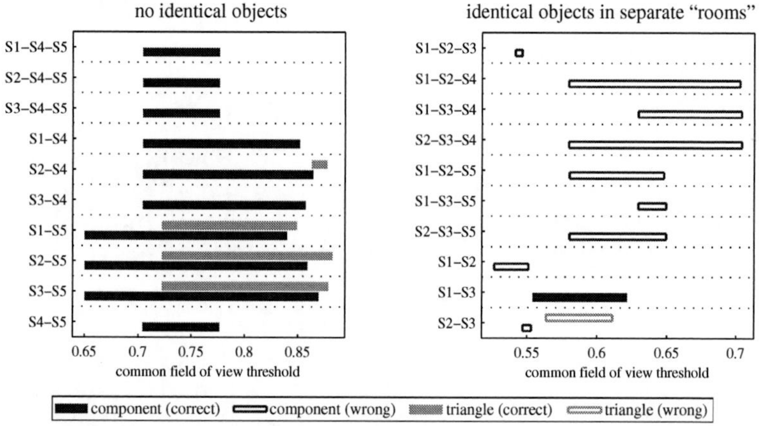

Figure E.12: Ranges of thresholds which separate the cameras into two or three groups, respectively. As in Figure 7.29, but without radial distortion correction. The influence of radial distortion correction on the room separation results is very small.

Bibliography

Alt, W. (2002). *Nichtlineare Optimierung*. Braunschweig/Wiesbaden: Vieweg.

Ameller, M.-A., Quan, L., and Triggs, B. (2002). Le Calcul de Pose : de nouvelles méthodes matricielles. In *Actes du 13ème Congrès AFCET de Reconnaissance des Formes et Intelligence Artificielle*.

Ameller, M.-A., Triggs, B., and Quan, L. (2000). Camera Pose Revisited – New Linear Algorithms. Technical report, INRIA Rhône-Alpes, Rapport Interne – Equipe MOVI.

Bajramovic, F. (2004). Kernel-basierte Objektverfolgung. Master's thesis, Computer Vision Group, Department of Mathematics and Computer Science, University of Passau, Germany.

Bajramovic, F. (2010). Multi camera calibration test data.

Bajramovic, F., Brückner, M., and Denzler, J. (2009). Using Common Field of View Detection for Multi Camera Calibration. In *Proceedings of the Vision Modeling and Visualization Conference (VMV)*, (pp. 113–120).

Bajramovic, F., Brückner, M., and Denzler, J. (2010). An Efficient Shortest Triangle Paths Algorithm Applied to Multi-Camera Calibration. *Journal of Mathematical Imaging and Vision, (submitted)*.

Bajramovic, F. and Denzler, J. (2007). Self-calibration with Partially Known Rotations. In *Proceedings of the 29th DAGM Symposium on Pattern Recognition*, (pp. 1–10).

Bajramovic, F. and Denzler, J. (2008a). An Efficient Shortest Triangle Paths Algorithm for Uncertainty-based Multi Camera Calibration. In *OMNIVIS'2008, the Eighth Workshop on Omnidirectional Vision, Camera Networks and Non-classical Cameras*.

Bajramovic, F. and Denzler, J. (2008b). Global Uncertainty-based Selection of Relative Poses for Multi Camera Calibration. In *Proceedings of the British Machine Vision Conference (BMVC)*, volume 2, (pp. 745–754).

Bajramovic, F. and Denzler, J. (2009). Experimentelle Auswertung von Unsicherheitsmaßen auf relativen Posen für die Multikamerakalibrierung. In *Publikationen der Deutschen Gesellschaft für Photogrammetrie und Fernerkundung (DGPF), 29. Tagung, Jena 2009*, (pp. 119–126).

Bajramovic, F., Koch, M., and Denzler, J. (2009). Experimental comparison of wide baseline correspondence algorithms for multi camera calibration. In *VISAPP 2009: Proceedings of the Fourth International Conference on Computer Vision Theory and Applications*, (pp. 458–463).

Baker, P. and Aloimonos, Y. (2000). Complete Calibration of a Multi-camera Network. In *Proceedings of the Workshop on Omnidirectional Vision (OMNIVIS)*, (pp. 134–144).

Baker, P. and Aloimonos, Y. (2003). Calibration of a Multicamera Network. In *Proceedings of the Workshop on Omnidirectional Vision (OMNIVIS)*.

Baker, S. and Matthews, I. (2004). Lucas-Kanade 20 Years On: A Unifying Framework. *International Journal of Computer Vision*, *56*(3), 221–255.

Barreto, J. P. and Daniilidis, K. (2004). Wide Area Multiple Camera Calibration and Estimation of Radial Distortion. In *Proceedings of the Workshop on Omnidirectional Vision (OMNIVIS)*.

Bergen, J. R., Anandan, P., Hanna, K. J., and Hingorani, R. (1992). Hierarchical Model-Based Motion Estimation. In *Proceedings 2nd European Conference on Computer Vision (ECCV92)*, number 588 in Lecture Notes In Computer Science, (pp. 237–252).

Bobick, A. F., Intille, S. S., Davis, J. W., Baird, F., Pinhanez, C. S., Campbell, L. W., Ivanov, Y. A., Schütte, A., and Wilson, A. D. (1999). The KidsRoom: A Perceptually-Based Interactive and Immersive Story Environment. *Presence*, *8*(4), 369–393.

Brand, M., Antone, M. E., and Teller, S. J. (2004). Spectral Solution of Large-Scale Extrinsic Camera Calibration as a Graph Embedding Problem. In *Proceedings of the Eighth European Conference on Computer Vision*, volume 2, (pp. 262–273).

Brückner, M., Bajramovic, F., and Denzler, J. (2008). Experimental Evaluation of Relative Pose Estimation Algorithms. In *VISAPP 2008: Proceedings of the Third International Conference on Computer Vision Theory and Applications*, volume 2, (pp. 431–438).

Brückner, M., Bajramovic, F., and Denzler, J. (2009). Geometric and Probabilistic Image Dissimilarity Measures for Common Field of View Detection. In *Proceedings of the IEEE Conference on Computer Vision and Pattern Recognition (CVPR)*, (pp. 2052–2057).

Brückner, M., Bajramovic, F., and Denzler, J. (2011). Intrinsic and Extrinsic Active Self-calibration of Multi-camera Systems. In *(unknown, to be submitted)*.

Brumitt, B., Meyers, B., Krumm, J., Kern, A., and Shafer, S. A. (2000). EasyLiving: Technologies for Intelligent Environments. In *Proceedings of the 2nd international symposium on Handheld and Ubiquitous Computing*, (pp. 12–29).

Chang, T.-H. and Gong, S. (2001). Tracking Multiple People with a Multi-Camera System. In *WOMOT '01: Proceedings of the IEEE Workshop on Multi-Object Tracking (WOMOT'01)*, (pp.$\tilde{1}$9).

Chen, X., Davis, J., and Slusallek, P. (2000). Wide Area Camera Calibration Using Virtual Calibration Objects. In *Proceedings of the IEEE Conference on Computer Vision and Pattern Recognition (CVPR)*, volume 2, (pp. 2520–2527).

Chippendale, P. and Tobia, F. (2005). Collective Calibration of Active Camera Groups. In *International Conference on Advanced Video and Signal Based Surveillance*, (pp. 456–461).

Collins, R. and Tsin, Y. (1999). Calibration of an Outdoor Active Camera System. In *Proceedings of the IEEE Conference on Computer Vision and Pattern Recognition (CVPR)*, volume 1, (pp. 528 – 534).

Conn, A. R., Gould, N. I. M., and Toint, P. L. (2000). *Trust-Region Methods*. Philadelphia: SIAM Society for Industrial and Applied Mathematics.

Cormen, T. H., Leiserson, C. E., Rivest, R. L., and Stein, C. (2001). *Introduction to Algorithms* (2nd ed.). Cambridge, Mass. and Boston, Mass.: MIT Press and McGraw-Hill.

Cox, D. A., Little, J., and O'Shea, D. (2005). *Using Algebraic Geometry* (2nd ed.). Graduate Texts in Mathematics. Berlin, Heidelberg: Springer.

Davis, J. and Chen, X. (2003). Calibrating pan-tilt cameras in wide-area surveillance networks. In *Proceedings of the IEEE International Conference on Computer Vision (ICCV)*, (pp. 144–149).

Domke, J. and Aloimonos, Y. (2006a). A Probabilistic Notion of Camera Geometry: Calibrated vs. Uncalibrated. In *Symposium of ISPRS Commission III Photogrammetric Computer Vision (PCV)*, (pp. 260–265). ISPRS.

Domke, J. and Aloimonos, Y. (2006b). A Probabilistic Notion of Correspondence and the Epipolar Constraint. In *Proceedings of the International Symposium on 3D Data Processing, Visualization and Transmission*.

Doubek, P., Geys, I., Svoboda, T., and Gool, L. V. (2004). Cinematographic Rules Applied to a Camera Network. In *Proceedings of the Workshop on Omnidirectional Vision (OMNIVIS)*.

Doubek, P., Svoboda, T., and Van Gool, L. (2003). Monkeys — a Software Architecture for ViRoom — Low-Cost Multicamera System. In *3rd International Conference on Computer Vision Systems*, (pp. 386–395).

Engels, C. and Nistér, D. (2005). Global Uncertainty in Epipolar Geometry via Fully and Partially Data-driven Sampling. In *ISPRS Workshop BenCOS: Towards Benchmarking Automated Calibration, Orientation and Surface Reconstruction from Images*, (pp. 17–22).

Faugeras, O. D. (1993). *Three-Dimensional Computer Vision*. MIT Press.

Faugeras, O. D. and Luong, Q.-T. (2001). *The Geometry of Multiple Images*. MIT Press.

Fischler, M. A. and Bolles, R. C. (1981). Random sample consensus: a paradigm for model fitting with applications to image analysis and automated cartography. *Communications of the ACM*, *24*(6), 381–395.

Frahm, J.-M. (2005). *Camera Self-Calibration with Known Camera Orientation*. PhD thesis, Institut für Informatik, Universität Kiel.

Frahm, J.-M. and Koch, R. (2003). Camera Calibration with Known Rotation. In *Proceedings of the IEEE International Conference on Computer Vision (ICCV)*, volume 2, (pp. 1418–1425).

Freeman, W. T. and Adelson, E. H. (1991). The design and use of steerable filters. *IEEE Transactions on Pattern Analysis and Machine Intelligence (TPAMI)*, *13*(9), 891–906.

Fusiello, A. (2000). Uncalibrated Euclidean reconstruction: a review. *International Journal of Image and Vision Computing*, *18*(6–7), 555–563.

Gill, Murray, and Wright (1998). *Numerical linear algebra and optimization*, volume 1. Reading, MA: Addison-Wesley.

Golub, G. and van Loan, C. (1996). *Matrix Computations* (3rd ed.). Baltimore, MD, USA: John Hopkins University Press.

Gonzalez, R. C. and Woods, R. E. (2002). *Digital Image Processing*. Upper Saddle River, New Jersey: Prentice Hall.

Goshen, L. and Shimshoni, I. (2006). Balanced Exploration and Exploitation Model Search for Efficient Epipolar Geometry Estimation. In *Proceedings of the European Conference on Computer Vision (ECCV)*, volume 2, (pp. 151–164).

Gross, M. H., Würmlin, S., Näf, M., Lamboray, E., Spagno, C. P., Kunz, A. M., Koller-Meier, E., Svoboda, T., Gool, L. J. V., Lang, S., Strehlke, K., Moere, A. V., and Staadt, O. G. (2003). blue-c: A Spatially Immersive Display and 3D Video Portal for Telepresence. *ACM Transactions on Graphics*, *22*(3), 819–827.

Grossberg, M. D. and Nayar, S. K. (2001). A General Imaging Model and a Method for Finding its Parameters. In *Proceedings of the Eighth International Conference On Computer Vision (ICCV)*, volume 2, (pp. 108–115).

Hager, G. D. and Belhumeur, P. N. (1998). Efficient Region Tracking With Parametric Models of Geometry and Illumination. *IEEE Transactions on Pattern Analysis and Machine Intelligence*, *20*(10), 1025–1039.

Harris, C. and Stephens, M. (1988). A Combined Corner and Edge Detector. In *Proceedings of The Fourth Alvey Vision Conference*, (pp. 147–151).

Hartley, R. and Sturm, P. (1997). Triangulation. *Computer Vision and Image Understanding*, *68*(2), 146–157.

Hartley, R. and Zisserman, A. (2003). *Multiple View Geometry in Computer Vision* (2nd ed.). Cambridge: Cambridge University Press.

Hartley, R. I. (1997). Self-Calibration of Stationary Cameras. *International Journal of Computer Vision (IJCV)*, *22*(1), 5–23.

Hayman, E. and Murray, D. W. (2002). The Effects of Translational Misalignment in the Self-Calibration of Rotating and Zooming Cameras. Technical Report OUEL 2250/02, Oxford University Engineering Library.

Hayman, E. and Murray, D. W. (2003). The Effects of Translational Misalignment when Self-Calibrating Rotating and Zooming Cameras. *IEEE Transactions on Pattern Analysis and Machine Intelligence (TPAMI)*, *25*(8), 1015–1020.

Heikkilä, J. and Silvén, O. (1997). A four-step camera calibration procedure with implicit image correction. In *CVPR '97: Proceedings of the 1997 Conference on Computer Vision and Pattern Recognition (CVPR '97)*, (pp. 1106–1112).

Horn, B. K. P. (1987). Closed Form Solution of Absolute Orientation using Unit Quaternions. *Journal of the Optical Society A*, *4*(4), 629–642.

Huber, P. J. (2004). *Robust Statistics*. New York: Wiley. (reprint of 1981).

Ji, Q. and Dai, S. (2004). Self-Calibration of a Rotating Camera with a Translational Offset. *IEEE Transactions on Robotics and Automation*, *20*(1), 1–14.

Jolliffe, I. T. (2002). *Principal Component Analysis*. Berlin, Heidelberg: Springer.

Kahl, F. and Hartley, R. (2007). Multiple View Geometry Under the L_∞ Norm. *IEEE Transactions on Pattern Analysis and Machine Intelligence*, *30*(9), 1603–1617.

Kahl, F., Triggs, B., and Åström, K. (2000). Critical Motions for Auto-Calibration When Some Intrinsic Parameters Can Vary. *Journal of Mathematical Imaging and Vision*, *13*(2), 131–146.

Kähler, O. (2009a). *Model-based Online 3D Reconstruction from Image Sequences*. PhD thesis, Friedrich Schiller University of Jena.

Kähler, O. (2009b). *Model-based Online 3D Reconstruction from Image Sequences*. PhD thesis, Friedrich Schiller University of Jena, Department for Mathematics and Computer Science.

Kanatani, K., Sugaya, Y., and Niitsuma, H. (2008). Triangulation from Two Views Revisited: Hartley-Sturm vs. Optimal Correction. In *Proceedings of the British Machine Vision Conference (BMVC)*, (pp. 173–182).

Khan, S., Javed, O., Rasheed, Z., and Shah, M. (2001). Human Tracking in Multiple Cameras. In *Proceedings of the 8th IEEE International Conference on Computer Vision (ICCV)*, volume 1, (pp. 331–336).

Kim, K. and Davis, L. S. (2006). Multi-camera tracking and segmentation of occluded people on ground plane using search-guided particle filtering. In *Proceedings of the European Conference on Computer Vision (ECCV)*, volume 3, (pp. 98–109).

Kitahara, I., Saito, H., Akimichi, S., Ono, T., Ohta, Y., and Kanade, T. (2001). Large-scale Virtualized Reality. In *Proceedings of the IEEE Conference on Computer Vision and Pattern Recognition (CVPR), Technical Sketches.*

Läbe, T. and Förstner, W. (2006). Automatic relative orientation of images. In *Proceedings of the 5th Turkish-German Joint Geodetic Days.*

Lee, L., Romano, R., and Stein, G. (2000). Monitoring Activities from Multiple Video Streams: Establishing a Common Coordinate Frame. *IEEE Transactions on Pattern Analysis and Machine Intelligence (TPAMI)*, *22*(8), 758–767.

Levi, N. and Werman, M. (2003). The Viewing Graph. In *Proceedings of the IEEE Conference on Computer Vision and Pattern Recognition (CVPR)*, volume 1, (pp. 518–524).

Lindeberg, T. (1994). *Scale-Space Theory in Computer Vision.* Dordrecht, Netherlands: Kluwer Academic Publishers.

Lowe, D. G. (2004). Distinctive Image Features from Scale-Invariant Keypoints. *International Journal of Computer Vision (IJCV)*, *60*(2), 91–110.

Lucas, B. D. and Kanade, T. (1981). An Iterative Image Registration Technique with an Application to Stereo Vision. In *International Joint Conference on Artificial Intelligence*, (pp. 674–679).

Ma, Y., Soatto, S., Košecká, J., and Sastry, S. (2004). *An Invitation to 3D Vision.* Berlin, Heidelberg: Springer.

MacKay, D. J. C. (2003). *Information Theory, Inference, and Learning Algorithms.* Cambridge University Press.

Mantzel, W. E., Choi, H., and Baraniuk, R. G. (2004). Distributed Camera Network Localization. In *Proceedings of the 38th Asilomar Conference on Signals, Systems and Computers*, volume 2, (pp. 1381–1386).

Martinec, D. and Pajdla, T. (2006). 3D Reconstruction by Gluing Pair-Wise Euclidean Reconstructions, or "How to Achieve a Good Reconstruction from Bad Images". In *3DPVT '06: Proceedings of the Third International Symposium on 3D Data Processing, Visualization, and Transmission (3DPVT'06)*, (pp. 25–32).

Martinec, D. and Pajdla, T. (2007). Robust Rotation and Translation Estimation in Multiview Reconstruction. In *Proceedings of the IEEE Conference on Computer Vision and Pattern Recognition (CVPR)*, (pp. 1–8).

Mikolajczyk, K. (2002). *Detection of local features invariant to affines transformations.* PhD thesis, INRIA Grenoble Rhone-Alpes, INPG, Grenoble.

Mikolajczyk, K. and Schmid, C. (2002). An affine invariant interest point detector. In *Proceedings of the European Conference on Computer Vision (ECCV)*, volume 1, (pp. 128–142).

Mikolajczyk, K. and Schmid, C. (2005). A Performance Evaluation of Local Descriptors. *IEEE Transactions on Pattern Analysis and Machine Intelligence (TPAMI)*, *27*(10), 1615–1630.

Mikolajczyk, K., Tuytelaars, T., Schmid, C., Zisserman, A., Matas, J., Schaffalitzky, F., Kadir, T., and Gool, L. V. (2005). A Comparison of Affine Region Detectors. *International Journal of Computer Vision (IJCV)*, *65*(1–2), 43–72.

Nistér, D. (2003). An Efficient Solution to the Five-Point Relative Pose Problem. In *Proceedings of the IEEE Conference on Computer Vision and Pattern Recognition (CVPR)*, volume 2, (pp. 195–202).

Nistér, D. (2004). An Efficient Solution to the Five-Point Relative Pose Problem. *IEEE Transactions on Pattern Analysis and Machine Intelligence (TPAMI)*, *26*(6), 756–777.

Nocedal, J. and Wright, S. J. (1999). *Numerical Optimization.* Springer Series in Operations research. Berlin, Heidelberg: Springer.

Philip, J. (1996). A non-iterative algorithm for determining all essential matrices corresponding to five point pairs. *Photogrammetric Record*, *15*(88), 589–599.

Philip, J. (1998). Critical point configurations of the 5-,6-,7-, and 8-point algorithms for relative orientation. Technical Report TRITA-MAT-1998-MA-13, KTH Royal Institute of Technology.

Philips, S. (2009). Nicht-lineare Optimierung zur Multikamerakalibrierung. diploma thesis. Lehrstuhl Digitale Bildverarbeitung, Friedrich-Schiller-Universität Jena.

Pizarro, O., Eustice, R., and Singh, H. (2003). Relative Pose Estimation for Instrumented, Calibrated Imaging Platforms. In *Proceedings of Digital Image Computing Techniques and Applications*, (pp. 601–612)., Sydney, Australia.

Pless, R. (2003). Using Many Cameras as One. In *Proceedings of the IEEE Conference on Computer Vision and Pattern Recognition (CVPR)*, volume 2, (pp. 587–593).

Pollefeys, M., Verbiest, F., and Gool, L. J. V. (2002). Surviving Dominant Planes in Uncalibrated Structure and Motion Recovery. In *Proceedings of the 7th European Conference on Computer Vision (ECCV)*, volume 2, (pp. 837–851).

Press, W., Teukolsky, S., Vetterling, W., and Flannery, B. (1994). *Numerical Recipes in C* (2nd ed.). Cambridge, UK: Cambridge University Press.

Prince, S., Cheok, A. D., Farbiz, F., Williamson, T., Johnson, N., Billinghurst, M., and Kato, H. (2002). 3D Live: Real Time Captured Content for Mixed Reality. In *Proceedings of the International Symposium on Mixed and Augmented Reality (ISMAR)*, (pp. 7–15).

Quan, L. and Triggs, B. (2000). A Unification of Autocalibration Methods. In *Proceedings of the Fourth Asian Conference on Computer Vision*, (pp. 917–922).

Remagnino, P. and Foresti, G. L. (2005). Ambient Intelligence: A New Multidisciplinary Paradigm. *IEEE Transactions on Systems, Man, and Cybernetics – Part A: Systems and Humans*, *35*(1), 1–6.

Rubner, Y., Tomasi, C., and Guibas, L. J. (1998). A metric for distributions with applications to image databases. In *Proceedings of the IEEE International Conference on Computer Vision (ICCV)*, (pp. 59–66).

Schiller, I. (2009). Mip - multicameracalibration. http://www.mip.informatik.uni-kiel.de/tiki-index.php?page=Calibration. last visited 2010-01-14.

Schiller, I., Beder, C., and Koch, R. (2008). Calibration of a pmd camera using a planar calibration object together with a multi-camera setup. In *The International Archives of the Photogrammetry, Remote Sensing and Spatial Information Sciences, Volume XXXVII. Part B3a*, (pp. 297–302). XXI. ISPRS Congress.

Schmidt, J. and Niemann, H. (2001). Using Quaternions for Parametrizing 3-D Rotations in Unconstrained Nonlinear Optimization. In *Proceedings of the Vision Modeling and Visualization Conference*, (pp. 399–406).

Sedgewick, R. (1988). *Algorithms* (2nd ed.). Reading, MA: Addison-Wesley.

Shashua, A. (1998). Omni-Rig Sensors: What Can be Done With a Non-Rigid Vision Platform? In *Proceedings of the 4th IEEE Workshop on Applications of Computer Vision (WACV)*, (pp. 174–179).

Shi, J. and Tomasi, C. (1994). Good Features to Track. In *Proceedings of the IEEE Conference on Computer Vision and Pattern Recognition (CVPR)*, (pp. 593–600)., Seattle, WA. IEEE Computer Society Press.

Sinha, S. N. and Pollefeys, M. (2004a). Synchronization and Calibration of Camera Networks from Silhouettes. In *Proceedings of the 17th International Conference on Pattern Recognition (ICPR)*, volume 1, (pp. 116–119).

Sinha, S. N. and Pollefeys, M. (2004b). Towards Calibrating a Pan-Tilt-Zoom Camera Network. In *Proceedings of the Workshop on Omnidirectional Vision (OMNIVIS)*.

Sinha, S. N., Pollefeys, M., and McMillan, L. (2004). Camera Network Calibration from Dynamic Silhouettes. In *Proceedings of the IEEE Conference on Computer Vision and Pattern Recognition (CVPR)*, volume 1, (pp. 195–202).

Slabaugh, G. G., Culbertson, W. B., Malzbender, T., and Schafer, R. W. (2001). A Survey of Methods for Volumetric Scene Reconstruction from Photographs. In *Proceedings of the Joint IEEE TCVG and Eurographics Workshop on Volume Graphics*, (pp. 81–100).

Slabaugh, G. G., Culbertson, W. B., Malzbender, T., Stevens, M. R., and Schafer, R. W. (2004). Methods for Volumetric Reconstruction of Visual Scenes. *International Journal of Computer Vision (IJCV)*, *57*(3), 179–199.

Snavely, N., Seitz, S., and Szeliski, R. (2008). Modeling the World from Internet Photo Collections. *International Journal of Computer Vision (IJCV)*, *80*(2), 189–210.

Stewénius, H. (2005). *Gröbner Basis Methods for Minimal Problems in Computer Vision*. PhD thesis, Centre for Mathematical Sciences LTH, Lund University, Sweden.

Stewénius, H., Engels, C., and Nistér, D. (2006). Recent Developments on Direct Relative Orientation. *ISPRS Journal of Photogrammetry and Remote Sensing*, *60*(4), 284–294.

Stewénius, H., Nistér, D., Oskarsson, M., and Åström, K. (2005). Solutions to Minimal Generalized Relative Pose Problems. In *Proceedings of the Workshop on Omnidirectional Vision (OMNIVIS)*.

Strang, G. (1993). *Introduction to Linear Algebra* (3rd ed.). Wellesley, MA, USA: Wellesley-Cambridge Press.

Sturm, P. (1997). Critical Motion Sequences for Monocular Self-Calibration and Uncalibrated Euclidean Reconstruction. In *Proceedings of the IEEE Conference on Computer Vision and Pattern Recognition (CVPR)*, (pp. 1100–1105).

Sturm, P. F. and Ramalingam, S. (2004). A Generic Concept for Camera Calibration. In *Proceedings of the 8th European Conference on Computer Vision (ECCV)*, volume 2, (pp. 1–13).

Süße, H. and Ortmann, W. (2003). Robust matching of affinely transformed objects. In *Proceedings of the IEEE International Conference on Image Processing (ICIP)*, volume 2, (pp. 375–378).

Süße, H., Ortmann, W., and Voss, K. (2006). A Novel Approach for Affine Point Pattern Matching. In *Proceedings of the Third International Conference on Image Analysis and Recognition (ICIAR 2006)*, volume 2, (pp. 434–444).

Svoboda, T. (2003). Quick guide to multi-camera self-calibration. Technical report, Computer Vision Lab, Swiss Federal Institute of Technology, Zurich.

Svoboda, T. (2005). A Software for Complete Calibration of Multicamera Systems. In *Image and Video Communications and Processing, Proceedings of SPIE–IS&T Electronic Imaging, SPIE volume 5685*, (pp. 115–128).

Svoboda, T., Hug, H., and Gool, L. J. V. (2002). ViRoom — Low Cost Synchronized Multicamera System and Its Self-calibration. In *Proceedings of the 24th DAGM Symposium on Pattern Recognition*, (pp. 515–522).

Svoboda, T., Martinec, D., and Pajdla, T. (2005). A Convenient Multi-Camera Self-Calibration for Virtual Environments. *PRESENCE: Teleoperators and Virtual Environments*, *14*(4), 407–422.

Tordoff, B. and Murray, D. W. (2000). Violating Rotating Camera Geometry: The Effect of Radial Distortion on Self-Calibration. In *Proceedings of the International Conference on Pattern Recognition (ICPR)*, volume 1, (pp. 1423–1427).

Tordoff, B. and Murray, D. W. (2004). The impact of radial distortion on the self-calibration of rotating cameras. *Computer Vision and Image Understanding (CVIU)*, *96*(1), 17–34.

Torr, P. and Zisserman, A. (2000). MLESAC: A New Robust Estimator with Application to Estimating Image Geometry. *Computer Vision and Image Understanding*, *78*(19), 138–156.

Triggs, B. (1998). Autocalibration from Planar Scenes. In *Proceedings of the European Conference on Computer Vision (ECCV)*, volume 1, (pp. 89–105).

Triggs, B., McLauchlan, P. F., Hartley, R. I., and Fitzgibbon, A. W. (1999). Bundle Adjustment — A Modern Synthesis. In *Proceedings of the International Workshop on Vision Algorithms: Theory and Practice*, (pp. 298–373).

Trivedi, M. M., Huang, K., and lvana Mikic (2000). Intelligent Environments and Active Camera Networks. In *Proceedings of the IEEE International Conference on Systems, Man and Cybernetics*, volume 2, (pp. 804–809).

Trivedi, M. M., Mikic, I., and Bhonsle, S. K. (2000). Active Camera Networks and Semantic Event Databases for Intelligent Environments. In *IEEE Workshop on Human Modeling, Analysis and Synthesis*.

Trucco, E. and Verri, A. (1998). *Introductory Techniques for 3D Computer Vision*. Englewood Cliffs: Prentice-Hall.

Tukey, J. W. (1977). *Exploratory Data Analysis*. Reading, MA: Addison-Wesley.

van Gool, L. J., Moons, T., and Ungureanu, D. (1996). Affine/photometric invariants for planar intensity patterns. In *Proceedings of the European Conference on Computer Vision (ECCV)*, volume 1, (pp. 642–651).

Vedaldi, A. (2007). An open implementation of the SIFT detector and descriptor. Technical Report 070012, UCLA CSD.

Vergés-Llahí, J., Moldovan, D., and Wada, T. (2008). A New Reliability Measure for Essential Matrices Suitable in Multiple View Calibration. In *VISAPP 2008: Proceedings of the Third International Conference on Computer Vision Theory and Applications*, volume 1, (pp. 114–121).

Vergés-Llahí, J. and Wada, T. (2008). A General Algorithm to Recover External Camera Parameters from Pairwise Camera Calibrations. In *ICIAR '08: Proceedings of the 5th International Conference on Image Analysis and Recognition*, (pp. 294–304).

Wang, L., Kang, S. B., Shum, H.-Y., and Xu, G. (2001). Error Analysis of Pure Rotation-Based Self-Calibration. In *Proceedings of the IEEE International Conference on Computer Vision (ICCV)*, volume 1, (pp. 464–471).

Wang, L., Kang, S. B., Shum, H.-Y., and Xu, G. (2004). Error Analysis of Pure Rotation-Based Self-Calibration. *IEEE Transactions on Pattern Analysis and Machine Intelligence (TPAMI)*, *26*(2), 275–280.

Weispfenning, V. and Becker, T. (1998). *Gröbner Bases*. Berlin, Heidelberg: Springer.

Wilburn, B., Joshi, N., Vaish, V., Talvala, E.-V., Antunez, E., Barth, A., Adams, A., Horowitz, M., and Levoy, M. (2005). High Performance Imaging Using Large Camera Arrays. *ACM Transactions on Graphics*, *24*(3), 765–776.

Willson, R. (1994a). *Modeling and Calibration of Automated Zoom Lenses*. PhD thesis, Robotics Institute, Carnegie Mellon University, Pittsburgh, PA.

Willson, R. (1994b). Modeling and Calibration of Automated Zoom Lenses. In *Proceedings of the SPIE #2350: Videometrics III*, (pp. 170–186).

Xu, W. and Mulligan, J. (2008). Robust relative pose estimation with integrated cheirality constraint. In *Proceedings of the International Conference on Pattern Recognition (ICPR)*, (pp. 1–4).

Zhang, Z. (1998). Determining the Epipolar Geometry and its Uncertainty: A Review. *International Journal of Computer Vision (IJCV)*, *27*(2), 161–195.

Zhang, Z. (1999). Flexible Camera Calibration by Viewing a Plane from Unknown Orientations. In *Proceedings of the IEEE International Conference on Computer Vision (ICCV)*, (pp. 666–673).

Zhang, Z., Deriche, R., Faugeras, O., and Luong, Q.-T. (1995). A robust technique for matching two uncalibrated images through the recovery of the unknown epipolar geometry. *Artificial Intelligence*, *78*(1–2), 87–119.

Zimmermann, T. (2007). Objektverfolgung in Multikamerasystemen. diploma thesis. Lehrstuhl Digitale Bildverarbeitung, Friedrich-Schiller-Universität Jena.

Zomet, A., Wolf, L., and Shashua, A. (2001). Omni-Rig: Linear Self-Recalibration of a Rig with Varying Internal and External Parameters. In *Proceedings of the IEEE International Conference on Computer Vision (ICCV)*, volume 1, (pp. 135–141).

List of Own Publications

Bajramovic, F., Brückner, M., and Denzler, J. (2010). An Efficient Shortest Triangle Paths Algorithm Applied to Multi-Camera Self-Calibration. *Journal of Mathematical Imaging and Vision (submitted).*

Bajramovic, F., Brückner, M., and Denzler, J. (2009). Using Common Field of View Detection for Multi Camera Calibration. In *Proceedings of the Vision Modeling and Visualization Conference (VMV)*, (pp. 113–120).

Brückner, M., Bajramovic, F., and Denzler, J. (2009). Geometric and Probabilistic Image Dissimilarity Measures for Common Field of View Detection. In *Proceedings of the IEEE Conference on Computer Vision and Pattern Recognition (CVPR)*, (pp. 2052–2057).

Bajramovic, F. and Denzler, J. (2009). Experimentelle Auswertung von Unsicherheitsmaßen auf relativen Posen für die Multikamerakalibrierung. In *Publikationen der Deutschen Gesellschaft für Photogrammetrie und Fernerkundung (DGPF), 29. Tagung, Jena 2009*, (pp. 119–126).

Bajramovic, F., Koch, M., and Denzler, J. (2009). Experimental comparison of wide baseline correspondence algorithms for multi camera calibration. In *VISAPP 2009: Proceedings of the Fourth International Conference on Computer Vision Theory and Applications*, (pp. 458–463).

Bajramovic, F. and Denzler, J. (2008a). An Efficient Shortest Triangle Paths Algorithm for Uncertainty-based Multi Camera Calibration. In *OMNIVIS'2008, the Eighth Workshop on Omnidirectional Vision, Camera Networks and Non-classical Cameras.*

Bajramovic, F. and Denzler, J. (2008b). Global Uncertainty-based Selection of Relative Poses for Multi Camera Calibration. In *Proceedings of the British Machine Vision Conference (BMVC)*, volume 2, (pp. 745–754).

Brückner, M., Bajramovic, F., and Denzler, J. (2008). Experimental Evaluation of Relative Pose Estimation Algorithms. In *VISAPP 2008: Proceedings of the Third International Conference on Computer Vision Theory and Applications*, volume 2, (pp. 431–438).

Bajramovic, F., Deutsch, B., Gräßl, C., and Denzler, J. (2008). Efficient Adaptive Combination of Histograms for Real-Time Tracking. *EURASIP Journal on Image and Video Processing, special issue Video Tracking in Complex Scenes for Surveillance Applications, 2008*, 1–11.

Bajramovic, F. and Denzler, J. (2007). Self-calibration with Partially Known Rotations. In *Proceedings of the 29th DAGM Symposium on Pattern Recognition*, (pp. 1–10).

Bajramovic, F., Mattern, F., Butko, N., and Denzler, J. (2006). A Comparison of Nearest Neighbor Search Algorithms for Generic Object Recognition. In *Advanced Concepts for Intelligent Vision Systems*, (pp. 1186–1197).

Bajramovic, F., Gräßl, C., and Denzler, J. (2005). Efficient Combination of Histograms for Real-Time Tracking Using Mean-Shift and Trust-Region Optimization. In *Proceedings of the 27th DAGM Symposium on Pattern Recognition*, (pp. 254–261).

Deutsch, B., Gräßl, C., Bajramovic, F., and Denzler, J. (2005). A Comparative Evaluation of Template and Histogram Based 2D Tracking Algorithms. In *Proceedings of the 27th DAGM Symposium on Pattern Recognition*, (pp. 269–276).

Bajramovic, F., Gruber, C., and Sick, B. (2004). A Comparison of First- and Second-Order Training Algorithms for Dynamic Neural Networks. In *Proceedings of the IEEE International Joint Conference on Neural Networks*, volume 2, (pp. 837–842).

List of Algorithms

List of Figures

List of Tables

List of Theorems, Definitions, etc.

Index